New Ways of Looking at Learning Disabilities

Connections to Classroom Practice

Edited by

Lou Denti
Lawton Love Distinguished Professor of Special Education
Center for Collaborative Education and Professional Studies
California State University, Monterey Bay

Patricia Tefft Cousin
Indiana University
Purdue University Indianapolis

LOVE PUBLISHING COMPANY
Denver • London • Sydney

Published by Love Publishing Company
Denver, Colorado 80222

All rights reserved. No part of this publication may be reproduced, stored in a retrieval system, or transmitted, in any form or by any means, electronic, mechanical, recording or otherwise, without the prior written permission of the publisher.

Library of Congress Catalog Card Number 00-104332

Copyright © 2001 Love Publishing Company
Printed in the United States of America
ISBN 0-89108-270-0

Contents

Preface xi
Introduction xii

Section One: Looking at Learning Disabilities in New Ways 1

1 Reconceptualizing Learning Disabilities by Reconceptualizing Education 5
Curt Dudley-Marling
  Some Assumptions Implicit in Traditional Schooling 7
  Reconceptualizing Schooling 13
  Summary 15

**2 Reconceptualizing the Learning Disabilities Paradigm:
  Multicultural Imperatives** 19
Bridgie Alexis Ford and Helen Bessent Byrd
  The LD Construct 21
  Present and Anticipated Phenomena Supporting a Multicultural Perspective 25
  Reformation of the Learning Disabilities Paradigm 34
  Summary 35

3 A Personal Journey: Changing Concepts of Learning and Disability 41
Cheryl Ames

**4 Critical Cultural Knowledge in Special Education:
  Reshaping the Responsiveness of School Leaders** 51
Khaula Murtadha-Watts and Edy Stoughton
  Intersections of Cultural Difference and Labeling 53
  Becoming a Multicultural Leader Through Disembedding Cultural Biases 54
  Critical Cultural Mirroring and Culturally Focused Dialogue 55
  Challenges for Curriculum Development:
    Culturally Focused Dialogue About Curriculum 56

Parents and the Formation of School Communities   58
Appendix   62

Section Two: Assessing and Supporting Student Learning and Understanding in New Ways   65

5   Transforming Children's Experiences of Failure Into Stories and Narratives of Competence   69
Dudley J. Wiest, Susan Brotherton, Dennis A. Kreil, and Joseph M. Cervantes
Reconceptualizing Pathology as Help   70
Postmodern Approaches to Counseling   72
Narrative Therapy   74
The Case of Adam   75
Use of Narrative Principles in the Classroom   79
Summary   81

6   Curriculum-Based Measurement: Cheaper, Faster, and Better Assessment of Students With Learning Disabilities   85
Michelle M. Gilbert and Mark R. Shinn
What Assessment Strategies Work in Medicine   86
Similarities Between Curriculum-Based Measurement and Medical Assessment   91
Cheaper and Faster Assessment   92
Cheaper and Faster Is Not Enough   93
Use of CBM as "Better" Assessment   93
Case Studies Using CBM   97
Summary   107

7   Personalized Grading Plans: A Systematic Approach to Making the Grades of Included Students More Accurate and Meaningful   111
Dennis D. Munk and William D. Bursuck
Key Grading Issues   112
Proposed Process for Making Grading Adaptations   121
Summary   126

8   Andrew, Stuck in Words: A Retrospective Miscue Analysis Case Study in Revaluing   129
Alan D. Flurkey and Yetta M. Goodman
Andrew's Reading and Writing at School and at Home   130
Reading Words   131
An Analysis of Andrew's Reading   132
Andrew Needs to Revalue Reading and Revalue Himself as a Reader   138
Retrospective Miscue Analysis and Revaluing   140
Andrew Comes Unstuck   140
Summary   147
Appendix: Markings for Miscue Analysis   149

9   Taking an Aesthetic Stance Toward Teaching and Assessment   151
Beth Berghoff
Assumptions Behind an Aesthetic Stance Toward Literacy   154
Peter's Story   159
Summary   169

10. **Successful Teacher Strategies in a Multicultural Language Arts Classroom: Organization, Techniques, and Discipline** 173
Angela E. Rickford
    Background and Profile of Students   174
    Strategies Used to Design the Multicultural Classroom   175
    Strategies Used to Inspire and Challenge Students   177
    Innovative Instructional Techniques   179
    Church-Based Discipline   184
    Implications and Summary   186

Section Three: Student-Centered Curriculum Approaches   189

11. **Necessary Conversations: Reframing Support in General Education Classrooms for Students With Learning Disabilities** 193
Elizabeth Althardt
    A Context for Change   194
    Important Questions for Special and General Educators to
       Discuss Prior to and During a Collaborative Arrangement   196
    Summary   198

12. ***"Traigon sus vidas, yo traigo la mía: Shared Reading for Older Emergent Readers in Bilingual Classrooms*** 199
Tomás Enguídanos and Nadeen T Ruiz
    Research on Effective Literacy instruction for
       Linguistically Diverse Students in Special Education   200
    Research-Based, Effective Literacy Instruction: The OLE Project   203
    Shared Reading as a Link Between Classroom Research and Practice   203
    Implementing Shared Reading for Older Emergent Readers   206
    Eliciting Personal Reaction/Constructing Meaning   212
    Skill Work: Daily Practice   215
    Performance and Extension (Going Public)   218
    Getting Started Writing Poetry   218
    Summary   219

13. **Tools for Reconceptualizing the Inclusive Classroom: Computers and Cooperative Learning** 223
Mary Male
    Cooperative Learning Groups Versus Traditional Learning Groups   224
    Synergy of Cooperative Learning and Computers   225
    Essential Components of Cooperative Computer Lessons   226
    Learning Together: A Cooperative Learning Strategy   229
    The Computer Lab   230
    Classroom Designs to Promote Social Development   230
    Summary   235

14. **Creating Opportunities for Success by Teaching Study Skill Strategies** 237
Mary M Gleason and Anita L. Archer
    Selection of Study Skill Strategies for Instruction   238
    Teaching Learning Strategies   239
    Teaching Organization Skills   256

Teaching Study Skills   260
Maintenance of Study Skill Strategies   261
Summary   263

15 High-Access Instruction: Practical Strategies to Increase Active Learning in Diverse Classrooms   267
Kevin Feldman and Lou Denti
Why Change the Way We Teach?   368
The Challenge of Incorporating High-Access Instruction in School Classrooms   269
High-Access Instruction: What Is It?   269
What Does Not Work: A Brief Look at Common Low-Access Teaching Practices   270
High-Access Instructional Strategies   273
Low- and High-Access Instruction Contrasted   282
Summary   282

16 Using Student Investigation to Water Up Content-Area Instruction for Adolescents With Learning Disabilities   287
Edwin S. Ellis, Carol Schlichter, and Charlotte A. Sonnier
What Is Project-Based Learning?   288
How Projects Address Goals of a Watered-Up Classroom   288
Project-Based Instruction   292
Project-Based Strategies   299
Facilitating the Use of Project Strategies   310

17 Sociocultural Scaffolding as a Means Toward Academic Self-Regulation: Paraeducators as Cultural Brokers   315
Robert Rueda and Michael Genzuk
Cognition and Learning: Sociocultural Considerations   316
From Theory to Practice: A Focus on Diverse Learners   317
Conceptualizing Everyday Knowledge   318
The Role of Paraeducators in Effective Instructional Programs   320
Paraeducators as Teachers: Some Classroom Examples   320
A Note on Collaborative Practice   323
Summary   323

Foreword

Patricia E. Swanson, Ph.D.
Department of Elementary Education
San José State University

When asked, as an assistant professor in the Department of Elementary Education to write the foreword for a book entitled, *New Ways of Looking at Learning Disabilities: Connections to Classroom Practice,* I quickly agreed seeing it as an excellent learning opportunity. Indeed, I hoped the book would provide me with a window into the current issues shaping special education. In addition, I could clearly see from the chapter headings that I would gain a wealth of new ideas to incorporate into my courses and work with classroom teachers. While reading this book admirably fulfilled these purposes, what I did not expect was the degree to which it would push me to reexamine my own practice, and reconceptualize my understanding of learning disabilities and how best to meet the needs of all children in inclusive classrooms.

As a bilingual elementary school teacher I have always worked in academically and linguistically diverse classrooms. Encompassed within this diversity were students with learning disabilities, some identified, some whom I identified, and probably more than a few who fit the definition (such as it is), but remained unidentified by us all. As a teacher educator, I watch my students grapple with even greater diversity than I knew as a teacher, and more students identified with learning disabilities. Of those identified an ever increasing number represent students who live in poverty, students of color, and language minority students. A label, designed to provide diagnostic information on the cognitive processing of language has become ambiguous, a psychological phenomena indistinguishable from the social context in which language develops. This book articulates the critical need to reexamine the concept of learning disability, both in terms of its utility and its flaws, and to rethink how we use this label, and translate it into instructional practice.

How did this book lead me to view learning disabilities in new ways? First, it has made me cautious in the use of the term "learning disabled" and reminded me that all labels must be viewed from multiple perspectives. As a classroom teacher I placed a great deal of scientific faith in the derivation of the label. To my mind, specialists, using specialized testing instruments, diagnosed specific differences in the cognitive functioning of certain children. Their job (the specialists) was to clearly communicate to me (the classroom teacher) the nature of the cognitive disability and the classroom adaptations necessary to meet the child's needs. It was a medical model, and with the humility of one trained in the social sciences, I placed a degree of faith in it. As I read the first section, *Looking at Learning Disabilities in New Ways*, I developed a healthy skepticism for the term "learning disabled." I do not disregard it, for it contains information on how children process information that is crucial to the classroom teacher. But I read with interest Ford's chapter clearly delineating the ambiguities associated with a legislated definition which makes some children eligible for special services and others not. Dudley-Marling's chapter reminded me of the moral implications of using any label that places blame for failure on the child while absolving the schools of guilt. The final two chapters in this section give voice to both the teacher and the site administrator grappling with the instructional and organizational changes necessary to create inclusive schools for all children.

In the second section, *Assessing and Supporting Student Learning and Understanding in New Ways*, I was reminded of the very human tendency to see what we look for. If we look for deficits then this is what we will see. Good teaching must surely involve identifying not just deficits but strengths, and teaching the child to overcome the former while building on the latter. This section provides not just a philosophical perspective shift but a wide range of strategies for assessment and instruction that capitalize on the rich repertoire of experiences, strategies, and cognitive strengths that all children bring to the classroom. The first chapter provides a compelling argument for helping students to address their disability as external to themselves, a specific problem to be solved and often one for which they have already developed worthy coping strategies. I was struck by the power of semantics and the shattering difference between talking about a *learning disabled student* versus a *student with a learning disability*. The difference is profound, not just in how we view the child, but in how the child comes to view himself.

The next two chapters in this section provide both a framework and practical strategies for an assessment system that focuses on instructional planning, and an inclusive and fair process for developing personalized grading plans for students with learning disabilities. The final three chapters each provide vivid case studies of teachers and classrooms where students with learning disabilities are experiencing success — classrooms in which teachers stress learning strategies rather than rote skills, and challenging multiple ability tasks provide access and opportunities for struggling readers. In the final chapter of this section, Rickford takes us beyond the notion of learning disabilities, to grapple with the challenges the teaching a class of uniformly poor readers in a culturally diverse, low socio-economic, inner-city seventh grade class. She describes a teacher who melds his diverse group of adolescents into a classroom community, and who utilizes the "cultural strengths of his students as the bedrock for learning and literacy."(page cite) It is a powerful piece that reminds us that good teaching is not just a question of understanding how students learn, but of knowing the social context in which they learn.

As a sociologist, trained to examine the effect of social context and group perceptions on the individual, I am struck by the separateness with which I previously viewed children labeled with learning disabilities. Theirs was a different kind of instructional challenge, requiring individual adaptations designed to meet their unique language processing needs. In the third section of this book, *Student Centered Curriculum Approaches,* I came to see inclusion not as a set of individual adaptations but rather as a necessary shift in perspective accompanied by a wide repertoire of instructional strategies.

These strategies share fundamental features. They are constructivist in nature, cognitively challenging, and designed to promote problem solving rather than rote skills. They stress the development of language skills through meaningful communication and are structured to maximize student interaction. They utilize curricular activities designed to capitalize on students' background, experiences, and interests. They require multiple intellectual abilities, providing students with access into the task, and the teacher with opportunities to recognize the wide range of intellectual contributions made by different students. They were strategies I recognized and taught in my classes as essential for teaching culturally diverse students and second language learners. They are the strategies too often reserved for the "gifted" class, which are essential for students with learning disabilities. They are strategies for all children.

The final section of this book made me want to rush back to the classroom to try out a wealth of new ideas. Althardt's chapter made me wish that I had had the opportunity to co-teach with a special education teacher. While there are clearly challenges, her advice is both sensitive and practical, and the learning opportunities for both teachers are great. The following chapter on shared reading in upper grade bilingual classrooms made me eager to rework a poetry unit I had recently modeled to better incorporate the elements of choice and personal connection to poetry captured in the chapter title, " *Traigan sus vidas, yo traigo la mia.* " (Bring Your Life [experiences], I'll Bring Mine). Similarly, Male's compelling argument for using computers as a catalyst for student interaction made me eager to incorporate carefully structured cooperative learning computer lessons into my social studies methods course.

The following two chapters, the first focusing on teaching learning strategies and organizational skills and the second on promoting "high access instruction" provide an essential balance in this section focused on challenging, student centered learning activities. The authors note that students with learning disabilities will not, and cannot, participate in these activities without access to the content and the organizational skills that would allow them to succeed. Gleason and Archer provide a detailed analysis and practical strategies for teaching the learning strategies and organizational skills that *all* students must have for meaningful participation in an inclusive and challenging classroom. Feldman and Denti provide a set of easily learned strategies for increasing student participation, interaction, and conceptual understanding during content instruction. These chapters should be required reading for all classroom teachers.

The final two chapters circle back to themes running throughout the book, the importance of providing students with a rich curriculum and opportunities for authentic problem solving, and the necessity of attending to sociocultural factors in student learning. Each remind us of the complex blend of cognitive and social factors embedded in meaningful learning and good teaching.

This book does indeed bridge the gap between special education and general education. The strategies are recognizable as best practices for all children. In an educational and political context that places increasing emphasis on the development of basic skills, the teachers challenge is to tenaciously hang-on to the idea that basic skills are best taught within the context of a meaningful and challenging curriculum. All children deserve access to such a curriculum. It takes a skilled, knowledgeable, talented, and caring teacher to provide it.

Children with learning disabilities are an essential element in the mix of any classroom. Their coping strategies and intellectual strengths add to the rich diversity of the whole. While I would not ignore the diagnostic information embedded in the many labels we give students, I have come to view learning disabilities as not just a "medical truth", but a social construct — one that operates in an institution driven by the need to sort and classify students. In this sense the label becomes superfluous, just another way of saying that all children are different. They learn in different ways and bring different strengths. Understanding children, centering not just on their cognitive deficits, but on their strengths and interests, their learning styles and aptitudes, their homes and communities — this is the key to the truly inclusive classroom.

Preface

This book emanates from a panel discussion that took place at the Council for Learning Disabilities (CLD) Conference held in Nashville, Tennessee, in 1996. Edwin Ellis, one of the contributors to this book, had asked me (Lou Denti) to chair a panel discussion on reconceptualizing the learning disabilities paradigm. Five people who would later contribute to the volume, Bridgie Ford, Curt Dudley-Marling, Pat Tefft Cousin, Dudley Wiest, and Dennis Kreil, joined me on the panel. We were surprised by the interest in this topic and equally surprised by the concerns voiced by the participants about the prevailing behaviorist model of instruction in special education that made, as one person said, "feel boxed in."

The bulk of the discussion centered around shifting the current behaviorist paradigm and how we, as special educators, could begin to systematically include general education perspectives based on more of a constructivist point of view into our vision of teaching and educational leadership. The participants believed that students with learning disabilities could profit from opportunities to create meaning from interacting with peers, teachers and the core curriculum. Many expressed strong feelings that separating students with learning difficulties from the regular classroom and then using a traditional behaviorist approach to instruction robbed them of a chance to learn in an environment where students were challenged to perform at high levels and meet state and district standards.

Of course, the participants were also concerned about compromising the integrity of special education preservice and professional development by overfocusing on general education. As the session progressed, however, a bridge between special and general education was masterfully constructed, with state-of-the-art instruction and curriculum undergirding the roadway to success for students with learning disabilities. It was in that rare conference moment that presenters and audience members could sense the triumph of possibility over resignation.

In the 3 years since the CLD Conference, much has transpired. Pat Tefft Cousin and I worked to bring a wonderful group of contributors together to address the theme for this book. The contributors' willingness to "hang in there" through the ups and downs of this project is worthy of celebration. Both Pat and I were honored to be in such distinguished company. Sadly, Pat passed away after an extended battle with cancer. Her lifeblood and spirit flow through this book. She was a remarkable teacher—brimming with compassion, conviction, and courage. Her energy and commitment to children, parents, and the field of education live on through this project.

Introduction

This book focuses on new perspectives related to learning disabilities and their meaning for classroom practice. Based on both theory and research, the text bridges the gap between general and special education pedagogy by including constructivist, humanist, critical pedagogical, sociocultural, and multicultural points of view. Through case studies and discussion, readers will see how classroom practices based on these perspectives can change the way educators work with students with learning disabilities. Readers will visit classrooms where students are experiencing success using student-centered curricular approaches, thematic teaching, multiage grouping, peer-mediated instruction, multiculturally oriented curricula, and authentic assessment.

The book is organized around three main thematic areas; (a) looking at learning disabilities in new ways, (b) assessing and supporting student learning and understanding in new ways, and (c) student-centered curriculum approaches. Each section is anchored by one or two "thought pieces" that present some of the main issues and questions brought about by the new perspectives. The thought pieces are followed by practical, teacher-accessible chapters that show the reader what such views look like in practice with real teachers and children. The text also covers an area that is rarely addressed—how to access the perspectives of the students who are being taught. This section of the text shows how to use different activities to find out what students think about their learning challenges, how they learn best, and how to use this information for curriculum planning.

Section 1

Looking at Learning Disabilities in New Ways

We, as educators, usually look at learning disabilities by focusing on the learners' problems and/or how their disabilities have been defined, leading us to think about learning disabilities as person specific rather than as a construct defined and perpetuated by societal beliefs and actions. This section provides readers with an opportunity to consider learning disabilities from a framework based on broader issues related to schooling in our society. The two thought pieces in this section, one discussing learning disabilities in relationship to school reform (Chapter 1) and the other wrestling with general issues related to diversity (Chapter 2), help us in this process of reconceptualization. Such a change of viewpoint is critical if we are to begin to think differently about children with learning disabilities and how we might best support them in school.

In the first chapter accompanying the thought pieces (Chapter 3), a public school educator chronicles her journey related to changing both her beliefs and her practices in working with children with learning disabilities. As she read and studied the field of learning disabilities in relationship to more general issues of schooling, she was able to better understand and operationalize educational practice that focused on students' strengths, thus achieving more success in the classrooms in which she worked. As she reflected on her practices, she recognized that change had to also occur outside her classroom doors if there was to be a real shift in how others viewed the education of children encountering difficulty in school. The accompanying chapter (Chapter 4) addresses and analyzes program coordination and leadership issues required to institutionalize this type of change at the school level.

Both the thought pieces and the subsequent chapters of this first section create the context for the rest of the book, where contributors provide further examples of how and why we must reconceptualize how we understand learning disabilities and change what we do in the classroom. This conceptual shift has made a huge difference for those of us involved in this project and also for the children for whom we work.

Reconceptualizing Learning Disabilities by Reconceptualizing Education

1

Curt Dudley-Marling

It is no coincidence that the field of learning disabilities emerged during the late 1950s and early 1960s, a period when concerns about the quality of education in American schools led to substantial increases in federal, state, and local resources earmarked for schools (Sleeter, 1987). Because learning disabilities, generally understood in terms of failure in school, exist within the structures of schooling (see Skrtic, 1991), efforts to reconceptualize the field of learning disabilities must begin by considering questions about how we currently understand schooling as well as questions about the current conceptualizations of learning disabilities. Following this line of argument, those who wish to consider alternative paradigms for serving students identified as learning disabled need to begin by asking two fundamental questions: What is the category learning disabilities for? and What are schools for?

A significant body of research exists that questions the effectiveness of special and remedial education programs in general (e.g., Allington & McGill-Franzen, 1989; Carlberg & Kavale, 1980; Glass, 1983) and learning disabilities programs in particular (e.g., Parkay & Bartnick, 1991; Smith, 1986; Taylor, 1991). Allington and McGill-Franzen (1989), for example, concluded that "the expectation that participation in remedial or special education will enhance [students'] access to larger amounts of higher quality instruction remains yet unfulfilled" (p. 85). On the average, programs for students with learning disabilities may be less effective than we wish. I am certain, however, that all of us who have worked with students labeled learning disabled believe that our efforts on behalf of these students have made a difference in the lives of individual students. This viewpoint supports the commonsense observation that learning disabilities programs are for children.

I believe that programs for students with learning disabilities have benefited—and will continue to benefit—individual children. And I do not dispute that programs for students labeled learning disabled have provided relief to overburdened teachers and comfort to guilt-ridden parents searching for explanations for their children's struggles in school (Dudley-Marling, 2000). I do argue, however, that learning disabilities programs do not *just* serve the needs of children, teachers, and parents. School-based learning disabilities programs—like special and remedial education programs more generally—also satisfy institutional needs (e.g., Dudley-Marling & Dippo, 1995; Dudley-Marling & Murphy, 1997; Skrtic, 1991; Sleeter, 1987). Arguably, special education, by signaling that the institution of schooling is responding to individual school failures, relieves pressure on schools to change the basic structures of schooling that produced so much failure in the first place. Tom Skrtic (1991) put it this way:

> Because schools are public organizations and therefore must be responsive to public demands for change, they relieve pressure for change by signaling the environment that change has occurred. That is, they create the illusion that they have changed when, in fact, they remain largely the same.... In this way, schools maintain their legitimacy and support... in the face of being unable to conform to environmental demands for change. (p. 166)

By helping to preserve the basic structures of schooling, the current learning disabilities paradigm—like special and remedial education more generally—also functions to preserve the ideological assumptions underlying the institution of schooling.[1] As Christine Sleeter (1987) put it, when we accept commonly used categories for children, "we also tacitly accept an ideology about what schools are for, what society should be like, and what the 'normal' person should be like" (p. 211). Yet these "commonly used categories" rest on values and assumptions that are not objective, cannot be proven, and serve the needs of some people (read: white, middle class, and upper-middle class) better than others (Gee, 1990; Sleeter, 1987). By locating school failure within the individual (i.e., *she* has a learning disability), for example, the current learning disabilities paradigm reinforces cultural assumptions that hold individuals solely responsible for their achievements in and out of school and efface the ways that such factors as racism, sexism, homophobia, and poverty affect people's life chances (Dudley-Marling & Murphy, 1997).

---

[1] I am using the term *ideology* here to refer to "values and viewpoints about the relationships between people and the distribution of social goods" (Gee, 1990, p. 144) including "life, space, time, 'good' schools, 'good' jobs, wealth, status, power, or control" (Gee, 1990, p. 23).

In the following sections, I discuss several assumptions underlying traditional models of schooling and examine ways in which the learning disabilities field is sustaining these assumptions. Then I briefly present an alternative set of assumptions that I believe ought to inform efforts to reconceptualize schooling and, by implication, the field of learning disabilities.

Some Assumptions Implicit in Traditional Schooling

Hard Work, Effort and a Good Education Are the Keys to Success in (and Out of) School.

Americans have an enduring faith in the potential of education to overcome any obstacle arising from an individual's background or experience. This conviction is at the heart of the Horatio Alger myth, which promises that with hard work and a good education, every citizen can reasonably hope to achieve some measure of social and economic success. However, the reality is that, for many people, education and hard work are insufficient to surmount the crippling effects of poverty or racial, gender, or religious discrimination. The evidence suggests that the stories of the rare individuals who have overcome disadvantage and/or discrimination to achieve high levels of economic or social success less demonstrate the possibility of success than reveal the effectiveness of institutional barriers in restricting access to social and vocational success to members of dominant groups.

Graff's (1979) study of the role of literacy in 19th-century Canada, for example, demonstrated that increased literacy was not advantageous to poorer groups in terms of income or power. The extent to which literacy was efficacious—at least in terms of vocational opportunities—depended on people's race, religion, and ethnicity. In 19th-century Canada, "being [black or Irish Catholic rendered literacy much less efficacious than it was for English Protestants" (Gee, 1990, p. 61). More recent evidence indicates that there continues to be an uneven relationship between effort and achievement in North American societies. Horsman (1990), for example, found that improved literacy, by itself, did little to improve the vocational prospects of rural women living in Nova Scotia. Similarly, Carnoy and Rothstein (1997) reported that the wage gap between young minority and young white people in California *grew* between 1980 and 1995 despite steady improvements in minority students' educational attainments over the same period. It may be true, as McCarthy and Crichlow (1993) asserted, that "the intolerable level of minority failure in schooling has to do with the fact that minority . . . cultural heritage is suppressed in the curriculum" (p. xv), but there is little reason to hope that improved curricula—however necessary—will be sufficient to transform the vocational and social prospects of students outside the cultural and economic mainstream.

The conclusion that education is a relatively ineffective agent for overcoming the effects of poverty and discrimination is discouraging enough, but there is an even more serious concern for educators. That is, that schools may *actively participate* in maintaining a status quo in which people have unequal access to our country's social and economic riches (e.g., Apple, 1996; Bowles & Gintis, 1975; Curtis, Livingstone, & Smaller, 1992; Jencks, 1972). A strong argument exists that schools help to maintain the social and economic status quo by functioning as gatekeepers that make it especially difficult—though not impossible—for members of nondominant groups to achieve either social or economic success. As indicated by a significant body of research, school discourse practices favor students who enter school with a certain kind of "cultural capital" (Bourdieu & Passeron, 1977)—specifically, those ways of talking, thinking, acting, doing, and valuing associated with white, able-bodied, middle- and upper-class males (Gee, 1990). White, middle-class students find, for example, that school literacy practices that stress storybook reading, being overly explicit, and learning to talk about literacy as much as doing literacy closely resemble the literacy practices in their homes (Gee, 1990; Heath, 1983). Therefore, middle- and upper-middle-class do not so much learn literacy in school as practice what they already know, making them appear to be quick studies compared to their less privileged classmates (Gee, 1990). As Banks (1993) put it, because "school knowledge is more consistent with the cultural experiences of most White middle-class students than for most other groups of students, these students have generally found the school a more comfortable place than have low income students and most students of color—the majority of whom are also low income" (Banks, 1993, p. 8). Therefore, rather than mediating the effects of poverty and discrimination, our schools—by favoring the discourse practices of white, middle-class, male students—actively participate in sorting students on the basis of race, culture, class, and gender (Bowles & Gintis, 1975; Gee, 1990; Swann, 1992).

Schools also favor those students, generally middle and upper-middle class, whose parents are able to bring to bear a range of social and economic resources in support of their schooling (Lareau, 1989). In general, middle- and upper-middle-class parents are better able, for example, to cultivate relationships with principals and teachers—by virtue of their similar backgrounds—than are lower income parents, making it more likely that their demands for specific curricular or programmatic resources (e.g., gifted programs, requests for particular teachers, and so on) for their children will be met (Dudley-Marling, 2000; Lareau, 1989). By contrast, poor and working-class parents may be unaware of even the possibility of making special requests of schools (Lareau, 1989). And if schools do not comply with the special requests of middle- and upper-middle-class parents, these parents typically have the economic resources to secure alternative support for their children outside of school (e.g., tutoring, private schools). Such options are rarely available to poor and working-class families.

Schooling may be about learning, but schools are not *just* about learning. As novelist and essayist Barbara Kingsolver put it, schooling is "two parts ABCs to fifty parts Where Do I Stand in the Great Pecking Order of Humankind?" (1995, p. 58). To the degree that students are sorted, at least partly, on the basis of who they are, where they are from, and how they speak (see Valdés & Figueroa, 1994), schools actively participate in maintaining a social and economic order that is strongly influenced by race, class, gender, and language.

Of particular interest here, learning disabilities programs, like other remedial and special education programs, reduce the pressure for meaningful educational reforms that address class, race, gender, and language bias in schooling by placing the responsibility for school failure upon the *student*. After all, it is the *student* who is removed from the classroom, not the teacher. It is the *student* who fails to learn to read as expected because *he* or *she* has a learning disability. Learning disabilities programs, by insisting that some student failure is due to problems residing within the individual (Miller, 1959), assist schools in portraying school failure as *personal trouble,* not as a public or social issue (Fulcher, 1989), and give no reason for educators and others to contemplate the possibility that school failure may be the result of an environment that systematically alienates and excludes significant sectors of the student population (Shapiro, 1980). To the degree that members of dominant groups allow themselves to be convinced that the blame for vocational and academic failure resides within individuals (who are unmotivated, irresponsible, unskilled, disabled, and so on), there is no reason to wonder about the possibility that the more privileged among us participate in, and benefit from, systemic discrimination that makes it difficult for some people (e.g., blacks, Hispanics, Native Americans) to succeed academically, vocationally, and socially no matter how motivated they are. Recent attacks on affirmative action in California, for example, ignored the reality that individual responsibility is often unrelated to vocational success (measured in terms of wages) (Carnoy & Rothstein, 1997). Ironically, the voters of California used a plebiscite—a demonstratively democratic exercise—to affirm a self-absorbed, self-interested individualism (Saul, 1995) that is an anathema to an inclusive democracy that makes a place for the voices of all of its citizens and finds ways to ensure that those voices are heard. Democracy is incompatible with racism, sexism, and poverty, in which the voices of many citizens are excluded or silenced. Arguably, this is the whole point of the Bill of Rights.

As indicated by the evidence cited here, better or different teaching techniques will be insufficient to overcome the effects of discrimination and poverty, which, for many students, are the real causes of school failure. By extension, learning disabilities programs—as they are currently constructed—are perhaps necessary but are ultimately insufficient for overcoming the failure of students disadvantaged by poverty and discrimination. Just as important, learning disabilities programs, by relieving pressure for substantive school change, help to maintain unfair school practices that bestow unearned privileges on students from middle- and upper-middle-class backgrounds.

School Knowledge Is Objective and Ideologically Neutral

There is an assumption in the way we talk about schooling that children are innocents who must be free from the political debates that occur outside of school. Forcing a particular ideological perspective on innocent children is generally considered to be a bad thing, and, therefore, most people assume that school knowledge is—or, at least, ought to be—ideologically neutral. In general, there is a preference in our society for objective knowledge untainted by human subjectivities. An important tenet of mainstream academic knowledge, for example, is that it is "neutral, objective, and . . . uninfluenced by human interests and values" (Banks, 1993, p. 9). However, since knowledge *always* implies a point of view, and since social and cultural factors *always* influence points of view, all knowledge, including school knowledge, is necessarily ideological. The Ebonics controversy, which made headlines across the country a couple of years ago, illustrates this point well, although a case can be made that all school knowledge—even learning to count to 100—implies a point of view (Davis, 1996).

In late 1996 the Oakland, California, school board declared that Black or African-American Vernacular English (Wolfram & Christian, 1989), also called Ebonics, was a legitimate language that could be used as the foundation for helping (some) black children learn "standard English" (McMillen, 1997). This decision sparked a furor among editorialists and media commentators, who have condemned the Oakland school board's actions as an assault on *proper English*. Presumably, if students who use Black Vernacular English (read: *bad* English) somehow come to believe that theirs is a legitimate language, as the Oakland school board has encouraged them to do, they will have no incentive to learn to speak *properly* (read: as the editorialists and commentators speak).

There is, however, reason to doubt this conclusion. As proponents of the Ebonics resolution noted (Perry, 1997), there is reason to believe that respecting students' nonstandard dialects will help them learn standard English (Linguistic Society of America, 1997; Perry & Delpit, 1998; Wolfram, 1998) and, perhaps, will positively affect their academic performance (McMillen, 1997). In addition, there is unassailable linguistic evidence that Black English is as systematic, complex, and rich as standard dialects of English (Labov, 1972; Wolfram & Christian, 1989).

As the Ebonics controversy made clear, Standard English is preferred not because it is correct or proper, but because it is the variety of English spoken by dominant groups; and Black English is devalued not because it is incorrect or inferior, but because it is spoken by a group of people who historically have been marginalized in our society. Simply put, schools are basically middle-class institutions that are staffed by members of the middle class who, not surprisingly, prefer their ways of speaking (i.e., *standard* English) over other people's ways of speaking English (e.g., the dialects of African-Americans largely excluded from the middle class). If African-Americans dominated our social, political, and educational institutions, there is every reason to believe that our schools would prefer African-American Vernacular English as the *standard*.

Language practices in our schools clearly favor the dialect(s) of some students over the dialect(s) of other students, and since some students (usually middle- and upper-middle class white students) come to school having already mastered preferred ways of speaking, children from dominant groups are much more likely to succeed in school and enjoy the rewards of schooling (higher education, better jobs)

(Gee, 1990). It is important to state again that there is no *rational* reason to prefer one dialect of English over another. Elevating one dialect as *the standard* is a subjective (albeit often unconscious) judgment, and since it implies "values and viewpoints about the relationships between people and the distribution of social goods" (Gee, 1990, p. 144), it is an inherently ideological practice. Equally disturbing, privileging one group's dialect also has the effect of masking the unfortunate reality that, ultimately, it is *who speaks* and *not how he or she speaks* that matters. Dialect is more often a marker of social class than a means for attaining a level of social and economic success.

Similar sociocultural arguments can be made about the ways schools equate middle- and upper-middle-class literacy practices with a universal literacy (e.g., Mitchell & Weiler, 1991). According to linguist James Gee (1990), people do not learn to *read* so much as they learn to read *particular* texts in *particular* ways appropriate to their social group. From this perspective, school literacy in the general classrooms does not just involve mastering a set of technical skills for making sense of print. It also involves learning to read in ways appropriate to dominant groups. Learning to talk *about* language, learning to talk *like books*, and learning to *tell fanciful stories* are not as much about learning to read as they are about learning to read, write, and talk like white, middle-class people (Gee, 1990; Heath, 1983; Michaels, 1981). Children who come to school already familiar with these discourse practices (i.e., middle- and upper-middle-class students) enjoy an advantage over their less privileged schoolmates that has at least as much to do with their sociocultural background as their ability to learn in school.

Through a kind of *ideological discourse laundering,* schools transform middle- and upper-middle-class ways of talking-reading-writing-thinking-believing into *right* ways of talking-reading-writing-thinking-believing. The result is that the dominant culture believes that schools offer students an ideologically free, level playing field but that just isn't so. If children are to succeed in school they must adopt middle-class ways of talking-reading-writing-thinking-believing, but if they come to school already possessing these ways of talking-reading-writing-thinking-believing their chances of success are greatly enhanced. In the end, much of what goes on in schools has the effect of affirming for middle- and upper-middle-class children that they are the "right sort of people" (Gee, 1990) with the right sort of background and values. Arguably, this type of ideological work is one of the primary functions of schooling.

The current learning disabilities, paradigms by defining learning problems primarily in terms of students' performance on standardized achievement tests, ratify the behavioral assumptions that underlie those tests. Further, by portraying school learning as a technical activity—that is, that learning to read, write, speak, listen, compute, and so on, are matters of mastering finite *sets of skills*—learning disabilities programs participate in masking the ideological implications of school learning. The learning disabilities field—indeed, all of special education—leaves unchallenged the questions of what counts as knowledge and who gets to decide which (or whose) knowledge counts (Scott, 1995).

It Is "Normal" to Fail in School

It is generally understood that school achievement, like most human behaviors, will distribute in a pattern similar to a bell curve. This means that a small number of children will do very well in school, a similarly small number will do very poorly, and the largest number will cluster around the middle range (i.e., *average*). It is also understood that half of the students in our schools will, by definition, test below average in terms of achievement and/or ability. In a society where *below average* is taken as both a pejorative and a statistical fact for half the population, it is not surprising that schools prefer to emphasize children's academic performance relative to their ability that is, their position on a bell curve rather than emphasizing their relative standing.

The naturalness of the normal distribution is open to question, however. Many (perhaps most) human behaviors do not distribute normally (reaction time is one of many examples of behaviors that do not). Most often, the normal distributions we have come to take as *natural* are a product of the tools we use to measure human behavior. Norm-referenced, standardized tests used to measure achievement and intelligence, for example, produce normal distributions because test developers insist that they must. Producing hierarchical distributions is at least as important to the people who develop and use these tests as are issues of validity and reliability.

For proponents of the normal curve it has explanatory as well as descriptive power. It provides, for example, a natural explanation for various social and economic hierarchies in our society. Statistician and eugenicist Ronald Fisher found the normal curve to be a potent explanation for racial hierarchies he believed to be *natural*. Contemporary neo-conservatives find the normal curve to be a *natural* explanation for the persistent and rapidly increasing gap between the rich and the poor. Herrnstein and Murray's (1994) book, *The Bell Curve*, is a contemporary fulfillment of Fisher's wish to find a "scientific" explanation for the persistent poverty of particular racial, social, and cultural groups. Herrnstein and Murray would have us believe that, in general, people are poor because they are less able (i.e., less intelligent) and, in what is a great comfort to the rich and powerful, that the privileged among us are privileged because they are more able (i.e., more intelligent).

Expectations that there are normal distributions in all human affairs blunt criticism that it is unfair for a small number of people to control a significant portion of our nation's economic resources. After all, if this is natural, it cannot be unfair. It is just the hand that nature dealt us. Tied to the doctrine of individualism, the concept of the normal curve produces a social Darwinism that both explains extreme poverty as *natural* and blames the poor for their condition (see Lugg, 1996).

The concept of normality is also used to protect the social and economic status quo, with *normal* being equated with the traditions of dominant groups. "Family values," for example, is equated with the norms of white, middle- and upper-middle-class Christian families, excluding the norms of significant numbers of minorities. For members of dominant groups, values are not deemed worthy unless they are the dominant (read: *normal*) values. The poor are poor because they don't have the right sort of values (i.e., middle-class values). Similarly, multiculturalism and affirmative action are often portrayed as threats to narrow and putatively traditional conceptions of what counts as normal (Scott, 1995). Here, outsiders (minorities) embody behaviors that jeopardize the very basis of a civilized society. Ebonics is a good example. By portraying the ways other people speak (dialects) as substandard or improper (i.e., not normal), it is possible to justify discriminatory practices that exclude people whose language, if accepted, would threaten orderly discourse. Of course, the real meaning behind criticism of Ebonics is not quite so noble. That is, if we accept nonstandard dialects, we will also have to accept the people who speak them. And, more critically, if all dialects were equal, some of us would no longer be able to justify our privilege on the basis of the ways we speak (that is, we do well because we speak well). Perhaps the most serious consequence of the concept of normality is the tendency to equate *normal* with *natural* and *abnormal* with *unnatural,* which justifies discrimination against gays and lesbians, for example, as a *normal* reaction to *unnatural behavior.*

Arguably, the learning disabilities field participates in sustaining the concept of normality in a number of ways. Perhaps most fundamental is its reliance on the so-called normal curve. Notions of "above average intelligence" and discrepancies between ability and achievement explicitly reference children's relative placement on taken-for-granted distributions of human ability. The learning disabilities field also reinforces statistical conceptions of normality by explaining the anomaly in intelligence testing of why some children fail to perform as predicted on various measures of academic achievement with the response: "They have a learning disability." Without the concept of learning disabilities, some people might question the meaning of IQ scores and the assumption of normality underlying the technology of intelligence testing. More seriously, of course, challenges to the "normal curve" might force us to reconsider the cultural myth that it is *natural* for human behavior and human accomplishments to distribute hierarchically.

Reconceptualizing Schooling

Ultimately, the meaning of learning disabilities is tied closely to the meaning of schooling, and the available evidence indicates that schools are not *just* about learning. Schools are also about sorting students on the basis of who they are, where they are from, and how they speak. The fact that such a strong relationship exists between school failure and the social, cultural, and economic backgrounds of students indicates that school reform is as much a moral as a technical issue.

If schooling is about sorting students and perpetuating social and economic inequities, then the field of learning disabilities, by helping to sustain the structures of schooling, also plays a role in maintaining a status quo in which relatively few control the lion's share of our country's social and economic resources. Reconceptualizing learning disabilities, then, is linked to our efforts to rethink what schools are for.

So what are the alternatives to today's schools that provide a ready means for organizing people into economic and social strata based on their social and cultural backgrounds? Can we imagine schools where students are not immersed in an ideology of individualism and narrow conceptions of normality that efface all of the social forces that affect people's lives? Can we imagine schools that are understood not in terms of teaching marketable skills that construct workers and citizens on the basis of the needs of the economy but rather in terms of teaching skills that construct an economy based on human needs?

Yes, I think we can, but we need to be explicit about what we want our schools to do. That is, we need to be explicit about what schools are for. For example:

▶ We want our schools to prepare good citizens, but we have to imagine models of good citizenship that go beyond filling students with cultural myths designed to create good and loyal Americans. "Feel good" patriotism based on self-serving historical narratives (Loewen, 1995) and unquestioned allegiance "to the flag and the country for which it stands" makes our students vulnerable to the forces of authoritarianism. Schools must not be thought of as means for passing on *truths* from one generation to another. They must encourage questioning and doubt which are central to citizen-based democracy (Saul, 1995). As noted by Saul (1995), "The virtue of uncertainty is not a comfortable idea, but then a citizen-based democracy is built upon participation, which is the very expression of permanent discomfort" (p. 195).

▶ We want our schools to cultivate the values of democracy, but we must reject circumscribed notions of democracy that equate democracy with consumer choice, an unregulated free market, majority rule, and the unfettered exercise of individual rights. Democratic societies make room for the range of human voices, and "good citizens" see beyond the needs of the individual to take responsibility for the common good.

▶ Working together is a fundamental idea in building and maintaining a democratic society (Saul, 1995), so we need to imagine schools where students negotiate and construct learning cooperatively and collaboratively. Democracy is about community (Greene, 1993), and school reformers must think about creating schools that are congenial to the range of differences children bring with them to school each day. Difference must not be thought of as something to be accommodated or tolerated but something to be celebrated as a means of enriching all of our lives.

▶ Schools must continue to develop the skills individuals need to get along in their lives—including their working lives—but we must also allow for the possibility of intellectual and artistic pursuits for the pure joy of it. Schooling should not be thought of as a commodity. People need to learn how to work, but they also need to learn to find pleasure in their lives. Currently, our society makes little room for people to find pleasure either in school or in the workplace.

These are, of course, just a few of the considerations for rethinking the purpose of schooling in the United States.

Summary

Most proposals for school reform do not challenge the basic assumptions of schooling. They merely seek more efficient means for achieving the same ends. Rarely do school reformers even consider the fundamental question of what schools are for. If we are serious about addressing the educational, social, and economic failures of so many of our citizens, we must face up to the fact that the struggle to reform our schools is more political and moral than it is technical. A learning disabilities field that seeks only to "fix" individual kids guarantees that significant numbers of children in our schools who are disadvantaged by poverty and discrimination will continue to fail with or without our efforts.

References

Allington, R. L., & McGill-Franzen, A. (1989). Different programs, indifferent instruction. In D. K. Lipsky & A. Gartner (Eds.), *Beyond special education: Quality education for all* (pp. 75–97). Baltimore: Paul H. Brookes.

Apple, M. W. (1996). Dominance and dependency: Situating the Bell Curve within the conservative restoration. In J. L. Kincheloe, S. R. Steinberg, & A. D. Gresson III (Eds.), *Measured lies: The Bell Curve examined* (pp. 51–69). New York: St. Martin's Griffin.

Banks, J. A. (1993). The canon debate, knowledge construction, and multicultural education. *Educational Researcher, 22,* 4–14.

Bourdieu, P., & Passeron, J. C. (1977). *Reproduction in education, society, and culture.* Beverly Hills, CA: Sage.

Bowles, S., & Gintis, H. (1975). *Schooling in capitalist America.* New York: Basic Books.

Carlberg, C., & Kavale, K. (1980). The efficacy of special versus regular class placement for exceptional children. *Journal of Special Education, 14,* 295–309.

Carnoy, M., & Rothstein, R. (1997). Are black diplomas worth less? *The American Prospect,* Jan.-Feb. (No. 30), 42–46.

Curtis, B., Livingstone, D. W., & Smaller, H. (1992). *Stacking the deck: The streaming of working-class kids in Ontario schools.* Toronto: Our Schools/Ourselves Educational Foundation.

Davis, B. (1996). *Basic irony: Troubling foundations of school mathematics.* Unpublished manuscript, York University, Toronto.

Dudley-Marling, C. (2000). *A family affair: How school troubles come home.* Portsmouth, NH: Heinemann.

Dudley-Marling, C., & Dippo, D. (1995). What learning disability does: Sustaining the ideology of schooling. *Journal of Learning Disabilities, 28,* 408–414.

Dudley-Marling, C., & Murphy, S. (1997). A political critique of remedial reading programs: The example of Reading Recovery. *The Reading Teacher, 50,* 460–468.

Fulcher, G. (1989). *Disabling practices? A comparative approach to education policy and disability.* Philadelphia: Falmer Press.

Gee, J. P. (1990). *Social linguistics and literacies.* Philadelphia: Falmer Press.

Glass, G. V. (1983). Effectiveness of special education. *Policy Studies Review, 2,* 65–78.

Graff, H. J. (1979). *The literacy myth: Literacy and social structure in the 19th century city.* New York: Academic Press.

Greene, M. (1993). Imagination, community, and the school. *Review of Education, 15,* 223–231.

Heath, S. B. (1983). *Ways with words: Language, life, and work in communities and classrooms.* Cambridge: Cambridge University Press.

Herrnstein, R. J., & Murray, C. A. (1994). *The bell curve: Intelligence and class structure in American life.* New York: Free Press.

Horsman, J. (1990). *Something in my mind besides the everyday: Women and literacy.* Toronto: Women's Press.

Jencks, C. (1972). *Inequality.* New York: Harper Colophon Books.

Kingsolver, B. (1995). *High tide in Tucson: Essays from now or never.* New York: HarperCollins.

Labov, W. (1972). *The language of the inner city.* Philadelphia: University of Pennsylvania Press.

Lareau, A. (1989). *Home advantage: Social class and parental intervention in elementary education.* Philadelphia: Falmer Press.

Linguistic Society of America. (1997). *LSA resolution on the Oakland "Ebonics" issue.* [http://www.lsadc.org/ebonics.html]

Loewen, J. W. (1995). *Lies my teacher told me: Everything your American history textbook got wrong.* New York: Touchstone.

Lugg, C. A. (1996). Attacking affirmative action: Social Darwinism as public policy. In J. L. Kincheloe, S. R. Steinberg, & A. D. Gresson III (Eds.), *Measured lies: The Bell Curve examined* (pp. 367–378). New York: St. Martin's Griffin.

McCarthy, C., & Crichlow, W. (1993). Theories of identity, theories of representation, theories of race. In C. McCarthy & W. Crichlow (Eds.), *Race, identity and representation in education* (pp. xiii–xxiv). New York: Routledge.

McMillen, L. (1997, January 17). Linguists find the debate over "Ebonics" uninformed. *The Chronicle of Higher Education,* p. A16.

Michaels, S. (1981). "Sharing time": Children's narrative styles and differential access to literacy. *Language in Society, 10,* 423–442.

Mills, C. W. (1959). *The sociological imagination.* Oxford: Oxford University Press.

Mitchell, C., & Weiler, K. (Eds.). (1991). *Rewriting literacy: Culture and the discourse of the other.* Toronto: OISE Press.

Parkay, F. W., & Bartnick, W. M. (1991). A comparative analysis of the "holding" power of general and exceptional education. *Remedial and Special Education, 12*(5), 17–22.

Perry, T. (1997). "I 'on know why they be trippin'." *Rethinking Schools, 12*(1), 3–5.

Perry, T., & Delpit, L. (1998). *The real Ebonics debate: Power, language, and the education of African-American children.* Boston: Beacon Press.

Saul, J. R. (1995). *The unconscious civilization.* Concord, Ontario: Anansi.

Scott, J. W. (1995). The campaign against political correctness: What's really at stake. In J. Williams (Ed.), *PC wars: Politics and theory in the academy* (pp. 22–43). London: Routledge.

Shapiro, H. (1980). Society, ideology and the reform of special education. *Educational Theory, 30,* 211–223.

Skrtic, T. M. (1991). *Behind special education: A critical analysis of professional culture and school organization.* Denver, CO: Love.

Sleeter, C. E. (1987). Why is there learning disabilities? A critical analysis of the birth of the field in its social context. In T. S. Popkewitz (Ed.), *The formation of school subjects: The struggle for creating an American institution* (pp. 210–237). Philadelphia: Falmer Press.

Smith, C. R. (1986). The future of the LD field: Intervention approach. *Journal of Learning Disabilities, 19,* 461–472.

Swann, J. (1992). *Girls, boys, and language.* Oxford, UK: Blackwell.

Taylor, D. (1991). *Literacy denied.* Portsmouth, NH: Heinemann.

Valdés, G., & Figueroa, R. (1994). *Bilingualism and testing: A special case of bias.* Norwood, NJ: Ablex.

Wolfram, W. (1998). Dialect awareness and the study of language. In A. Egan-Robertson & D. Bloome (Eds.), *Students as researchers of culture and language in their own communities* (pp. 167–190). Cresskill, NJ: Hampton Press.

Wolfram, W., & Christian, D. (1989). *Dialects and education: Issues and answers.* Englewood Cliffs, NJ: Prentice-Hall Regents.

2

Reconceptualizing the Learning Disabilities Paradigm: Multicultural Imperatives

Bridgie Alexis Ford and Helen Bessent Byrd

Across the nation, a common factor in every neighborhood is the school. In the inner-city ghetto, barrio, or regentrified center city; in the suburb created by "white flight" and changed by the arrival of middle-income persons of color; in the rural communities of the South, New England, Appalachia, the plains, or the West Coast—everywhere, states require schooling for children and youth. With the diversity of the population on multiple variables, school systems are challenged to effectively serve all students. As a consequence, children who evince differences proven or perceived to be deficits are labeled with a disability and provided special services as appropriate. This effort has resulted in a potpourri of special education categories.

One category of special education that has remained nebulous and complex from its inception is learning disabilities (LD). For years there has been advocacy for an educational mechanism to provide services for youth exhibiting characteristics that make them eligible for the category currently termed *Specific Learning Disability*. Professionals across the field are now calling for a reconceptualization of the LD paradigm that examines the construct from multidimensional perspectives (Adelman & Taylor, 1993; Artiles & Trent, 1997; De Leon & Gonzales, 1991; Garcia, 1992; Lyon, 1996; and Obiakor & Utley, 1997) This chapter explores the relevant issues and offers a reconceptualization focused on clarity of the definition and multicultural factors.

One of the factors that supports revisitation and reformation of the current LD construct is the fact that the construct is so poorly defined that it is ineffective in gatekeeping (Lyon, 1996; Ysseldyke, Algozzine, & Epps, 1983). With the advent of federally mandated services (Education of All Handicapped Children Act [EHA], 1975) for students labeled as having learning disabilities, large numbers of students were rapidly and consistently identified for placement. The majority of these youth were white and/or middle class (Harry, 1994; U.S. Department of Education, 1996). Parents who were supposedly informed on disability and placement options, as well as teachers, were instrumental in the identification of many students as youth with learning disabilities. The LD category became loosely referred to as the category for privileged white children and youth who experienced learning and behavioral problems in school. Indeed, the inadequacy of the definitions provided for identifying youth for LD placement has resulted in a surge of inappropriate placements.

Current demographic changes also support a revisitation and reconceptualization of the LD paradigm. Statistics on changes in population groups during the 1990s and forecasting into the 21st century show that collectively those identified as today's ethnic minority groups will soon constitute a majority of America's society (Grossman, 1998; Harry, 1994; U.S. Department of Education, 1996). The continuing challenges surrounding both the overidentification and the underidentification of ethnic minority children as having specific learning disabilities make it imperative that there be systemic inclusion of knowledge about children of color (and their families and communities) in this reconceptualization.

Yet another factor supporting a reconceptualization of the current LD construct is the inadequate preparation of school personnel for teaching culturally diverse students. The literature continues to report that special educators experience feelings of inadequacy when making educational decisions about quality programming for ethnic minority youth with disabilities. Obiakor, Algozzine, and Ford (1993), for example, emphasized that both general and special education have failed to deliver quality programming for African-American youth with disabilities because both systems continue to view these youth from a deficit perspective. Furthermore, demographic shifts toward a white, female teaching workforce reveal that unless effective proactive measures are conducted, ethnic minority youth will not see themselves in the faces of the teachers in their schools. In light of these facators, a multicultural approach to the schooling process is essential for special educators to acquire the competencies that foster equity in quality educational opportunities for students. There is equivocation over what term to use to describe the population of persons from culturally/ethnically diverse groups. The term "minority" is used in this chapter because of its familiarity; however, the term is used judiciously for several reasons. First, due to rapidly changing demographics, student populations that are traditionally included under the minority umbrella may be the majority in certain school systems, especially in the inner cities (Grossman, 1998; Harry, 1994; Obiakor et al., 1993; U.S. Department of Education, 1996; Wald, 1996). Second, the term extends beyond numbers and captures the inequities faced by minorities in the distribution of political and economic power. Third, some individuals from culturally diverse groups find the term *minority* to be offensive, carrying a negative connotation (Council for Exceptional Children—National Black Caucus of Special Educators, 1995; Wald, 1996).

Unless and until serious attention is given to understanding the impact of culture on school personnel interactions with children and youth whose worldview and approaches to learning are different from the monolithic orientation of the school, such youth, their families, and their communities are going to remain at a disadvantage (Cummins, 1986; Franklin, 1992; Melendez & Ostertag, 1997; Obiakor, 1999; Obiakor et al., 1993; Rueda, Ruiz, & Figueroa, 1995; Shade, 1989; Voltz, 1995; Wald, 1996). While it has always been a moral requirement to respond to diversity in the classroom, the current population shifts make it a practical requirement as well.

In this chapter, the LD construct is analyzed within the context of a multicultural paradigm. Two questions undergird the discussion: What policies and practices associated with the current LD paradigm lead to inequities in educational opportunities for ethnic minority learners? How might the situation be remedied? These concerns are addressed by (a) an examination of the current LD construct, (b) a review of the present and anticipated phenomena that necessitate a multicultural perspective for any LD paradigm, and (c) discussion of issues that must be addressed in the reformation of the LD paradigm.

The LD Construct

The LD construct was introduced during the early 1960s, and the definition used by the public school system today is the one that was proposed by the National Advisory Committee on Handicapped Children in 1968. It was incorporated into EHA (PL 94–142; now the Individuals With Disabilities Education Act of 1997, or IDEA, PL 105–17), and, as such, it is the definition tied to federal funding for special education services for the LD population. It reads, in part, as follows:

> The term specific learning disability means a disorder in one or more of the basic psychological processes involved in understanding or in using language, spoken or written, which may manifest itself in an imperfect ability to listen, speak, read, write, spell, or do mathematical calculations. The term includes such conditions as perceptual handicap, brain injury, minimal brain dysfunction, dyslexia, and developmental aphasia. Such terms don't include children who have learning difficulties which are primarily the result of visual, hearing, or motor handicaps, of mental retardation or emotional disturbance, or of environmental, cultural, or economic disadvantage. (*Federal Register,* 1977, p. 65083)

The diagnostic criteria of the federal definition have led to at least two major problems that have complicated the identification process for the LD category. The first problem derives from the discrepancy clause included in the definition; the second derives from the exclusionary clause.

Problems With the Discrepancy Clause of the LD Definition

One diagnostic criterion of the federal definition of learning disability requires the presence of a significant discrepancy between potential (as indicated in IQ scores) and academic achievement (as determined by achievement measures) of the student. In other words, the child with learning disabilities is one who exhibits unexpected academic difficulty. However, the validity of the elements constituting the discrepancy clause has been called into question (Harry, 1994; Lyon, 1996; U.S. Department of Education, 1996). For example, Lyons revealed that the IQ/achievement discrepancy does not differentiate a poor reader with average to above average intelligence from a poor reader whose intelligence is commensurate with his or her low reading ability. In other words, discrepant readers (high IQ) and nondiscrepant readers did not differ on cognitive and neurological assessment measures.

Another problem with the discrepancy clause is that different, often ambiguous criteria have been used across and within states to determine a "significant discrepancy." Students who are classified as having a learning disability in one state may not meet the criteria in another state. The same may be true for students in different schools within the same district. As a result, teachers, parents, and other concerned citizens have asked, time after time, "What is LD?" The question clearly brings to light the ambiguity of the LD construct. In Harry (1994) commentary on disproportionate representation, this ambiguity in determining a significant discrepancy is a contributing factor in the shift in the racial composition of LD classes to include more ethnic minority youth.

A key element to the discrepancy clause requirement is the existence of average intelligence based on IQ test results. Thus, the academic failure of youth who score low on IQ tests (often ethnic minority youth) is oftentimes considered to be expected and commensurate to their low intellectual ability based on the IQ test results.

Some ethnic minority children and youth, in particular those from poor backgrounds, often do not score in the average to above average range on IQ tests. The validity of IQ tests, however, has been called into question. According to numerous studies, these tests (a) ignore the different manifestations of cultural and social experiences of individuals in the United States, (b) disregard the inequities in educational opportunities afforded to many ethnic minority youth, (c) fail to recognize that all who take the test do not have equal facility with "standard" English language, (d) dismiss the cumulative historical and present-day experiences resulting from the dynamic interplay between the perpetual political, social, and economic forces on the value system of many ethnic minorities, (e) assign differences in scores as representing deficits in mental abilities rather than differences in behavior styles, and (f) fail to take into consideration assessor bias (Baca & Cervantes, 1984; Dent, 1976; Hilliard, 1995; Midgette, 1995; U.S. Department of Education, 1996).

Although the use of intelligence test results for decision making is wrought with unresolved flaws, all too often, other facts (e.g., family structure and family size) shape perceptions of student abilities and their placement into LD special education programs (Artiles, 1998).

According to Slaughter and Epps (1987), in the perception of school personnel, the community and family replace IQ in determining the learning potential of children in economically depressed communities. The school personnel have deficit mind-set when thinking about these children, which contributes to negative attitudes and low expectations and leads to differential treatment of many ethnic minority students within both general and special classes. By ascribing the principal cause of school difficulties (viewed as resulting from lowered intelligence due to poverty) of minority learners to external, out-of-school factors, school personnel are justifiably relieved of accountability and responsibility pertaining to their attitudes, quality of teaching, and overall service delivery to minority students.

Although socioeconomic factors do play a role in accounting for academic variance, research (Comer, 1989; Croninger, 1990; Cummins, 1986; Ford, 1995; Wang, Haertel, & Walberg, 1993–1994) delineating factors that make a difference in the provision of quality programming and student outcomes has specifically emphasized the determinant effect of school-related variables, such as teacher expectations, teacher-student interaction, curriculum, classroom climate, and parent involvement. Poor communities are generally cursed with ill-equipped schools, inferior educational services, and inexperienced teachers (Ford, 1995; Harry, 1994; Kozol, 1991).

According to statistics from the U.S. Department of Education's 18th Annual Report to Congress (U.S. Department of Education, 1996), African-American youth in the inner city are more overrepresented in the mental retardation category than in the LD option and are overrepresented in the LD category as compared to non-inner-city youth. Despite the special education reforms that have occurred since the 1960s, the effectiveness of special education classes for students in general and ethnic minority students in particular remains controversial. However, because of their socially acceptable status and their emphasis on average to above average students, LD placements usually offer a less watered-down curriculum than mental retardation placements, and, theoretically, teachers tend to hold higher expectations.

Given the problems surrounding the use of IQ tests for certain ethnic minority groups, coupled with the continued deficit paradigm about poor ethnic minority children, more varied, alternative authentic measures of intellectual abilities (Cheng, Ima, & Labovitz, 1994; Midgette, 1995; Suzuki, Meller, & Ponterotto, 1996) are imperative if the IQ/achievement discrepancy clause remains a part of the LD diagnostic criteria. As Midgette (1995) stated, any assessment of ethnically or racially different exceptional students must involve programmatic efforts on the part of psychologists, teachers, administrators, parents, and other community stakeholders.

Problems With the Exclusionary Clause of the LD Definition

The other major problem with the current LD diagnostic criteria derives from the exclusionary clause. This portion of the federal definition stipulates, in essence, that the child who does not fit any other category of disability and who is not learning in school may be identified as having a learning disability. Supposedly, the definition excludes children and youth who manifest difficulties due to economic and cultural disadvantages. That being the case, the classification of LD is not a realistic option for a large segment of ethnic minority children whose families reside in economically depressed areas. Two questions come to mind at this point: Are these youth to be excluded from LD services because lowered intelligence is presumed? What general educational services are to be systematically provided to underachieving average youth from poor communities?

In practice, as noted by Shapiro (1996), poor ethnic minority students are the target for LD classes despite the fact that these youth do not have identifiable learning disabilities. Likewise, data from the 18th Annual Report of the U.S. Department of Education (U.S. Department of Education, 1996) indicated a growing inclusion of ethnic minority students in LD programming as well as an overrepresentation of certain groups (e.g., Hispanic Americans and Native Americans) in this programming.

Other Problems With the Definition

An underlying assumption for LD eligibility is that academic failure is occurring despite the fact that the child has been exposed to appropriate instruction. This brings into question the issue of equity in educational opportunity. Child-centered culturally responsive curriculum models, instructional strategies, and managerial techniques designed to build on children's culturally influenced learning experiences have not been a part of special education programming. Scholars (Ford, 1995; Ford, Obiakor, & Patton, 1995; Franklin, 1992) continue to point to the lack of adequately prepared educators, administrators, and other significant school personnel to work with ethnically and racially diverse learners and their families. As a result of this deficiency, many of these youth are not exposed to appropriate instruction and indeed fail, at least in part because of noncomplementary teaching procedures.

Collectively, the LD definition lacks the clinical specificity that is evident in some other disability definitions, such as those for orthopedic impairment and visual impairment. The reasoning embedded within the LD definition is, simply, "If it is not *(A)* or *(B)* then it must be *(C)*. In other words, the LD definition is based on the elimination of other disability categories. Thus, the construct of learning disabilities has become a catchall, an invitation for placement of children who are not learning in school for disparate reasons.

As previously stated, poor ethnic minority students are often identified as LD despite the fact that a specific disability is not evident. Even with scholarly discussions about the need to move from a deficit paradigm to one of "difference" regarding ethnic minority students and their families, daily practices suggest that neither general nor special education has integrated a difference model in the schooling process. As a consequence of all the factors mentioned thus far, a new paradigm that clearly defines the LD construct and appropriately distinguishes the children who require services is warranted.

Present and Anticipated Phenomena Supporting a Multicultural Perspective

Several important factors support the need to construct a new LD paradigm using a multicultural perspective. They include but are not limited to the following:

- Changing student demographics
- Inadequate teaching workforce
- Disproportionate representation of ethnic minority youth in LD programs
- Poor personnel preparation
- Limited parental involvement and home-school-community networks

These factors are discussed in the following sections.

Changing Student Demographics

As mentioned earlier in this chapter the population statistics for ethnic groups in America are changing. A condition that has been called the "browning of America" is occurring. The number of Americans and other Americans commonly referred to as ethnic minority groups (including African-Americans, Hispanic Americans, Asian Americans, and American Indians) is rising in proportion to the number of white Americans. This shift is primarily the result of higher birthrates among these minority groups. It follows that the impact of these changes in numbers is being felt in the schools before it impinges on the workforce.

From an analysis of demographic data from varied government reports, Smith-Davis and Smith (1993) found that the percentage of non-Hispanic white Americans in the population declined from 83.5% in 1970 to 75.6% in 1990. They also found that the states that were growing the fastest were those with the greatest number of persons from ethnic minority groups. With regard to children and youth, they found that the total (or collective) minority rose from 26.2% of the population in 1980 to 31.1% in 1990.

By this year, over one third of the students in U.S. public schools is expected to be from culturally diverse backgrounds. The three fastest growing groups are Hispanic Americans, African Americans, and Southeast Asian Americans. The two largest minority groups, African Americans and Hispanic Americans, will constitute almost one third of the total school enrollment (Grossman, 1998). Presently, 23 of the 25 largest school systems in the country are heavily composed of students from ethnic minority groups, with approximately 75% of the students being African Americans.

Along with the increase in minority students in U.S. schools, there has been an increase in the number of minority group members identified as being learning disabled. Today, the percentages of selected minority groups in LD programs are almost equal to the percentage of white Americans in those programs (African Americans, 5.8%; Hispanic Americans, 5.3%; white Americans, 5.3%). If current patterns of differential educational treatment continue, an even higher number of ethnic minority students in our schools will be classified as needing of remedial and/or special education services.

Inadequate Teaching Workforce

Consideration of the demographics of those who teach is as important as the study of the demographics of those who learn. There are two critical supply-and-demand issues that require attention: (a) fairness in the proportion of teachers to students based on ethnicity, and (b) the supply of credentialed teachers of students with learning disabilities. The incommensurate numbers of ethnic minority special education teachers in U.S. schools necessitate a revisiting of recruitment, retention, and graduation issues as well as certification or licensure issues. The reasons posited in the literature for attention to this matter include (a) enhancement of student self-concept, (b) eradication of negative attitudes in the teaching force, (c) the promise of fair assessment, (d) increased knowledge of the student and the appropriate context for learning, (e) provision of role models for ethnic minority group children, and (f) facilitation of cross-cultural understanding (Byrd, 1995; Ford, 1995; Hilliard, 1995; Midgette, 1995; Obiakor, 1995; Smith-Davis, 1995; Wald, 1996).

The low numbers of minority teachers in the LD field have received much attention in recent years. These low numbers are just one part of the fallout from the integration brought about by the *Brown v. Board of Education* (1954) court decision. With regard to African American teachers, Witty (1982) offered the following recommendations:

- ▶ Reduce the disparity in equal access to teachers of the same race by employing black teachers in sufficient numbers to make the ratio of black teachers to black children equal to the ratio of white teachers to white children
- ▶ Assure fair representation of blacks on the administrative staff, boards, task forces, committees, and commissions that make and administer educational policy
- ▶ Identify black parents and community organizations that set black children as a goal of highest priority and provide linkages to the schools
- ▶ Expand the professional component (of teacher preparation programs) to include emphasis on the teacher's self-concept

In a recent study that addressed the ethnic demographics of special education teachers, Wald (1996) noted that the diminished supply of teachers from minority groups (with 86% of the teachers being white, 10% black, 2% Hispanic, and 2% "other") is the result of several factors. She cited failure to reach the point of having the option to enter teaching due to poverty, the attraction of other majors, difficulty completing the preservice education programs due to alienation and racism, and the adverse effect of the requirement of meeting a criterion on standardized tests.

It was predicted that the number of ethnic minority teachers would drop to approximately 5% by the year 2000. Although the projected shortage of minority teachers will be a tremendous loss to all students, the loss will be particularly detrimental for ethnic minority students, who will lose out on many opportunities to have school personnel from their culture as leaders, role models, and mentors. The decrease in the number of ethnic minority teachers will mean ethnic minority students will, on a long-term basis, engage in the interpersonal teaching-learning process with persons whose worldview and cultural and experiential backgrounds are significantly different from their own. Wald cited the report "Schools and Staffing in the United States: 1990–91" which indicated that 13.5% of the U.S. teaching force during the 1990 school year was composed of people of color, whereas 31.4% of all students represented diverse populations.

An issue that is often neglected is the importance of white students having the experience of being educated by ethnic minority teachers (Smith-Davis, 1995). If a goal of education is to adequately prepare youth to function in our culturally pluralistic society, then *all* students are better prepared for life when they are systematically exposed to cultural diversity in the school, which is society's primary formal learning environment.

Another issue that must be addressed is the dramatic shift that has been occurring toward a female teaching force. According to the U.S. Department of Education (1996), women make up 68% of the teaching force. Since teachers often serve as role models for ethnic minority youth, the decline in the number of male teachers in general and ethnic minority males in particular is problematic. Recruitment efforts to increase the number of male teachers should be a priority.

Disproportionate Representation of Ethnic Minority Youth in LD Programs

After years of educational and civil rights reform, ethnic minority students continue to receive differential forms of treatment by the educational system. The controversial issue of disproportionate representation—the over- and underrepresentation of ethnically and culturally diverse students in special education services and programs—remains alive (Artiles & Trent, 1994; Harry, 1994). Governmental reports (e.g., the 18th Annual Report of the U.S. Department of Education, 1996) continue to indicate that the disproportionate representation of racial and ethnic minorities occurs not only in the disability categories that require professionals to make more complex judgments about placements, such as mental retardation, serious emotional disturbance, or learning disability, but also in such categories as deaf/blindness, visual impairment, and orthopedic impairments. The issue of representation is further compounded by the fact that minority youth now constitute the majority in many inner-city school systems. Despite this demographic shift, data consistently evidence disproportionate representation of ethnic minority youth in special education programming (Harry, 1994).

Learning disability is the fastest growing disability category and, as previously stated, is a socially acceptable one because of its focus on children with average or above average intellectual ability. Representation of ethnic minority students in the LD category varies from state to state, district to district, and school to school. However, a national profile reveals that from the 1980s to the 1990s, Hispanic Americans and American Indians have been overrepresented in LD programs, African Americans have been roughly proportionately represented, and Asian Americans have been underrepresented.

An Office of Civil Rights (OCR) report contrasting inner-city with non-inner-city schools for the 1992-93 school year found that the non-inner-city areas had higher percentages of their total enrollment of African American and Hispanic students identified as having specific learning disabilities than did inner-city districts. Although the inner city districts enroll a larger percentage of students living in poverty, a larger percentage of students with limited English proficiency, and a larger percentage of students from racial/ethnic minority groups, the OCR report (as cited in U.S. Department of Education, 1996) suggested that inner-city districts served similar percentages of students in special education as suburban and rural districts served. Differences existed in the representation per special education category. These differences (e.g., the higher percentage of LD students in non-inner-city compared to inner-city schools) were described as being due to higher rates of poverty among minorities. The label of mental retardation was more frequently associated with inner-city placement. The label of mental retardation was more frequently associated with inner-city placement.

In an article entitled "A Separate and Unequal Education for Minorities With Learning Disabilities," Shapiro (1996) discussed the results of a study based on the school records of more than 65,000 students in special education in Connecticut regarding "who gets labeled." The study concluded that males from minority groups are more than twice as likely to be labeled as having a serious emotional disturbance, than white American males, and even when minority students are diagnosed as having learning disabilities they are more than twice as likely to remain in separate classes. Placement in full-time separate LD classes in inner-city district was a trend also found in the OCR data. The OCR report revealed that students classified as having specific learning disabilities living in inner cities were more likely to be placed in full-time restrictive learning environments than less restrictive settings. In addition, the data indicated 36.4% full-time LD placement for the inner city compared to 19% full-time for the non-inner city.

As previously stated, the effectiveness of special education classes for many youth from poor backgrounds remains questionable. When they are placed in separate classes or schools for most of the day, their chances of being exposed to motivating and culturally responsive curriculum and instruction diminishes even more.

Finally, the data on outcomes for youth with disabilities in inner cities is not positive. Studies show that they are less likely than their peers in suburban and rural areas to graduate from high school and are more likely to drop out of school. The National Longitudinal Transition Study of Special Education Students (NLTS), cited in the 18th Annual Report of the U.S. Department of Education (U.S. Department of Education, 1996), listed drop-out percentages for youth with disabilities at 36.6% in urban areas, 24.6% in suburban areas, and 31.4% in rural areas. The graduation rates for these students were reported to be 50.8% in urban areas, 66.9% in suburban areas, and 60.8% in rural areas. The remaining students either were suspended/expelled or left school after reaching maximum age. Studies also show that the adverse consequences for adolescents who drop out of high school are magnified by pregnancy, underemployment, or unemployment, involvement in the juvenile justice system, and substance abuse (National Education Association, 1990; U.S. Department of Education, 1996). Overall, the data suggest the need to reconsider factors impacting placement patterns of ethnic minority youth.

Poor Personnel Preparation

Another factor that supports the need to revisit the LD paradigm from a multicultural perspective is personnel preparation. Any paradigm that fails to include appropriately trained personnel is doomed. Teacher education programs today should ensure that preservice teacher preparation provides knowledge, skills, and abilities for teaching culturally diverse students. In addition, continued learning opportunities should be a part of inservice personnel development programs. Both pre-service and in-service training programs should assist trainees and practitioners in (a) acquiring an overall appreciation and valuing of cultural diversity, (b) obtaining an understanding of the cultural and language backgrounds of LD students who are from minority backgrounds, (c) becoming more knowledge about the impact of mismatches among cognitive structures, speech patterns, and behavior used in homes and schools, and (d) affording more respect for the skills and knowledge offered by culturally diverse parents and communities (Byrd, 1995; Ford, 1992, 1998, 2000; Harry, 1995; Obiakor & Utley, 1997; Ortiz, Yates, & Garcia, 1990).

To deliver effective education for students with learning disabilities, general and special educators must be provided with learning experiences that prepare them to create and orchestrate a multicultural education for all students. Byrd's (1994) multicultural multicognitive model (see Figure 2.1) is one means of preparing teachers to provide a supportive environment for the learning experiences of all children. The model consists of four overlapping circles, each of which represents a significant component of the milieu in which the child learns (or fails to do so). The components are cognitive style, cultural context, curricular content, and pedagogical tactics. By preparing teachers to address all of these factors, the model ensures that the overall milieu for the child's learning experience will be supportive.

The importance of ascertaining the learner's cognitive style and cultural context and then achieving a match of the two has been well documented. The learner's cognitive style may be determined in a number of ways. One way is to ascertain the learner's preference of sensory modalities for both input and output. In other words, a learner may learn best via auditory, visual, or tactile, kinesthetic input and may best express himself or herself through the same or a different mode. Another popular means of classifying cognitive styles is to use Gardner's multiple intelligences model (Armstrong, 1993; Gardner, 1993). While it is important to hone the learner's

FIGURE 2.1

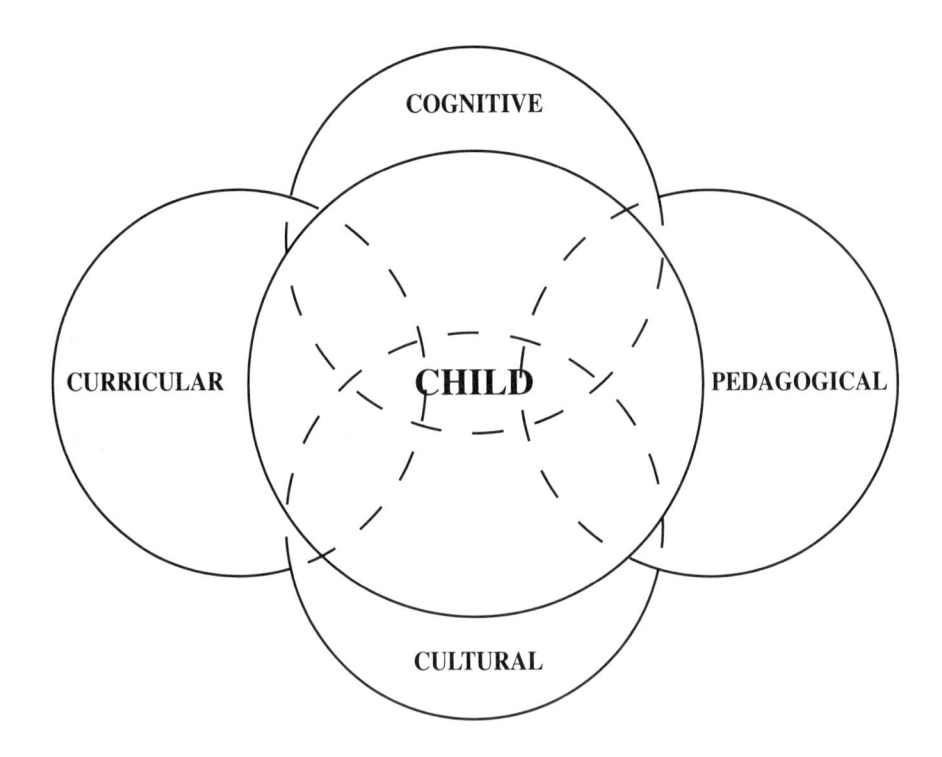

Multicultural Multicognitive Model

skills in each of the intelligences, it is even more critical that the preferred type of intelligence be determined to enhance the rate of content mastery.

After ascertaining the learner's cognitive style, the next step in Byrd's multicultural multicognitive model is to determine the learner's cultural context. To accomplish this, it is necessary to seek to know the learner's background by gathering data from the family and community. Various schemes have been developed for determining the tenets of a learner's cultural context. For example, Wilson (1972) differentiated indigenous values of black Americans from Anglo Americans, and more recently, Nichols (1987) described four philosophical aspects of cultural difference between European, African, and Asian peoples (Anderson, 1988; Lynch & Hanson, 1992; Shade, 1989).

Curricular content is another of the circles of inclusion specified by this model. In addition to all of the other reasons for selecting certain concepts and skills for students to master, it is important that the content reflect the learner (i.e., the learner needs to see himself or herself in the curricular content). Byrd (1995) described three ways to accomplish this, each reflecting a different degree of integration: (a) supplantation, or the replacement of existing course content with new content about the cultures of specific groups; (b) supplementation, or the addition of content on the specific group, e.g., African-Americans, to the existing curriculum; and (c) permeation, or the infusion or integration of the standard Eurocentric curriculum with content about the specific group. Most people would agree that the third alternative is the most appropriate, since it provides for adequate interspersion and sequencing of subject matter into the overall curriculum and accentuates both the interrelatedness of subject matter and the interdependence of cultural groups.

The final circle of inclusion in the model is pedagogical tactics, or the strategies used for the delivery of instruction. A plethora of such strategies exist. The four that follow are ones that Byrd (1994) deemed critical for multicultural education. They are (a) conflict resolution skill development—peaceable strategies for reducing hostilities and solving differences, (b) antiracist learning/teaching—confronting prejudice, racism, stereotypes, and discrimination through discussions, (c) role-playing—experiencing situations through forced compliance or value discrepancy study, and (d) cultural immersion experience—removing the student from a familiar environment and placing him or her in another cultural setting 24 hours per day 7 days per week for a prescribed period. Some additional effective pedagogical strategies include cooperative learning and metacognitive skills development.

Byrd's multicultural multicognitive model provides a means of creating an effective learning environment for children and youth. It is only when personnel are trained to create such environments that students will be given greater opportunities to realize their potential.

Limited Parental Involvement and Home-School-Community Networks

The positive effects of parental involvement on ethnic minority students' motivation and academic attainment have been well documented (Ascher, 1987; Banks, 1997; Brandt, 1998; Comer, 1989; Croninger, 1990; Epperson, 1991; Ford Foundation and John D. & C. T. MacArthur Foundation, 1989; Harry, 1995). Research documents that collaborative school/community initiatives are important components of schools that make a difference, those that optimize the educational service delivery for youth and their families (Comer, 1989; Cummins, 1986; Ford Foundation and John D. & C. T. MacArthur Foundation, 1989; Hatch, 1998). Collaborative initiatives between schools and *significant resources* from local communities are beneficial to all students. However, this relationship is especially advantageous in enhancing the schooling process for youth from ethnic minority populations. *Significant resources* are organizations, agencies, and individuals that local community residents perceive as providing valuable services. The service may encompass educational, advocacy, financial, legal and/or empowerment assistance (Ford, 1998). For some members of ethnic minority groups, *significant community resources* often operate as friendly domains to acquire vital information (e.g., educational related information), develop and practice empowering skills, and to express opinions (Banks, 1997; Ford, 1995, 1998; Rueda, 1997; Telesford, 1994). The importance of school/community collaboration is explicitly described in Lewis and Morris' (1998) discussion of the *Communities in Schools* project (formerly known as Cities in Schools) founded in 1977. Given the current escalation of academic and social crises confronted by many ethnic minority youth within schools (e.g., persistent disproportionate representation in special education programs and significant decrease in ethnic minority teachers to serve as adult role models and mentors), the mission of *Communities in Schools* "to champion the connection of needed community resources with schools to help young people successfully learn, stay in school, and prepare for life" (p. 34) is equally crucial today and for the near future. However, most schools have not systematically attempted to capitalize on the expertise and pockets of strengths of ethnic minority families and communities respectively. IDEA requires extensive parental participation, including parental consent for identification, involvement in assessment, and participation in the development of the individualized education program. (IEP). Beyond that, however, authentic partnerships between ethnic minority parents and the school, whereby parents are in empowering positions, are more the exception than the rule. This lack of participation is detrimental in many ways, one being that parents who are not "empowered" in this way will seldom bring about changes in identification, assessment policies and practices, and service delivery.

Although, ethnic minority parents historically have advocated for better services for their youth (e.g., the *Brown v. Board of Education* landmark case), participation by individual families with local school personnel is often at low levels. Several factors contribute to the lack of involvement by ethnic minority families at levels that lead to systemic changes in policies and procedures. These factors include both school- and family-imposed barriers, such as (a) the negative perception by school personnel of ethnic minority families and their contributions to the schooling process, (b) conflicts in values, (c) conflicting parent work schedules, (d) feelings of powerlessness and alienation by parents, (e) limited English proficiency, (f) child care and (g) transportation problems, and other competing priorities that take precedence over IEP meetings and other school conferences (Ford, 1995; Harry, 1995; Rueda, 1997; U.S. Department of Education, 1996).

Oftentimes, ethnic minority parents do not have adequate, in-depth knowledge about special education procedures and their rights as parents (Harry, 1995; Marion, 1980). If schools are to effectively form collaborative relationships with parents, school personnel must first evidence positive attitudes about the contributions of ethnic minority parents and next establish meaningful networks to arm parents with knowledge. As aforementioned for certain ethnic minority groups *significant* community-based organizations provide an arena for the dissemination of information in nonthreatening environments as well as offer "comfort" and a place to develop empowering skills. A major problem associated with the current and predicted teaching force that impacts school-community linkages is that school personnel are less and less connected to the communities of the children they serve. The majority of teachers do not and will not reside in the communities of their students. Consequently, they may not have knowledge of and access to *significant* individuals and organizations that provide invaluable education-oriented services to families in those communities (Ford, 1998). It therefore becomes imperative that schools connect with *significant* organizations of the communities they serve. Any reconceptualization of the LD paradigm must be holistic—that is, it must recognize the importance of the sociocultural background of each child. Empowered parents, as their children's primary teachers, can provide critical information to help ensure quality decision making.

Ford (1995, 1997, 1998, 2000) outlined a three-phase model (see Figure 2.2) to help provide preservice trainees and inservice-level school personnel with experiences that enhance authentic home/school/community collaboration. As shown in the figure, Phase 1 focuses the attention of the trainees and school personnel on themselves, helping them to reshape and redefine their personal attitudes regarding ethnic minority families and communities.

In Phase 2, the emphasis is on the development of an accurate knowledge base. In this phase of the model, preservice and inservice-level persons acquire information about the kind and degree of past and present school/community collaborative

---

Phase 1— **Reshaping Attitudes and Personal Redefinition**

Phase 2— **Development of Accurate Knowledge Base**
- **Analysis of historic and present school/community collaborative activities**
- **Identification of** *significant* **Community Organizations**

Phase 3— **Productive School/Community Networks**
- **Establishment of inclusive school/community partnerships**
- **Utilization of** *significant Community Resources* **by school personnel**

Source: Ford, B. A. & Reynolds, C. (2000). Connecting with Community Resources: Optimizing the Potential of Multicultural Students with Mild Disabilities. In F. E. Obiakor & C. Utley (eds.). 1997.

FIGURE 2.2

Three-Phase Preservice/Inservice Model for
Promoting Productive School and Community Collaborative Networks

efforts within their local district. In addition, trainees and practicing school personnel identify and make contact with *significant* individuals and traditional and nontraditional community-based organizations that provide important educationally related services for ethnic minority youth. The goals are for them to (a) become acquainted with the local ethnic minority communities and to obtain information regarding the kind of services offered, (b) determine if and how the services may benefit children and youth with disabilities in either an out-of-school or an in-school arrangement, and (c) share educational information with community organizations for dissemination to residents; i.e., parents as needed. Since a critical feature of many community-based organizational programs is parental involvement, the systematic observation of parents engaged in active and empowering roles by trainees and school personnel is a key component of Phase 2.

Phase 3 concentrates on application. It requires trainees and school personnel to demonstrate how the information obtained during Phase 2 can be used to enhance educational service delivery for ethnic minority youth with disabilities and their families.

Reformation of the Learning Disabilities Paradigm

There is consensus that serious problems exist with using the current LD construct to identify children and youth with learning disabilities. For various reasons already cited in this chapter, the problems magnify when the LD paradigm is used with ethnic minority learners. As a result, there is often a mixed response to this population. Sometimes there is a disproportionately high representation of ethnic minority learners in LD programs. On the other hand, sometimes ethnic minority learners are either not identified or they are disproportionately placed in other categories such as mental retardation. The following recommendations are posited to promote more competent identification practices and to help ensure equity in educational opportunities for ethnic minority youth in need of special services to reach their learning potential.

1. The LD paradigm must be reformed in a fashion that makes it an exclusive category among the disabilities. It must no longer be a catchall category but must instead by precisely delineated. In addition, the discrepancy and exclusionary clauses must be eliminated. The concept that this population has deficits in phonological awareness has promise (Lyon, 1996). However, greater facility and economy of testing and intervention will be necessary for this to be a meaningful reformation of the paradigm.

Further, the paradigm must be inclusive enough to appropriately identify students from various economic and culturally and linguistically diverse backgrounds. For example, measures of intelligence and academic or skill deficits used to determine eligibility must have a multicultural frame of reference. A variety of alternative assessments must be conducted to obtain comprehensive and accurate understanding of the strengths and weaknesses of individual ethnic minority children and youth.

2. The recruitment of ethnic minority school personnel must become a priority. Colleges of education have awesome roles to play in this regard. At the same time, current administrators, teachers, and other significant school personnel must be trained in the use of multicultural practices to guide decision making. A primary goal of multicultural education is to help educators acquire an adequate understanding of the integral components and underlying dynamics of culture and consequent educational implications for both the curriculum and the pedagogical process. Collectively, multicultural education attempts to equip school personnel with (a) the knowledge base and skills for determining what constitutes culture, (b) an awareness of and understanding that everyone has a culture, (c) a personal understanding of how one's own and one's students' cultural beliefs guide behavior, attitudes, and interactions, (d) knowledge about the types of cultural characteristics (e.g., verbal and nonverbal communication patterns, learning styles/child rearing approaches) that are relevant to school personnel and how these traditional and contemporary characteristics may manifest themselves in the schooling process, and (e) the skills for making decisions based on a holistic understanding of the individual child.

3. The authentic inclusion of parents in collaborative decision-making roles that lead to the delivery of effective services for their children and youth must be an integral component underlying reform efforts. In addition, with dwindling school resources and the multidimensional problems confronted by educators today, ongoing networking with community organizations concerned about the well-being of youth is desperately needed. Such partnerships have the potential to aid school personnel in obtaining a genuine understanding of the needs of the student population they serve. Furthermore, community organizations in which parents actively participate can be used as recruiting grounds for soliciting the help of concerned parents with leadership qualities. The resulting networks may also function as mechanisms for disseminating vital school-related information to parents. However, in order to accomplish these school/community linkages, school personnel must be adequately trained. Thus, colleges of education and inservice training programs must provide trainees and school personnel with specific experiences that imbue them with the appropriate attitudes and skills.

Summary

In an effort to equip school personnel with the tools to make appropriate decisions about programming, federal definition of learning disabilities must be reconsidered and the LD paradigm must be rethought. The concepts in the discrepancy and exclusionary clauses of the federal definition have complicated the identification process. Related literature discussed in this chapter leads to the conclusion that current cognitive and neurological assessment measures cannot differentiate a poor reader with average or above average intelligence from a poor reader with low intellectual functioning, putting the validity of the discrepancy clause into question. Further, it is surmised that many ethnic minority learners who exhibit academic failure are disproportionately branded with the mental retardation label rather than the more socially acceptable LD classification. With regard to the exclusionary clause, not only does it result in the LD category being a catchall for students with many different problems, but it also does not embrace students who manifest academic difficulties due to economic and cultural disadvantages.

It is our strong belief that the LD construct must be revisited from a muticultural perspective and that all students will be better prepared for life if they are systematically exposed to cultural diversity in school. With changing student demographics, the disproportionate representation of ethnic minority youth in LD programs, the unrepresentative teaching workforce, poor personnel preparation, and limited parental involvement, and inadequate home-school-community networks, it is necessary to reconsider factors impacting placement patterns of ethnic minority students and the types of curriculum offered. To that end, we presented educational constructs to support the preparation of teachers for multicultural education and authentic home-school-community collaboration. The multicultural, multicognitive model described by Byrd (1994) provides for a supportive learning environment for the students that takes into account cognitive style, cultural context, curricular content, and pedagogical strategies. The home-school-community collaboration model described by Ford (1997) delineates ways to systematically expose preservice and inservice-level trainees to experiences that increase the proclivity toward genuine partnerships with ethnic minority parents and communities. It is our belief that a movement toward equity must be the ultimate goal of the formal public schooling process for all children and youth.

References

Adelman, H. S. & Taylor, L. (1993). *Learning problems and learning disabilities: Moving forward.* Belmont, CA: Brookes/Cole.

Algozzine, B., & Ysseldyke, J. E. (1994). Why inclusion may fail and what teachers can do to prevent it. *Educators' Forum '94.* Boston: Houghton Mifflin.

Anderson, J. A. (1988). Cognitive style and multicultural populations. *Journal of Teacher Education, 39*(1), 2-9.

Armstrong, T. (1993). *7 kinds of smart: Identifying and developing your many intelligences.* New York: Penguin Group.

Artiles, J., & Trent, S. (1994). Over-representation of minority students in special education: A continuing debate. *Journal of Special Education, 27,* 410-437.

Artiles, J. & Trent, S. C. (1997). Building a knowledge on culturally diverse students with learning disabilities: The need to enrich research with a sociocultural perspective. *Learning Disabilities Research & Practice. 12,* 80–81.

Artiles, J. (1998). Predicting placement in learning disabilities: Do predictors vary ethnic group. *Teaching Exceptional Children, 64,* 543–559.

Ascher, C. (1987, December). *Improving the school-home connection for poor and minority urban students* (ERIC/CUE Trends and Issues Series No. 8). New York: Columbia University, Institute for Urban and Minority Education.

Baca, L. M., & Cervantes, H. T. (1984). Parent and community involvement in bilingual special education. In L. M. Baca & H. T. Cervantes (Eds.), *The bilingual-special education interface* (pp. 213-232). St. Louis, MO: Times Mirror/Mosby.

Banks, C. A. M. (1997). Parents and teachers: Partners in school reform. In J. A. Banks & C. A. M. Banks (Eds.), *Multicultural education: Issues and perspectives.* Boston: Allyn and Bacon.

Banks, J. A. (1993). Approaches to multicultural curriculum reform. In J. A. Banks & C. A. Banks (Eds.), *Multicultural education: Issues and perspectives* (2nd ed.). Boston: Allyn & Bacon.

Brandt, R. (1998). Listen first. *Educational Leadership,* 25–30.

Byrd, H. B. (1994, April 7). *Inclusive curricula for African-American exceptional students.* Paper presented at the seventy-second annual convention of the Council for Exceptional Children, Denver, CO.

Byrd, H. B. (1995). Curricular and pedagogical procedures for African American learners with academic and cognitive disabilities. In B. A. Ford, F. E. Obiakor, & J. M. Patton (Eds.), *Effective education of African American learners: New perspectives* (pp. 123-150). Austin, TX: PRO-ED.

CEC—National Black Caucus of Special Educators. (1995). Roundtable debate at the April 1995 Council for Exceptional Children Annual Convention, Indianapolis, IN.

Cheng, L. L., Ima, K., & Labovitz, G. (1994). Assessment of Asian and Pacific Islander students for gifted programs. In S. Garcia (Ed.), *Addressing cultural and linguistic diversity in special education: Issues and trends* (pp. 30-45). Reston, VA: Council for Exceptional Children.

Comer, J. P. (1989). The school development program: A psychosocial model of school intervention. In G. L. Berry & J. K. Asaman (Eds.), *Black students: Psychologic issues and academic achievement* (pp. 264-285). Newbury Park, CA: Corwin Press.

Croninger, B. (1990). African-American parents . . . Seeing them as colleagues, neighbors, and friends? *Equity Coalition for Race, Gender and National Origin 1*(2), 8-9.

Cummins, J. (1986). Empowering minority students: A framework for intervention. *Harvard Educational Review 56*(1), 18-35.

DeLeon, J., & Gonzales, E. (1991). An examination of bilingual special education and related training. *Teacher Education and Special Education, 14,* 5–10.

Dent, H. (1976). Assessing black children for mainstreaming placement. In R. L. Jones (Ed.), *Mainstreaming and the minority child* (pp. 77-92). Minneapolis, MN: Leadership Training Institute.

Epperson, A. I. (1991). The community partnership: Operation rescue. *Journal of Negro Education, 60(3),* 454–458.

Education for All Handicapped Children Act (1995).

Federal Register. 1997. (1997, December 29). (65082-65085). Washington, DC.

Ford, B. A. (1992). Multicultural training for special educators working with African American youth. *Exceptional Children, 59,* 107–114.

Ford, B. A. (1995). African American community involvement processes and special education: Essential networks for effective education. In B. A. Ford, F. E. Obiakor, & J. M. Patton (Eds.), *Effective education of African American exceptional learners: New perspectives* (pp. 235-272). Austin, TX: PRO-ED.

Ford, B. A. (1998). Productive school and community partnerships: Essentials to improve educational outcomes for ethnic minority students. In A. Freeman, H. Bessent-Byrd, & C. Morris (Eds.). *Enfranchising urban learners for the twenty-first century* (pp. 91–113). Kearney, NE: Morris.

Ford, B. A. & Reynolds, C. (2000). Connecting with community Resources: Optimizing the potential of multicultural students with mild disabilities. In F. E. Obiakor & C. A. Utley (Eds.), Thomas Publishing Company.

Ford Foundation and John D. & C. T. MacArthur Foundation. (1989). *Visions of a better way: A Black appraisal of public schooling.* Washington, DC: Joint Center for Political Studies. (ERIC Document Reproduction Service No. ED 312320).

Franklin, M. (1992). Culturally sensitive instructional practices for African-American learners with disabilities. *Exceptional Children 59,* 115-122.

Fuchs, D., & Fuchs, L. S. (1994). Inclusive schools movement and the radicalization of special education reform. *Exceptional Children, 60,* 294-308.

Garcia, S. B. (1992, Fall/Winter). A model for staff development in bilingual special education: The interagency collaboration project. *The Bilingual Special Education in Perspective, 12,* 1–6.

Gardner, H. (1993). *Multiple intelligences: The theory in practice.* New York: HarperCollins.

Grossman, H. (1998). *Ending discrimination in special education.* Springfield, IL: Charles C. Thomas.

Harry, B. (1994). *The disproportionate representation of minority students in special education: Theories and recommendations.* Alexandria, VA: National Association of State Directors of Special Education.

Harry, B. (1995). African American families. In B. A. Ford, F. E. Obiakor, & J. M Patton (Eds.), *Effective education of African American exceptional learners: New perspectives* (pp. 211-233).

Hatch, T. (1998). How community contributes to achievement. *Educational Leadership,* 16–19.

Lewis, R., & Morris, J. (1998). Communities for children. *Educational Leadership,* 34–36.

Hilliard, A. G., III (1995). Culture, assessment, and valid teaching for the African American student. In B. A. Ford, F. E. Obiakor, & J. M. Patton (Eds.), *Effective education of African American exceptional learners: New perspectives* (pp. ix-xvi).

Kozol, J. (1991). *Savage inequalities: Children in America's schools.* New York: Harper Perennial.

Lynch, E. W., & Hanson, M. J. (1992). *Developing cross-cultural competence.* Baltimore: Paul H. Brookes.

Lyon, G. R. (1996). The state of research. In S. C. Cramer & W. Ellis (Eds.), *Learning disabilities: Life-long issues* (pp. 3-61). Baltimore: Paul H. Brookes.

Marion, R. L. (1980). Communicating with parents of diverse exceptional children. *Exceptional Children, 46*(8), 616-623.

Melendez, W. R., & Ostertag, Z. (1997). *Teaching young children in multicultural classrooms: Issues, concepts, and strategies.* New York: Delmar.

Midgette, T. (1995). Assessment of African American exceptional learners: New strategies and perspectives. In B. A. Ford, F. E. Obiakor, & J. M. Patton (Eds.), *Effective education of African American exceptional learners: New perspectives* (pp. 3-26).

National Education Association. (1990). *Academic tracking: Report of the NEA Executive Committee/Subcommittee on Academic Teaching.* Washington, DC: Author (ERIC Document Reproduction Service No. ED 322 642).

Nichols, E. (1987). *The philosophical aspects of cultural difference.* Unpublished manuscript.

Obiakor, F. E. (1995). Self-concept model for African American students in special education settings. In B. A. Ford, F. E. Obiakor & J. Patton (Eds.). *Effective Education of African American Exceptional Learner: New Perspectives* (pp. 71–88). Austin, TX: Pro Ed Publishing Co.

Obiakor, F. E. (1999, Fall). Teacher expectations of minority exceptional learners: Impact on "accuracy" of self-concepts. *Exceptional Children, 66,* 39–53.

Obiakor, F. E., Algozzine, B., & Ford, B. A. (1993). Urban education, the general education initiative, and service delivery to African American students. *Urban Education, 28*(3), 313-327.

Obiakor, F. E., & Lumpkins, R. (1993). *The "reach one" male education program.* Arkadelphia, AR: Henderson State University.

Obiakor, F. E., & Utley, C. A. (1997). Rethinking preservice preparation for teachers in the learning disabilities field: Workable multicultural strategies. *Learning Disabilities Research & Practice, 12,* 100–106.

Obiakor, F. E., Mehring, T. A., & Schwenn, J. O. (1997). *Disruption, disaster, and death: Helping students deal with crisis.* Reston, VA: Council for Exceptional Children.

O'Neil, K. (1993). "Inclusive" education gains adherents. *Update, 35*(9), 1.

Ortiz, A. A., Yates, J. R., & Garcia, S. B. (1990, Spring). Competencies associated with serving exceptional language minority students. *The Bilingual Special Education Perspective, 9,* 3–4.

Rueda, R. (1997, January). *FIESTA EDUCATIVA.* Paper presented to the Family/School/Community Strand at the Council for Exceptional Children—Division for Culturally and Linguistically Diverse Exceptional Learners Multicultural Symposium, New Orleans, LA.

Rueda, R., Ruiz, N. T., & Figueroa, R. A. (1995). Issues in the implementation of innovative instructional strategies. *Multiple Voices for Ethnically Diverse Exceptional Learners, 1,* 12-22.

Shade, B. J. (1989). *Culture, style and the educative process.* Springfield, IL: Charles C Thomas.

Shapiro, J. P. (1996). A separate and unequal education for minorities with learning disabilities. In S. C. Cramer & W. Ellis (Eds.), *Learning disabilities: Life-long issues* (pp. 109-112). Baltimore: Paul H. Brookes.

Slaughter, D. T., & Epps, E. (1987). The home environment and academic achievement of black American children and youth: An overview. *Journal of Negro Education, 56*(1), 3-20.

Smith-Davis, J. (1995). *Issues arising from insufficient diversity among education personnel.* Albuquerque: Outreach Alliance Project, University of New Mexico.

Smith-Davis, J., & Smith, D. (1993). *Demographic, social, and economic trends affecting children and youth in the United States: A synthesis.* Albuquerque: Outreach Alliance Project, University of New Mexico.

Suzuki, L. A., Meller, P. J., & Ponterotto, J. G. (Eds.). (1996). *Handbook of multicultural assessment: Clinical, psychological, and educational application.* San Francisco: Jossey-Bass.

Telesford, M. C. (1994, Summer). Tips for accessing and involving families of color in a significant way. *Focal Point,* p. 11.

Twelve principles for successful inclusive schools. (19XX). *CECToday, 1*(2), 3.

U.S. Department of Education. (1996). *To assure the free appropriate public education of all children with disabilities* (Eighteenth annual report to Congress on the implementation of Individuals With Disabilties Education Act). Washington, DC: Author.

Voltz, D. L. (1995). Learning and cultural diversities in general and special education classes: Frameworks for success. *Multiple Voices for Ethnically Diverse Exceptional Learners, 1,* 1-11.

Wald, J. L. (1996*). Culturally and linguistically diverse professionals in special education: A demographic analysis.* Reston, VA: National Clearinghouse for Professions in Special Education.

Wang, M. C., Haertel, G. D., & Walberg, H. J. (1993-1994). What helps students learn? *Educational Leadership, 51*(4), 74-79.

Wilson, T. (1972). Notes toward a process of Afro-American education. *Harvard Educational Review, 42*(3), 374-389.

Witty, E. P. (1982). *Prospects for black teachers: Preparation, certification, employment.* Washington, DC: ERIC Clearinghouse on Teacher Education.

Ysseldyke, J., Algozzine, B., & Epps, S. (1983). A logical and empirical analysis of current practice in classifying students as handicapped. *Exceptional Children, 50*(2), 160-166.

3
A Personal Journey: Changing Concepts of Learning and Disability

Cheryl Ames

In the early 1970s I began my journey to become a special education teacher. The beginning of this journey was exhilarating! I finally had found an undergraduate program that intrigued me—one where I would learn how to teach students with emotional and behavior disorders. I was enrolled in one of the top special education training programs in the country, on my way to what I believed would be an engaging, rewarding career. As I participated in my courses, I had no doubt that I was gaining the teaching and management strategies that would enable me to teach any mildly handicapped student. One spring I remember walking across campus after an evening class and exclaiming to myself, "I can teach anyone!" I believed it! I was fully armed with behavior modification techniques and task analysis strategies. I could analyze baseline data and design a reinforcement program to change any behavior. I could teach any child to read through analyzing the decoding skills necessary to read a particular book and creating a series of minutely sequenced lessons that would guarantee success.

After graduation I landed a job teaching elementary students with behavioral and learning difficulties. I found I was able to engineer a classroom that controlled behavior. Through mostly one-to-one instruction I assisted students in gaining math and reading skills.

A few of my students even successfully returned to general education classrooms. But something was missing for me. Although I enjoyed my students and the success I experienced in helping them learn more constructive behaviors, I felt that I wanted to focus more on teaching academics, particularly reading. So I enrolled in a graduate program in special education, with a focus on learning disabilities (LD).

The idea of "learning disability" fascinated me. I truly wanted to learn how to teach these bright students who were challenged by neurological problems that resulted in extreme difficulties in learning to read fluently, spell correctly, understand math concepts, or even control a pencil well enough to write legibly. I learned about the parts of the brain that might be damaged and thus affect a child's ability to decode words and understand them. I studied the efforts of pioneering professionals who searched for new neurological pathways and advocated motor patterning, training visual/perceptual skills, and honing auditory discrimination. However, my professors were clear in communicating that although these early efforts were important contributions to the field, training "underlying process deficits" had been shown to not be successful in increasing academic performance. My classmates and I were told instead to rely on the behavioral approaches I had begun learning in my undergraduate program. I studied how to analyze reading errors to pinpoint problems, perfected my task analysis skills, and explored direct instruction techniques that ensured mastery learning.

After obtaining a master's degree, I became a resource teacher and worked with elementary and middle school students. As a member of multidisciplinary teams, I participated in evaluating students who were struggling in school and helped to decide if they had a "learning disability." I enjoyed the prestige and mystique that surrounded the career of working with children who were impaired in their learning but capable intellectually. My students liked coming to the resource room and working on the activities I had planned, although I frequently had to devise incentive programs to encourage them to fully engage and try their best, particularly during the last part of each school year. I found that after a few years I again was not fulfilled by my work and found it too routine. I assumed that I had reached a pinnacle in my professional development and was ready to consult and supervise, to assist teachers in developing the effective teaching strategies that I had mastered through training and experience. After all, strategies developed early on in the LD field and now out of favor were still quite apparent in the work of some of my colleagues, as they tested for perceptual problems and designed programs to remediate them. I had become proficient with behavioral interventions such as task analysis and knew I could assist teachers in gaining these skills and understanding the lack of research supporting perceptually based approaches.

A new and different job did not emerge during this time, but I did discover a new topic to learn about and add to my teaching repertoire—writing. Educators were beginning to talk more about teaching students to write—even young elementary children. I began to challenge my notion that it was senseless to work on writing without first establishing strong reading skills. I read whatever I could find on teaching students to write, even though I suspected that articles written by general educators were not entirely appropriate for students with learning disabilities. (There was still little focus in special education on writing—just spelling and handwriting skills). I read and believed that students should write frequently, even daily, and that topics for writing needed to be relevant to their lives. I utilized the task analysis strategies I was familiar with to create a series of lessons ascending in difficulty, involving sentence combining strategies and capitalization and punctuation skills in the context of the sentence combining activities. I assigned topics related to my students' lives and helped them analyze their writing to combine sentences and correctly capitalize and punctuate. I designed individualized spelling programs based on high frequency words and the words my students misspelled when they wrote. I helped my students find books with patterns and encouraged them to write and "publish" their own patterned books. I found that regardless of my students' reading skills, they could learn to write and enjoyed writing activities. And finally, I was feeling more satisfied in my profession, as I designed my own curriculum, challenged traditional ideas about learning disability and writing, and formally shared my work with others during inservice presentations.

Exciting events continued to unfold. I joined my school's writing project and learned that students should write by choosing their own topics and proceed through experiences similar to how "real" writers write. I discovered that even students with learning disabilities could do this and that it was rewarding and challenging to teach this way. A book was finally published on teaching writing by an educator whose name I saw repeatedly in journal articles—Donald Graves (1983). Along with other teachers in my school, I purchased Graves's book and experimented with his suggestions. My writing instruction became more and more child centered. I learned how to support my students as they chose topics from their own experiences, planned their writing, wrote drafts utilizing developmental spelling, read and reread their writing to make the meaning clear, and carefully checked the conventions prior to publishing some of their pieces.

At this same time, a woman named Dorothy Watson was invited to conduct a 2-day workshop on literacy with special education staff in my school district. While I understood that Watson was not a special educator and wondered what relevance her presentation would have to my work, I was quite curious. After all, I was committed to Graves's ideas about the teaching of writing, and Graves also was not a special education professional.

Watson talked about a new way of conceptualizing reading and writing instruction. Her strategies for teaching reading were the antithesis of what I had been practicing but were strangely connected to my new way of teaching writing. I was convinced not only to try these new strategies but to entirely abandon my task-analyzed specific skills techniques. I would use only predictable, well-written reading material, read to my students, and teach skills in the context of these books and my students' writing. I knew that I needed to be careful in how public I would be about my work, however. Watson had experienced vehement opposition from some of the special education staff in my group, and during the following months many of them voiced strong concern about the direction our special education department was taking.

Back at my school, I was feeling more professionally rewarded than ever before. Not only were other teachers in my school experimenting with writing instruction, many were also beginning to teach reading through children's literature, journal writing, and contextualized mini-lessons about reading skills and strategies. I joined forces with a new Chapter I reading teacher, who had just finished a reading endorsement program based on these "progressive" ways of teaching literacy. We shared professional books and teaching activities. I abandoned any professional reading in special education journals and books and conversations with most of my special education colleagues. I felt somewhat guilty and isolated by doing so, but I didn't want to be branded as a maverick.

My learning curve took a steep incline. Except for pattern books, I had not paid much attention to children's books since my undergraduate children's literature class many years before. I added the librarian to my circle of indispensable colleagues. Real books became the source of my teaching material, rather than phonics books, reading kits, and high-interest, low-vocabulary series. I learned how to facilitate shared reading lessons from large print books, conduct individual reading conferences, respond constructively to children's oral reading miscues, and create books from my students' voices using the language experience approach. I literally threw away a decoding program that I had designed and had at one time considered trying to publish (although it was painful to do this).

My new approach for teaching reading was challenging, however. I worried about skills I might not be teaching that would lead to deficiencies in my students. I really struggled with understanding how to teach children who could not yet read connected text. I knew that these students were labeled "emergent" readers, but I didn't know how to make the act of reading emerge from them. However, when I tried a return to my behaviorist strategies from earlier years, my students disengaged, sending me a clear signal with their heads in their arms on the table. I definitely had more to learn in order to optimize the learning experiences of my students, but I felt that I was on the right track, and I had the support of the primary teachers and Chapter I teacher in my school. Finally after my second child was born, I came to understand how to teach emergent readers while reading Don Holdaway's *Foundations of Literacy* (1979), as I nursed my new son during the midnight hours.

A number of other professional books highly influenced my thinking during these years. Brian Cambourne's *The Whole Story* (1988) supported my understanding of the conditions for language learning; later I was fascinated to observe language and literacy learning happen in my own two young children in just the way Cambourne described. Frank Smith's *Insult to Intelligence* (1986) made me committed to initiate all of my students into the literacy club and propelled my search for more authentic and meaningful evaluation strategies. Regie Routman's *Transitions* (1988) and Curt Rhodes and Lynn Dudley-Marling's *Readers and Writers With a Difference* (1988) expanded my teaching repertoire and assured me that my new understandings truly applied to special education students.

During this time of struggling with how to teach reading, I received one of my biggest rewards. Tim, a fourth-grade student who had not learned to become an independent reader through the direct instruction DISTAR program, was becoming a reader through rereading predictable books and his dictated stories that I typed. He seemed to be liberated as I taught him to use "the strategies that good readers use": using synonyms for unknown words, skipping unknown words and reading on, monitoring for meaning and correcting himself if the miscues did not make sense. As I learned not to interrupt him while he read to create meaning from text, he gained the power of a reader who could proceed through a text independently without an adult to tell him words he could not decode. One day after I had been absent to attend an inservice session, he reported to me that my substitute didn't know how to be a good reading teacher, since she stopped him each time he made an oral reading error!

I became even more excited about my teaching, but I remained wary of some special education teachers' opinions of what was being labeled "whole language." In my monthly meetings with other resource teachers in my district, I was careful about my contributions. Nevertheless, following one inservice presentation that I had facilitated the news spread about how I had advocated meaning-based ways of teaching reading skills rather than the isolated instruction characteristic of remedial materials. I was quite shaken one afternoon when I received a confrontive phone call from another resource teacher in my district, who literally yelled at me for "damaging" the students in my program.

I continued to find positive support in my own school, however, as well as from a few special education teachers who were also exploring whole language concepts. I understood myself as an emergent whole language teacher, and I continued to learn and benefit my students. I also became more reflective about my teaching, which allowed me to profit more from conversations with others in my school, gain insights from my own teaching, and connect my professional reading with day-to-day practice.

When I looked back on my experiences of the past several years, I realized that I had drastically changed my paradigm for understanding teaching and learning. I no longer believed learning could most effectively occur if I broke down the tasks into small, sequenced parts. Instead, I believed that children needed to learn to read and write whole texts and work on the patterns of language within those texts. Instead of directing all aspects of learning in my resource room, I supported students in making many of their own decisions about what to read, what to write about, and what activities we might use to help them become more literate. I began to see my students' errors as signs of their development and opportunities for developmentally appropriate teaching, rather than as mistakes to eradicate. I considered both myself and my students as learners, always moving toward higher levels of competence.

My students were now demonstrating the top end of their development rather than the lower range (Ruiz, 1995). They were readers and writers. They published books. They criticized my writing and the writing of the authors of the high-interest, low-vocabulary books they occasionally discovered in the library. They talked about their favorite books and authors and could explain why they liked them. I began to view them as more like the students who were not identified to receive help in the resource room, than as the neurologically impaired students I originally endeavored to teach. What was their disability, anyway?

About this time, a book with a strange but compelling title was recommended to me by an inservice presenter: *The Learning Mystique: A Critical Look at "Learning Disabilities"* (Coles, 1987). The author, Gerald Coles, directly challenged the notion of learning disabilities (LD) and claimed that a student's learning difficulties were the product of an interaction of social relationships, individual behavior, and *differences* in neurological functioning, rather than *dys*function. His ideas made sense to me. My students certainly had differences in learning as compared to their "nondisabled" peers, but so did other students who did not qualify as LD because they were presumed to have less intellectual ability, to have emotional problems, or to have socioeconomic factors contributing to poorer school performance (the "exclusionary factors" for determining learning disabilities). The Chapter I reading teacher and I sometimes contemplated about the differences between our students, but we always concluded that they were more alike than different.

I realized that my students varied in many characteristics just like their nondisabled peers: Some were unusually short or tall, some were overweight or skinny, some were exceptionally talented in music or drawing or had no skill in this area, some were great athletes and others did not care at all about sports, some had social charisma while others were more shy and preferred solitary activities. I began to wonder why there shouldn't be natural significant variation in academic learning as well, which, as Coles suggested, would interact with other variables in a student's life to make academic learning more or less effective.

I also became more aware of the variation in skills and interests in my own two sons. My youngest son, in particular, had unique talent in drawing and spatial abilities. For example, he learned to write his name at age 3 by noticing how it was written on a plaque on his wall, and he reported at age 5 that he learned how to tie shoes by watching his father tie his wingtips every morning. But in spite of exposure to classical music at home, to an older brother who played the violin, and to an outstanding music program at school, he could not sing a song on tune—at all! It's a good thing he did not have this neurological difference in reading or math, I thought, or he might be identified as having a "learning disability."

It was not long before I began having discomfort with the process of labeling referred students as learning disabled. As I began again to do more reading in the special education field and to pay more attention to the articles in popular magazines, I became aware that although the notion of LD was being challenged, the predominant popular and professional view still was that the learning difficulties of intellectually normal children were usually caused by some kind of internal neurological deficit, not difference. These students were learning disabled and needed to be fixed, to experience some kind of educational program that would remediate their learning problems. My difficulty with labeling existed on a personal level as well. On my multidisciplinary team I had primary responsibility to test for and identify learning disability. I resolved this conflict by reporting to my team and to parents that an individual child "met the criteria for the category of learning disabilities" and thus was "eligible for special education services," rather than stating the child "<u>was</u> learning disabled."

My new concept of learning disability was now harmonious with my beliefs about how literacy learning most effectively occurs. My students had not changed, but my understanding of them, their strengths and needs, and how they learn had certainly changed immensely.

Soon after this time I was offered the opportunity to work on developing curriculum with various groups of special education, Chapter I, and English as a Second Language teachers. For 2 years I collaborated with teachers of special needs students in developing curriculum units and learning activities based on holistic, constructivist theory. I was blissfully separated from the process of identifying students as having a disability.

As is often the case with the "ideal" job, my position was eliminated after a grant expired and budgets were reduced. I was thrust back into the realities of day-to-day special education processes, only this time as a "program specialist" for learning disabilities, providing district-level direction and support for special education teachers. Among other responsibilities, my job involved operationalizing state procedures for identifying learning disability and providing technical assistance to special education teachers and other multidisciplinary team members at each school, an interesting challenge considering the paradigm change I had experienced in the previous years!

Although my current position frequently presents dissonance between what I believe and the tasks I must accomplish, I continue to support teachers in working toward holistic, constructivist practice in teaching students with disabilities. I have found abundant professional development opportunities for special education teachers in my school district who are seeking to change from traditional, behaviorist approaches. Vast supplies of children's literature, predictable books for emergent readers, and other teaching materials are available for implementing state-of-the-art instruction, and professional resources abound for the teacher seeking change. General education classroom teachers in my district are supported with *First Steps* (Heinemann, 1995), an inservice program in assessment and strategies for promoting literacy and providing a community of learners in each school. Even with this context of support, however, special education teachers face the challenge of transforming their conceptualization of teaching and learning from the traditional special education training that most received in preparing to become special education teachers (Denti & Katz, 1995). They must also break ties with the deeply entrenched neurological, deficit-based conceptualization of learning disability.

Although there is currently a great deal of discussion about paradigm shift and alternative frameworks for conceptualizing LD in the professional literature, the day-to-day practice of professionals who interact with children typically does not reflect this thought, in my experience and the experience of others (Wiest & Kreil, 1995). But what difference does this make, as long as effective teaching and learning happen in the classroom? I am finding that deficit-driven definitions of learning disability (and other disabilities, and even conceptualizations of other children with special learning needs, such as Chapter I and English as a Second Language students) subtly impact even the teacher who professes holistic, constructivist philosophy. Students who are viewed as having deficits are more likely to receive interventions that attempt to "fix" their problems rather than interventions that treat them as learners who are capable of actively learning and functioning independently. They are likely to be helped more often in their literacy attempts, continuing their dependency upon adults, rather than supported in learning independent strategies to proceed with reading and writing. In contrast, teachers who view learning disability as also shaped by social forces are more likely to support the student by adjusting environmental factors, such as encouraging parent involvement and collaborating with the general education classroom teacher in arranging congruent, mutually supportive learning activities in both the special education and general education classrooms.

I am also concerned about the amount of time that is spent in assessing, deliberating, and reporting about the student who is identified as having a learning disability. When a multidisciplinary team treats the learning disability as reality instead of a definition created by policy makers, they often prolong the identification process and complete additional testing to determine if the student "really" has a learning disability or to understand the "type" of learning disability the child has. They often look for signs of neurological dysfunction, of "dyslexic" behavior, and bemoan the fact that they just don't find many "classic" cases anymore. They find it extremely difficult to rule out exclusionary factors such as low socioeconomic level and frequent change of schools. And with the increase in disability categories to consider in the past several years, they worry that the student may really be "other health impaired" because of attention deficit disorder or may be high functioning autistic.

My biggest concern is how a definition based on neurological deficit and the accompanying identification process impacts students. By the time students are referred for a special education evaluation, they have struggled with academic learning and developed negative concepts of themselves as readers and writers. They attempt to avoid engaging in literacy activities, and the quality of their performance shows it. The typical response of well-meaning teachers as they break down the learning into "easier" parts and provide the student with "remedial" materials can further discourage these students, who at this time are demonstrating only the low end of their potential performance. Then, when the evaluation process begins and these students experience standardized tests with ceilings of "six consecutive errors," they further believe that something is wrong with them and that they "can't" read and write. It is quite difficult even for the very sensitive evaluator, who is also looking for the student's strengths, to prevent the student from feeling like an academic failure. (For a poignant account of the blinding impact of the special education process on professionals in understanding what a student can do, see Denny Taylor's book, *Learning Denied* (1991).)

Where am I now, after 25 years of my journey in special education? In my day-to-day work I have had opportunities to converse with professionals in the schools about the social construction of learning disability and other disabilities as well. I am finding that these ideas provide relief to many professionals. No longer burdened with having to decide if students "are" a specific disability, they are able to proceed with policy definitions of disability and to decide more efficiently if students meet the criteria for the disability. We have a long way to go, however. I recently completed a research project involving interviews and focus group discussions with special education teachers regarding their conceptualizations of learning disability. Although I interviewed 13 teachers who were recommended as knowledgeable in their field, including several teachers who represented constructivist practice, none gave any hint of challenging the traditional, deficit-driven conceptualization of LD. All of the teachers communicated frustration with the special education identification process, but there was overwhelming acceptance of the notion that a certain percentage of students in school represent "true" learning disability (Ames, 1998).

Recently a student in one of the special education classrooms I support introduced himself to me by saying, "Hi, my name is Chris. I have a reading disability." Many students, like Chris, are framed by their disabilities; it is the major part of who they are. They are defined by what they *can't* do, rather than by their strengths and interests. With both constructivist, holistic teaching practice *and* socially framed ideas of disability, I believe that we as practitioners in the field can create school experiences for our students that shape positive self-statements about what they *can* do. As I continue my journey as a special education professional and learner, I will always be working toward that goal.

References

Ames, C. K. (1998). *What is learning disability? A study of special education teacher beliefs.* Unpublished doctoral dissertation, Portland State University, Portland, OR.

Cambourne, B. L. (1988). *The whole story: Natural learning and the acquisition of literacy.* New York: Scholastic.

Coles, G. (1987). *The learning mystique: A critical look at "learning disabilities."* New York: Pantheon.

Denti, L. G., & Katz, M. S. (1995). Escaping the case to dream new dreams: A normative vision for learning disabilities. *Journal of Learning Disabilities, 28,* 415–424.

Education Department of Western Australia, (1994). *First Steps.* Heinemann.

Graves, D. (1983). *Writing: Teachers and children at work.* Portsmouth, NH: Heinemann.

Holdaway, D. (1979). *Foundations of literacy.* New York: Ashton Scholastic.

Rhodes, L. K., & Dudley-Marling, C. (1988). *Readers and writers with a difference: A holistic approach to teaching learning disabled and remedial students.* Portsmouth, NH: Heinemann.

Routman, R. (1988). *Transitions: From literature to literacy.* Portsmouth, NH: Heinemann.

Ruiz, N. T. (1995). The social construction of ability and disability: II. Optimal and at-risk lessons in a bilingual special education classroom. *Journal of Learning Disabilities, 28,* 491–502.

Smith, F. (1986). *Insult to intelligence: The bureaucratic invasion of our classrooms*. Portsmouth, NH: Heinemann.

Taylor, D. (1991). *Learning Denied*. Portsmouth, NH: Heinemann.

Wiest, D. J., & Kreil, D. A. (1995). Transformational obstacles in special education. *Journal of Learning Disabilities, 28,* 399–407.

Critical Cultural Knowledge in Special Education: Reshaping the Responsiveness of School Leaders

Khaula Murtadha-Watts and Edy Stoughton

Issues related to the cultural diversity of students, faculty, and communities increasingly dominate the current debate in education. Race, class, gender, and disability have all been important foci for researchers interested in school restructuring (see the American Educational Research Association Annual Meeting Program, 1998). Much of the discussion has been framed by scholars promoting multicultural curricula and better teacher preparedness for working with children who differ in ethnicity and social class. Other scholars are attempting to enhance the competence of teachers for working with children who have special needs. Still others are drawing attention to the interconnectedness and effects of ableism, sexism, classism, and racism. Very little research, however, has been directly linked to the cultural preparedness of school administrators who are responsible for curricular, instructional, pupil service, financial, and community relations leadership. The need for culturally responsive leaders is even more dramatic when we look at the effect of issues of culture and difference on special education. Many teachers in special education often work with school administrators who are responsible for providing instructional leadership and influencing overall school climate but have little knowledge of the specific learning theories and teaching strategies used with children who have special needs or of the multicultural issues that affect placement and services.

We begin this chapter with a discussion of the political and ideological dimensions of culture, cultural difference, and labeling. We follow with the assertion that administrators' beliefs, as expressions of personal values, are connected to their instructional behaviors and their leadership roles in schools (Hart & Bredeson, 1996). Therefore, we make the argument that an administrator's personal commitment to becoming a multicultural person, concerned with disembedding deep-seated cultural biases and self-reflection will contribute to schoolwide preparedness and responsiveness to cultural diversity and inclusion.

Next, we suggest that an important leadership role which is missing from the principal preparation literature is critical cultural mirroring, that is, speaking and acting across difference, to reflect to the staff possible biases, prejudice, and stereotyping that may exist while supporting school cohesion and a unifying climate. This role should serve as a foundation for working with teachers to help them recognize those times when multicultural issues are distinct from special educational needs as well as those times when issues of cultural diversity and learning problems are symbiotic. This dimension of multicultural education is sometimes minimized or neglected by administrators, who may think of their role as being a curriculum development leader who is concerned only with *content* related to ethnic, racial, or other cultural groups.

Finally, we suggest that leaders who are attentive to cultural diversity and special education, prioritize forming school communities as projects of possibilities, where students' successes are collective responsibilities rather than solitary struggles by individual teachers. Both special and general educators face major challenges in working together and with parents to provide appropriate, individualized education to students with disabilities from culturally diverse backgrounds. Recognizing the importance of parental input and that parents must be considered an integral part of the school community, we employ social contact theory to provide an understanding of the problems that occur in formal and informal situations when parents and educators from diverse backgrounds interact.

Our aim in this chapter is to enhance professional practice by drawing attention to the inadequacy of traditional leadership models and the way they respond to cultural differences, particularly for students who are in need of special education. In our view, leaders need to have a personal commitment to becoming multicultural people, to engage in critical cultural mirroring, and to develop parent collaborators in the school community. In these ways, critically reflective, morally caring educators can do a great deal to bring about change in culturally diverse school settings.

Central to this discussion is an understanding of our use of the term culture. We chose not to follow Geertz's (1973) well-known approach to thinking about culture as the "templates" or "webs of meaning" by which we organize "social and psychological experience." It appears to be devoid of the political and ideological dimensions important to our work. Bullivant (1993) defined culture as a group's program for survival in and adaptation to its environment. In this chapter, we use a critical cultural perspective, that draws attention to the asymmetrical power relations of the society that are maintained in schools and the deficit view of minority students that school personnel often uncritically and unknowingly hold (Bartolome, 1996). We believe that an education for students with special needs must take into account concerns for how groups struggle to make sense of their existence and thus requires an alternative leadership model embodying critical cultural knowledge for today's demographically changing schools.

Intersections of Cultural Difference and Labeling

Considered a reform movement, multicultural education is designed "to bring about a transformation of the school so students from both genders and from diverse cultural and ethnic groups will have an equal chance to experience success" (Banks,1997). As noted by Banks and many others, some students, because of their backgrounds and particular characteristics, have a better chance to succeed in school as it is currently structured than do other students. The highly disproportionate number of male African Americans and Hispanics classified as learning disabled indicates the extent to which students from culturally diverse backgrounds experience discrimination or inadequate educational programs. Data from the U.S. Department of Education Office of Civil Rights (OCR, 1995) point to the many discriminatory practices in our schools that result in the overrepresentation of students from ethnic groups in special education. These data reveal differences in all of the following areas:

▶ Prereferral intervention (e.g., districts with predominantly White students have more extensive prereferral programs than do schools with predominantly African American students)
▶ Reasons for referrals for special education evaluations (e.g., for African American students, there is greater emphasis on behavioral reasons than on academic reasons for special education referral)
▶ The factors used in the evaluations (e.g., greater reliance is placed on IQ tests in the evaluation of African American students)
▶ Placement in more restrictive settings (e.g., a disproportionate number of African American students are labeled as having mental retardation, the category in which students are most likely to be in separate settings) (OCR: 1995)

Students who have limited English proficiency face similar problems. The difficulties that teachers and clinicians have in distinguishing between language difference and language disability are documented in psychological and language assessment research. The use of a standardized language assessment approach has proved to be deficient and inadequate in assessing the dual language abilities of bilingual students.

As noted by Meadmore (1993, cited in Lipsky & Gartner, 1997) "race, gender and class intersect in discrimination and social injustice" (p.2). At the time of Meadmore's study for example,

▶ approximately 40% of secondary students in the general population came from households with annual incomes of less than $25,000; for secondary students with disabilities, the percentage was 68%, and

▶ whereas 25% of secondary students, in the general population were living in single-parent families, 37% of youth with disabilities had a single parent.

Along a similar vein, Podell and Soodak (1993), who studied the referral of children from families of low socioeconomic status (SES), concluded that low-SES students may be at greater risk for referral because of teacher, rather than student, factors. In other words, teachers' "decisions about poor children are susceptible to bias when teachers perceive themselves as ineffectual" (p. 251).

School leadership must play a major role in drawing attention to racist and classist language, social, and gender inequities. To implement successful inclusive education programs, the support of the superintendent of schools and school board members is critical. However, we agree with Lipsky and Gartner (1997) that the role of the principal is central, as the school site is the key locus of educational services.

Becoming a Multicultural Leader Through Disembedding Cultural Biases

How does a principal lead a school to become a caring, culturally supportive community? Why does he or she need to? What are the compelling reasons for such a leadership initiative? In an attempt to be color-blind and to treat all students equally, to be impartial and fair, many educators do not want to acknowledge cultural differences. In a sincere fashion, they often say "I don't see black or white, rich or poor. I see only students." However, as Gollnick and Chinn (1998) informed us, teachers base their expectations about student achievement on such characteristics such as first language, race, socioeconomic status, and gender. Principals need to recognize the impossibility of cultural neutrality among fellow administrators, staff, and students and their own efforts to be objective may in fact impede the goal of providing the best education for all students. Many teachers prefer to think that students' lack of interest and poor academic achievement are due solely to conditions in their homes or are innately a part of diverse students' cultures—the cultural deficit myth (Contreras & Delgado-Contreras, 1991). If an educator sees the cultures of people of color and people from low socioeconomic class as a problem, his or her attention is likely to be deflected from understanding that the majority group in this society perpetuates discrimination and inequality. These patterns have several implications for educational leadership interested in improving the academic achievement of all children as well as their life chances.

For instance, the patterns suggest that school leadership is a moral activity. "Moral" is being used here in its professional, cultural, and ethical sense. As Foster (1986) pointed out, the moral side of administration has to do with those attempts administrators make to bring resolution to dilemmas as they present themselves in day-to-day life in schools. School leaders must raise questions about cultural dilemmas, including beliefs about linguistic, gender, ethnic, and ability differences. Further, they need to ask about poverty and equity. Because we are all part of a society that is racist and stratified by ability, class, and language, all of us (both children and adults) have consciously and subconsciously internalized some of these ideologies.

As Nieto (1996) cautioned, a reeducation process— learning new things and unlearning some of the old—can be difficult and sometimes painful. One important step is to have a greater level of self-knowledge. This means critically reflecting on culturally informed behaviors, beliefs, and values and naming the historical situatedness of cultural phenomena. For the moral leader, this naming act–this surfacing—serves to identify his or her location in the process of learning and knowing. It is our belief that an administrator's self-reflection may contribute to schoolwide responsiveness to cultural diversity.

Freire and Macedo (1996) noted that the process of learning and knowing requires dialogue in which the sharing of experiences needs to be infused with an ideological analysis and a political project capable of eradicating oppressive practices and institutions both in education and society. Principals may develop these perspectives when they become deeply dissatisfied with the trivialization of complex educational and societal problems and the simplistic remedial plans that result from this kind of thinking. For some, a sense of mission is a driving force in their fight against oppression and inequity. For others, a desire for radical change, through special relationships with colleagues, friends, and mentors with whom they have an honest sharing of previously unexamined values.

Critical Cultural Mirroring and Culturally Focused Dialogue

We have coined the term *critical cultural mirroring* to refer to the ability of a school leader to speak and act across difference to reflect to the staff possible biases, prejudice, and stereotyping. Critical cultural mirroring is, for example, needed to raise the awareness that differential treatment is given to students based on their presumed deficits and teacher bias. Discourse is also needed to uncover the sedimented layers of beliefs and biases that result in students from low-income families and children from marginalized groups being mislabeled and inappropriately targeted for special education programs.

Critical cultural mirroring is similar to Gitlin and Smyth's (1989) dialogical approach to understanding. As a part of staff professional development, teacher evaluation, and program assessment, educators—both teachers and administrators alike–must begin to question why things are the way they are. Through culturally focused dialogue, they can begin to see how social, historical forces affect their own students, advantaging some and disadvantaging others. If this dialogue does not exist in the school culture, there are several roles that principals must play. They must be initiators of change, supporters for multicultural curriculum development, and facilitators for collaboration.

Leaders are crucial for initiating organizational change "because they act as a constant source of pressure to think in ways that deviate from the current culture" (Louis & Kruse, 1995, p. 39). They can stimulate a slow-to-change staff with the urgency and seriousness of dialogue about curriculum that examines the impact of cultural beliefs on content and instructional strategies that are planned and in place, both explicit and implicit. (In such dialogue, it is crucial to discuss what we *do not* teach in schools as well as what we *do*.) Because the process of making curriculum decisions is so important, we need to understand how educators make such decisions and to consider how the process can and should be questioned. This is the focus of the next section of this chapter.

Challenges for Curriculum Development: Culturally Focused Dialogue About Curriculum

A cycle of culturally focused dialogue helps bring to the surface embedded beliefs and instructional practices. An example of a culturally focused dialogue would be one where school leadership recognized a deficit model of teaching and learning and brought it to the attention of faculty as a schoolwide, ongoing concern. The point might be raised that educators who are invested in "fixing" defects within the child are not involved in examining how the climate and academic curriculum may have contributed to learning or behavior problems.

Questions that would support such a cycle of dialogue includes the following:

- How does the content of the curriculum (or specific lessons) serve certain established interests and points of view while marginalizing or excluding others? Whose culture is valued?
- How can the curriculum be constructed and connected to the lived experiences of children and families from different cultural backgrounds? What fit exists?
- How can instruction include inquiry by teachers and students that increases understanding?
- What social responsibility and social action will the education lead to?

Classrooms in which a majority of the students are uninvolved, off task, and not learning are commonplace across the country (Goodlad, 1984). Yet, rather than examining ways to change the climate and curriculum to engage the students, many teachers cling to the belief that the students themselves are the problem. A vicious cycle begins in which low-achieving students from poor and minority backgrounds receive instruction that emphasizes low-order skills and repetitious drills (Maeroff, 1998). If they don't respond to the watered-down instruction, they are likely to then be referred for testing for special education. Special education placement has, in this way, been the result of a continuum of misreading student behavior, beginning with an inadequate understanding of divergent learning styles and cultures, with the end result being a continuation of the same low-order thinking skills curriculum that did not work in the first place.

The responsibility of administrators in such situations is to engage in the process of cultural mirroring with the teacher. One way that cultural mirroring could be carried out is to examine communication styles, including the messages people send, often unintentionally, as they interact (Flinders, 1994). Many communication problems can occur between teachers and students from different cultures simply because they are behaving in ways that are accepted and normative in their own cultures but problematic in the culture of the other person. As an example, children who are being considered for special education services often indicate, when questioned, that they "shut themselves off" from responding to a particular teacher because they are convinced that she or he "doesn't like them" (Silverstein & Krate, cited in Franklin, 1992). The entire affective climate in such situations can be altered by pinpointing the cultural messages that are being misunderstood by the students and teachers. In some cases, this will lead to a reconsideration of the need of special education services.

In addition to sensitizing school personnel to communication discrepancies between cultures, administrators need to be aware of how mismatches between the curriculum and the learning styles of certain students can lead to failure. When students are labeled mentally retarded and yet function well in all areas of their lives except for school, it is important to examine what other factors could be contributing to the academic problems. Again, are we looking for deficits within these children when we should be examining how schools are failing to reach them? Are we asking if curriculum and instruction are relevant to them? Are we building on the strengths that they are able to demonstrate in other environments? Is assessment bias leading us to see students as deficient rather than culturally different and leading to further bias in placement decisions?

An important goal of administrators is to pose these types of critical questions to teachers and to work with them to reorganize instruction to engage students' specific interests and prior knowledge. The questioning brings to light the problems inherent in teaching that avoids cultural responsiveness; the goal should be to draw attention to ways in which teachers can develop culturally responsive teaching practices. A shift must occur from cultural deprivation to increased attentiveness to the uniqueness of children.

School leaders (including lead teachers) must work with teachers, observing and creating analytical self-reflective texts about their teaching and helping them to unpack their assumptions about the curriculum. School leaders must also help teachers to provide learning that truly engages students and at the same time is authentic, rigorous, and thought provoking. Good teachers facilitate a safe, risk free learning environment that values each student's contributions. The understanding that exemplary education takes place when each student's gifts and talents are valued, when young people and adults learn to respect each person's individual strengths and weaknesses, has provided the vision that undergirds the move to inclusionary classrooms.

In evaluating their teaching, most teachers use a number of criteria. Three criteria that we suggest follow. Ross, Bondy, and Kyle (1993) pointed out that many teachers tend to focus only on the first of these. They noted that the second and third are evaluative questions that make teaching a profession as opposed to a technical skill. The criteria are:

1. Does what I am doing work? Is it possible for me to implement a particular strategy or approach?
2. Are my teaching approaches educationally sound? Are the children learning appropriate attitudes, values, concepts, and skills using methods that are consistent with good pedagogy?
3. Are my teaching approaches ethically defensible? Are the children learning in ways that will enable them to grow up to be responsible members of their community and as citizens who can participate fully and intelligently in a democratic society? Am I treating each child with dignity and respect and with regard to his or her specific needs? Are the children developing capacities for caring and being cared for or concern about others in the world?

These criteria are also useful to teachers who wish to engage in dialogue with their colleagues about teaching practices with children with special needs from diverse cultural groups.

Parents and the Formation of School Communities

After many years of research, the link between parental involvement and student achievement is undeniable. Nevertheless, many parents remain distant from their child's school and see the school as an uninviting place. We believe that certain ethical behaviors and characteristics supported by all school community members can contribute to and emerge from effective collaborative relationships with parents. As noted by Friend & Cook (1996), "these include beliefs and values that support collaboration, mutual trust, mutual respect, and establishment of a sense of community."

The idea of community and its importance for moving beyond artificial structures of individualism has become popular in contemporary scholarship. We find it useful in this discussion about special education and cultural diversity because teachers have traditionally viewed their work in isolation and exclusion, rarely looking critically at teaching and learning except when being evaluated or through self-criticism. If we are to change what happens in schools, an alternative model should be embraced that supports collaboration, team building, and cooperative work. It should be a model through which teachers can not only examine their classrooms and those of other teachers but can also engage with parents, administrators, other staff members, and students in deciding how educational environments can be improved for a changing society.

According to social contact theory (Allport, cited in Bennett, 1995), at least four basic conditions are necessary if social contact between groups of diverse cultural backgrounds is to be strengthened. To lessen prejudice and lead to attitudes and behaviors that support learning, the following conditions must be met:

1. Contact must be sufficiently intimate to produce reciprocal knowledge and understanding between groups.
2. Members of various groups must share equal status.
3. The contact situation should lead people to do things together. It should require intergroup cooperation to achieve a common goal.
4. There must be institutional support and authority and/or a social climate that encourages intergroup contact.

Social contact theory is useful for understanding the formal and informal situations in which parents and educators from diverse backgrounds communicate. The second condition for strengthening social contact between groups, raises issues of power and authority in schools, that is, that members of the groups share equal status. All parents, especially those of low income, are not accorded the same standing or an equal standing with educators, when decisions or plans are made in schools.

Two of the formal occasions in which parents of students with special needs and educators meet are when the initial placement assessment process has been completed and in the required annual case review meeting during which plans are made for the child's individualized educational program (IEP) for the following school year. Both of these conferences are mandated by law, and both are expected to be conducted in compliance with a set of federal guidelines as set out in the Individuals With Disabilities Education Act (IDEA). The purpose behind these conferences and their structure is to ensure that parents of children with disabilities will play an integral and important part in the educational plans instituted for their children. Unfortunately, in many instances, the very process intended to provide a more active role for parents has actually tended to cause parents to be less involved.

From their research, concerning parent involvement in special education, Meyer, Harry, and Sapon-Shevin (1997) found that whereas the law focuses on the creation of objectively verifiable documentation by parents and professionals, the volume and content of paperwork tends to be confusing, overwhelming, and intimidating for parents. It can be embarrassing for parents to indicate confusion or to ask for clarification and explanations. These same authors found that the structure of formal conferences, which focuses on written verification casts parents in a passive role unless they possess the knowledge base and professional language enables them to actively contribute to the process. There is, therefore, a cultural dissonance between all but the most sophisticated parents and educational personnel which creates a chasm of uncertainty and discomfort that is hard to surmount. This is in addition to the intimidation felt by minority parents as a consequence of the environment itself, in which they are frequently the only minority people in a room of "experts."

For special educators and other concerned school personnel to comprehend how the context of the formalized placement or case review conference frames the participation level of many parents, it is necessary to step back from a milieu that is comfortable and familiar to those of us who are professional educators and view this same milieu through the lenses of those who may be extremely uncomfortable in this environment. Although the intent of IDEA is for parents to be partners with the school system in planning for their children, parents are not given enough information to question effectively, and if they disagree with plans being made they are often placed in an adversarial position. Evans, Salisbury, Palomboro, and Goldberg (1994) reported that professionals tend to have low expectations of parent participation, expecting parents to limit their contributions to agreeing with the professional recommendations and signing the forms.

Another barrier to the full and equal partnership between all parties involved with planning for a child's educational future is the manner in which disabilities are viewed. School personnel tend to view children through the medical model. This viewpoint sees the child in a clinical fashion, assuming that knowledgeable experts with sophisticated assessment tools can pinpoint with scientific accuracy remedial methods to correct the problem. The medical model identifies a disability through testing and then prescribes therapies in the form of IEPs. Because professionals possess information and terminology that are generally not possessed by parents, they become the experts controlling the discourse. Professional jargon lends authority to the educators' opinions while devaluing parent knowledge. Those parents without the social capital that permits participation in the conversation about their child are further alienated (Harry, 1997).

These asymmetrical power relations are rarely negotiated and maintain a barrier of silence that is buttressed by the formal, impersonal communication style that educators typically use during the meetings. Many parents become aware of the unequal balance of power and become resentful of this form of discussion. A basic mistrust develops that intensifies as parents consider the manner in which students are selected for special education programs, including the assessment tools and procedures that are used. Their feelings of mistrust can be exacerbated by awareness of the overrepresentation of African-American children in special education programs and discomfort over the practice of locating learning problems solely within the child with no critical discussion about school contexts (Howe & Miramontes, 1992).

Another problem is that, in most instances, assessment has already been completed and the educational personnel are in basic agreement about how they wish to proceed before the parents are brought into the picture. During the first meeting with parents, the proposed plan is explained to the parents; they are given the opportunity to ask questions; and then they are expected to sign the paperwork to indicate agreement with the plan. If parents disagree with the committee's recommendations, they can find themselves in a confrontive posture, faced with the consternation and disapproval of educational experts who sincerely believe that they know what is best for the child. Additionally, if parents disagree with some of the proffered strategies or feel the need to add or correct information to provide a better understanding of the child, they are often viewed as being adversarial and therefore as alienating the educators who are needed as allies. This is a far cry from a partnership of all concerned parties who are sharing their input on an equal basis and collaborating on an appropriate educational plan. Educators need to ask themselves whether the participation they desire is merely consent to a legal document, or is a true dialogue that has the purpose of discerning the nature of a child's learning or emotional need and how best to proceed with educational program planning.

The intention on the part of many school personnel in case conference meetings is not to ignore or intimidate parents. The conference is, however, often viewed by school personnel as a timeconsuming, cumbersome legality that should be completed as quickly and efficiently as possible. Because of the volume of paperwork school personnel must set aside extensive periods of time from already full teaching schedules just to complete the pages of written documentation in a perfunctory way. All too often, educators view this process as taking them away from their real work rather than as being an integral part of their work. Many also think parents are equally inconvenienced by the length of time the meeting takes, and they justify the tendency to expedite matters as sensitivity to parent work schedules and child care needs. However, this impatience with the volume of work and time required can translate to parents as a lack of desire to include them in the process. The cultural gap widens when parents perceive judgments about their skills in raising their children.

In light of all of these factors, the temptation for parents is strong to simply agree with what the experts are recommending and get through the process as quickly as possible. Teachers, too, may be uncomfortable and worry about possibly being "put on the spot" or having their expertise called into question by dissatisfied parents. Nevertheless, in looking at placement and annual educational plan reviews, where so much is at stake regarding a child's education, it is crucial that everyone has an opportunity to have input into plans for the child.

One way to improve the level of discourse would be for principals to monitor the affective atmosphere of the conference. By facilitating the discourse, principals can help to make the experience more beneficial to everyone involved. Parents should be welcomed on a respected basis as partners in the process, and there should be an understanding that their comments are no less credible because they are subjective and personal than are the technical assessments of the professional educators. Indeed, parents' comments provide invaluable insight into the cultural and social environment of the child. Because it is necessary to view children holistically, anecdotal and environmental information is crucial. Information about where the child is successful, about his or her experiences outside of the school, and about the quality of interactions in the settings of family and community is extremely important for seeing the child's strengths and weaknesses and for preventing a deficit view of the child.

Communication with parents could further be enhanced by bringing them into the process at an earlier point, that is, before assessment is complete and decisions have been made. If parents are an integral part of the assessment and planning team from the beginning, they will know that their role is not simply to agree or disagree with an already formulated plan but to provide input throughout the process. This involvement would also help prevent the commonly held perception that referral of a child for testing is tantamount to a decision that she or he is a special education student. With parents and educators working more closely together in an atmosphere of mutual sharing and respect, there would be a greater understanding of the roles of all participants, and a leveling of the hierarchy. There would likely also be greater openness to points of disagreement and differences of opinion. The learning community would be viewed as a place for possibility, a place where an ethic of care is important, where trust is not taken for granted but worked for, and where openness to critique is available.

As schools struggle to become culturally responsive inclusive communities, their members must address such questions as the following:

> Do we value diverse cultures entering the school community? If so, do we demonstrate this?
> What kinds of reflective work will be necessary so that educators, parents, and children will see themselves as necessarily connected in a school community?

The responsibilities of educational administrators for developing schoolwide critical cultural knowledge go beyond merely citing legal requirements and developing job descriptions. Adminstrators must engage discourses of change that transcend the cacophony of special interests and the disinterest of those unwilling to be a part of a collaborative community. They must struggle for an environment where the voices of marginalized children and their families are not only heard but valued. Their most critical task is to enable others to act. (See appendix to this chapter.)

The principal's role as the leader-manager of a school is pivotal according to the effective schools literature. Yet, each building principal faces a unique set of challenges. While principals attempt to address various students' learning needs, they must also respond to parents' concerns, teachers' attitudes and professionalism, and a myriad of administrative duties. When administrators take seriously the moral imperative of responsiveness to the cultural differences of teachers, students, and families, they work to support inclusion while raising a critical cultural mirror to the staff and themselves. They schedule time for teachers to plan and to learn new knowledges and skills, fostering epistemological curiosity. Professional development about multicultural education is ongoing, just as our society is changing socially, politically, and economically. Intentional in their focus to build a school that is culturally responsive, that involves parents from diverse backgrounds, and that insures the appropriate education for children with special needs, school leaders understand that tensions and conflicts may arise but that even those tensions will lead to the growth of the learning community.

Appendix

Friend (1998) offered the following list of administrative responsibilities in inclusive schools. In our view, the list is highly useful as a starting point but does not reach far enough for critically thinking leaders.

1. Understand the legislative and legal requirements of least restrictive environment for students with IEPs.

2. Develop knowledge of and commitment to inclusive education as a philosophy that addresses all students with special needs, including those with disabilities. Make clear, public, and repeated statements setting inclusive practices as a standard for the school.
3. Understand and address accountability issues related to the provision of services for students with IEPs in inclusive settings.
4. Know common teacher concerns and questions about inclusive education and strategies for responding to them.
5. Know common parent concerns and questions about inclusive education and strategies for responding to them.
6. Provide needed staff development for all personnel affected by inclusive practices (e.g., teachers, paraprofessionals, tutors).
7. Involve staff in decision making concerning scheduling, student assignment, and other critical aspects of inclusive education.
8. Encourage staff to use innovative and experimental strategies for providing services to students. Strategies should relate to specific instructional approaches, service delivery models, the use of school personnel, and the allocation of time.
9. Create job descriptions that set expectations for staff to adopt and implement inclusive practices.
10. Establish hiring and personnel evaluation practices that foster the development of inclusive schools.
11. Work with staff to obtain "seed money" and other funds to foster the development of inclusive practices.
12. Address the needs of students with IEPs in the development of school policies, including testing and assessment, curriculum development, discipline policies, and report card grading.
13. Facilitate the creation and implementation of a plan for evaluating school initiatives related to inclusive education.
14. Create and use vehicles for involving all constituent groups in the development of school practices related to inclusion (e.g., parent groups, unions, and local advocacy groups for individuals with disabilities).

References

American Educational Research Association. (1998). Annual meeting program. San Diego, CA.

Banks, J. (1997). Multicultural education: Characteristics and goals. In J.A. Banks & C.A.M. Banks (Eds.). *Multicultural education: Issues and perspectives* (3rd ed., 3-31). Boston: Allyn and Bacon.

Bartolome, L. (1996). Beyond the methods fetish: Toward a humanizing pedagogy. In P. Leistyna, A. Woodrum & S. Sherblom. Eds. *Breaking free: The transformative power of critical pedagogy.* (229-252). Cambridge, MA: President and Fellows of Harvard College .

Bennett, C. (1995). *Comprehensive multicultural education: Theory and practice.* (3rd ed.). Boston: Allyn&Bacon.

Bullivant, B. (1993). Culture: Its nature and meaning for educators. In J.A. Banks & C.A.M. Banks (Eds.). *Multicultural education: Issues and perspectives* (2nd ed.), 29-47. Boston: Allyn and Bacon.

Cinnamond, J. (1995). Safeguarding empowerment. In B. Kanpol & P. McLaren (Eds.). *Critical multiculturalism.* Westport, CT: Bergin & Garvey.

Evans, I. M., Salisbury, C., Palomboro, M., and Goldberg, J. S. (1994) Children's perception of fairness in classroom and interpersonal situations involving peers with disabilities. *Journal of the Association for Persons with Severe Handicaps,* 19, 326-332.

Ford, A., Davern, L, & Schorr, R. (1992). Inclusive education: "Making sense" of the curriculum. In S. Stainbeck & W. Stainbeck. *Curriculum considerations in inclusive classrooms.* (37-61). Baltimore: Paul H. Brookes.

Foster, W. (1986). *Paradigms and promises: New approaches to educational administration.* Buffalo, NY: Prometheus Books.

Franklin, M. (1992). *Exceptional Children.* 59 (2) 115-122.

Freire, P., & Macedo, D. (1996). A dialogue with Paulo Freire. In P. McLaren & P. Leonard. (eds.) *Paulo Freire: A critical encounter.* London: Routledge..

Friend, M. (1998). Collaboration the key to urban educational success. Paper presented at the first Indiana Urban Superintendent's Association/ IUPUI Conference, July. Indianapolis, IN.

Friend, M., & Cook, L. (1996). *Interactions: Collaboration skills for school professionals.* New York: Longman.

Geertz, C. (1973). *The interpretation of cultures.* New York: Basic Books.

Gitlin, A. & Smyth, J. (1989). *Teacher evaluation: Educative alternatives.* New York: Falmer Press.

Gollnick, D.M. & Chinn, P. (1998). *Multicultural education in a pluralistic society* (5th ed.). Upper Saddle River, NJ: Merrill.

Goodlad, J. (1984). *A place called school.* New York: McGraw-Hill.

Graden, J. & Bauer A. (1992). Using a collaborative approach to support students and teachers in inclusive classrooms. In eds. Stainbeck, S. & Stainbeck, W. *Curriculum considerations in inclusive classrooms.* 85-100. Baltimore, Md. Paul Brookes Publishing.

Harry, B. (1997). *Cultural diversity, families, and the special education system: Communication and empowerment.* New York: Teachers College Press.

Hart, A. & Bredeson, P. (1996). *The principalship: a theory of professional learning and practice.* New York: McGraw-Hill.

Howe, K., & Miramotes, O. (1992). *The Ethics of Special Education,* New York: Teacher's College Press.

Lipsky, D., & Gartner, A. (1997). *Inclusion and school reform: transforming America's classrooms.* Baltimore, MD. Paul H. Brookes.

Louis, K., & Kruse, S. (1995). *Professionalism and community.* Thousand Oaks, CA: Corwin Press.

Maeroff, G. (1998). *Altered destinies.* New York: St. Martin's Press.

Marion, R. (1979). Minority parent involvement in the IEP process. A systematic model approach. *Focus on Exceptional Children,* 10(8), 1-16.

Meyer, L., Harry, B., and Sapon-Shevin, M. (1997). School inclusion and multicultural issues in special education. In J.A. Banks & C.A.M. Banks (Eds.). *Multicultural education: Issues and perspectives* (3rd ed.). 334-354.

Podell & Soodak (1993). *The Journal of Educational Research.* 88 (1), 44-51.

Ross, D., Bondy, E., & Kyle, D. (1993). *Reflective teaching for student empowerment.* New York: Macmillan.

Section 2

Assessing and Supporting Student Learning and Understanding in New Ways

This section focuses on an orientation toward assessment that highlights learners' strengths and provides insights into learners' difficulties in light of these strengths. Special education assessment usually looks at learners' deficits rather than considering the talents and challenges of each learner. The constructivist orientation toward learning disabilities on which this book is based, promotes a reframing of all areas of education practice, including assessment. With regard to the topic of this section, it focuses on recasting the goals and use of assessments, both formal and informal, with labeled students.

The thought piece (Chapter 5) shares a cogent rationale for this reframing, presenting and discussing the necessity for a major shift from the traditional assessment perspectives on which the field of learning disabilities has been established. The authors challenge traditional concepts on which labeling and identification have been based and replace them with perspectives that focus on what the learner can do, not what he or she cannot do.

The accompanying pieces focus on two different areas. Chapters 6 and 7 look at how to organize and document students' competencies and how to use such assessments within typical school structures that have focused on and continue to highlight student deficits. Chapters 8–10 offer specific examples of how teachers can collect and interpret different types of data using a theoretical framework based on students' strengths. Specific techniques for gathering, organizing, and using assessment data with students with learning disabilities, which readers of this section can use in their classrooms, are shared in these chapters. In this section, as in the first section of this book, readers are asked to reflect on new paradigms and orientations toward learning and to consider how these new perspectives push us to view learning disabilities in new ways.

5

Transforming Children's Experiences of Failure Into Stories and Narratives of Competence

*Dudley J. Wiest, Susan Brotherton,
Dennis A. Kreil, and Joseph M. Cervantes*

In earlier publications we argued the position that Western culture must consider new ways of thinking about the field of education. Special education requires reconceptualization from the legalistic refer-test-placement mentality, which often results in poor home-school relationships and low success rates relative to intervention (Wiest & Kreil, 1996). School psychology continues to struggle with the transformation of reductionistic roles into more holistic means of service delivery (Wiest & Kreil, 1997). Teachers need to conceptualize and utilize more authentic and contextual techniques in the areas of curriculum, instruction, and evaluation within both general and alternative education classrooms (Poplin, Wiest, & Thorson, 1996; Wiest, 1996). In addition, schools are encouraged to utilize their communities and cultural norms in interventions for students who display learning and behavior problems (Wiest, Kreil, Ramirez, & Gonzalez, 1997).

Here, we argue that special education, and especially the field of learning disabilities, is struggling to cope with the problems of identifying children, adolescents, and even adults as disabled. The area of learning disabilities is arguably the most controversial area of special education. Students are sometimes identified as having a learning disability by the system of special education in an effort to placate general education teachers who feel overwhelmed with the prospect of educating children from multiple diverse backgrounds. Adding to the problem, the taxonomy for diagnosis varies from state to state despite the Individuals With Disabilities Education Act (IDEA) and its regulations. In addition, the refer-test-placement mentality often leaves educators with a medical model that does little to address authentic, real methods of learning. Subsequently, the label required for special services too often becomes a "real" identity for the student. In other words, significant community and family members associated with the person identified as handicapped may assume that this label is definitive and reflective of the total person, thus limiting both current and future education, social, and vocational options. Finally, a number of systemic issues are associated with the assignment of labels. To compound the problem there is a finite level of resources and funding available for the implementation of services for the identified students. All of these factors create an imperfect and often inconsistent manner of classifying disabilities, with the decision often varying from professional to profession, school to school, district to district, and state to state.

This chapter addresses several issues related to reconceptualizing the notion of disability and subsequent issues of labeling from the practitioner perspectives of teacher, school counselor, school psychologist, and psychotherapist. All of these practitioner positions have multiple roles and functions, including assessment, counseling, guidance and prevention, consultation, research, and inservice. We begin with a review of the conceptual problem of "psychopathology" and then examine newer, postmodern approaches to intervention and counseling. Finally, we discuss narrative therapy as a perspective that offers great hope when intervening with children who display learning and behavior problems.

Reconceptualizing Pathology as Help

Public schools have multiple specialists working in various capacities with students to address specific problems related to learning, socialization, and development. Speech and language therapists, adaptive physical education specialists, occupational and physical therapists, full inclusion facilitators, behavioral specialists, resource specialists, reading teachers, special day class teachers, vision and hearing specialists, vocational and community facilitators, counselors, school psychologists, and mental health therapists all have unique and specific roles and focuses within the school setting. Simultaneously, they are also bound by a central core belief and postulate—that is, that the children they serve are pathological.

We are not saying that these children see themselves as pathological or impaired in some way, at least initially. Rather, the adults who determine policy and decisions relative to program placement, curriculum, access to the mainstream, and availability to peers make this assumption. These "authorities" make up a powerful social constituency that the child must assume reflects reality. After all, don't all adults have a child's best interest at the core of their beliefs and subsequent decisions? In essence, children are forced to accept labels and placements based on the beliefs of primary adults in their lives.

At first glance, it seems logical that adults are making these decisions for children. After all, experts are often consulted in various life situations to clarify tasks, evaluate systems, classify problems, propose solutions, and implement interventions. The practice represents a logical, natural manner of working with problems within the system or, in this case, the child.

However, children are not "systems" to be evaluated, "outcomes" to be understood, or "pathologies" to be cured. As basic as it may sound, children are people. They are human. They are affective, spontaneous, dynamic, thoughtful, impulsive, creative people. They are also judged relative to "standard behavior," average "development," and typical "learning patterns." If children are not at least lower average or better in these various measures of normalcy (e.g., cognition, intelligence, academics, fine motor skills, language, mental health, physical health, vision, and hearing), they are considered deviant or pathological. According to its definition, pathology means "abnormal" and deficient relative to others. Additionally, abnormality suggests inferiority. Educationally, the child who is labeled with a pathology has just experienced failure. The child has just been defined as "not successful." No matter how adults frame the situation, the child begins to suspect that something is wrong, and the thing that is wrong is clearly defined as the child, not the curriculum, teaching methods, school and cultural expectations, teachers, or parents.

Adults do not use such words as disabled, impaired, diagnosis, and pathology in their conversations with children struggling with academic and social problems. However, even without the use of such vocabulary, the children understand that significant others believe that these words apply to them, are real, and have validity.

Culturally, society has committed resources to help children with "pathological" symptoms. The logic is simple: Help people with problems, and they may have a more positive outcome in life experiences within the culture. It is also more cost effective to address problems early (i.e., during childhood), so that future problems have less likelihood of arising. Irrespective of motivation, culturally we want to help children, and we have followed the model of medicine for doing so.

Medicine addresses illness and disease with an emphasis on pathological vocabulary. The language of categories allows medical staff to communicate in a clear way about the problems of the patients. Specialists use precise vocabularies that reflect definite diagnostic dimensions of illnesses. In addition, the vocabulary and taxonomic systems used allow professionals to conduct research and study "illness," "pathology," "disease," and "dysfunction." Such research is presumed to enable practitioners to "cure" the patient in the most efficacious manner.

The fields of education and psychology have modeled much of their work after the medical model of pathology. For students or clients who struggle, professionals in these fields employ taxonomies that reflect the language of impaired. The fourth edition of the *Diagnostic and Statistical Manual of Mental Disorders* (DSM-IV) and criteria from the Individuals With Disabilities Education Act (IDEA) provide taxonomic structures for labeling behavior in a uniform manner with a common language. Theoretically, this language allows professionals to communicate about problems with more clarity, to conduct research relative to solutions and intervention approaches, and to instruct others in appropriate ways of resolving problems.

The problem with this logic is that often there is an insidious process that transforms people into taxonomic criteria and labels. Notice the language of professionals, those who train individuals to intervene with their children, those who directly teach, counsel, or assess children, those who create policy, those who lobby lawmakers about policy, those who assist in the norming, or not norming, of behavior for culture. Far too many times, professionals will say "He's an LD kid," "She's depressed," John is "social maladjusted," "Jeremy belongs in that program. After all, he's SED," or "Allison is anorexic."

The implication is clear. These children are considered to be the problem. They do not have a problem; they are referred to as the problem.

It is important to note how children initially conceptualize problems. Children seldom refer to themselves as a " problem"; rather, they refer to themselves as themselves *with* a problem. The problem is the problem, not the student. However, well-meaning adults, parents and professionals, unwittingly use language based on the assumptions of pathology that all behavior implies a consistent and real presence. These assumptions are then accepted and employed as taxonomic truths, without consistent and systematic attempts to critically evaluate their veracity. Subsequently, children tend to learn and accept these assumptions, internalizing them into their construct of self.

What is wrong in the field of special education, specifically learning disabilities, is what is wrong with the concept of mental health. All of these fields conceptualize problems as pathology, use language to describe them, personalize the language to the child, and assume that the child is the problem. Children are then faced with a difficult dilemma. Do they not trust what adults assume to be true about them (as demonstrated with their specific labels, programs, techniques, meetings, and interventions), or do they accept these definitions and begin believing them? There is little middle ground. This position may seem to be extreme and rather dualistic, but it is what nearly always happens.

Postmodern Approaches to Counseling

Traditional psychological theory and practice have their foundation in modernistic interpretation. The approach is one of a scientific search for truth and knowledge. It was believed that scientific principles could be applied to just about any topic for the purpose of greater understanding (Jones & Wilson, 1987). This era peaked during the 1950s and 1960s when the need for singular definitions of reality gave comfort to a world that was experiencing radical changes as a result of newly developed technologies. Modernism attempted to discover universal codes, structures, and definitions of "normal" psychological constructs. Those who supported this philosophical approach have been called *structuralists, positivists, functionalists,* and/or *modernists.* Irrespective of name and definition, these theorists were unified by the belief that universal notions and questions of truth exist that can be discovered through scientific answers. The hallmark of modernism's desire for measurement was the creation of psychiatric and scientific management of humans (Tierney, 1993). It was believed that with universal understandings of normal, one might well be able to predict human behavior.

Psychologists, educators, and counselors know the canons of modernism well. Its roots are impacted in the very soil of their daily work in schools. Taxonomies of diagnosis that label the presence or absence of pathology are a prime example. With the ammunition of scientific "truth," psychological authorities in children's lives hold immeasurable power in their attempts to reflect an acceptable reality. Here, the traditional researcher or scientist (psychologist) sees himself or herself as an unbiased, neutral interpreter of the truth. Yet, what happens if the truth does not "fit all"?

The 1970s and 1980s brought about a challenge to modernism that is often described as *postmodernism.* Theorists began to see the scientific approach as repressive, homogeneous, and domineering in terms of epistemology, sexuality, politics, and culture (Kellner, 1988). Postmodernism is far from having a clear definition that truly reflects its position of truth and reality. For clarity, we can describe it, as Brotherton (1996) did, as being in "multiple perspectives and viewed through multiple lenses" (p. 77). According to William Doherty, "While modernism comprised an aesthetic of purity, clarity, order, and analytical abstraction, postmodernism tends toward elaboration, eclecticism, ornamentation, and inclusiveness" (p. 40). Postmodernists are suspicious of what they call "great subjects," "grand narratives," and "objective truths," claiming that these are instruments of social power and are inherently political. Therefore, postmodernism attempts to "deconstruct" totalities of absolutes and notions of "truth" by pushing for redefinitions of previously unquestioned universal concepts. The contention of postmodernists is that there can be no single idea of common good since some groups and individuals within society will be silenced because of their differences from the norm (Tierney, 1993).

Postmodernism rejects the belief that experts control interpretation. As noted by Brotherton (1996), "A consequence of this is that the relationship between researcher-researched shifts from one of powerful-powerless, where one holds the knowledge and the other is kept in the dark, to a relationship where each is a collaborator and a participant. Thus, relationships equalize and a power shift occurs" (p. 78). The notion of singular truths vanishes when experts no longer have control over interpretations. An obvious outcome is the possibility of multiple interpretations, multiple realities, and shifts in perceptions. Realities become fluid in nature, allowing for different stories with different endings.

To live in postmodern times means to live among competing realities, vast choices, and conflicting notions. As Maureen O'Hara and Walter Anderson (1991) described it, people "are shoppers in the great marketplace of realities that the contemporary Western world has become: here a religion, there an ideology, over there a life-style" (p. 20). Some shoppers are changing not only their identities but also their ideas about what identity means. The current wave in the ocean of humanity is that of diversity and multicultural perspective. No longer can one live in isolation, untouched by multiple beliefs, multiple realities, and a profusion of world views. To once again quote O'Hara and Anderson (1991), "We can choose among these, but we cannot choose not to make a choice" (p. 20).

One influence of postmodernism on psychotherapeutic practice is the focus on ideas regarding human text and narrative. As noted by Lax (1992), "Much attention is given to the importance of dialogic/multiple perspectives, self-disclosure, lateral versus hierarchical configurations, and attention to process rather than goals" (p. 69). To take it one step further, postmodernism is characterized by the following focus:

> The self is conceived not as a reified entity, but as a narrative; text is not something to be interpreted, but is an evolving process; the individual is considered within a context of social meaning rather than as an intrapsychic entity; and scientific knowledge or what could be considered undeniable "facts" about the world yields to narrative knowledge with emphasis placed more upon communal beliefs about how the world works. (Lax, 1992, pp. 69–70)

Narrative Therapy

Central to postmodernism is a focus on language. This is a major shift from the modernist's emphasis on the essential nature of "things" (McNamee, 1992). A feature of emerging postmodern influence in counseling is the increasing use of narrative in clinical practice. A narrative, one's voice in personal story, is suggested to be a root metaphor in human experience (Sarbin, 1986). As stated in Lax (1992), "The narrative view holds that it is the process of developing a story about one's life that becomes the basis of all identity and thus challenges any underlying concept of a unified or stable self" (pp. 70–71).

The sharing of our lived experience, our narrative, is something that human beings do with another. It is an interactive process where the storyteller acts as a human agent on his or her own behalf, thus holding the power to reshape the world in which he or she lives. Lax (1992) described it as "the process of defining who we are in interaction with other people's perceived understandings of us" (p. 71). Narratives exist within the contexts of the experiences people find themselves, including economic, social, political, and cultural constructs. One's sense of self does not become "revealed" as a result of conversation with others; rather it *is* the discourse with others. A forthright explanation was offered by Lax, who wrote: "A permanent self is merely an illusion that we cling to, a narrative developed in relation to others over time that we come to identify as who we are" (1992, p. 71).

The postmodern approach of narrative therapy and counseling supports the notion that the client and therapist/counselor are interdependent. In other words, the new story, which holds new insights and can reinterpret and embellish our life history, is being continually re-created and reconstructed as a result of the person-to-person discourse. When clients describe their lives in ways that limit their ability to expand beyond their previously told story about their life situation or concepts of self, it is the therapist's job to join with the clients in the development of a new story about their lives; a story that in some way opens the story line with alternative views. Thus, this therapeutic intervention allows for changing/co-constructing narratives of fluidity, inclusion, and shifts in the power-holders of truth. Postmodern influences give rise to multiple ways of knowing and being.

Operationally, we utilize Michael White and David Epston's (1990) interview model in our narrative work with children and adolescents. With their emphasis on externalization of the problem, the use of influencing questions, and the utilization of the written word in the therapeutic process, White and Epston have created new roles for the therapist and counselor. No longer in search of pathological interpretations of the client's story, they emphasize the exploration of personal knowledge and power over the problem. In addition, instead of assuming that the problem lies within the client, they speculate that the problem is the problem. This problem is conceptualized as emanating from the dominant culture and those who exercise power over the construction of realities. When this model is followed, the counseling session becomes a joint venture of rewriting these problem-oriented stories, which often have had profound implications for the client. The counselor joins with the client to label this problem. The following case study illustrates the use of narrative therapy.

The Case of Adam

Adam is a 15-year-old youngster who attends a local high school. He has been in special education since the sixth grade, and he struggled all during elementary school with writing, reading, and calculation. Along with the obvious learning problems, he has a long history of inattentiveness and fear, culminating with formal diagnoses of obsessive-compulsive disorder (OCD), learning disabilities (LD), and attention-deficit/hyperactivity disorder (ADHD). Much of his life has been organized around the fear that accompanies his obsessions and the possibility of failing in the classroom. When he was referred for private therapy at age 12, he was sleeping in his parents' bed nearly every night because of recurring fear and anxiety. Daily decisions that most of us take for granted, such as which chair to sit in, how much paper to use on an assignment, and which door to use when going to another room tormented him internally. Troubled with the fear that if he made the wrong decision either he or his parents would die, he battled the seemingly endless barrage of interior, obsessive thoughts of danger and death.

Now, at age 15, he is involved in narrative therapy. During an early session rather than label *himself* as the problem, such as "obsessive-compulsive, learning disabled kid," he labeled the problem "the OCEEDEES," thus externalizing it. This allowed him to conceptualize the problem as something he could fight, not something that he is. He seemed to know intuitively that it is the belief that "one is" that creates the sense of impotence and helplessness.

When Adam identified this problem, in his personal, linguistic format, the counselor began a series of interview questions that mapped the influence of problem over Adam's life. "How do the OCEEDEES keep you from making friends? How do the OCEEDEES affect your schoolwork? When do the OCEEDEES seem the most powerful? What are you doing when they appear to be most powerful? What do your friends/Mom/relatives notice when the OCEEDEES are most strong? How do the OCEEDEES keep you tricked into believing that you can't be a good student? How old were you when the OCEEDEES first started to attempt to convince you that you could not do well in school? How have the OCEEDEES convinced your teachers over the years that you are not a competent student? How have the OCEEDEES affected your confidence as a student? Friend? Son? How have the OCEEDEES influenced others to treat you differently than you've wanted to be treated? What would you be doing differently as a 15 year old freshman in high school if you did not have to battle the OCEEDEES?"

Adam is not the problem. The OCEEDEES are the problem. Through the interactional narrative, he began to see the problem with a wider lense and new definition. He began to understand the historical development of the OCEEDEES and their impact on self, social relationships, and family. He became aware that the OCEEDEES were separate from his own identity and sense of self. He began to conceptualize an opponent, and he began to lose hopelessness and develop a story with goals of mastery.

The counselor then asked Adam about his influence and power over the OCEEDEES. Often clients, whether they are children, adolescents, or adults, perceive the problem as all powerful and may be surprised when questions of their own competence and mastery of the problem are posed. Among the questions Adam was asked were the following: "When are times when you realized that the OCEEDEES could have been present, but they weren't? When was a time when the OCEEDEES were trying to control or discourage you, but you were able to fight back? What new knowledge have you discovered about yourself that leads you to feel more powerful over the OCEEDEES? What do your friends notice about you when you have been able to defeat the OCEEDEES? What changes in your relationship with your parents when you gain some mastery over the OCEEDEES?"

With children, adolescents, and even adults, drawing is often helpful to develop the concept of the external problem. The pictorial image cements the idea of a problem residing outside of the person and thus susceptive to influence from the person. Adam's pictures embellish his sense of the problem. In one of his drawings (reprinted here as Figure 5.1), which he titled "BAD OCD," he created a stick man with no face, hands and feet. The person is confronted with decisions on each side of himself, and he is unsure about which option to choose. He is confused. He feels hopeless and frightened. Someone else (the circle) rescues him from the decision (see the arrow), and he no longer feels the fear of the obsession.

In addition, Adam drew the OCEEDEES as a dark, sinister figure that comes calling at the door (see Figure 5.2). He equated the figure with death and forces of evil. This is not surprising, considering that one of his fears was that if he made the

FIGURE 5.1

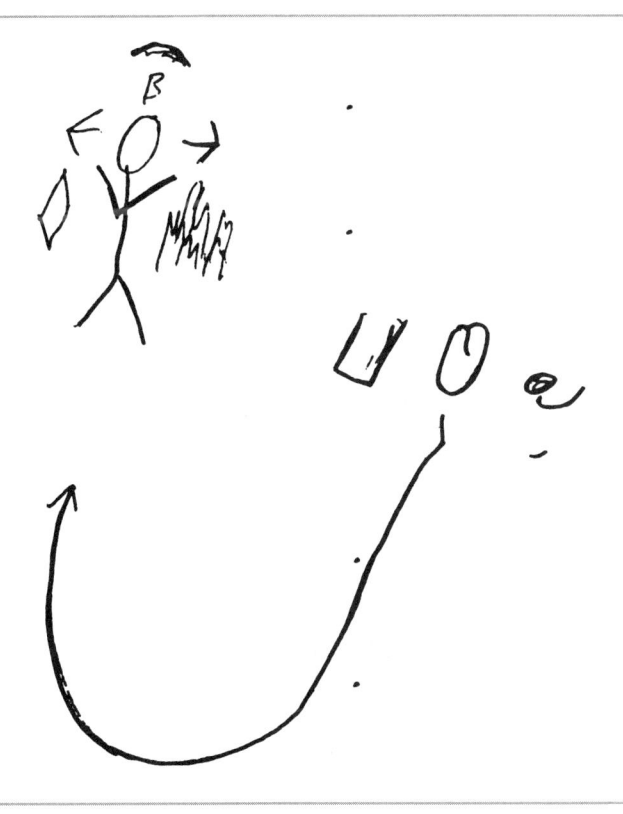

Transforming Children's Experiences

wrong decision regarding food, clothing, chair, doorway, when to go to bed, or how many dots to put on a homework paper, he would eventually be controlled by Satan. However, after reviewing his drawing, he felt a stronger sense of power and a clearer definition of the distortion of his fear.

Following the session, the counselor drafted a letter to summarize the important knowledge that crystalized from the interview. Using words, phrases, imagery, and new conceptual knowledge from the interview in the letter, the counselor developed a new story of competency and mastery. This was a new dialogue to replace the pathological narrative that accompanied Adam. Adam's mother noted that he enjoyed the letter when he received it, and in a later session Adam admitted that, the day the letter came, he had stayed home from school because of a particularly bad day with the OCEEDEES. He opened the mail, and the letter allowed him to fight

FIGURE 5.2

Transforming Children's Experiences

the obsessions and rituals that were so powerful earlier in the day. The counselor's letter read as follows:

> Dear Adam,
> For some time now you have helped me understand the difficulty of living with OCD (or as you say it, the OCEEDEES). It is clear that OCD has a powerful impact on your life. It has

intense power to make you feel anxious and worried. You become so worried about your future that you will do almost anything to get rid of it, including using rituals and tricking your mother. OCD has also prevented you, to some degree, from developing as rich a spiritual life as you would like to experience. It also prevents you from having closer friendships.

What is also clear is how courageous you are in the battle to deny OCD dominance in your life. The thoughts continue to pummel you on some days, and the rules and rituals can be exhausting, but you appear determined to fight on. You have defeated ideas about couches, doors, and Satan. You have become so much more independent, walking home from school, helping set your school schedule, and studying for a career as an emergency medical technician. You are more open, humorous, and insightful than when we first met some 2-3 years ago.

I wonder what knowledge you have gained about yourself in the past few years. What transformations are surprising to you? How have these transformations changed the relationship between you and your mom? What new stages would you like to develop for yourself? What new relationship would you like to improve between you and your mom? Between you and your grandfather?

I am anxious to hear more about your new ideas next session.
Sincerely,
Dr. W.

Adam's ideas about himself, constructed with the counselor's assistance (Dr. W.), became a written form that allowed additional summaries and conceptualizations to develop. The written word allowed ideas formed through a new set of lenses to be carried out of the therapy office to home and school. The letter allowed Adam to speculate about future implications and create new perspectives of self in the world. As Nylund and Thomas (1994) noted, these questions and observations after the session allow the opening of space for new possibilities. Thus, the previous chronicles, which supposedly represented the truth and reduced the client to pathology, are dismissed as myths or the tales are reinvented with new plot and details that depict competence, vision, and hope.

Use of Narrative Principles in the Classroom

The use of narrative therapy techniques and principles is hardly restricted to the school counselor, school psychologist, or therapist's office (Winslade & Monk, 1999). Narrative emerges, after all, from paradigmatic beliefs. Those using it are not bounded by vocation; rather, narrative may be employed by parents, teachers, administrators, and virtually any person who thinks in terms of alternative stories.

Within the typical classroom, the themes, stories, and discourse that evolve from dominant culture are transparent. For better or worse, the norms, values, and beliefs that are the bedrock of American culture are typically transmitted there, as well as in the other social institutions that play a part of culture. It is no surprise that children often are perceived in our schools in reductionistic ways that reflect a culture organized around a medical model of problems. In this view, problems are more than problems; they are diagnoses and pathology.

Narrative interaction can have a powerful impact on normal day-to-day classroom activities for children who are developing in expected patterns, which are reflected in curriculum and instructional practice. It also allows new discourse to evolve between the teacher and the student who struggles to be competent in the typical educational model. Such children are referred to as disabled, slow learners, educationally challenged, below grade level, underachievers, unmotivated, and lazy.

Narrative interaction requires narrative thinking. In other words, to effectively develop the spaces of exception, competence, resilience, and autonomy, one must believe that people are adversely affected by stories of pathology and blame. One must consider the possibility that negative symptoms and problems are not within the person but are simply problems to be solved. One must not succumb to the institutional practices that ultimately define people with pathological descriptions.

Teachers who embrace the underlying principles of narrative interaction have an opportunity to reauthor stories that children have begun to integrate as truths. For a child who is struggling, the teacher can challenge these beliefs by engaging the child in a collaborative verbal exchange that elicits the child's perceptions of the problem. By doing so, the teacher can help the child develop and articulate the externalized problem ("What do you consider to be the problem? What do you call this problem?"). Then the teacher can engage the child in a question/answer exchange that helps to map the influence of the problem on the child's life ("How does _____ interfere with your life? In what ways has _____ kept you from being the kind of kid you want to be? What differences would there be in your life if you didn't have to put up with _____ [the problem]? How has _____ kept you from making the friends in this class that you wanted to make? How does _____ trick you into doing behavior you would rather not do?").

The teacher can also search with the child for exceptions to the problem, for times when the child has competently been able to fight the problem or solve the problem. Through questions, the teacher can help the child explore ways of thinking about the problem that seem incongruous to the previous definition ("When is a time you were able to not let _____ get the best of you? What are other examples of times you were able to keep away _____? When is a time you were sure _____ would be strong, but it wasn't? What did you notice about yourself when this occurred? What did other people notice?"). These and the previous questions are replicated in an interview format in Figures 5.3 and 5.4 for use in the school or community.

1. What do you consider to be the problem?
2. What do you call this problem? (If the child has trouble labeling the problem, help the child search for words reflective of his or her vocabulary and experiences.)
3. How does (the problem) interfere with your life?
4. In what ways has _____ kept you from being the kind of kid you want to be?
5. How does _____ hurt your relationship with your mom? Dad? Brothers and sisters?
6. How does _____ affect your relationships with other kids? Do you see yourself making better or worse friends with this problem?
7. How does _____ trick you into doing things you would rather not do?
8. What kind of feelings do you have after _____ has tricked you into doing things you don't want to do?
9. What differences would there be in your life if you didn't have to put up with _____?
10. What will happen to your life, at home, at school, in the community, in sports, etc., if this problem keeps defeating you?

FIGURE 5.3

Intensity Interview: Mapping the Influence of the Problem on the Child

Note that, through dialogue, the teacher has coauthored a new conceptualization that places the problem outside of the child. The child sees the impact of the problem upon his or her life and simultaneously begins to understand how much control he or she exerts over this problem. The teacher can then send a letter that summarizes the knowledge gained from the verbal interchange and daily classroom/playground observations and allows new possibilities and hope to coexist with the problem.

Summary

Transforming children's experiences of failure ultimately entails transforming our own thoughts about what constitutes a problem. We, as practitioners and parents, must reconsider our basic assumptions of behavior. What makes a behavior "normal"? What is "normal" development? What are the everyday, typical kinds of change we can expect from children and adolescents? What does it mean if the

1. When is a time when <u>(the problem)</u> could have tricked you, but it didn't? (Help the child explore concrete examples.)
2. When you stopped or changed _____, what were you doing?
3. What affect did fighting against _____ have on your friendships?
4. When you got the upper hand, that is, beat _____, what changed for you and your relationship with your teacher?
5. What changed between you and your parents when you fought _____ and won?
6. What was different between you and your siblings, grandparents, etc., when you fought _____?
7. What happened to your ability to be a good student when you beat _____?
8. What are other examples of times you were able to fight _____ or not let _____ get the best of you?
9. When is a time you were sure _____ would be strong, but it wasn't? What did you notice about yourself when this occurred? What did other people notice?
10. What is the best thing that has happened since you found a way(s) to fight back against _____?

FIGURE 5.4

Exceptions Interview: Mapping the Influence of the Child on the Problem

behavior of these young people does not reflect these expected beliefs? As a culture, how do we conceptualize helping children to grow to their potential? Do we require the medical model and subsequent emphasis on pathology as a vehicle to ensure optimal opportunity for growth and development?

Answering these questions should instill a certain amount of discomfort within those of us who practice our vocations in the school and the community. Assumptions implicit in these questions suggest that much of what we consider to be problematic and pathological behavior is strongly influenced by the attempts of intervention by professionals and community members who have the good intentions of help but embrace fundamentally flawed paradigmatic assumptions of the world (see Poplin, 1986a, 1986b, for an explanation of this argument). Such assumptions expect the world to operate in a linear, mechanistic, medical model. Thus, problems become conceptualized as pathology, and pathology must be "cured." This model may work for tumors, but it falls short in addressing the needs of children.

Thinking about children as more than their problems and in more holistic terms may not be popular in a political sense. Clearly, those who do not value education and services for children will not conceptualize growth and development from a holistic and broad lens. This is not unexpected, but what is surprising is how adamant certain advocacy groups demand pathological and reductionistic models for children who have problems or struggle. They cling to deviancy and abnormal development archetypes in order to garner the political support to fund intervention and laws to protect these students. Unfortunately, the same groups for which they advocate protection and services are at risk for potential abuse in a different manner. Labeling, pathologizing, and inferring dominant models of dysfunction have the long-term effect of crippling one's autonomy, competency, and overall development.

Transforming children's experiences begins with our own individual relationships with our children, students, and clients. It requires rethinking our own ideas about problems and interventions. This reexamination of our ideas allows us to take problems seriously but resolve them in the context of a child's experience (Freeman, Epston, & Lobovits, 1997). Finally, transforming children's experiences mandates that culture reexamine the requisite beliefs of paradigm that become the foundation for policy, law, and intervention.

References

Brotherton, S. (1996). *Counselor education for the twenty-first century.* Westport, CT: Bergin & Garvey.

Freeman, J., Epston, D., & Lobovits, D. (1997). *Playful approaches to serious problems.* New York: W.W. Norton.

Jones, J., & Wilson, W. (1987). *An incomplete education.* New York: Ballantine Books.

Kellner, D. (1988). Reading images critically: Toward a postmodern pedagogy. *Journal of Education, 170 (3),* 31-52.

Lax, W. D. (1992). Postmodern thinking in clinical practice. In S. McNamee and K.J. Gergen (Eds.), *Therapy as social construction* (pp. 69-85). Newbury Park, CA: Sage Publications.

McNamee, S. (1992). Reconstructing identity: The communal construction. In S. McNamee and K.J. Gergen (Eds.), *Therapy as social construction* (pp. 188-199). Newbury Park, Ca: Sage Publications.

Nylund, D. & Thomas, J. (1994). The economics of narrative. *Family Therapy Networker, 18,* (6), 38-39.

O'Hara, M., & Anderson, W.T. (1991). Welcome to the postmodern world. *The Family Therapy Networker, 15* (5), 19-25.

Poplin, M., Wiest, D., & Thorson, S. (1996). Alternative instructional strategies to reductionism: Constructive, multicultural, feminine, and critical pedagogies. In W. Stainback & S. Stainback (Eds.), *Controversial issues confronting special education.* (Pp. 169-183). Boston: Allyn & Bacon.

Sarbin, T. (Ed.). (1986). *Narrative therapy.* New York: Praeger.

Tierney, W. G. (1993). Self and identity in a postmodern world: A life story. In D. McLaughlin & W. G. Tierney (Eds.), *Naming silenced lives: Personal narratives and processes of educational change* (pp. 119–134). New York: Routledge.

White, M., & Epston, D. (1990). *Narrative means to therapeutic ends.* New York: W.W. Norton.

Wiest, D., & Kreil, D. (1996). Transformational obstacles in special education. In M. Poplin & P. Cousins (Eds.), *Alternative views of learning disabilities: Issues for the 21st century* (pp. 15–32). Austin, TX: PRO-ED.

Wiest, D., & Kreil, D. (1997). Organizational impediments to the reformation of school psychology into a holistic model of service delivery. In T. Jennings (Ed.), *Restructuring for integrative education and learning.* (pp. 53–76). Westport, CT: Bergen & Garvey.

Wiest, D., Kreil, D., Ramirez, J., & Gonzalez, A. (1997). A community-systems approach to intervention with high school students with at-risk behaviors. *Issues in Teacher Education.* 6, (2), 5–10.

Winslade, J., & Monk, G. (1999). *Narrative counseling in schools.* Thousand Oaks, CA: Corwin Press.

6

Curriculum-Based Measurement: Cheaper, Faster, and Better Assessment of Students With Learning Disabilities

Michelle M. Shinn and Mark R. Shinn

With the exception of an emphasis on the diagnosis of learning disabilities as a physical "disease" that exists solely within the student, special education assessment is remarkably unlike the field of medicine. How ironic it is, then, that one of the most frequent criticisms of learning disabilities assessment is an emphasis on the so-called medical model (Bardon, 1988).

In this chapter, we do not focus on the problems, including a lack of science, inherent in a "within-the-person" medical model disability perspective on learning disabilities. Numerous other professional articles (Ysseldyke & Thurlow, 1984), books (Kavale & Forness, 1985; Salvia & Ysseldyke, 1995), book chapters (e.g., Reschly, 1987; Shinn, Good, & Parker, 1998), and task force reports (National Association of School Psychologists/National Association of State Directors of Special Education, 1994) have covered this ground in significantly more detail than space provides in this chapter. Instead, we initially focus on what assessment strategies work in medicine with the idea that this metaphor will set the stage for understanding the need for a critical shift in the focus of special education assessment from identification for determining to identification for treatment planning and evaluation. Then, we specify and describe a valid set of measurement tools Curriculum-Based Measurement (CBM) that allow special education teachers to shift their assessment focus to treatment planning and evaluation.

We emphasize that CBM is an assessment technology that is designed to work like key health indicators in medicine (e.g., temperature and weight), allowing teachers to make vital decisions about students with learning disabilities' "academic health," namely treatment planning and evaluation decisions. We argue that this assessment technology is *cheaper, faster,* and *better* than conventional assessment tools. Although cheaper and faster are desirable features in an assessment and decision-making system for students with disabilities, it is the concept of *better* assessment that is paramount. We emphasize that CBM is a "better" assessment technology because it (a) provides a continuous database for systematic decision making, (b) is consistent with the intent and language of the reauthorization of the Individuals With Disabilities Education Act, and (c) is tied to improved achievement outcomes with students with learning disabilities. Finally, we conclude with a case study that illustrates how special education teachers can use CBM in a Problem-Solving model for identifying problems, for writing individualized education program (IEP) goals as part of treatment planning, and for evaluating progress toward these IEP goals to allow for treatment evaluation.

What Assessment Strategies Work in Medicine

Assessment is a process that is naturally embedded in the field of medicine. However, unlike education and, in particular, *special education,* assessment in medicine is conceptualized quite differently with respect to three interrelated areas: (a) focus, (b) frequency, and (c) intensity. In medicine, the assessment focus is conceptualized as the principal purpose(s) of the assessment, assessment frequency is a question of how often the assessment should be done, and assessment intensity is a question of cost in terms of time and expense.

Assessment Focus

In medicine, as in special education, the most *visible* assessment activities center around diagnosis: testing to determine what is causing an illness. However, diagnosis of illness is only a *part* of medical assessment. Beyond diagnosis, the substantial portion of routine medical assessment, albeit important, goes largely unnoticed. This portion of assessment is tied to *growth* or *change* of the individual over time for the purposes of *promoting* healthy development, *preventing* problems of development, and *evaluating the effects* of treatment. From birth, children's development is tracked routinely on key growth indicators such as height and weight. From birth, children's weight forms the basis for decisions about healthy development. Especially in the first year, children routinely and frequently visit the physician's office, where they are weighed as part of "well checks." Weight is assessed and recorded in graphic form to allow for judgments to be made about healthy development. When the "well checks" indicate healthy growth, it is assumed that the child is developing "on track." Babies significantly below and, on occasion, above standard developmental trajectories for weight may be identified as at risk and/or assessed further to identify potential variables that may be contributing negatively to healthy development. Treatments may be prescribed and, logically, their effects evaluated by changes in weight over time. Goals of this "well check" process are to document healthy growth and assure appropriate intervention as soon as possible, *before* developmental problems become more severe and perhaps less amenable to treatment.

Even after healthy growth has been established in the early years, in part by tracking changes in weight, assessment of this health indicator does not stop. In fact, most readers will recall that during their last visit to a physician's office, their own weight was recorded, regardless of their age! Despite its simplistic nature, this type of information is relevant to medical decision making; in times of managed care, if the information were not useful, its collection would be dropped from standard practice.

In addition to its use in diagnosis, promoting healthy develoment, and preventing problems of development, medical assessment is also used for evaluating treatments that are prescribed. It is not just early intervention treatments that are evaluated. In medicine, nearly all interventions are evaluated as soon as possible after treatment begins, and evaluation then occurs as frequently as necessary to determine if the treatment is working.

In contrast, the assessment focus in education is *not* for purposes of promoting development and preventing problems. Proactive assessment over time to assure healthy development and facilitate early identification and intervention is not what educators routinely do. Instead, the focus of assessment in education is almost exclusively *reactive,* for purposes of identifying pathology within students with severe problems that, relatedly, may be less amenable to treatment. And, despite rhetoric, the focus of assessment in special education is not on evaluating the effects of interventions. At best, evaluation of treatment outcomes remains a once-a-year phenomenon, and tools that may not be related to the intervention are deployed to try to determine effects (*National Agenda to Improve Outcomes for Students With Disabilities,* 1994; Salvia & Ysseldyke, 1995; U.S. Department of Education, 1994).

How do we explain the differences in assessment focus between standard practices in medicine and in education? Surely the differences do not occur because educators are not interested in the promotion of positive development, prevention, and early identification and treatment. Surely they do not occur because educators are not interested in determining if their interventions are working or require modification. We believe the reason is technological; that is, unlike medicine, education as a whole has failed to develop, or implement, assessment technologies that can be used in a promotion and prevention focus.

Medicine has a number of validated "indicators" of health that can be used across the age range, time, and circumstances to provide a database for positive health and to assist in problem solving when it appears that a patient may be unhealthy. In addition to weight, physicians routinely assess height for many years, as well as blood pressure, heart rate, and body temperature. These indicators do not measure *all* aspects of health, but they do measure simple, general, and vital aspects. Take, for example, body temperature. This simple index, assessed accurately in seconds, can be used to make general decisions about a patient's health. When a patient's temperature falls within the average range and no other signs or physical concerns are reported, a physician may conclude that the person is "healthy." However, if the patient's temperature is significantly different from average, other problem solving can be done to determine, for example, the following factors:

1. Whether there may be a health problem that warrants further investigation. A temperature of 101.5°F is significantly higher than normal and would suggest closer examination of the patient's health.
2. Whether the problem is serious and may require special treatment. A temperature of 104°F is more severe than one of 101°F and would suggest that something serious may be wrong.
3. What the goals are for the medical treatment. The intervention should reduce the temperature to 98.6°F.
4. Whether the medical treatment is effective. A temperature that has been reduced to 100.3°F after the administration of Tylenol would suggest that the treatment has been effective.
5. If the treatment is no longer necessary. When the patient's temperature has reached the goal temperature of around 98.6°F special treatment may not be required.

As this example shows, temperature as an index of general health can be used both proactively in the promotion of healthy development (i.e., monitoring over time to assure maintenance of an average temperature) and for remediation and problem solving (i.e., for determining the need for treatment and for evaluating treatment effects). It is important to note that as a health indicator, temperature does not tell the physician *directly* what the treatment should be or what has caused a high temperature. However, this deficiency does not diminish its utility as an important health indicator.

Assessment Frequency

In medicine, assessment is *ongoing* and conducted as frequently as possible. The more severe the problem, the more frequent the assessment activity. Babies' height, weight, and temperature are assessed at least biweekly during the first 6 months and monthly thereafter for the first year. Persons in the hospital have their temperature monitored at least every 6 hours, regardless of the presenting problem. Persons with cardiac problems are connected to machines that evaluate their heart rate continuously.

In special education, *objective* assessment is not ongoing; it occurs infrequently. The principal source of any ongoing assessment remains teacher judgment, which is usually based on clinical impressions of student performance during instruction or student outcomes on teacher-made tests. Neither is satisfactory in and of itself for making judgments about student progress and intervention effectiveness. In particular, teacher judgment has not been shown to be reliable with regard to student progress (Fuchs & Fuchs, 1984). Most objective assessment information is collected at three major events in the experience of a student with learning disabilities: (a) testing to determine eligibility, (b) the annual review, and (c) the 3-year review. Outside of these major events, teacher decision making is usually tied to subjective judgments or is informally constructed.

By any definition, these three time frames cannot be considered "frequent" when compared to assessment conducted in the medical field. In fact, the "static" nature of special education assessment practice has been the target of criticism in nearly every one of the four major *federally* supported white papers and priorities in the past 5 years:

1. The *National Agenda for Achieving Better Results for Children and Youth With Disabilities* (1994)
2. The *U.S. Office of Special Education Research Strategic Targets* (1994)
3. The National Association of State Directors of Special Education's (NASSDE) *Leading and Managing for Performance* (1994)
4. The NASDSE and the National Association of School Psychologists's *Assessment and Eligibility in Special Education: An Examination of Policy and Practice with Proposals for Change* (1994)

Perhaps the strongest criticisms of special education assessment among these task forces were the conclusions and recommendations in the *National Agenda for Achieving Better Results for Children and Youth With Disabilities* (1994). Starting from the ground up, this task force produced a consensus document from the voices of national representatives from major disability advocacy groups, direct service providers, families, related services personnel, researchers, teacher trainers, teachers, and administrations supported by the U.S. Department of Education. The task force reduced the problem(s) in assessment to one statement (National Agenda, 1994, p. 20): "The current assessment process is being overused for labeling and placement purposes rather than for instructional planning. Alternative methods of assessing the skills and needs of children and youth should be developed." Among the concerns the National Agenda voiced was the conclusion that the "assessment process is often static rather than dynamic" (p. 21). Among the solutions proposed was the use of "continuous progress measures and ongoing assessments to maintain and support appropriate teaching strategies" (p. 22).

The infrequent collection of assessment information does *not* result from a lack of interest in objective information about student progress and intervention effectiveness. Surely, special educators are highly motivated to know if what they are doing on a daily basis for students with learning disabilities is effective. In our view, the explanation, again, is technological. Special education has failed to develop, or implement, valid assessment technologies that can be used on a continuous and frequent basis.

Assessment Intensity

We have defined assessment intensity for the medical field as issues of logistics and expense. In medicine, because standard, ongoing assessment is normative practice, assessment must be as economical as possible. That is, it should be inexpensive in terms of time and money. Time-consuming and expensive assessment should be done only when necessary and not as standard practice. An example illustrating this concept is the contrast between taking a patient's temperature and giving the same patient a CAT scan. The former can be undertaken in a matter of seconds and with low-cost instruments. Further, a wide range of medical personnel can collect temperature information. Therefore, it is logistically feasible to perform this assessment with a focus on promotion, prevention, and evaluating remediation. Incorporation into standard practice is simply a matter of commitment to using the information.

A CAT scan, conversely, takes a considerably longer period of time. Furthermore, the equipment is very costly and must be managed by highly trained and costly personnel. Although the CAT scan is important for particular types of health problems, logistics barriers preclude its use for anything but highly selective medical cases.

In education and special education, most objective assessment procedures are more like taking a CAT scan than taking a patient's temperature. Special education assessment, indeed, can be characterized as low-frequency, high-stakes assessment. There is little doubt that the three major assessment events—eligibility, annual reviews, and 3-year reevaluations—are expensive in terms of time and personnel (see again the four major white papers). For example, intellectual assessment for the purpose of determining eligibility is estimated to require 8–10 hours on average for testing, report writing, and meeting to share results. School psychologists, among the most highly trained educational personnel, typically spend between 67 and 76% of their professional time collecting information for the purpose of determining eligibility (Fagen & Wise, 1994; Hutton, Dubes, & Muir, 1992). Given the general professional consensus that the types of information typically collected for these low-frequency, high-stakes decisions do not contribute to improving outcomes for students with learning disabilities, one must question why special educators and school psychologists persist in collecting the information. The issue becomes even more disturbing when one considers that these types of assessment activities may prevent special educators and school psychologists from using their time to contribute to better treatment programs.

Here, too, we do not see the persistence in using expensive and time-consuming information that may not be useful for improving outcomes as a lack of interest in more logistically feasible and useful information about student progress and intervention effectiveness. Surely, special educators want to use their assessment time wisely to know if what they are doing on a daily basis for students with learning disabilities is effective. And surely, they desire to assess *as little as is needed to make good decisions* so that they can focus more of their time on providing treatments.

Again, our explanation is technological; special education has failed to develop, or implement, valid assessment technologies that can be used on a continuous and frequent basis for purposes of promotion, prevention, and effective remediation.

Similarities Between Curriculum-Based Measurement and Medical Assessment

We have proposed that special education's failure to adopt an assessment focus, frequency, and intensity similar to what occurs in the medical field as the result of a lack of appropriate technology or a failure to implement available technology. In a number of content areas (e.g., history, social studies, science), it is clear that a technology similar to medical health indicators does not exist (Espin & Tindal, 1998). However, in the basic skill areas (reading, mathematics computation, written expression, and spelling), such technology does exist. In these areas, the problem is more accurately characterized as a failure to implement on a widespread basis a technology that has been validated for the purposes described in this chapter. Curriculum-Based Measurement was developed to allow for a "medical model" of assessment and decision-making practice (a) with a *focus* on promotion and prevention as well as remediation, (b) with high-*frequency* data collection, and (c) at low *intensity* in terms of time and money. However, the use of CBM with students with or without disabilities remains a very localized practice, with the exception being in the state of Iowa, where CBM has been incorporated into standard assessment practices within the statewide special education reform process. See Tilly and Grimes (1998) for more on the use of CBM as standard assessment practice in Iowa.

CBM is a set of standard, simple, short-duration fluency measures of reading, spelling, written expression, and mathematics computation. It was developed to serve as dynamic indicators of basic skills (DIBS; Deno, 1985; 1986; Shinn, 1998) or general outcome indicators (Fuchs & Deno, 1991) by measuring key indicators or "vital signs" of student achievement in important areas of basic skills or literacy. Using the example presented earlier in this chapter from medicine, the CBM measures were designed to function as "academic thermometers" to monitor students' growth in important skill domains relevant to school outcomes. For more information on how CBM measures were developed as indicators of general basic skill achievement see Deno (1985, 1992), Fuchs and Deno (1992), and Shinn and Bamonto (1998).

CBM consists of the following testing strategies:

1. In reading, students read aloud from reading passages typically drawn from general education readers for 1 minute. The number of words read correctly constitutes the basic decision-making metric. Maze, a multiple-choice cloze reading technique, also has been validated as a CBM testing strategy (Fuchs & Fuchs, 1992). With Maze, the number of correct word choices per 5 minutes is the primary metric.

2. In spelling, students write words from randomly selected general education annual spelling curricula that are dictated at specified intervals (either 5, 7, or 10 seconds) for 2 minutes. The number of correct letter sequences and the number of words spelled correctly are counted.
3. In written expression, students write a story for 3 minutes after being given a grade-level-appropriate story starter (e.g., "Pretend you are playing on the playground and a spaceship lands. A little green person comes out, calls your name, and . . ."). The number of words written, spelled correctly, and/or correct word sequences are counted.
4. In mathematics, students write answers to computational problems selected randomly from general education computational objectives using 2- to 5-minute probes. The number of digits written correctly is counted.

Cheaper and Faster Assessment

Most apparent from these descriptions of the typical CBM measures is the short duration of the testing periods. For example, the general reading achievement measure, reading aloud from passages derived from general education texts, requires students to read for 1 minute. Typically, trained teachers can administer the test—reading the directions, having the student read, and scoring and recording the scores—in a little over 2 minutes total time per passage (Wesson, Fuchs, Tindal, Mirkin, & Deno, 1986). Administration of the written expression measure takes about 5 minutes total to read the directions, have the students write their story, and score and record the results. Short tests allow frequent testing (e.g., weekly to assess progress toward IEP annual goals) to be logistically feasible, and information can be collected without a major distraction or diversion from instruction.

Less apparent is the "cheaper" aspect of the assessment. Cheaper is, in part, a result of the fact that the basic CBM assessment strategies, from directions to scoring rules, are available in the public domain. Special education teachers or other persons who use CBM do not have to purchase consumable test protocols, scoring templates, computerized scoring packages, or interpretive manuals. Testing materials from most commercially available reading and spelling programs that can be used to develop CBM materials have been developed by local school systems and teachers around the country and are available for the costs of photocopying and mailing. Once teachers have administration directions, scoring rules, and test materials, maintenance expenses are simply for photocopying.

Other factors also contribute to making CBM inexpensive. Not only are the assessment materials available for a very low cost, but CBM also requires less time for training and completing an assessment (i.e., test administration, scoring) than traditional assessment measures and has lower personnel costs for the person who conducts the testing. With CBM, *quality* training for a variety of educational personnel, from aides to administrators, can be accomplished in a short period of time. Because the testing skills can be taught to a wide range of personnel, the most costly personnel (i.e., school administrators and school psychologists) need not be involved in "routine" assessment. With the low cost, it is easier to make timely, ongoing decisions in special education—decisions that are similar to those made in medicine. However, the real "cost savings" is in increasing *instructional productivity,* or the amount of student learning that occurs per instructional minute. If students with disabilities are learning at a high rate, their special education programs have high instructional productivity. If students with disabilities are learning at a low rate, their special education programs have low instructional productivity. When CBM is used on an ongoing basis to evaluate the effects of an instructional program, special education teachers can detect in 4–6 weeks when programs are or are not working. For programs that are not working, instructional productivity can be increased by changing the program in some meaningful way.

Cheaper and Faster Is Not Enough

It is not enough to have short, fast, inexpensive tests that can be managed by a wide range of education personnel. The tests must also be *quality* tests; that is, they must be accurate and valid. Length limits for this chapter prevent us from describing in detail the information on the technical adequacy of CBM from traditional perspectives (see Marston, 1989) or from more contemporary perspectives (see Good & Jefferson, 1998). Beginning almost 20 years ago, and continuing through today, researchers have undertaken serious efforts to develop short-duration, easy-to-administer-and-interpret, quality educational tests that can be used as indicators. As a result of these efforts, educators can read the professional literature to evaluate the quality of CBM efforts just as they can with any achievement test.

Use of CBM as "Better" Assessment

CBM comprises short-duration, quality tests of basic skills that we argue are cheaper and faster than the achievement tests used conventionally. We also argue that they are "better." By "better," we mean that they meet the following criteria:

1. They allow for a broader assessment focus that includes promotion and prevention in addition to remediation, creating a continuous database for systematic decision making.
2. They are tied to federal law regarding the educational needs for persons with disabilities.
3. They result in improved learning outcomes when used with students with disabilities.

Broader Focus and a Continuous Database

Earlier in this chapter we discussed that CBM can be used like a thermometer in medicine. Like the medical thermometer, CBM can be used proactively, preventively, and remedially. Because of the cheaper and faster logistics benefits, CBM can form the basis of standard education practice in the basic skill areas.

General education teachers can use the CBM tools to promote positive development and prevent learning problems by using them monthly to track growth and development from kindergarten on. See Kaminski and Good (1998) for more information on the use of CBM in the primary grades.

Standard CBM data also can be used in a Problem-Solving model when educational concerns arise. The problem-solving model as described by Deno (1989) involves five steps for decision making: (a) problem identification, (b) problem certification, (c) exploring solutions, (d) evaluating solutions, and (e) problem solution. When CBM is used in a Problem-Solving model, assessment procedures and materials are selected to provide answers to specific questions at each step regarding the student's "academic health" in basic skill acquisition. As in medicine, the assessment process begins with determining what question(s) one is trying to answer and then using an ongoing, data-based evaluation process to inform decision making at each step. Information collected at one step in the model is used to determine whether to continue to the next step or to discontinue assessment, therefore making the assessment process question-driven and economical. Assessment is discontinued when enough information has been collected to answer the referral question(s) and/or the problem(s) have been resolved. Table 6.1 shows the similarities in the use of the thermometer in medicine and the use of CBM in reading as well as showing how CBM in reading can be used in a problem-solving model. Because a standard assessment tool has been used, a database is established that all educators (and parents) can understand and that can be used to make a broad range of assessment decisions, not just decisions about special education eligibility.

Tied to the Assessment Language of IDEA

CBM is predicated, in part, on the use of testing materials that are linked to the content of general education basic skills curriculum. The correspondence of the materials need not be perfect, but there should be some relation. See Fuchs and Deno (1992) for more detail on this topic. CBM also is predicated on its principal use as a tool for writing observable and measurable IEP goals and for assessing the achievement of students with disabilities in the basic skill areas on an ongoing basis. We believe that CBM is *better* than traditional assessment measures, in part, because it matches the language and intent of the original legislation for students with disabilities, the Education for All Handicapped Childrens Act of 1975. This "match" has been made more explicit with the reauthorization of the Individuals With Disabilities Education Act (1997). In Figure 6.1, we have highlighted some of the key language in the IDEA reauthorization that we believe links directly to the use of CBM.

Improving Student Achievement Outcomes

The ultimate criterion for "better" with regard to an assessment strategy is the degree to which the strategy contributes to effective treatment or, as described by Hayes, Nelson, and Jarrett (1987), the degree to which there is *treatment validity*. Since

TABLE 6.1
Comparison of Health and CBM Reading Decisions and the Use of CBM Reading in a Problem-Solving Model

Health	CBM Reading	Problem Solving
Routine collection of temperature information as standard practice; comparisons to standard development norms	Routine collection of reading information as standard practice; comparisons to standard development norms	Promotion of positive development
Periodic collection of temperature information when it is suspected that there is a *health* problem that warrants further investigation (e.g., a temperature of 102.5°F)	Periodic collection of reading information when it is suspected that there is a *reading* problem that may warrant further investigation (e.g., the student reads significantly slower than same-grade peers)	Problem identification
Quality information on temperature when the *health* problem is serious and may require special treatment (e.g., a temperature of 104°F is more severe than a temperature of 101°F)	Quality information on reading when the *reading* problem is serious and may require a special treatment (e.g., the student's reading skills and instructional needs fall outside of the range of typical treatments)	Problem certification/validation
Setting goals for the specialized treatment (reduce temperature to 98.6°F)	Set the goals of the specialized reading program (read the same number of words correctly as peers in 1 year)	Exploring solutions goals
Continuous monitoring of temperature to decide whether a given intervention is effective during the treatment process (a reduced temperature to 100.3°F after aspirin)	Continuous monitoring of reading to decide if the specialized reading intervention is effective during the course of treatment (the student is improving oral reading fluency at the rate projected by the goal)	Evaluating solutions
Periodic collection of temperature information to determine if a specialized treatment is no longer necessary (the goal temperature of around 98.6° has been reached)	Periodic collection of reading information to determine if the specialized reading program is no longer necessary (the student's reading skills fall within the range of typical peers)	Problem solution

Under "Definitions of an IEP":
"(i) a statement of the child's present *level of educational performance*, including—
"(I) how the child's disability affects the child's *involvement and progress in the general curriculum*"

Under "Evaluation Procedures":
"(A) use a *variety of assessment tools* and strategies to gather *relevant functional and developmental information* . . . that may assist in determining . . . the content of the child's individualized education program, including information related to enabling the child to *be involved in and progress in the general curriculum* . . .
"(ii) a statement of *measurable annuals goals* . . . related to—
"(I) meeting the child's needs...to enable the child to be *involved in and progress in the general curriculum;*
"(viii) a statement of—
"(I) how the child's progress toward the *annuals goals* . . . (ii) *will be measured*; and
"(II) how the child's parents *will be regularly informed* (by such means as periodic report cards), at least as often as parents are informed of their nondisabled children's *progress*"

Under "Revision of the IEP":
"(ii) *revises the IEP* as appropriate to address—
"(I) any lack of *expected progress toward the annual goals and in the general curriculum*"

*Throughout this figure, italics have been added.

FIGURE 6.1

Language in the Reauthorization of IDEA That Links to the Use of CBM*

1984 (Fuchs, Deno, & Mirkin, 1984), a series of studies have been conducted investigating the effect of using CBM and its decision-making features on student achievement. Most of these studies were conducted with students with disabilities, principally students with learning disabilities. The studies can be divided into three broad approaches: (a) those that used CBM to monitor student achievement without providing instruction on *how* to use the information obtained (informal decision making), (b) those that used CBM and provided systematic rules for making intervention effectiveness decisions, and (c) those that used CBM and provided feedback about how the students' performed on specific required curricular skills (instructional enhancements).

As summarized in Shinn and Hubbard (1992), irrespective of the approach, the use of CBM improved student achievement outcomes significantly. Average effects on achievement increased when systematic decision making was used (b, p. 96) as compared to when informal decision making was used (a, p. 96). The most powerful outcomes were observed when CBM was used with systematic decision making and feedback and skill analysis. Based on our analysis of the assessment literature, we have yet to find evidence that any other achievement measure or aptitude measure produces anywhere near the achievement outcomes seen with CBM for students with disabilities (Reschly & Ysseldyke, 1995).

Case Studies Using CBM

Earlier, we set forth the proposition that the use of CBM in a Problem-Solving model is cheaper, faster, and better than the use of other assessment approaches for students with learning disabilities. The following discussion, and the case study that is woven through the discussion illustrates how CBM can be used with a Problem-Solving model to collect information not only for identifying problems but also for treatment planning and evaluation.

Problem Identification

Once a referral is made, the first step in the Problem-Solving model is to identify whether a significant problem exists in student performance that warrants further assessment. Identification of the problem should be quick and efficient so that educators can focus precious time and resources on instructional planning and program evaluation.

Typically, someone with a concern (usually the general education teacher) has referred a student because of low performance in the general education classroom and/or curriculum. CBM can be used to identify whether a significant problem exists by providing a measure of the difference between the referred student's actual performance and the expected performance of typical same-grade peers. Therefore, a problem is defined as the difference between what is expected and what is occurring (Deno, 1989). Student performance is assessed with general education materials or materials typical students in that grade are expected to learn. Performance then is compared to the normative performance of same-grade peers on the same materials.

PROBLEM IDENTIFICATION FOR CRAIG

Consider the case of Craig, a third-grade boy referred by his general education teacher for reading difficulties. Craig's teacher stated that Craig's reading performance and grades were consistently below those of other students. To determine if Craig's performance in reading was significantly different from other students, a trained examiner tested Craig for 3 consecutive days by having him reading three different passages each day from the general education reading book that typical third graders were expected to be reading. Third graders in Craig's school were expected to be reading Level 3.1 in the *MacMillan Reading Series,* so passages were sampled from this level to conduct problem identification. Typically, expected instructional reading materials are considered to be materials at the level of the general education reading curriculum that corresponds with a student's grade placement (Lovitt & Hansen, 1976).

For each passage Craig read, the number of words read correctly (WRC) and the number of errors (E) in 1 minute were calculated. His scores are presented in Table 6.2. Medians for Craig's performance across all passages for each day are also given.

DETERMINING A "HEALTHY" SCORE

In medicine, a temperature obtained using a thermometer allows a physician, or other health care provider, with a means for determining whether a problem exists and whether further assessment should be conducted. The temperature that is obtained is compared to an expected temperature, and subsequent actions are based on the discrepancy between what is expected, a temperature of 98.6°, and what is occurring, a temperature of, say, 102°. Although the temperature does not tell the health care provider *what* is wrong, its utility in the assessment process is not diminished; it functions as an indicator of a larger problem and guides additional assessment and/or treatment.

In Problem Identification using CBM, local normative performance, or what is expected of typical students at a particular grade level, is the standard for determining whether an obtained score is a "healthy" score. A problem is identified when a significant discrepancy exists between a referred student's performance and the local normative performance of same-grade peers. Local school districts typically identify a cutting score to determine the existence of a problem and follow-up assessment. A common cutting score is student performance below the 16th percentile.

To determine whether a problem existed in Craig's reading performance, the examiner compared Craig's CBM reading scores on the third-grade reading material to the scores of his same-grade peers on the same material. If Craig's score were

TABLE 6.2
Problem Identification Using CBM Reading for Craig

Reading	Craig's CMB Scores Day 1	Day 2	Day 3	Median	Peer Median	Craig's Percentile Rank
Pass 1	34	30	48			
Pass 2	26	18	30			
Pass 3	35	35	33			
Daily Median	34	30	33	33	85	8th

below the 16th percentile, or one standard deviation below the mean, a problem warranting further assessment would be identified. Craig's median score of 33 WRC in third-grade material placed him at the 8th percentile compared to typical third graders, identifying a potential serious problem in reading (Table 6.2). A graphic display of Craig's performance compared to the third-grade local norms from Craig's school district is provided in Figure 6.2.

CHEAPER, FASTER, AND BETTER

The problem identification process for Craig took approximately 5 minutes a day for 3 days, which means that a total of 15 minutes were required for administration (including briefly removing Craig from his classroom) and scoring. Thus, in just 5 minutes a day, the examiner was able to get a *rich* sample of Craig's reading skills in his *general education* reading book. This sample of Craig's reading skills could be used to (a) conduct a skills analysis, (b) determine the appropriateness of materials for instructional purposes (i.e., too hard, too easy), and (c) identify subskill deficiencies. All of this information could be useful for planning interventions, regardless of the setting for service delivery.

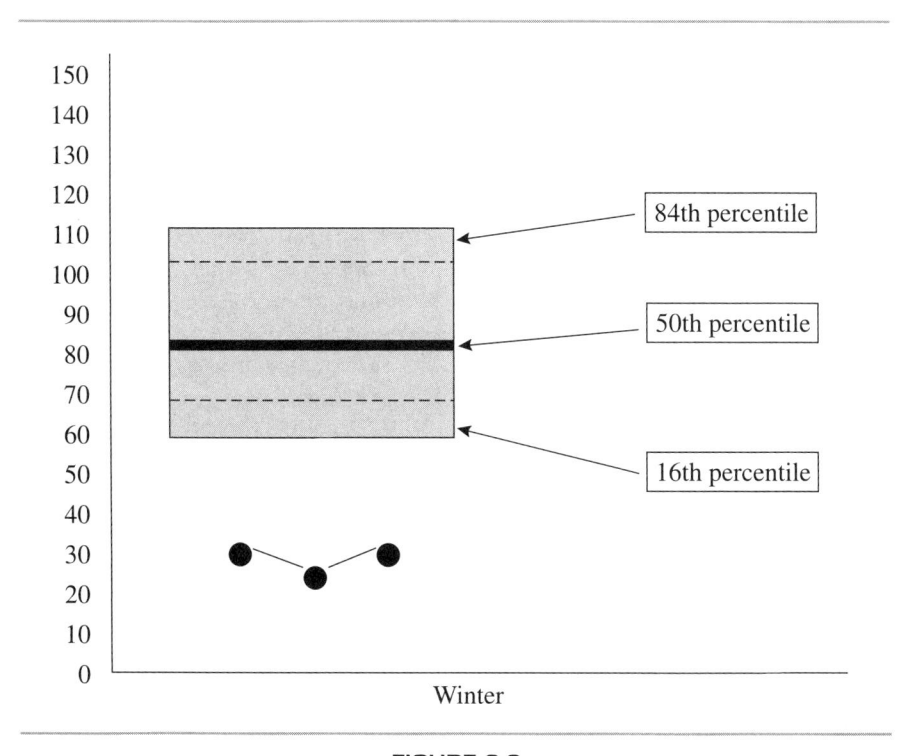

FIGURE 6.2

Graphic Display of Craig's Problem Identification Data

Typical published norm-referenced achievement and/or reading tests average 1 hour of administration time and, at best, allow the examiner to obtain a 2- or 3-minute sample of oral reading in materials that are unrelated to what the student is expected to be learning in his or her classroom. Thus, using CBM to make Problem Identification decisions not only is *cheaper* and *faster* in terms of cost of materials and time but also allows teachers to collect a *better* sample of student performance to use for error analysis and instructional planning.

Problem Certification

Should a potential problem be validated, the data collected during the Problem Identification decision-making process can be used as a beginning step in making Problem Certification decisions. Problem Certification is the process of determining whether an identified problem is serious enough to warrant a special program, including special education.

DETERMINING PROBLEM SEVERITY

A Survey-Level Assessment (SLA; Shinn, 1989) that uses CBM is completed in the Problem Certification decision-making step to determine problem severity, or the difference between a student's expected instructional placement and his or her actual instructional placement. SLA is the process of having students read multiple samples (usually three) in successively lower levels of the curriculum until an appropriate instructional level is identified (Shinn, 1989).

Expected instructional placement typically is considered the level of the general education reading curriculum that corresponds with a student's grade placement (Lovitt & Hansen, 1976). The expected instructional placement for Craig, a third grader, was Level 3.1 in the *MacMillan Reading Series,* the reading series that was used for instruction in Craig's general education classroom.

Actual instructional placement is considered the level at which a student can be appropriately placed for instructional purposes. Appropriate instructional materials generally are defined as materials that are not too hard and not too easy for instructional purposes (Taylor, Harris, & Pearson, 1988). Because Craig's performance in the Level 3.1 reader was significantly lower than that of his peers, the reader was considered too difficult for Craig for instructional purposes, and an SLA was conducted to determine Craig's appropriate instructional-level material. If the results of the SLA revealed a large discrepancy between expected and actual placement in the curriculum, the likelihood would be high that Craig's instructional needs would not be met in general education alone and that special education services might be necessary to reduce the performance discrepancy, assuming all procedural state and federal requirements were met.

PROBLEM CERTIFICATION FOR CRAIG

An SLA was completed to determine the difference between Craig's expected level of performance and his actual instructional level. In the SLA, Craig read three 1-minute passages at each of successively lower levels of the reading curriculum until an appropriate instructional level was identified. This process was completed in approximately 15 minutes with a trained examiner. The median WRC was used as the summary score for each level and compared to local normative performance at each level of the curriculum. Craig's score in Level 2.1, for example, was compared to typical second-grade performance in the same materials. His score in Level 1 was compared to first-grade norms. The assessment continued, using reading passages at lower levels in the *MacMillan Reading Series* until Craig's median WRC was above the 16th percentile when compared to local norms.

DETERMINING PROBLEM SEVERITY FOR CRAIG

The results of Craig's SLA are displayed in Table 6.3 and are graphically displayed in Figure 6.3. Testing for Craig was stopped at *MacMillan* Level 1 where his median WRC of 36 placed him at the 23rd percentile compared to typical first-grade readers. The discrepancy (three levels in the general education curriculum) between Craig's expected and actual instructional level was large enough to consider him eligible for special education and an individualized education program with an annual goal in reading. Although the eligibility team also considered other information for administrative purposes (e.g., classroom observations, teacher interview, record review), that information will not be reported in this example.

Percentile rank criteria typically are used in making Problem Certification or eligibility decisions using CBM (Marston & Magnusson, 1988; Shinn, 1989). In Craig's particular school district, Craig could have been considered eligible for special education services if his scores were below the 16th percentile of students one grade level below his expected grade placement. For example, Craig's performance in Level 2.1 materials (one grade level below his actual grade placement) was at the 10th percentile. Therefore, his performance was below the 16th percentile of students one grade level below, making him eligible for special education. However, this information alone was not enough to determine eligibility. The multidisciplinary team also had to decide whether Craig *needed* specially designed instruction to benefit from his educational program. It was determined that Craig needed specially designed instruction as his needs determined by the assessment could not solely be

TABLE 6.3
Survey-Level Assessment Using CBM for Craig

Curriculum and Level	Craig's Median Performance	Grade-Level Median Peer Performance	Craig's Percentile Rank
MacMillan 3.1	33	85	8th
MacMillan 2.2	27		No local norms
MacMillan 2.1	36	72	10th
MacMillan 1	36	66	23rd

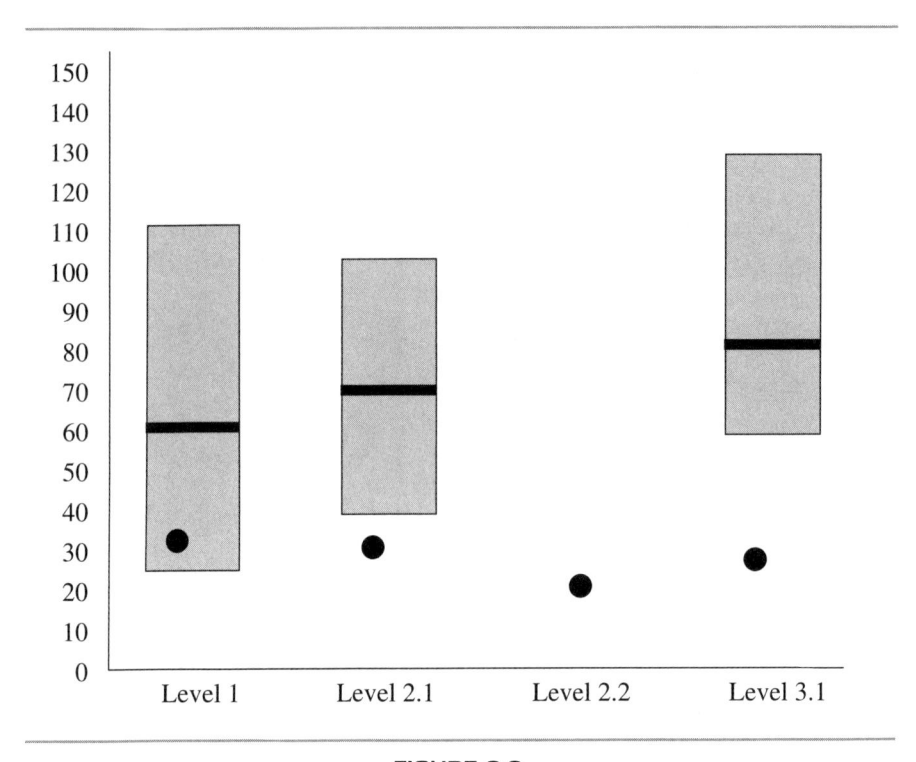

FIGURE 6.3

Graphic Display of Craig's Survey-Level Assessment

met in his general education classroom without the aid of supplemental services. Craig was determined eligible for special education with an IEP in reading, as his performance in materials one grade level below his current placement was at the 10th percentile and the multidisciplinary team determined that his instructional needs were extensive enough to require additional resources outside those provided solely in his general education classroom.

Exploring Solutions

Information collected during Problem Identification and Problem Certification (PI/PC) are used to explore potential solutions to reducing a performance discrepancy. The Exploring Solutions step in the Problem-Solving model includes (a) writing an annual IEP goal and (b) developing the content and process of the instructional plan for reducing the discrepancy between actual and expected performance. Because all the information needed to complete (a) and (b) will have been collected during PI/PC, program development and goal writing in the Exploring Solutions step are *time efficient, specific* to student needs, and tied to expectations in the general education curriculum, a common theme throughout IDEA.

USING CBM TO WRITE AN IEP GOAL

Annual IEP goals written using CBM emphasize broad, rather than specific, curricular achievement (Fuchs & Deno, 1991; Fuchs & Fuchs, 1986). For example, an annual CBM IEP goal would state the level of the curriculum at which the team wants the student to be performing successfully in 1 year, rather than stating the specific skills the student would need to master (e.g., short and long vowels, blends) to become a successful reader. The advantages of measuring performance with an annual IEP goal include (a) increased efficiency in monitoring progress as measurement material and task difficulty remain constant, (b) the ability to assess for generalization and retention in general education materials as intended in IDEA, and (c) support by technical adequacy data (Shinn, 1989, 1998). See Fuchs and Deno (1991) for details on the use of long-term and short-term measurement with CBM IEP goals.

Components of a CBM annual IEP goal include time, behavior to be measured, and criterion for success. The criterion for success is where the student should be performing in 1 year, including the level of the general education curriculum and the rate of performance in that level. SLA data are used to decide where the student should be expected to perform in 1 year given the student's instructional placement level and the instructional resources available.

In Craig's case, the IEP team wanted Craig to be performing successfully in Level 3.1 in 1 year. This goal was three levels higher than his actual instructional placement, Level 1, according to the publisher's scope and sequence chart. The criterion for success was defined by the performance of typical third-grade peers in the Level 3.1 reader. An annual goal was written that stated, "In 30 weeks, when given a randomly selected passage from *MacMillan* Level 3.1, Craig will read aloud 85 words in 1 minute."

Once an annual IEP goal is written, it is displayed graphically (Figure 6.4) to facilitate progress monitoring and program evaluation. The graph includes (a) time (horizontal axis), (b) unit of measurement (vertical axis), (c) current student performance, or baseline performance, and (d) the criterion for success as written in the long-term goal. The *aimline* represents the intersection between current performance, Craig's median baseline performance in Level 3.1, and expected performance, his goal of 85 WRC in 30 weeks in Level 3.1.

INSTRUCTIONAL PROGRAMMING

Student performance during SLA can also be used to develop the content and process of an instructional program. During SLA, a teacher (or examiner) obtains a 15- to 20-minute reading sample of student performance in various levels of the curriculum. This sample is large enough to conduct an in-depth error analysis and provide input into the development of an instructional program. For example, errors made while reading connected text may be typed on a separate list and read by a student during an untimed situation. Student responses would be recorded by an examiner and analyzed for specific patterns of skills a student may or may not demonstrate. Areas of particular skill deficiency could then be included in the instructional program.

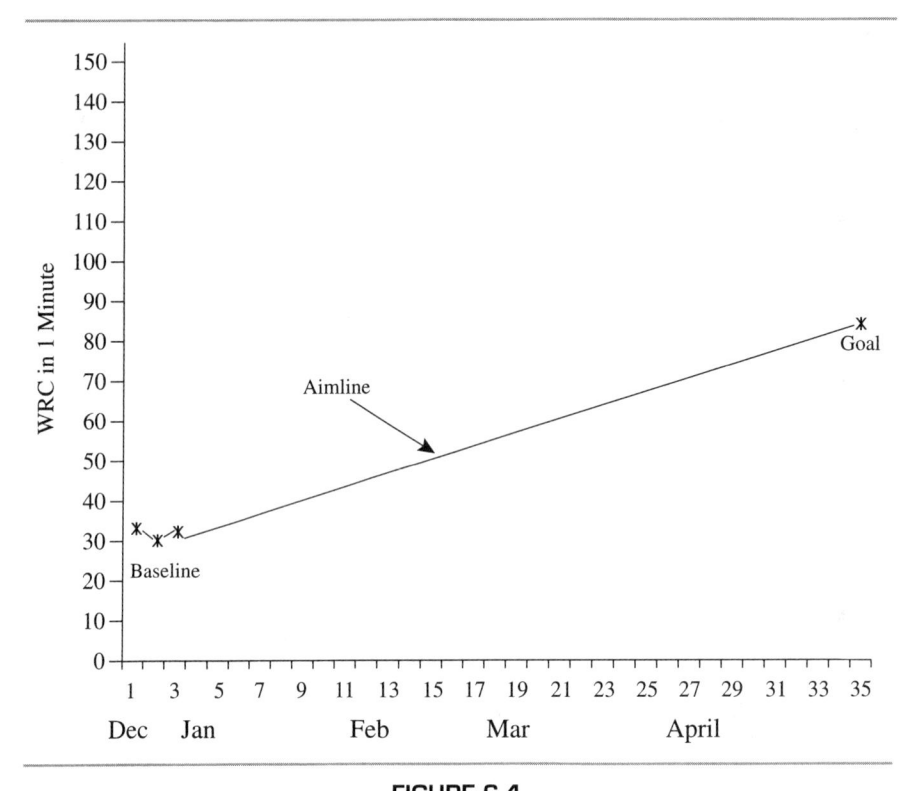

FIGURE 6.4

Graphic Display of Craig's Annual IEP Goal

Evaluating Solutions

Evaluating Solutions is the continuous measurement of student performance toward the annual IEP goal. Routine and frequent assessment of student performance is the "thermometer" for judging whether the special education instructional plan is working. Student performance is assessed continuously *during* instruction, and regular decisions are made as to whether performance toward the IEP goal is satisfactory or unsatisfactory. To evaluate whether student performance is satisfactory or not, actual student performance is compared to the aimline (or expected rate of progress), and decisions are made about programmatic changes or modifications. Increases in student performance typically indicate satisfactory performance toward the IEP goal and signal that a program is working and should be maintained. No increase or decreases in performance indicate unsatisfactory performance and a need for a change or modifications in the instructional program with the goal of improving student outcomes. See Fuchs and Shinn (1989) for more detailed instructions on decision-making rules regarding student progress.

Although different methods have been utilized to collect and analyze CBM performance data, it is typically teachers who collect, score, and graph the data. Fuchs, Deno, and Mirkin (1984) and Fuchs and Fuchs (1986) found that student achievement gains are greater when teachers are involved meaningfully in collecting and evaluating student performance data.

MONITORING PROGRESS FOR CRAIG

To evaluate Craig's performance toward his annual IEP goal, his special education teacher had Craig read a different 1-minute passage twice a week. Each time, the teacher graphed Craig's WRC on his progress monitoring chart (see Figure 6.5). After 7 weeks, Craig's special education teacher drew a trendline through his performance and compared his *actual* rate of performance (the trendline) to his *expected* rate of performance (the aimline) to determine whether Craig's program was working. Satisfactory progress would be indicated by Craig's trendline being parallel to, or steeper than, his aimline, a situation that would indicate that Craig's instructional program should be maintained. A trendline that was less steep would indicate unsatisfactory progress and a need for a change in the instructional program to improve Craig's performance.

As seen in Figure 6.5, the slope of Craig's trendline was increasing after 7 weeks of intervention, although not at a rate that would allow him to reach his goal of 85 WRC/minute. Because the intervention was not accomplishing what was intended, Craig's special education teacher made a change in his program to see if his rate of performance could be increased. The change in program is indicated by a solid vertical line separating Craig's performance during his first intervention and his performance after a change was made.

Even though Craig's special education teacher made a change in Craig's program, his annual goal remained the same and his progress toward that goal was monitored in the same manner. In medicine, this practice would be comparable to a physician making a change in medication for a patient to reduce a temperature and using the same thermometer to evaluate the effectiveness of the new medication.

After the change in Craig's program, his special education teacher continued having him read two 1-minute passages/week from the Level 3.1 book and continued to calculate and graph his scores. After 6 weeks of implementation of the modified program, Craig's teacher again evaluated his progress toward his goal. She computed a new trendline (as shown by the dashed line in Figure 6.4) and compared its slope to the aimline. The slope of the new trendline indicated that Craig now was making satisfactory progress toward his annual goal. Therefore, no further changes were made in his program.

Problem Solution

Assessment activities during Problem Solution are aimed at determining whether the discrepancy that was validated in Problem Identification has been reduced. A significant reduction in the discrepancy may indicate that special education services may

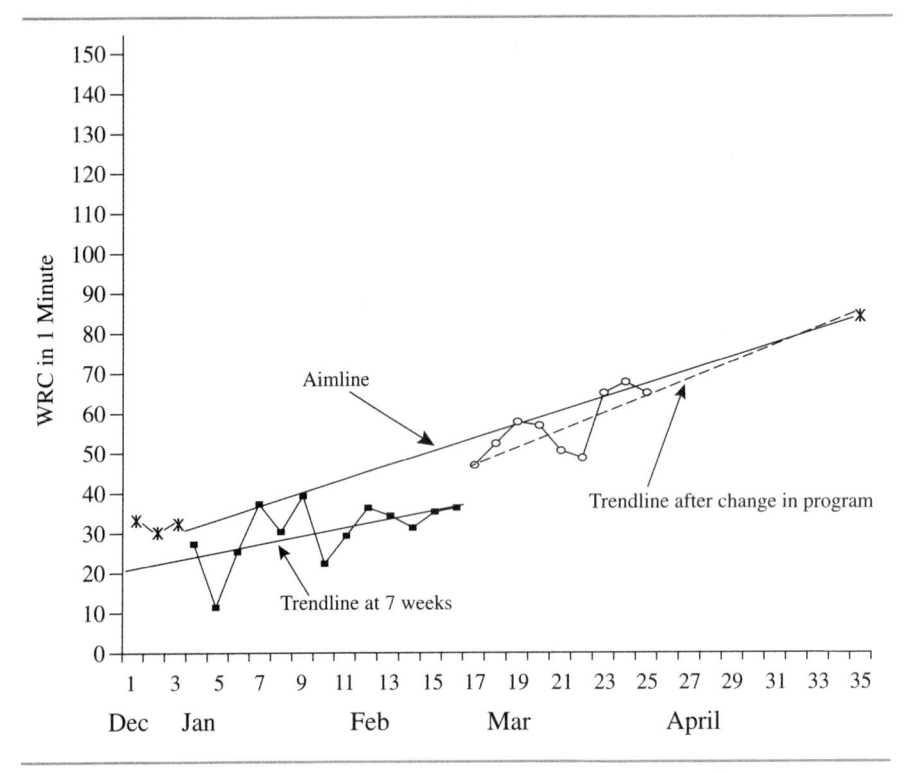

FIGURE 6.5

Progress Monitoring Chart for Craig

be reduced or eliminated. An increase, or no reduction, in the discrepancy may indicate continued need for specialized instruction through special education.

CBM can be used in two ways in Problem Solution decision making. The first method involves comparing current student performance to previous (baseline) performance and drawing conclusions about program effectiveness. The second method involves repeating the process used in problem identification where student performance at a specified point in time is compared to the performance of same-grade peers at that same time. Both methods can be used to conduct periodic and annual reviews of student performance. During annual reviews, an SLA is repeated to allow for comparisons of student performance to same-grade and lower grade peers. Data collected during the SLA serve as a basis for writing new long-term IEP goals and making program modifications.

In Craig's case, a review of his performance toward his annual goal after 5 months of intervention indicated that he was on track for achieving his annual goal. Peer-referenced assessment repeated in the spring revealed that his performance in third-grade materials was at the 34th percentile when compared to same-grade peers.

His initial performance had placed him at the 8th percentile when compared to his peers.

Even though Craig was performing within the average range when compared to his same-grade peers in the spring, the multidisciplinary team did not exit him from special education and continued his eligibility. They believed that although Craig had made satisfactory progress in the Level 3.1 book, he would be in fourth grade in the fall and his performance at that time could still be discrepant from his peers. Therefore, the team decided that Problem Identification, and an SLA if necessary, should be completed for Craig in the fall of fourth grade to determine if Craig's performance was discrepant from his peers' and, if so, whether the performance discrepancy would require intervention services through special education.

Summary

Curriculum-Based Measurement used in a Problem-Solving model combines a validated measurement technology with a decision-making model for *cheaper, faster,* and *better* assessment of students with learning disabilities. The assessment is cheaper and faster in that low-cost assessment tools are used to collect quality information in a short period of time, so that precious time and resources can be focused on treatment planning and evaluation. It is better in that the tools (a) allow for ongoing data-based decision making, (b) are in line with the intent and content of the newly reauthorized Individuals With Disabilities Education Act, and (c) lead to improved achievement outcomes for students with disabilities.

Curriculum-based measures are designed to work like key health indicators in medicine, allowing teachers to make vital decisions about the academic health of students with learning disabilities. When used within a problem-solving model, the assessment activities can be utilized not only for identifying problems but also for treatment planning and evaluation. Just like in medicine, the assessment activities (a) focus on prevention, promotion, and remediation of problems, (b) are ongoing and direct, allowing for continuous evaluation of treatment effects, and (c) are low cost with respect to logistics and expense. Time-consuming and expensive assessment should be done as needed, not as standard practice.

References

Bardon, J. I. (1988). Alternative educational delivery approaches: Implications for school psychology. In J. L. Graden, J. E. Zins, & M. C. Curtis (Eds.), *Alternative educational delivery systems: Enhancing instructional options for all students* (pp. 563–571). Washington, DC: National Association of School Psychologists.

Deno, S. L. (1985). Curriculum-based measurement: The emerging alternative. *Exceptional Children, 52,* 219–232.

Deno, S. L. (1986). Formative evaluation of individual student programs: A new role for school psychologists. *School Psychology Review, 15,* 358–374.

Deno, S. L. (1989). Curriculum-based measurement and special education services: A fundamental and direct relationship. In M. R. Shinn (Ed.), *Curriculum-based measurement: Assessing special children* (pp. 1–17). New York: Guilford.

Deno, S. L. (1992). The nature and development of curriculum-based measurement. *Preventing School Failure, 36*(2), 5–10.

Espin, C. A., & Tindal, G. (1998). Curriculum-based measurement for secondary students. In M. R. Shinn (Ed.), *Advanced applications of curriculum-based measurement* (pp. 214–253). New York: Guilford.

Fagen, T. K., & Wise, P. S. (1994). *School psychology: Past, present, and future.* White Plains, NY: Longman.

Fuchs, L. S., & Deno, S. L. (1991). Paradigmatic distinctions between instructionally relevant measurement models. *Exceptional Children, 58,* 488–500.

Fuchs, L. S., & Deno, S. L. (1992). Effects of curriculum within curriculum-based measurement. *Exceptional Children, 58,* 232–243.

Fuchs, L. S., Deno, S. L., & Mirkin, P. (1984). The effects of frequent curriculum-based measurement and evaluation on pedagogy, student achievement and student awareness of learning. *American Educational Research Journal, 21,* 449–460.

Fuchs, L. S., & Fuchs, D. (1984). Criterion-referenced assessment without measurement: How accurate for special education? *Remedial and Special Education, 5*(4), 29–32.

Fuchs, L. S., & Fuchs, D. (1986). Effects of systematic formative evaluation on student achievement: A meta-analysis. *Exceptional Children, 53,* 199–208.

Fuchs, L. S., & Fuchs, D. (1992). Identifying a measure for monitoring student reading progress. *School Psychology Review, 21,* 45–58.

Fuchs, L. S., & Shinn, M. R. (1989). Writing CBM IEP objectives. In M. R. Shinn (Ed.), *Curriculum-based measurement: Assessing special children* (pp. 130–152). New York: Guilford.

Good, R. H., & Jefferson, G. (1998). Contemporary perspectives on curriculum-based measurement validity. In M. R. Shinn (Ed.), *Advanced applications of curriculum-based measurement* (pp. 61–88). New York: Guilford.

Hayes, S. C., Nelson, R. O., & Jarrett, R. B. (1987). The treatment utility of assessment: A functional approach to evaluating assessment quality. *American Psychologist, 42,* 963–974.

Hutton, J. B., Dubes, R., & Muir, S. (1992). Assessment practices of school psychologists: Ten years later. *School Psychology Review, 21,* 271–284.

Kaminski, R. A., & Good, R. H. (1998). Assessing early literacy skills in a problem-solving model: Dynamic indicators of basic early literacy skills. In M. R. Shinn (Ed.), *Advanced applications of curriculum-based measurement* (pp. 113–142). New York: Guilford.

Kavale, K., & Forness, S. (1985). *The science of learning disabilities.* San Diego, CA: College Hill Press.

Lovitt, T. C., & Hansen, C. L. (1976). Round one: Placing the child in the right reader. *Journal of Learning Disabilities, 9,* 18–24.

Marston, D. B. (1989). A curriculum-based measurement approach to assessing academic performance: What is it and why do it. In M. R. Shinn (Ed.), *Curriculum-based measurement: Assessing special children* (pp. 18–78). New York: Guilford.

Marston, D. B., & Magnusson, D. (1988). Curriculum-based assessment: District-level implementation. In J. Graden, J. Zins, & M. Curtis (Eds.), *Alternative educational delivery systems: Enhancing instructional options for all students* (pp. 137–172). Washington, DC: National Association of School Psychologists.

National Association of School Psychologists/National Association of State Directors of Special Education. (1994). *Assessment and eligibility in special education: An examination of policy and practice with proposals for change.* Alexandria, VA: National Association of State Directors of Special Education.

Reschly, D. J. (1987). Learning characteristics of mildly handicapped students: Implications for classification, placement, and programming. In M. C. Reynolds, M. C. Wang, & H.

J. Walberg (Eds.), *The handbook of special education: Research and practice* (Vol. 1 pages 35–58). Oxford, UK: Pergamon.

Reschly, D. J., & Ysseldyke, J. E. (1995). School psychology paradigm shift. In A. Thomas & J. Grimes (Eds.), *Best practices in school psychology,* (Vol. 3, pp. 17–32). Washington, DC: National Association of School Psychologists.

Salvia, J., & Ysseldyke, J. E. (1995). *Assessment in special and remedial education* (5th ed.). Boston: Houghton Mifflin.

Shinn, M. R. (Ed.). (1989). *Curriculum-based measurement: Assessing special children.* New York: Guilford.

Shinn, M. R. (Ed.). (1998). *Advanced applications of curriculum-based measurement.* New York: Guilford.

Shinn, M. R., & Bamonto, S. (1998). Advanced applications of curriculum-based measurement: "Big ideas" and avoiding confusion. In M. R. Shinn (Ed.), *Advanced applications of curriculum-based measurement* (pp. 1–31). New York: Guilford.

Shinn, M. R., Good, R. H., & Parker, C. (1998). Noncategorical special education services with students with severe achievement deficits. In D. J. Reschly, W. D. Tilly, J. P. Grimes (Eds.), *Functional and noncategorical identification and intervention in special education* (pp. 65–84). Des Moines: Iowa Department of Education.

Shinn, M. R., & Hubbard, D. D. (1992). Curriculum-based measurement and problem-solving assessment: Basic procedures and outcomes. *Focus on Exceptional Children, 24*(5), 1–20.

Taylor, B., Harris, L. A., & Pearson, P. D. (1988). *Reading difficulties: Instruction and assessment.* New York: Random House.

Tilly, W. D., & Grimes, J. P. (1998). Curriculum-based measurement: One vehicle for systemic educational reform. In M. R. Shinn (Ed.), *Advanced applications of curriculum-based measurement* (pp. 32–60). New York: Guilford.

U.S. Department of Education. (1994). *The national agenda for achieving better results for children and youth with disabilities.*

Wesson, C., Fuchs, L., Tindal, G., Mirkin, P., & Deno, S. (1986). Facilitating the efficiency of ongoing curriculum-based measurement. *Teacher Education and Special Education, 9*(4), 166–172.

Ysseldyke, J. E., & Thurlow, M. L. (1984). Assessment practices in special education: Adequacy and appropriateness. *Educational Psychologist, 9,* 123–136.

This chapter was supported in part by Grant 84.029D60057, "Leadership Training in Curriculum-Based Measurement and Its Use in a Problem-Solving Model," sponsored by the U.S. Department of Education (USDE), Office of Special Education Research. The views expressed within this chapter are not necessarily those of the USDE. Some of the ideas expressed in this chapter are presented in more detail in "Advanced Applications of Curriculum-Based Measurement: 'Big Ideas' and Avoiding Confusion," by M. R. Shinn and S. Bamonto, in *Advanced Applications of Curriculum-Based Measurement, edited by M. R. Shinn, 1998,* New York: Guilford. Correspondence and questions about this chapter should be addressed to Michelle Shinn, College of Education, University of Oregon. Electronic mail may be sent via the Internet to mgilbert@oregon.uoregon.edu.

Personalized Grading Plans: A Systematic Approach to Making the Grades of Included Students More Accurate and Meaningful

Dennis D. Munk and William D. Bursuck

Tommy is a fifth grader with a learning disability that severely affects his ability to organize and write responses to questions. He has just received his first report card grades since being included in the general education social studies class. Tommy's teachers made several instructional adaptations for him, including providing him with study guides prior to tests. As he glances over his grades, Tommy is crestfallen to see the "D" in the social studies box. He knew he had not done well on the longer written tests in class, but he had worked hard to prepare, and he had attended regularly and completed all of his homework and in-class projects. What else could he do?

Samantha is a seventh grader with a learning disability that affects her reading and organizational skills. She is both excited and nervous as she receives her report card. Samantha is most concerned about her math grade, so she is surprised to see that she received a "C–" in science, a class she felt good about and in which the instructor seemed to treat her like all of the other kids. The class had worked in *cooperative learning groups the entire semester, and Samantha's group had worked well together. Their project on the causes and effects of erosion was interesting, and Samantha had learned a lot. Unfortunately, the group work was not counted toward her grade, and the project was only a part of her grade. Other assignments that required extensive reading and summarization were difficult for her, and Samantha knew she had not done as well on those.*

How unusual are the experiences of Tommy and Samantha? Do seemingly motivated students with learning disabilities work hard in general education classes only to receive lower grades than their peers? Donahoe and Zigmond (1990) found that 60–70% of students with learning disabilities passed their mainstreaming classes but received a below-average (below a C-) grade. A similar finding was reported by Valdes, Williamson, and Wagner (1990), whose survey results indicated that 60% of secondary students with learning disabilities had grade point averages (GPAs) of 2.24 or lower and 35% had GPAs below 1.74 (below a C–). In addition, at least one third of the students surveyed had received at least one failing grade. More recently, Wagner, Blackorby, and Hebbeler (1993; cited in U.S. Department of Education, 1994) reported that a nationwide sample of students with learning disabilities in grades 9–12 had an average cumulative GPA of 2.3; of particular concern was the performance of 9th and 10th graders, whose average GPAs were 1.9. Clearly, these research findings are of concern and should give educators pause to question the effectiveness of recent efforts to include students with disabilities in more challenging general education classes.

Although research findings suggest relatively poor outcomes under traditional grading practices, teacher adaptations of grades may serve to alleviate this problem. Grading adaptations are not a new idea, as evidenced by the fact that 50% of general education teachers report using them on an informal basis (Bursuck et al., 1996), and as many as 60% of school grading policies include stipulations for adapting the grades of students with disabilities (Polloway et al., 1994). However, a systematic process for selecting and implementing grading adaptations has not been reported. The purpose of this chapter is to provide an overview of key issues involved in making grading adaptations for students with disabilities and to propose a process for making such adaptations fairly, systematically, and effectively.

Key Grading Issues

When selecting grading adaptations for individual students, a number of key issues need to be considered. These involve the purposes of grades, options for adapting grades, the relationship of grading adaptations to district grading policies, the impact of grading adaptations on transitions to school and work, the interface of grading adaptations with instructional and curricular adaptations, and the acceptability of grading adaptations to teachers and students.

Grading **113**

Purposes of Grading

Letter grades (i.e., A–F) are so ingrained in our image of school, due in part to the fact that as many as 80% of schools require letter grades (Polloway et al., 1994), that it is easy to overlook the multitude of meanings or purposes that may be assigned to grades. Educators may have one purpose for grades (e.g., to indicate student performance relative to other students), while parents may feel the grades have a somewhat different purpose (e.g., to indicate how hard their children tried), and students may ascribe yet another purpose (e.g., to indicate that they passed their course and received credit toward graduation). In light of the different meanings attributed to grades, the process of considering the need for and type of an adaptation to report card grades must begin with agreement on the purpose of a grade. Figure 7.1 presents an overview of commonly cited purposes for grades (Bradley & Calvin, 1998; Carpenter, 1985; Ornstein, 1994) phrased as questions that educators, parents, and teachers may ask themselves when identifying a purpose for grades.

A proposed process for identifying and implementing grading adaptations is presented later in this chapter. The first step involves the educational staff, parents, and the student reaching agreement on the purposes of a grade. Such agreement may be difficult to achieve given the rigidity of current grading schemes as well as the lack of involvement parents and students have historically enjoyed in the grading process. Still, while time consuming, this initial step may be the most informative of all of the steps in the process and can result in the team agreeing to find ways to make report card grades meet multiple purposes.

Grading Adaptation Options

Table 7.1 presents an overview of grading adaptations, with potential advantages and disadvantages described for each. Several types of adaptations are covered, including

---

When I give a grade, review a grade, or receive a grade, do I expect the grade to . . .

- ▶ Communicate general achievement and quality of work on school curriculum?
- ▶ Communicate effort and work habits?
- ▶ Motivate me/student to keep working?
- ▶ Communicate progress on individual goals or mastery of specific content?
- ▶ Communicate how child's/my performance compares to that of other students?
- ▶ Communicate strengths and needs, and provide feedback on how to improve?
- ▶ Provide direction for planning for future, after-school life?
- ▶ Provide information to teachers for planning instruction?
- ▶ Convey abilities to postsecondary schools or employers?
- ▶ Provide information to teachers about which students may need special help or programs?

FIGURE 7.1

Questions for Identifying the Purpose of a Report Card Grade

changing grading criteria (e.g., varying the weight of assignments, modifying curricular expectations for graded work, developing on individualized contract with the student, grading on the basis of improvement), *providing supplemental information to letter and number grades* (e.g., adding written comments, adding information from the student activity log, adding information from portfolios or performance-based assessments), and *using alternatives to letter and number grades* (e.g., using pass-fail grades, using competency checklists). It is important to note that not all of these adaptations has been empirically validated, although the perceived acceptability of specific adaptations to teachers and students has been investigated as will be discussed later.

District Grading Policies

Polloway et al. (1994), in a nationwide survey of 225 school districts, found that 65% of the districts had written grading policies; of those districts having written grading policies, 60% included some guidelines for adapting grades for students with disabilities. When we reviewed the grading policies of several school districts, we found significant variation in the conditions under which an adaptation might be warranted, the process for selecting and documenting an adaptation, and the process for receiving approval for the use of an adaptation. Because of the variation that exists in grading policies, we recommend that prior to selecting a grading adaptation, the team consult the school district grading policy, if there is such a policy.

Adaptations that involve changing grading criteria—including varying the weight of assignments, modifying curricular expectations, using contracts and modified course syllabi, and grading on improvement—are most consistent with practice in inclusive settings and are therefore less likely to require special approvals or consideration. Such adaptations should be documented in a student's individualized education program (IEP). Prior to adding a grading adaptation to an IEP, however, it is important to determine if the adaptation overlaps with instructional and curricular adaptations already required by the IEP. Effective use of instructional and curricular adaptations may mitigate the need for a grading adaptation, and the distinction between types of adaptations suggested and required should be clarified prior to implementing a grading adaptation. Only grading adaptations that do not overlap with present IEP components should be added.

Another policy concern involves how teachers may indicate that a student is receiving adapted grades. At the time of this writing, we have received differing accounts of what may or may not appear on a student's report card. Before implementing an adaptation involving a change to a letter/number grade, such as adding written comments to report cards, educators should consult their district and statewide policies covering these circumstances.

Future Transitions to School and Work

Often, the motivation for making grading adaptations is to enhance the quality of feedback provided to educators, parents, and students. However, one must also keep

TABLE 7.1
Overview of Grading Adaptations

Adaptation	Description	Example	Advantages	Disadvantages
Adaptations That Involve Changing Grading Criteria				
Vary weighting of assignments.	Vary how much certain assignments count toward grade.	Increase proportion of final grade determined by performance on in-class science experiments.	Ease of implementation; assignments can be tailored to student abilities.	All assignments may be equal in difficulty; may require extra time for teacher.
Modify curricular expectations for graded work.	Prioritize specific curriculum to be used to determine grade.	Write on individualized education program (IEP) that grading in geography will be based on research on Wisconsin while rest of class covers entire region.	Ease of implementation; requires no change to curriculum.	Important content may be excluded; may require individualized assessment.
Develop individualized contract with student.	Teacher and student agree on quality, quantity, and timeliness for work completion.	Contract indicates that student will receive an "A–" for completing all assignments at 80% accuracy, attending all classes, and completing one extra-credit report.	Can be tailored to student strengths; student has input; may include classwide assignments.	Requires judgment due to lack of standards; student may not be given input; may require individualized assignments.
Grade on basis of improvement.	Assign extra points toward final grade for improvement in achievement or effort since last marking period.	Change a "C" to a "B" if student's total points were significantly higher than for prior marking period.	Reflects change in performance; may motivate student; requires no change to curriculum.	Required amount of change requires judgment; requires separate record keeping.

Grading **115**

TABLE 7.1 (Continued)

Adaptation	Description	Example	Advantages	Disadvantages
Supplemental Information to Letter and Number Grades				
Add written comments.	Add comments on products, performances, and other criteria used to determine final grade.	Write on report card or attachment that grade reflects performance on combination of IEP objectives and other class requirements.	Provides more detailed information to parents and student; may indicate areas for improvement.	Policy may prevent writing on report card (teachers should check policy before marking report card).
Add information from student activity log.	Maintain daily notes or ratings of student performance in specific areas.	State on student's report card that while the student's grade was the same this period, daily records indicate improvement in completing assignments on time.	Provides more detailed information to parents and student; may indicate areas for improvement.	Policy may prevent writing on report card; maintaining daily log may be time consuming.
Add information from portfolios and/or performance-based assessment.	Collect and summarize student work that reflects student effort, progress, and achievement.	State on report card that student's written language showed an increase in word variety, sentence length, and quality of ideas.	Provides detailed information to parents and student; may indicate areas for improvement; may draw attention to student strengths.	Determining products to collect requires judgment; products may be difficult to summarize; assembling portfolio may be time consuming.

TABLE 7.1 (Continued)

Alternatives to Letter and Number Grades

Adaptation	Description	Example	Advantages	Disadvantages
Use pass-fail grades.	Give student a "pass" if he or she meets the preestablished requirements for the class.	Give student a "pass" for completing 80% of daily work with at least 65% accuracy and attending at least 90% of classes.	Establishes clear criteria for student to follow; reduces emphasis on letter grades.	Postsecondary programs and colleges may require letter grades on transcripts.
Use competency checklists.	Construct a list of goals and objectives for marking period and mark completion.	Attach a checklist to report card indicating that during the last quarter the student mastered addition facts, 2-digit addition with regrouping, and counting change to $1.00.	Provides detailed information on content mastered and remaining; based on actual curriculum.	Postsecondary programs or colleges may require letter grades on transcripts.

an eye on the future if alternatives to letter/number grades, such as pass-fail grades and competency checklists, are used. High schools rely almost exclusively on letter/number grades for calculating GPA and class rank, both of which are used for college admissions. In addition, training programs and colleges may not grant credit to classes in which an alternative grade was given. Before choosing these adaptations, the team should consider the student's postsecondary plans, perhaps as part of the regular transition planning process. If the student plans to attend a particular postsecondary program or institution, contacts should be made to determine how alternatives to letter/number grades will affect admission or scholarship status.

Interface With Instructional and Curricular Adaptations

Considerable attention has been given to instructional and curricular adaptations, or adapted instruction, for students with disabilities included in general education classes (e.g., Friend & Bursuck, 1999; Fuchs, Fuchs, Hamlett, Phillips, & Karns, 1995; Keogh, 1988; Schumm & Vaughn, 1995; Zigmond & Baker, 1994). The resulting body of literature suggests adaptations in the areas of classroom organization (e.g., placing a student's desk in close proximity to teacher; implementing an individualized behavior contract for class transitions), classroom grouping (e.g., using small-group rather than large-group instruction; adopting peer tutoring to provide extra practice), instructional materials (e.g., using taped textbooks; making study guides to accompany readings; using assistive technology), instructional methods (e.g., providing extra teacher-directed instruction; using hands-on experiments and multimedia presentations; assigning fewer homework problems), and evaluation (giving oral tests; allowing extended time on tests; using individualized grading contracts). The use of these adaptations may obviate the need for grading adaptations, as is the case with the following two scenarios.

In one scenario, the aforementioned adaptations or methods are implemented classwide, with all students participating in very similar activities and producing like performances and products. For example, a science teacher may use hands-on experiments to enhance the motivation and performance of all students, including those with disabilities who struggle with comprehending dense texts and memorizing technical terms. In such a situation, students with and without disabilities may be graded on the same criteria. There would be an underlying assumption that the instructional methods used had effectively equalized expectations and facilitated success for students with disabilities.

In an alternative scenario, individual adaptations may be made for one or more students with disabilities while no attempt is made to adapt the classwide methods being used. For example, in the science class just mentioned, students with learning disabilities in written expression may be allowed to make oral lab reports. In this situation, the individual adaptations would be intended to equalize the expectations, and students with disabilities would still be graded according to the classwide criteria.

If we assume that the general and special educators in the scenarios just described collaborated to provide the best possible learning environment for students with disabilities, then can we also assume that those students will receive the grades they "deserve" and that the grades will serve their intended purpose? A firm and confident response to this question is often difficult, because no clear criterion for making such a judgment exists. Further complication may occur because of differing interpretations of guidelines requiring schools to provide adequate, if not optimal, conditions for student success. In the absence of a clear criterion for determining when instructional and curricular adaptations have been properly selected, implemented, and monitored, we cannot judge when it is appropriate to grade a student based on classwide criteria or when a grading adaptation would be helpful. The matter is further complicated by the likelihood that some students who do receive exemplary instruction and support will still receive relatively low grades. Thus, while the type and extent of instructional adaptations being used and the resulting grade are important pieces of evidence when considering the need for a grading adaptation, these factors may not be as important as the purposes for grading identified by the team in the first place. Indeed, even low grades may communicate accurate and helpful information, though perhaps to the detriment of student effort and self-efficacy.

Teachers' and Students' Perceptions of Grading Adaptations

In the absence of empirically validated standards for determining the need for a grading adaptation or for matching a particular adaptation to student characteristics, additional factors, such as the perceived acceptability of specific adaptations, may inform a decision to make an adaptation. Perceived acceptability of a grading adaptation can be defined as the extent to which teachers find the adaptation helpful in accurately describing a student's performance (Polloway, Bursuck, Jayanthi, Epstein, & Nelson, 1996). When Bursuck and colleagues (1996) surveyed 368 elementary and secondary general education teachers on the use and utility of grading practices and adaptations, the results indicated that while number and letter grades were most commonly used, teachers found the less often used adaptations of pass-fail grades, checklists, and written comments actually more helpful for students with disabilities. However, the teachers indicated that letter and number grades could be adapted for students with disabilities by (in descending order of perceived helpfulness) (a) basing grades on process instead of product, (b) basing grades on amount of improvement, (c) basing grades on progress on IEP objectives, (d) adjusting grade weights based on assignment and ability, and (e) basing grades on criteria met in an individual contract. Adaptations the teachers rated as less helpful were basing grades on less content, using a modified grading scale, assigning a passing grade for effort, or assigning a passing grade no matter what.

Evidence that teachers consider grading adaptations an appropriate and viable strategy for improving the accuracy and purposefulness of grades is found in the fact that 50% of the teachers in the study by Bursuck et al. (1996) reported that they had used specific grading adaptations for students without disabilities. Thus, adapting grades is not considered solely an intervention for special education students.

An explanation for teacher preferences for specific grading adaptations may be student preference; teachers may be unlikely to use adaptations that are perceived negatively by their students (Schumm & Vaughn, 1995). A recent study by Bursuck, Munk, and Olson (1999) sheds light on student preferences in this regard. The researchers surveyed 275 high school students, including 15 with learning disabilities, about the fairness of nine commonly used grading adaptations. For each of these adaptations, students were asked whether they thought making the adaptation for some students in class but not for other students in the class was fair. For each one, a majority or better of the students felt that making the adaptation for some students but not others was unfair, although significant variation in responses was evidenced across the various adaptations. Students thought that raising grades when students tried their hardest and giving two grades, one for effort and one for achievement or quality of product, were the most fair adaptations. The adaptations that students thought were least fair included changing grading weights, using a different grading scale, and passing students no matter what. A majority also thought that grades in more difficult classes should count more toward overall GPA. The students believed that a grading system should treat everyone equally; therefore, they felt that any adaptation made available to only certain students was unfair.

Perhaps not surprisingly, students with disabilities viewed at least two of the adaptations more favorably than did their peers without disabilities. Two thirds of the students with disabilities thought it was fair to grade some students using a different scale and to have grades count the same toward GPAs regardless of the difficulty of the class.

Educators looking to student and teacher perceptions for guidance in selecting an adaptation might draw several conclusions. First, the use of adaptations seems to be acceptable to teachers, who report using them with students with and without disabilities. However, students without disabilities think that using adaptations for some, but not all, students is unfair. Thus, some teachers may be reluctant to use adaptations that cannot be applied classwide, such as changes made for tracking IEP objectives and alternatives to letter and number grades. Teachers may be particularly reticent to make individualized adaptations for students with learning disabilities whose differences are not obvious and who are not likely to require an alternative curriculum. Second, teachers and students seem to be sensitive to the impact of grades on the motivation of students with disabilities, a purpose for grading listed in Figure 7.1. Encouraging news is that adaptations that could have a positive effect on student motivation, such as grading on the basis of improvement, weighting assignments, and grading on effort and achievement, were considered by teachers and students to be more fair. A third theme is found in the overwhelming perception that passing students no matter what they do is unfair and will discourage effort by those students as well as their peers. Finally, the perceptions of teachers and students seem to reinforce the overarching need for implementing a grading adaptation only when a mutually agreed upon purpose is identified by the teacher, parent, and student. This important step, along with others in a potential process for implementing a grading adaptation, is presented next.

Proposed Process for Making Grading Adaptations

Obviously, the decision to implement a grading adaptation involves a considerable degree of professional and parental judgment. We have recently completed an exploratory study of a process for developing personalized grading plans that include one or more grading adaptations (Munk & Bursuck, in press). Our model is outlined in Figure 7.2.

The first two steps involve the identification of purposes for grading. We recommend that teachers spend time prior to the first meeting with the parents and student developing a clear sense of the purposes that grades may have, including identifying specific examples for each. The teacher can then clearly explain the grading purposes listed in Figure 7.1 to the parents and student at the beginning of the first meeting and encourage the parents and student to ask for additional examples or clarification. Once the potential purposes for grades have been discussed, each participant should take several minutes to write down the purposes he or she perceives for grades. After everyone has had the opportunity to generate one or more purposes, the teacher should record everyone's responses and begin the process (Step 3) of selecting, by weighting or ranking, 2–3 purposes that the group will use to guide the selection of an adaptation.

Once the first three steps are completed, the team should proceed to Step 4, in which they identify, discuss, and compare the learner's characteristics and the

---

Step 1   Clarify teacher purposes for grades (i.e., the information the grade should convey).

Step 2   Clarify parent and student purposes for grades (i.e., the information parents and students want to receive).

Step 3   Arrive at mutually agreed upon purpose(s) for grades.

Step 4   Examine student learning characteristics (achievement level, impact of disability, areas of strength, limitations) and classroom demands that will contribute to the student's grade. Identify potential grading problems (learner characteristics interacting with class requirements and grading system).

Step 5   Review current grading system and determine if grade could be higher and/or more meaningful if a grading adaptation was implemented.

Step 6   Select an adaptation that meets agreed upon purposes and addresses the grading problems identified previously.

Step 7   Document the adaptation in the individualized education program and begin implementation.

Step 8   Monitor the effectiveness of the adaptation. (Does it meet the purposes identified?)

FIGURE 7.2

Protocol for Implementing a Grading Adaptation

classroom demands (i.e., assignments, activities, behavioral expectations). The discussion should begin with a review of the class requirements and demands that will contribute to the course grade. The discussion can be expedited if the teacher has already completed a worksheet that includes demands (assignments, activities, behavioral expectations) for the marking period and indicates how much weight each will have in computing the final grade. Next, the team should compare the student's characteristics to the course demands and grading system and project how the interaction of the demands and learner characteristics will affect the student's course grade. Although the teacher should retain a facilitator's role in this step, it is important that the discussion not be centered around standardized testing results, as might be the case in a multidisciplinary conference. Rather, this discussion should be frank and should center around the requirements for the class (e.g., tests, in-class assignments, homework) and how the student's disability causes him or her to be more or less successful on these requirements. The outcome of this step should be a list of activities on which the student is most successful and a list of those activities that exacerbate the student's limitations. This discussion may include a brief review of existing curricular and instructional adaptations. For example, the team might conclude that a student's algebra grade is low not because the student is unable to solve complex equations but because he or she has problems remembering math facts, which is causing lower test scores and hence lower grades. The team might then decide that giving the student a calculator to use when problem solving may eliminate the need for a grading adaptation.

Step 5 involves a review of the current grading system for the class. Having already highlighted classroom demands that may interact with the student's characteristics to produce more or less success, the team would be prepared to project the student's grade for the course. Two questions can be used to establish the need for a grading adaptation: (a) Could the student's grade be higher if a grading adaptation were implemented?, and (b) Could the student's grade be more meaningful (meet the desired purposes) if a grading adaptation were implemented? A positive response to either question would prompt the team to enter Step 6, which involves the selection of an adaptation. Step 6 begins with a review of the types of grading adaptations and identification of one or more adaptations that would address student characteristics and meet the purposes for grading identified in Step 3. Here again, the teacher should prepare ahead of time by becoming familiar with each adaptation and developing examples for parents and students. Once an adaptation is identified, an addendum to the IEP describing that adaptation should be written and attached to the IEP (Step 7). Finally, before the team meeting is adjourned, the participants should pinpoint expected grading outcomes and agree to a timeline for reviewing the effectiveness of the adaptations (Step 8). As evaluation will be ongoing, this step should involve periodic written communication between the teacher and the parents.

It should be obvious by now that parents and students would be active participants in the protocol, a role for which they may be neither accustomed nor prepared. In general, team meetings will be more productive if parents are made to feel welcome, their perceptions and concerns are carefully considered, they are treated as important, and professionals work with them to address student needs (Friend & Bursuck, 1999). More specifically, parents may feel more comfortable if, as suggested in the protocol, they are allowed to identify the purposes they feel grades should have before being asked to participate in a discussion of adaptations. Educators should also provide parents and students with clear, nontechnical information about the school's grading policy and potential adaptations. As students are not accustomed to participating in decisions regarding their grades, they will likely benefit from receiving concrete examples of how adaptations would affect their assignments and grades in a specific class. Students may also benefit from direct instruction in how to contribute to a team meeting (see Van Reusen and Bos, 1994, for a specific strategy).

Because we are still in the process of investigating this protocol for identifying and implementing a grading adaptation, we can only hypothesize what will transpire when a team meets to begin the process. The following is one possible scenario involving Samantha, one of the students profiled at the beginning of this chapter, her parents, and her teachers.

A Grading Adaptation for Samantha

Both Samantha and her parents were disappointed with the C– Samantha received in science and felt that the grade was unfair because Samantha liked the class and had always received positive feedback from the general and special education teachers. Following a call to Mrs. Stoneman, the science teacher, a meeting was scheduled to discuss the possibility of using a grading adaptation for the next marking period. Mrs. Simon, the special educator, prepared a "reader-friendly" handout on the grading adaptations that were allowed under the school's grading policy. When the team met, Mrs. Simon opened the meeting by reviewing the list of purposes for grades. Then, each person took 5 minutes to prioritize the purposes from most to least important. Each team member then shared his or her list with the group.

Not surprisingly, differences existed in the lists. Samantha thought her grade should indicate how hard she had worked because she did everything her teachers had requested. Her parents had a similar view; however, Samantha's father also thought that he should be able to ascertain from a grade how much of the material Samantha had mastered and what she needed to improve on. Both parents gave a high ranking to the importance of a grade communicating the probability that Samantha would be able to go on to college. Mrs. Simon indicated that grades should serve many purposes, with the most important being communicating achievement and measuring effort. Mrs. Stoneman added that grades are usually used to provide information on how a student's performance compares with that of other students, although she did not necessarily agree with that emphasis. After an enlightening discussion, the team agreed that the most important purpose of Samantha's grade in science should be to measure effort and communicate the quality of her work.

Mrs. Stoneman then led the team through a review of Samantha's learning characteristics and the demands of the science class. This was accomplished by writing Samantha's strengths and limits on a large sheet of poster board and then outlining the class demands on a second piece of poster board. By comparing the two boards, the team could quickly see that Samantha's limits in responding to timed, written production test items would interact with the exams for the class, which involved several open-ended questions requiring students to integrate and summarize multiple concepts and write clearly and quickly.

Having identified the potentially negative interaction between Samantha's learning characteristics and their likely affect on her grade, the team responded to the questions "Could Samantha's grade be higher" and "Could Samantha's grade be more meaningful?" with a unanimous yes. Everyone agreed that the C– she had received was unsatisfactory because it was so heavily influenced by just three in-class exams rather than taking into account her day-to-day performance in group work and on exercises completed when reading.

Thus, the team reviewed the possible adaptations and reached consensus that a grading adaptation involving an individual contract was desirable, because the contract could include measures of effort, such as questions asked during class, attendance, and preparation, as well as formal projects and assignments. Furthermore, the contract would allow Samantha's parents to monitor her performance in each area and to determine areas in which they might help her when needed.

Mrs. Simon and Samantha wrote the contract, which indicated that Samantha's grade would be based on the following performances or activities: completion of reading guides prior to class, participation (questioning, explaining, notetaking) during cooperative learning group activities and projects, and word-processed responses to reading questions. Criteria for accuracy and timeliness were established for each type of assignment. Both Samantha and her parents recognized that Samantha's workload would not be reduced but rather would be prioritized so as to take advantage of her strengths and motivation to succeed. The team agreed to meet again halfway through the marking period to assess the effectiveness of their choice. An example of what Samantha's grading contract might look like is presented in Figure 7.3.

A report card grade for the third marking period (12 weeks) will be based on the following assignments:
1. **Reading Guides:** Samantha will receive a study guide from her science teacher each time a reading assignment is given. Reading assignments will be given 2 days per week. Each guide will include questions about the reading and may include simple activities or experiments. Each guide will be worth 10 points. Points will be deducted for incorrect or missing answers. Incorrect answers can be corrected by the next class to earn back 1/2 point.
2. **Participation in Group Activities/Experiments:** Samantha will participate in group activities or experiments 2 days per week. Each of those days she will earn 0–10 points for fulfilling her role as notetaker, questioner, or summarizer. Roles will be assigned by her teacher. Samantha will receive daily feedback on a checklist that includes the responsibilities for each of the three roles. Points will be deducted when Samantha is not prepared for her role or does not pay attention during the activity.
3. **Answers to Essay Questions Using a Word Processor:** At the end of each of the four chapters in the text, Samantha will complete three essay questions that require summarization and synthesis of information covered by the text and in class. She will outline her answers to these questions while other students take the chapter test. She will complete her answers during her free period and at home using a word-processing program. The teacher will assign a due date. Each of the four sets of questions will be worth 0–40 points.

A report card grade will be based on the following criteria:

Study Guides:	12 weeks × 2 guides per week × 10 points each	= 240 points
Participation Grades:	12 weeks × 2 grades per week × 10 points	= 240 points
Essay Questions:	4 chapters × 40 points each	= 160 points
		Total 640 points

Grading Scale:
  576–640 points = A   384–447 points = D
  512–575 points = B   383 or below   = F
  448–511 points = C

Signatures

Samantha _____

Parents _____

Special Educator _____

Science Teacher _____

Principal _____

Guidance Counselor _____

FIGURE 7.3

Samantha's Grading Contract

Summary

The practice of making grading adaptations is certainly not new. For years, teachers have made informal adaptations based on student characteristics and classroom requirements. Interest in a more systematic approach to making adaptations has no doubt been sparked by the increase in the number of students with disabilities, particularly learning disabilities, being included in general education classes.

The purpose of this chapter was to provide an overview of the types of grading adaptations and to discuss the factors that might influence the selection of a particular adaptation. A protocol that has been field-tested was described, with the caveat that educators should be prepared for a variety of responses from parents and students about the purposes of grades. Indeed, the step of identifying the purpose(s) of a grade promises to be enlightening.

Regarding the grading adaptations themselves, several findings from the fairness research may be useful. Teachers interested in implementing grading adaptations only for students with disabilities might expect some protest from other students. Future research might address the effects of informing general education students about the rationale for grading adaptations on student perceptions of fairness. The importance of using grades to acknowledge effort and improvement by students for whom school is difficult is also evident. Adaptations that involve giving two grades, one for effort and one for achievement, or that involve varying grading weights, are perceived by students as more fair and may have a positive impact on student motivation to succeed. Such adaptations are also attractive in that they require relatively less effort by the teacher and communicate more information about the student's performance. We hope that research on the relative effectiveness of specific adaptations will become available. Until that time, the protocol for making grading adaptations will be built primarily upon the cooperation and judgment of teachers, parents, and students.

References

Bradley, D. F., & Calvin, M. B. (1998). Grading modified assignments: Equity or compromise? *Teaching Exceptional Children, 31*(2), 24–29.

Bursuck, W. D., Munk, D. D., & Olson, M. (1999). The fairness of report card grading adaptations: What do students with and without disabilities think? *Remedial and Special Education, 20*(2), 84–92.

Bursuck, W. D., Polloway, E. A., Plante, L., Epstein, M. H., Jayanthi, M., & McConeghy, J. (1996). Report card grading and adaptations: A national survey of classroom practices. *Exceptional Children, 62*, 301–318.

Carpenter, D. (1985). Grading handicapped pupils: Review and position statement. *Remedial and Special Education, 6*(4), 54–59.

Donahoe, K., & Zigmond, N. (1990). Academic grades of ninth-grade urban learning disabled students and low-achieving peers. *Exceptionality, 1*, 17–27.

Friend, M., & Bursuck, W. D. (1999). *Including students with special needs: A practical guide for teachers* (2nd ed.). Boston: Allyn & Bacon.

Fuchs, L. S., Fuchs, D., Hamlett, C. L., Phillips, N. B., & Karns, K. (1995). General educator's specialized adaptation for students with learning disabilities. *Exceptional Children, 61,* 440–459.

Keogh, B. K. (1988). Improving services for problem learners: Rethinking and restructuring. *Journal of Learning Disabilities, 21,* 19–22.

Munk, D. D., & Bursuck, W. D. (in press). Preliminary findings on personalized grading plans for middle school students with learning disabilities. *Exceptional Children.*

Ornstein, A. C. (1994). Grading practices and policies: An overview and some suggestions. *NASSP Bulletin, 78*(561), 55–64.

Polloway, E. A., Bursuck, W. D., Jayanthi, M., Epstein, M. H., & Nelson, J. S. (1996). Treatment acceptability: Determining appropriate interventions within inclusive classrooms. *Intervention in School and Clinic, 31,* 133–144.

Polloway, E. A., Epstein, M. H., Bursuck, W. D., Roderique, T. W., McConeghy, J., & Jayanthi, M. (1994). Classroom grading: A national survey of policies. *Remedial and Special Education, 15*(3), 162–170.

Schumm, J. S., & Vaughn, S. (1995). Getting ready for inclusion: Is the stage set? *LD Research and Practice, 10,* 169–179.

U.S. Department of Education. (1994). *Sixteenth annual report to Congress on the implementation of the Individuals With Disabilities Education Act.* Washington, DC: Author.

Valdes, K. A., Williamson, C. L., & Wagner, M. M. (1990). *The national longitudinal study of special education students* (Vol. 1). Menlo Park, CA: SRI International.

Van Reusen, A., & Bos, C. S. (1994). Facilitating student participation in individualized education programs through motivation strategy instruction. *Exceptional Children, 60,* 466–475.

Zigmond, N., & Baker, J. (1994). Is the mainstream a more appropriate educational setting for Randy? A case study of one student with learning disabilities. *LD Research and Practice, 9,* 108–117.

8

Andrew, Stuck in Words: A Retrospective Miscue Analysis Case Study in Revaluing

Alan D. Flurkey and Yetta M. Goodman

The language we use to talk about language is an important topic that is often overlooked in discussions of how to help struggling readers. We believe that this oversight is regrettable, because rich opportunities for growth come from raising readers' awareness of the reading process. By guiding readers through a close examination of their use of reading strategies, it is possible for readers to alter their fundamental beliefs about reading and about themselves as readers. This chapter tells the story of one student's shift in his stance toward reading and shows the language that we—and he—used to describe that shift.

> *Andrew Sandoval and his mother are heading out in the car to buy groceries. They live in an area that isn't as fully developed as some of the more dense suburbs in this large city in the Sonoran Desert. It's more open. As they drive over mild hills dotted with saguaro, paloverde, and mesquite, they pass signs and billboards by the side of the road. A billboard catches Andrew's eye. It shows a close-up of a thick peanut butter and jelly sandwich with a bite taken out. Andrew tentatively offers a guess as to what the words might say.*

"Mom, does that say, 'Got Milk'?" he asks.

"Yes! See, you're reading," she says, trying to convince him and support him. A desperate sort of enthusiasm is cracking through her voice. But Andrew takes no comfort from his mother's approval. He's not fooled. Those words don't count, he tells her. "Mom, they're baby words."

As told by his mother, this anecdote was typical of Andrew's stance toward his reading. We were introduced to Andrew by his school's principal and his fifth-grade teacher,[1] both of whom were concerned about Andrew's academic welfare. As they told us, Andrew was receiving learning disabilities pullout instruction in reading and writing. And even though Andrew was in a rich and supportive classroom with a highly talented and deeply committed teacher, concerns persisted about Andrew's reading—in particular, his attitude toward reading and toward himself as a reader.

Andrew believed reading to be difficult—strenuous. And he didn't think he was good at it. He certainly didn't recognize his own strengths. But Andrew did, indeed, have strengths—rich experiences and linguistic resources to draw from. Getting him to recognize his strengths and to enlist them to become a more effective reader became our primary concern.

Andrew's Reading and Writing at School and at Home

Andrew attended 2 years of preschool at a neighborhood church school and spent kindergarten and first grade at Mendoza Elementary School in the next neighborhood over. Then his family moved to another neighborhood, where Andrew repeated first grade at Greene Elementary. "Slowness in reading development" was the reason cited to his mother for retention. During that yeare, Andrew was tested and subsequently placed in special education for learning disabilities. He has been at Markley Elementary, his current school, since second grade. Markley is, thus, the third school he's attended, not counting preschool. When we met him, Andrew was 12 years old and in fifth grade.

Mrs. Sandoval's concern about Andrew's reading prompted her to send him to a commercial, national-chain "learning center" for 9 months. She recalled that he seemed to have fun and that the learning center's tests showed improvement, but she noticed no improvement at home and felt disillusioned with this approach to solving his reading difficulties. Later, she sent him to a different commercial tutoring business for 2 months but saw no noticeable results.

During the past 2 summers, Andrew attended his school district's special education summer school program. Describing the situation using Andrew's own words, his mother told us that Andrew was in a class of "normal LD" kids, but "the rest of the school was classes for nerds," possibly referring to students with developmental disabilities. On a couple of occasions she mentioned that Andrew *hated* it.

---

[1] The research team included Yetta Goodman, Alan Flurkey, and Prisca Martens.

Mrs. Sandoval remembered that Andrew's educational problems seemed to begin shortly after Andrew started getting homework. These first assignments included spelling words (Andrew does poorly on this type of assignment) and reading an easy book (this homework was done only if Mom read to Andrew—he would not read by himself at home).

Homework seemed to be a particularly contentious issue. Andrew needed to be pressured to do his homework, and he usually did not volunteer to do any writing. Andrew has recently improved with regard to writing assignments; however, he will write a story only if his mother spells the words. Even then, Andrew insists that each word *must* be right. If not, he is not satisfied that the assignment is complete. The only home writing that his mother mentioned was a note to his grandmother and an occasional Christmas list.

Andrew does not volunteer to read at home, but he always listens when his mother offers to read aloud. Books in *The Chronicles of Narnia* series are his favorites. He still asks his mother to read and reread them on a regular basis.

Andrew's mother reported to us that she feels positive about the learning disabilities resource teacher. The teacher told us that Andrew seems to have success if he reads to other students in the classroom. He also suggested the local University's reading clinic as a possible source for help.

Reading Words

Shortly after we began working with Andrew it became clear that he placed a great deal of importance on the word level of written language. The anecdote about reading the billboard and his insistence on having every word spelled correctly in his writing were evidence that helped to paint a picture of Andrew as a reader. The following responses that Andrew gave during our reading interview with him (Y. M., Goodman, Watson, & Burke, 1987) flesh out this portrait of Andrew as a person who views reading as a word-oriented enterprise. Notice that in no response did Andrew focus on units of language larger than the word. His references to the word level of reading are highlighted. In searching for details, the interviewer made use of Andrew's language but initiated no references to "words" herself.

Yetta: When you are reading and come to something you don't know, what do you do?
Andrew: I skip it.
Yetta: Do you ever do anything else?
Andrew: Sometimes I try to **sound it out**.
Yetta: Who is a good reader you know?
Andrew: Justin Fisher. In my class.
Yetta: What makes Justin a good reader?
Andrew: Because he can read fast and read good; he never comes to a **word** that he doesn't know.

Yetta: Do you think he ever comes to a word he doesn't know?
Andrew: Well, sometimes . . .
Yetta: When Justin does comes to something he doesn't know, what do you think he does?
Andrew: He **sounds it out.** I don't think he does anything else.
Yetta: If you knew someone was having trouble reading, how would you help that person?
Andrew: I'd read for him—a page . . . And I'd help him with the **words** he didn't know.
Yetta: And how would you help him with the words he didn't know?
Andrew: I'd **sound them out** for him.
Yetta: What would your teacher do to help that person read?
Andrew: Sometimes she'll—sometimes she tries to **sound it out**.
Yetta: Anything else?
Andrew: Sometimes she tells us to skip it.
Yetta: What would you like to do better as a reader?
Andrew: Like Justin Fisher. I'd like to be like he is. Sometimes he comes to a **word** and he **sounds it out real easy**.
Yetta: So you'd like to be able to do things real easy like he does?
Yetta: Do you think you are a good reader?
Andrew: Kind of.
Yetta: Why do you think you're kind of a good reader?
Andrew: Because sometimes Mr. Dahlstrom [resource teacher] tells me I am, and sometimes I say the **words**.

An Analysis of Andrew's Reading

To gather information about Andrew's reading, we periodically collected reading samples using miscue analysis procedures (Y. M. Goodman et al., 1987). Miscue data collection requires an uninterrupted, tape-recorded oral reading of a complete, authentic text. The reading is followed by a close-grained analysis of the quality and quantity of unexpected responses (miscues) produced by the reader. This analysis helps teachers and researchers get a sense of the strategies a reader uses as he or she reads.

Soon after we began working with Andrew, he was asked to read the folktale "The Man Who Kept House" (1962). It is an old traditional tale retold in many languages and cultures about a woodcutter and his wife.[2] As the story goes, the woodcutter complains that his work is much harder than his wife's housekeeping. To teach the woodcutter a lesson in humility (and provide a "reality check"), the wife offers to switch jobs with him for a day. When left at home to manage the household, the woodcutter is beset by a variety of calamities, including a pig loose in the house, a baby who gets lost, and a turn of events in which the woodcutter manages to get stuck in the chimney only to be rescued by his wife when she returns at the end of the day.

The miscue-marked typescript of Andrew's reading (Figure 8.1) provides further evidence of Andrew's word-centered view of reading. (An explanation of markings for miscue analysis is provided in the appendix to this chapter.) Inspection of this excerpt of typescript shows that Andrew's reading of this particular story was marginally effective and generally inefficient.[3]

Andrew's ineffectiveness was displayed in the numerous substitution miscues that were semantically unacceptable. For example, Sentence 2, beginning on Line 0103, was produced by Andrew as: *One evening when he came home from work, he said to his wolf, "What do you do all day with I'm away thinking wood?"*

Perhaps the most noticeable aspect of Andrew's ineffective reading was his frequent production of deliberate omissions. An omission is a text item (a word, a phrase, or a line of text) that has been "skipped" in oral reading. Deliberate omissions can be distinguished from nondeliberate omissions by taking into account the reader's intonation, the reader's use of pause and/or regression, and the syntactic features of the text that precede and follow the miscue. When readers produce deliberate omissions, they often assign hesitant-sounding intonation to what they are reading and/or pause or produce a regression at a point preceding something unfamiliar in the text. They sound tentative. And miscue analysis shows that less effective readers will generally produce structures that are semantically and syntactically unacceptable—structures that don't make sense. Nondeliberate omissions, on the other hand, usually produce no discernible signal to an interested listener that a miscue has been produced. In other words, the production of nondeliberate omissions rarely result in meaning loss, sound natural, and, like other nondeliberate miscues, are produced without the reader's awareness.

An analysis of Andrew's reading shows that the production of a deliberate omission was a strategy that he used indiscriminately and imprudently. He did not take optimum advantage of its "place holder" function—a function that enables efficient readers who judiciously employ this strategy to navigate unfamiliar text in a tentative, circumspect, hypothesis-driven manner while still successfully making sense.

---

[2]The syntax in the version Andrew read is relatively uncomplicated. Fry readability places this story at about a third-grade level.

[3]*Effective* reading results when a reader successfully constructs meaning for himself or herself. *Efficient* reading occurs when a reader samples the minimum number of print cues necessary to successfully make sense of text. *Proficient* reading is both effective and efficient. Proficient reading is relatively free of regressions and pauses (K. S. Goodman, 1996a).

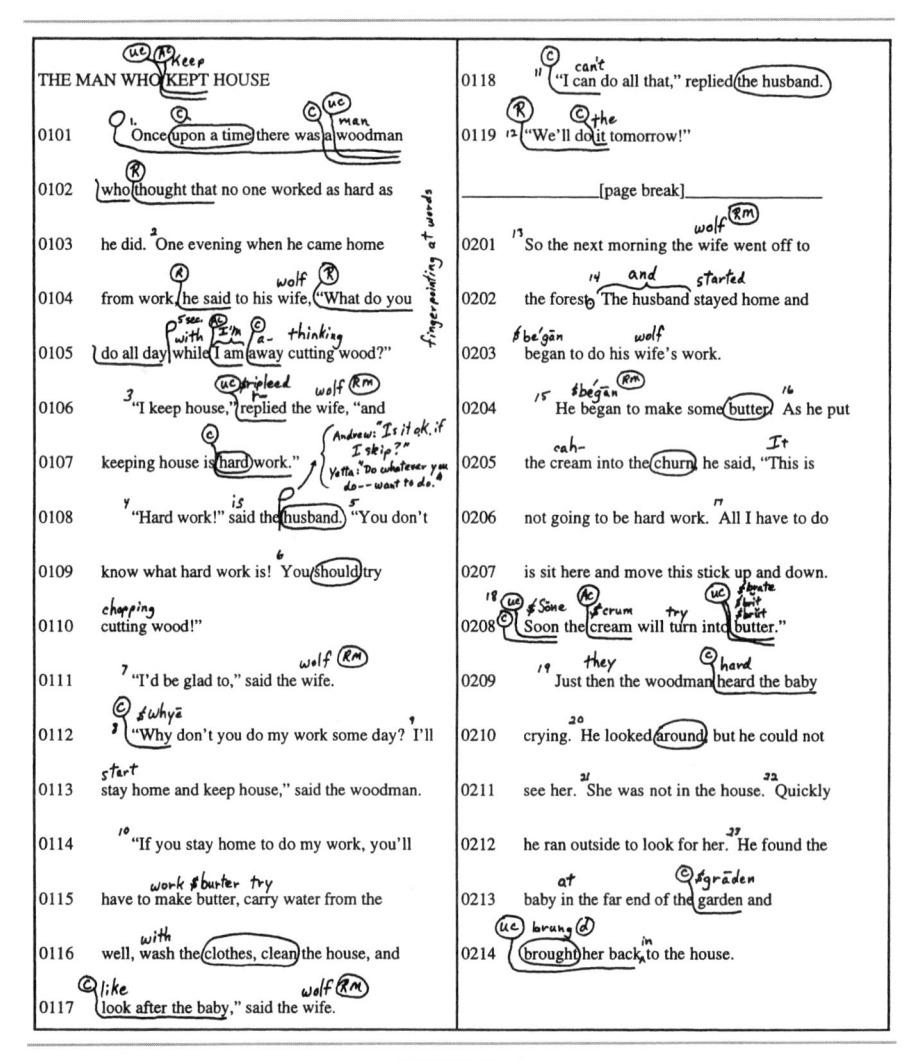

FIGURE 8.1

Marked Typescript of an excerpt of Andrew's First Reading of *"The Man Who Kept House"*

```
THE MAN WHO KEPT HOUSE                          0118  "I can do all that," replied the husband.
0101  Once upon a time there was a woodman      0119  "We'll do it tomorrow!"
0102  who thought that no one worked as hard as        _____[page break]_____
0103  he did. One evening when he came home     0201  So the next morning the wife went off to
0104  from work, he said to his wife, "What do you  0202  the forest. The husband stayed home and
0105  do all day while I am away cutting wood?"  0203  began to do his wife's work.
0106  "I keep house," replied the wife, "and    0204  He began to make some butter. As he put
0107  keeping house is hard work."              0205  the cream into the churn he said, "This is
0108  "Hard work!" said the husband. "You don't 0206  not going to be hard work. All I have to do
0109  know what hard work is! You should try    0207  is sit here and move this stick up and down.
0110  cutting wood!"                            0208  Soon the cream will turn into butter."
0111  "I'd be glad to," said the wife.          0209  Just then the woodman heard the baby
0112  "Why don't you do my work some day? I'll  0210  crying. He looked around but he could not
0113  stay home and keep house," said the woodman.  0211  see her. She was not in the house. Quickly
0114  "If you stay home to do my work, you'll   0212  he ran outside to look for her. He found the
0115  have to make butter, carry water from the 0213  baby in the far end of the garden and
0116  well, wash the clothes, clean the house, and  0214  brought her back to the house.
0117  look after the baby," said the wife.
```

In other words, Andrew was not sufficiently focused on constructing meaning to the point where he was able to determine when it was better to make a sensible guess and when it was better to skip and go on.

Note that Andrew asked permission to use this strategy: When Andrew encountered *husband* on Line 0108, he asked, *"Is it okay if I skip?"* Asking permission suggests that he was signaling a wish to suspend his internal protocol that says, "You need to get all the words right." This subtle signal is another indication that Andrew viewed reading as faithful text reproduction. In all, Andrew produced 29 uncorrected deliberate omissions and 0 nondeliberate omissions. Of the 68 sentences in the story, 40% were syntactically and semantically acceptable.

Even though Andrew's reading effectiveness was marginal, he still showed strengths—that is, signs that he could make sense of the text. For example, Sentence 5 on Line 0109 contains two miscues that are fully acceptable: *You try chopping wood*. Furthermore, most of the substitution miscues that resulted in meaning loss retained the same part of speech as their counterparts in the printed text (e.g., the substitution of *thinking* for *cutting* in Line 0105 and of *started* for *stayed* in Line 0202).

Andrew's retelling of the story (reprinted below) revealed a major strength. It showed that he was able to construct meaning for himself despite the fact that he substituted *wolf* for *wife* on each of 11 occurrences in the story. Indeed, the story he retold retained all of the major plot details and most of the minor details. The one misconception was that Andrew's version was constructed as a type of "fractured fairy tale" in which the wolf played the role of housekeeper and protector (to scare away burglars). The retelling seems all the more reasonable when one considers that children know that woodcutters and wolves go together in stories.

ANDREW'S RETELLING OF HIS FIRST READING OF "THE MAN WHO KEPT HOUSE"

Yetta: Now, Andrew, tell me everything you can remember about the story.

Andrew: The woodman thought he was the hardest worker until the wolf said, "You can take my job for one day." And so, um, [the woodman] did. He made a disaster. And when the wolf came home, everything was a mess. And the woodman would never work within the house again—housekeeper again. [long pause].

Yetta: Tell me about the characters in the story.

Andrew: There was an argument between the woodman and the wolf—[the woodman] said he was the hardest worker.

Yetta: What kind of work did he do that he was the hardest worker?

Andrew: Wood chopping.

Yetta: And what kind of work did the wolf do?

Andrew: He kept the house clean.

Yetta: Why do you think there was a wolf in the house?

Andrew: Burglars. Scare them away. I don't know.

Yetta: Oh. And then you said that the wolf said, "You can take my work for one day," and what did the wolf do?

Andrew: He went to go chop wood. And the woodman stayed home and did the wolf's job.

Yetta: And then you said "He made a disaster." I love that word. What did you mean by that?
Andrew: He did a whole bunch of things wrong.
Yetta: Like what? Do you remember any of it?
Andrew: He put a cow on the roof.
Yetta: That's pretty wrong?
Andrew: He fell of the roof.
Yetta: The cow fell off? Okay.
Andrew: And . . .
Yetta: Why did he put the cow on the roof?
Andrew: 'Cause he didn't have time to give him grass and he said "You'll find something to eat up there."
Yetta: Okay. And you said when the wolf came home everything was a mess? *What* was a mess?
Andrew: The house.
Yetta: In what way was it a mess?
Andrew: Uh, the cow fell off of it and the baby was crying.
Yetta: You said that the woodman never worked as a housekeeper again. What did you mean by that?
Andrew: Because of the big mess that he made and he didn't like it.
Yetta: Do you think that he thought he was the hardest worker still at the end of the story as he was at the beginning?
Andrew: No.
Yetta: How do you know that?
Andrew: Because the—what he did—what the wolf did, it's a lot harder than chopping wood.

The inefficiency in Andrew's reading resulted from the multiple regressions, unsuccessful attempts at correction, and frequent pauses. He read slowly and carefully. When one puts the issue of reading efficiency aside, though, Andrew's reading and retelling of "The Man Who Kept House" showed Andrew to be a much stronger reader than he believed himself to be.

On another occasion, Andrew read *Nate the Great* by Marjorie Sharmat. Our research team had been working with him for several weeks, and Andrew had begun to show greater effectiveness and efficiency in his reading. Immediately after he read the story, we asked Andrew how well he thought he had done:

Yetta: What do you think of yourself as a reader. Did you do a good job, average job, okay job, wonderful job?
Andrew: Average.
Yetta: Why? Why do you say that?
Andrew: About half—About half the words I didn't know.

Yetta:	Oohh. We're going to check that out. Next time, we'll show you what we find out about that.
Alan:	So you say 50% of the words you didn't know. Is that your prediction?
Andrew:	50 or 25%.
Yetta:	Well, that's a big difference.
Alan:	A big difference.
Yetta:	You made a prediction, and we're going to have to check it out.
Andrew:	50. 50. [adamantly]
Alan:	You say you didn't know 50% of the words. Okay. Uh, what percent of the story do you think you understood?
Andrew:	Uh, I didn't understand most of it.
Yetta:	Go ahead and tell us what it was about.
Andrew:	So they were digging for clues and they didn't find nothing and Nate the Great never likes to eat on the job so he was so hungry that he said, "To keep my strength up, I have to eat." So they went to Annie's friend who had cats. She was missing a cat and Nate the Great went into the house and he said—And this big cat jumped on Nate the Great and he said, "Get off," and Nate the Great stepped on something else—Super Hix or that other cat that was lost. And so he found a whole bunch of [unintelligible] somehow he found it. And they left and they went to go see her brother, Harry. So he went into his room and he saw the monster picture and he went back downstairs and talked and he said the monster picture is the dog. And this is the tail, this is the ear, and the other ear. And he just went home. After that, he just went home.
Yetta:	Did you talk about the color of the monster?
Andrew:	It was orange, and the other ones were red. He tried to make red out of the yellow, but it made orange. Harry, her brother.
Yetta:	How did that happen.
Andrew:	'Cause red and yellow make orange.

This excerpted transcript of the retelling shows that Andrew misjudged himself. In actual fact, Andrew not only understood the entire story (recounting characters, sequence, and major and minor plot points), but he quoted dialogue from memory. Regarding Andrew's estimation of the number of words he knew in the story, it is difficult to determine precisely what he meant when he said he didn't know "about half the words." What did "know a word" mean to Andrew? A miscue analysis of his reading showed that Andrew produced expected responses for 91% of the words in the story, not the 50% that he had estimated.

In light of this analysis, the questions we faced were, *How could Andrew have so completely misjudged himself?* and *How could we get Andrew to recognize his strengths and build upon those strengths to result in more efficient reading strategy use?*

Andrew's self-appraisal of his reading helped us to locate and define the issues that were causing him difficulty. For Andrew, "knowing words" was saying words. And saying words was "reading." "Making sense" did not seem to be part of Andrew's intellectual definition of reading. We believed, that his intellectualized definition of "reading" was hampering his proficient use of the reading process.

Andrew Needs to Revalue Reading and Revalue Himself as a Reader

When we shared with Andrew the insights that we gained from our close inspection of his reading and our appraisal of his linguistic strengths, the experience was unsettling for him. He had grown accustomed to thinking of himself as an incapable reader. His failures greeted him every time he dealt with print. Like so many readers who face difficulties, Andrew was unable to recognize his strengths. He was unable (or, perhaps, unwilling) to recognize that he was capable of effectively engaging in the act of reading. Such strengths conflicted with the picture he had painted of himself as a reader. Andrew seemed to believe that he didn't "get enough words right" to consider himself a capable reader.

The information provided by our miscue analyses of Andrew's readings allowed us to *revalue* Andrew as a reader. Revaluing refers to the practice of evaluating a reader's linguistic strengths as the reader constructs personal meaning from print (K. S. Goodman, 1996b). For parents, teachers, and researchers, "revaluing" is the result of discerning insights from the analyses of readers' miscues. The information about a reader that stems from a meaning-construction view sharply contrasts with the kind of information about a reader that proceeds from a deficit-oriented view of the reading process—a view that results from the use of standardized, skill-oriented tests and assessments.

Thus, the process of revaluing frees teachers from making deficit-oriented judgments about readers. Instead, the act of revaluing readers focuses on the following:

▶ The *effectiveness* with which readers employ reading strategies *as* they engage in the reading of a particular text (Ken Goodman, 1996a, called this an index of *comprehending*)

▶ An evaluation of how *efficiently* readers are able to employ those strategies in meeting their needs to understand a particular text

▶ The ability readers have to retell information and discuss a particular text they've read (comprehension)

Clearly, the portrait of a reader that results from this sort of appraisal is far richer—and fairer—than the portrait that is rendered from "standard scores" or "error rates."

To fairly represent Andrew, it bears mentioning that he was not marginally effective and inefficient in all that he read. There were particular texts over which Andrew demonstrated proficient control. On one occasion, Andrew was asked to bring in material that he liked to read. When he mentioned that he was uncertain which material would qualify for this activity, we brainstormed a list of readable material that he might have at home. It was then that he hit upon the idea of bringing in his collection of baseball cards.

As it turned out, Andrew (who was something of a sports fanatic, as young people can be) knew a great deal about baseball. Not only was he able to read the information on the baseball cards with ease, but he could also interpret and explain the information to those of us who were less familiar with the contents on the cards. For pitchers Andrew identified the win-loss column, earned-run average, number of games, saves, innings pitched, walks, and strikeouts. For fielders, he showed us batting average, number of games, at bats, runs, hits, home runs, and runs batted in. An excerpt from our discussion about the cards follows:

Alan: Tell us what this card is about.
Andrew: Um, this guy is a pitcher and he's on the Red Sox.
Alan: How did you know that?
Andrew: He has a "B" on his hat and he's throwing.
Alan: A "B." How did you know he didn't play for the Bluejays?
Andrew: There's socks in the picture.
Alan: Socks.
Andrew: And it says "Red Sox" on the baseball.
Alan: So you looked at the logo and read it. What's on back?
Andrew: Um, his, um, numbers about how good he is and stuff.
Alan: Like what?
Andrew: The number of games he was in and wins, hits, walks.
Alan: What are "SO.s"?
Andrew: Um, strikeouts I think. Yeah.
Yetta: How about this card, Andrew?
Andrew: That's Ken Griffey, Jr.
Alan: Tell us about him.
Andrew: He's with Seattle.
Alan: And what does the card say about him?
Andrew: It shows his batting average, home runs, RBIs, and like that.

Alan:	How do you find out how many home runs?
Andrew:	There. Under "HR" it says 22.
Yetta:	Wow, that's more than—I don't think I know what all those abbreviations stand for.
Alan:	Me either [laughs].
Yetta:	Andrew, do you know this is reading? You had to read this to understand it. Did you know that?
Andrew:	[pauses] Sort of. Yeah.

But for all of his control over the ability to understand and make use of the information on baseball cards, Andrew wasn't satisfied. Like the "baby words" on billboard signs, baseball cards didn't count as "real reading." For Andrew, real reading came from books with "long sentences with hard words," and Andrew didn't believe he was capable of real reading.

Retrospective Miscue Analysis and Revaluing

Retrospective miscue analysis (RMA) is a powerful tool for helping a reader to revalue his or her use of the reading process and for revaluing himself or herself as a reader. RMA is an invitation for a reader to join with a knowledgable person in an investigation of his or her use of the reading process. In effect, it is an invitation for a reader to "do miscue analysis" on his or her reading with a co-investigator to uncover his or her linguistic strengths in using the reading process. RMA procedures enable a teacher to present a reader with evidence of the strengths he or she brings to the act of reading (Y. Goodman & Flurkey, 1996). It is a presentation to the reader of a portrait of himself or herself as an effective and efficient reader.[4]

Andrew Comes Unstuck

Over a period of 12 weeks, we collected 10 tape-recordings of Andrew reading complete, authentic fiction and nonfiction texts. Each of the 10 reading sessions provided a rich data set for use in the 10 subsequent RMA sessions. Typically, our sessions began by engaging Andrew in a discussion of the previous week's oral reading. Our goal was to involve Andrew in a variety of discussions about the nature of written language. The topics of our sessions ranged from discussions about the quality of miscues that Andrew produced to explicit discussions about letter-sound relationships, to the strategies involved in the writing of predictable texts.

Our discussions focused on miscues that Andrew had produced and the strengths that those miscues indicated. For example, for several weeks we focused

---

[4]A detailed accounting of RMA procedures, as well as several case studies, can be found in *Retrospective Miscue Analysis: Revaluing Readers and Reading* by Y. M. Goodman and A. Marek (1996).

on Andrew's use of self-correction strategies and his production of fully acceptable noncorrected substitutions. After we sensed that Andrew had become comfortable pursuing these topics, we broached more sensitive issues, such as the production of partially acceptable or unacceptable, uncorrected miscues. Initially, we began the discussions by asking the following questions about each miscue (Y. M. Goodman & Marek, 1996):

RMA QUESTIONS

1. Does the miscue make sense?
2. Does the miscue sound like language?
3. a. Was the miscue corrected?
   b. Should it have been?

If the answers to Questions 1 and 3a were no, we asked:
4. Does the miscue look like what was on the page?
5. Does the miscue sound like what was on the page?

For all miscues, we asked:
6. Why do you think you made this miscue?
7. Did that miscue affect your understanding of the text?

But as Andrew quickly came to understand what we were asking, we were able to play a recording of his production of a miscue and ask, "What do you think happened here?" sometimes Andrew would volunteer an explanation without ever being prompted. We finished each RMA session by collecting a taped reading sample to be analyzed and used as grist for the next week's RMA session.

The following excerpt of a session transcript demonstrates the language we used to support Andrew's strategy use and to help Andrew revalue himself as a reader. In this excerpt, we were focusing the discussion on the various ways that Andrew made sense during his reading.

> Alan: Before we start reading, let's talk about your reading and some of the things that you do that are smart. Because that's the reason why we're here—we're fascinated by what readers do. So what are some of the good things that you do now when you come to something that you're not sure about.
> Andrew: The words . . . Sometimes I make up a word that makes sense or I skip it.
> Yetta: What else could you come to that you don't know in a story besides words?
> Andrew: Pictures.
> Yetta: What do you do when you come to a picture that you don't know?

Andrew: I read the words.
Yetta: So, do the words help you understand more about the picture?
Andrew: Yeah.
Yetta: Wow, that's interesting. Do both. Go in both directions.
Alan: You know, something struck me just now about what you said about putting in a word and about looking at the pictures is that you focused on making sense. And that's what readers do. They focus on making sense. So, as we go on reading, just go ahead and keep using those strategies.

As we continued our thoughtful, in-depth discussions about written language, we observed a change in Andrew's reading and in Andrew's stance toward his reading. Over the course of our sessions, Andrew displayed a shift in the quality of three reading-related dimensions: strategy use, metacognitive awareness, and confidence.

Strategy Use

Figure 8.2 shows an excerpt of the marked typescript of Andrew's second reading of "The Man Who Kept House," which he read 12 weeks after the first reading. Even a brief glance at the first page of the typescript shows that Andrew produced fewer miscues, higher quality miscues, and fewer omissions than during the first reading. A statistical analysis of Andrew's reading showed a shift in his reading proficiency. A comparison shows he was now apporoaching his reading more thoughtfully. He was applying strategies more judiciously and efficiently. (See Table 8.1.)

The analysis in Table 8.1 shows that Andrew produced a greater number of syntactically and semantically acceptable sentences in his second reading of "The Man Who Kept House" than in his first reading. This observation in itself is evidence of Andrew's improved effectiveness. But when we include a transcript of his retelling of the story with this statistical analysis, a fuller, more complete picture of Andrew's reading effectiveness emerges. Andrew's retelling was rich, confident, and complete, providing major and minor plot elements:

Alan: Would you pretend that we had never heard the story—or pretend a kid came in and wanted to know what the story is about? Could you please tell us what the story is about?
Andrew: The story was about a woodman and his wife. The woodman came home from work one day and he asked the wife, "What do you do all day?" And she said, "I keep the house clean." And they made a bargain that he'd stay home and she would cut the wood. And he was wrong—it was a hard job. Harder than cutting wood. And he never asked her again.

Andrew, Stuck in Words **143**

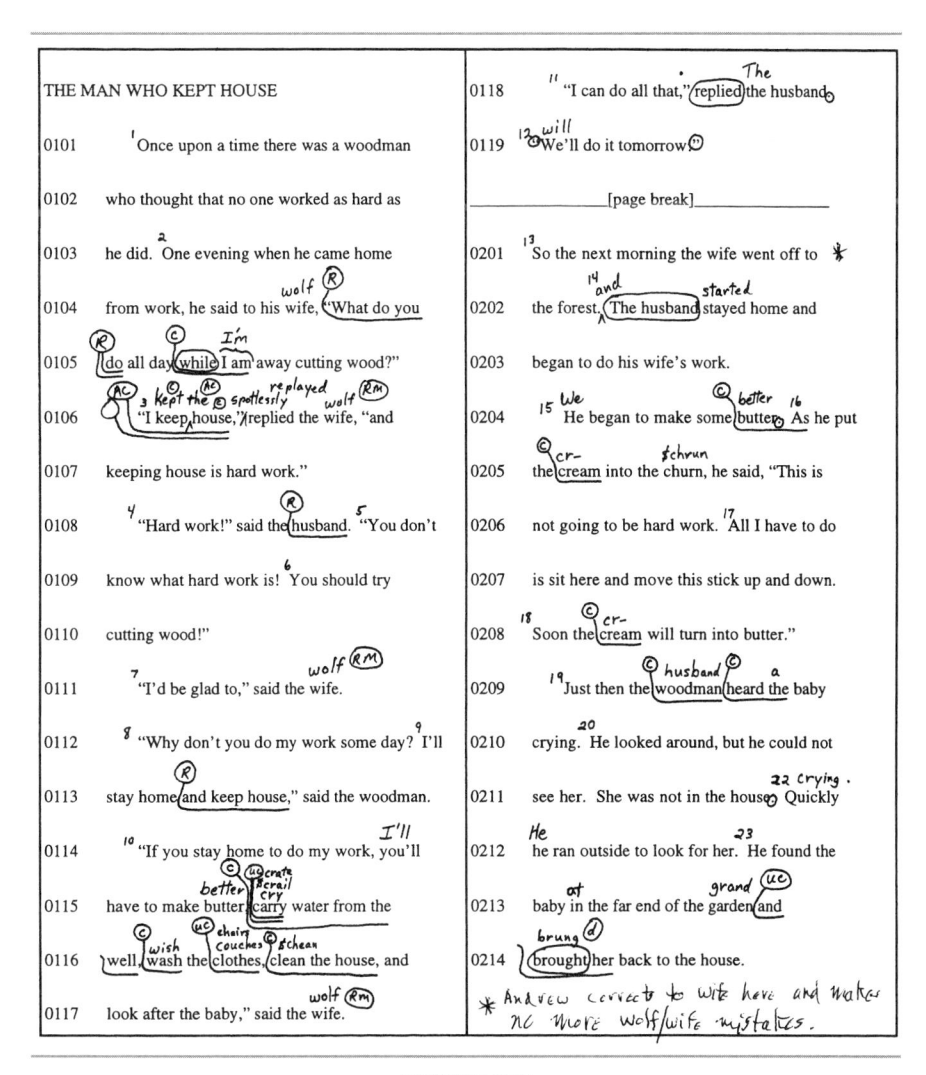

	THE MAN WHO KEPT HOUSE	0118	¹¹ "I can do all that," ~~replied~~ **The** the husband~~.~~
0101	¹Once upon a time there was a woodman	0119	¹² ~~We'll~~ **will** do it tomorrow~~.~~
0102	who thought that no one worked as hard as		_____[page break]_____
0103	he did. ²One evening when he came home	0201	¹³So the next morning the wife went off to
0104	from work, he said to his wife, "What do you **wolf** ®	0202	¹⁴ **and** ~~started~~ the forest. The husband stayed home and
0105	do all day ~~while~~ I am away cutting wood?" **I'm**	0203	began to do his wife's work.
0106	³kept the ~~spotlessly~~ **replayed** ~~wolf~~ "I keep house," replied the wife, "and	0204	¹⁵ **We** He began to make some butter. ¹⁶ As he put **better**
0107	keeping house is hard work."	0205	the cream into the churn, he said, "This is **cr- tchrun**
0108	⁴"Hard work!" said the husband. ⁵"You don't	0206	not going to be hard work. ¹⁷All I have to do
0109	know what hard work is! ⁶You should try	0207	is sit here and move this stick up and down.
0110	cutting wood!"	0208	¹⁸Soon the cream will turn into butter." **cr-**
0111	⁷"I'd be glad to," said the wife. **wolf**	0209	¹⁹Just then the woodman heard the baby **husband a**
0112	⁸"Why don't you do my work some day? ⁹I'll	0210	²⁰crying. He looked around, but he could not
0113	stay home and keep house," said the woodman.	0211	see her. She was not in the house. ²²Quickly **crying**
0114	¹⁰"If you stay home to do my work, you'll **I'll**	0212	**He** he ran outside to look for her. ²³He found the
0115	have to make butter, carry water from the **crate ~~cry~~ better ~~crail~~**	0213	baby in the far end of the garden and **at grand**
0116	well, wash the clothes, clean the house, and **wish chair couches tchean**	0214	**brung** brought her back to the house.
0117	look after the baby," said the wife. **wolf**		★ Andrew corrects to wife here and makes no more wolf/wife mistakes.

FIGURE 8.2

Marked Typescript of an excerpt of Andrew's Second Reading
of <u>*"The Man Who Kept House"*</u>

Yetta: Oh, boy, do I like the way you summed that up. And when you said he made a bargain. 'Cause you know the word "bargain" isn't in here, is it?

Andrew: [Shakes head no].

Yetta: So you had to think that through yourself. That's terrific. Can you tell us what the bargain was that they decided to do?

TABLE 8.1
Miscue Analysis Reading Profile

	Initial Reading	Final Reading
Percent of Sentences That Were Syntactically Acceptable	49%	80%
Percent of Sentences That Were Semantically Acceptable	41%	70%
Percent of Sentences That Involved Meaning Change	14%	4% (Another 4% involved partial meaning change)
Total Uncorrected Omissions		
Nondeliberate	0	2
Deliberate	29	2
	(97% meaning loss)	(0% meaning loss)

Source: From *Reading Miscue Inventory: Alternative Procedures* by Y. M. Goodman, D. J. Watson, and C. L. Burke (New York: Richard C. Owen, 1987, p. 107.

Andrew: Uh, he stays home and she cuts the wood.

Yetta: So what did he do when he stayed home? How did he find out that he was wrong? You said that he was wrong.

Andrew: Uh, it was very hard because the baby was crying, and he didn't know where the baby was. And he kept the door open and he went out to find the baby and a cow went in—I mean a pig went into the house and made a mess of it. Then he found the baby.

Yetta: How did the pig make a mess of it?

Andrew: He was running around, and when the woodman went back he told the cow to leave and he was yelling at it. And then he heard the cow, and the baby was still crying and he thought they were both hungry. And he was making the baby porridge and he doesn't have time to give the cow grass, so he puts him on the roof and he says, "You'll find something up here."

Yetta: And then what happens. Does the cow find something up there?

Andrew: No. And, so the cow wouldn't fall off, he tied a rope around its neck and threw the other side down the chimney and tied it onto his leg. And the cow fell off

	the roof and he was hanging up in the chimney. And the wife came and he cut the cow's—the rope that was hanging off the cow's neck. And he fell . . .
Yetta:	Who did the cutting?
Andrew:	His wife. And he fell down through the chimney. And the wife saw, and he was full of porridge.
Yetta:	Poor guy. Nothing like having hot, yucky porridge—do you know what porridge is?
Andrew:	Some kind of soup. Oatmeal or . . .
Yetta:	It could be either one depending on—In Canada, they use the word porridge to mean oatmeal. But porridge can also mean, in different countries, I think it can mean "heavy soup". What would you feel like if you took your head out of a pot and had hot oatmeal all over your head?
Andrew:	I'd run to a sink.
Yetta:	You'd run to the sink (laughs). Did you like the story or not?
Andrew:	Yeah.

Not only was Andrew's reading more effective that the first time, but analysis showed a corresponding shift toward more *efficient* strategy use as well. It is particularly revealing that Andrew shifted away from his indiscriminate use of the "skip and go on" strategy (deliberate uncorrected omissions), choosing instead to use that strategy sparingly and judiciously—and without producing sentences that resulted in meaning loss.

Compare lines 0118 and 0119 in each excerpt.

First reading:

0118   "I can do all that," replied the husband.
0119   "We'll do it tomorrow!"

(Produced as: *"I can't—I can do all that," replied...*(skips *the husband*) *"We'll do the—it— We'll do it tomorrow!"*

Second reading:

0118   "I can do all that," replied the husband.
0119   "We'll do it tomorrow!"

(Produced as: *"I can do all that." The husband will do it tomorrow.*

A comparison of Andrew's production of 29 deliberate omissions in the first reading with 2 deliberate omissions (with no resulting meaning loss) in the second reading gives us a sense the magnitude of Andrew's shift in strategy use.

Metacognitive Awareness

Our RMA work with adult, middle school, and elementary school readers has shown us that proficient and struggling readers alike are aware of and able to discuss the thinking processes that they use while they are reading for meaning (Y. Goodman & Flurkey, 1996; Marek, 1996). In fact, the results of our work contradict a widely held view that one of the causes of poor reading is the inability of poor readers to use metacognitive processes to regulate their reading (Y. Goodman & Flurkey, 1996, p. 102).

When we began working with Andrew, his focus in reading was almost exclusively on faithfully reproducing the printed text. The transcript of his retelling of his second reading of the "The Man Who Kept House" shows a different emphasis. Andrew's comments in our discussion of his retelling of the story show that he valued reading differently—that he now valued it as a process where focusing on meaning is the central concern.

Alan:	Can you remember some of the words that you knew this time that you didn't know the first time?
Andrew:	Wife. And I think porridge. And chimney. That's it.
Alan:	Think about what enabled you to get those words this time—wife, chimney, porridge. What was different?
Andrew:	The first time, when I said wolf it didn't make sense. Then I saw the picture of the lady with the ax and I said "wife" and it made sense.
Yetta:	The picture helped you. But you still had to know that you wanted to look at the picture so that you would know it would make sense to you. What else about sense? Do words help you make sense or does making sense of the story help you know the words?
Andrew:	Making sense of the story.
Yetta:	That has to come first sometimes, huh?
Andrew:	Yeah.

Andrew also demonstrated an awareness of his shift in strategy use. He was able to articulate that he had supplanted his less effective use of a "skip and go on" strategy with a procedure involving additional sampling of information with a focus on making sense.

Alan:	You know, when we first started working together, you would deliberately skip things—you know, we talked about that as a strategy. But you know what I noticed about this time? You did that in very, very few cases. I wonder what was going on. You had a different strategy that you used. Do you know what you did instead of skipping? Can you remember?

Andrew: Oh, if it didn't make sense, I'd go back to the word.
Yetta: That's a strategy. If it's making sense, you keep going—and you don't skip too many words. And then if it doesn't make sense you back up and say, "Hey wait a minute—let me back up and see if I can manage it."
Alan: Can you tell me what kind of clicked in your mind and why you're feeling better about going back and having a second look? Whereas before—
Andrew: —'Cause it didn't make sense. . . . That's why I went back.
Yetta: So you're worried about sense more.
Alan: Did you think [the first time you read the story] it was just a wacky story or something? Or did you think the problem was that you didn't understand it . . .
Andrew: I thought it was a wacky story.
Yetta: So sometimes you can ask people, "Is it supposed to be this? This is strange." It's okay to say, "I want more information about this story."

Reader Confidence

The third dimension in which a shift was noted was reader confidence. It has been our experience that one of the first signs that announces a reader's revaluing of himself or herself is a change in the reader's mien. This change in bearing manifests itself in the decisiveness with which the reader employs reading strategies. And decisiveness is an aspect of *efficient* reading—making swift and sure choices that result in better first guesses while sampling the fewest print cues necessary to continue to make sense (K. S. Goodman, 1982b).

Andrew's newfound confidence in himself as a reader came through in the transcript, as illustrated by the following dialogue. We take this as evidence of his revaluing reading and revaluing himself as a reader:

Alan: How do you think you did?
Andrew: Better than the first time.
Alan: Why?
Andrew: Cause I read through fast. . . . And there were some words in the first time I read it—there were a whole bunch of words I didn't know and the book didn't make sense. [But now] the book made sense.

Summary

For Andrew, reading had indeed begun to make sense. By the time the school closed for summer vacation, Andrew had undergone a fundamental shift in his approach to reading. He was using reading strategies more judiciously, and he was aware that he was thinking about making sense as he read. He was beginning to understand that reading has to make sense if it is to be a worthwhile activity and that "getting the words right"—reproducing the printed text—was not what reading was about.

Although a casual listener who is unfamiliar with miscue analysis might not easily have been able to detect Andrew's shift in reading proficiency, it is likely that the listener *would* have been able to discern a difference in Andrew's appraisal of himself as a reader. And for close observers of the reading process, Andrew's outward confidence would have foretold changes deep below the surface, like the sighting of the tip of an iceberg.

At our final meeting, Andrew told us that he was beginning to see himself as a "pretty good reader." And sometimes that simple shift—from "kind of good because sometimes I say the words" to "pretty good because the book made sense" is enough to make a difference. For Andrew, it was enough for him to come unstuck.

References

Goodman, K. S. (1982). Miscues: Windows on the reading process. In F. V. Gollasch (Ed.), *Language and literacy: The selected writings of Kenneth S. Goodman* (Vol. 1, pp. 93–102). Boston: Routledge.

Goodman, K. S. (1996a). *On reading.* Toronto: Scholastic.

Goodman, K. S. (1996b). Principles of revaluing. In Y. M. Goodman & A. M. Marek (Eds.), *Retrospective miscue analysis: Revaluing readers and reading* (pp. 13–20). Katonah, NY: Richard C. Owen.

Goodman, Y. M., & Marek, A. M. (Eds.). (1996). *Retrospective miscue analysis: Revaluing readers and reading.* Katonah, NY: Richard C. Owen.

Goodman, Y., & Flurkey, A. (1996). Retrospective miscue analysis in middle school. In Y. Goodman & A. Marek (Eds.), *Retrospective miscue analysis: Revaluing readers and reading* (pp. 87–106). Katonah, NY: Richard C. Owen.

Goodman, Y. M., Watson, D. J., & Burke, C. L. (1987). *Reading miscue inventory: Alternative procedures.* New York: Richard C. Owen.

Marek, A. M. (1996). Surviving reading instruction. In Y. Goodman & A. Marek (Eds.), *Retrospective miscue analysis: Revaluing readers and reading* (pp. 71–86). Katonah, NY: Richard C. Owen.

The man who kept house. (1962). In J. McInnes (Ed.), *Magic and make-believe* (pp. 282-287). Toronto: Thomas Nelson & Sons.

Substitutions
Substitutions are shown by writing the miscue directly above the word or phrase.

comfortable
He was sitting comfortably in the carriage.

Omissions
Omissions are marked by circling the omitted language structures.

"I can do (all) that," replied the husband.

Insertions
Insertions are shown by marking a proofreader's caret at the point of insertion and writing the inserted word or phrase where it occurs in the text.

some
"Now I've got ∧ more work to do," said the man.

Regressing and Abandoning a Correct Form
Abandonments are marked by drawing a line from right to left at the point at which the reader went back to repeat but abandoned the expected text. An inscribed (AC) is used to indicate this type of regression. In this example, the reader first reads *head against the wall*, then rejects this possibility and produces the more sensible *hand against the wall*.

(AC) *hand*
"How many times did I hit my head against the wall?" she asked.

Regressions or Repetitions
Linguistic structures that are reread are underlined to explicitly show how much the reader chose to reread. Regressions are marked by drawing a line from right to left to the point at which the reader went back to repeat. A circle inscribed with an (R) designates simple repetitions. Multiple repetitions, words or phrases that are repeated more than once, are underlined each time they occur.

(R) Why don't you do my work some day?

(R) All at once I was covered with red paint.

Regressing and Correcting the Miscue (Self-corrections)
Self-corrections are marked by drawing a line from right to left to the point at which the reader went back to repeat in order to correct the miscue. A circle inscribed with a (C) indicates a correction. (The (UC) is described in a following panel.)

The markings in this example show that the reader predicted *horses* (which he repeated twice), followed by a correction to *houses*, followed by the substitution *of* for *and*, followed by the correction to *houses and roads*. His multiple attempts are written and numbered in the order of occurrence above the sentence.

(C) 4. *houses and*
(C) 3. *houses of*
(UC) 2. *horses*
1. *horses*
These he made into blocks for building houses and roads.

Substitutions Often Called Reversals
An editor's transposition symbol shows which words have been reversed.

I sat looking down at Andrew.

Was something wrong with Papa?

APPENDIX
Markings for Miscue Analysis

Regressing and Unsuccessfully Attempting to Correct
Unsuccessful attempts to correct are marked by drawing a line from right to left to the point at which the reader began to repeat in an attempt to correct. An inscribed (UC) is used to designate this type of regression.

In this example, the reader repeats *river washed* twice, and this is marked as (UC), an unsuccessful attempt at correction.

And this he did with such might that soon the
(UC)   *washed*
river rushed over its banks, . . .

Nonword Substitutions
A dollar sign ($) indicates that a reader has produced a miscue that is not recognizable as a word in the reader's language. Retain as much of the original spelling of the text word as possible.

$*shrickled*
Judy shrieked and jumped up in her chair.

Partial Miscues
Partial miscues are marked by putting a dash after a partial word when a reader attempts but does not produce a complete word. Intonation is used to determine partials.

Often readers start to say a word and self-correct or attempt a correction before a word is completed. Here, the reader predicts *ability*. He only starts the word and immediately self-corrects to *able*. Partial attempts that are corrected are marked on the typescript with a dash following the partial.

There is nothing greater than man and the work
in his   ⊙*abil-*
he is best able to do.

Repeated Miscues
Repeated miscues are marked with an encircled (RM) to indicate the same miscue for the same text item.

can   *can* (RM)
Off came our boots. Off came our socks.

Intonation Shift
An accent mark indicates intonation shifts within a word. Intonation shifts are marked only if there is a change in meaning or grammatical structure of the original text.

He will récord her voice.

We want the próject to succeed.

Pauses
A ⌒ marks noticeable pauses in reading. It is useful to mark the length of unusually long pauses.

⌒ 12 sec.
⌒*when*   *always*
"What do you do all day| while I am away cutting wood?"

Dialect and Other Language Variations
Miscues that involve a sound, vocabulary item, or grammatical variation that is perceived as a dialect difference between the author and reader are marked by a balloon with an inscribed *d* .

headlights ⓓ
I switched off the headlamps of the car . . .
like ⓓ
. . . just about everybody likes babies.

From Goodman, Y. (1995). Miscue analysis for teachers: Some history and some procedures. *Primary Voices K–6, 3*(4), 2–9.

APPENDIX
Markings for Miscue Analysis (Continued)

9

Taking an Aesthetic Stance Toward Teaching and Assessment

Beth Berghoff

Almost every first grade has at least one Peter, one youngster with thick glasses halfway down his nose who comes to school wearing shoes without socks. He is a likeable guy, but he's always a little lost. His pencil is broken and chewed so that it barely writes, and he can't find his book even though it is in the pile of papers and books he is rummaging through. Peter is the child who delivers the important note from his mother at the end of the day instead of in the morning and who misses his bus because he detoured through the gym. The most troubling thing about Peter is that he is not making much progress toward learning to read and write. He has all the characteristics that mark him as being one of those children who will struggle throughout his school career.

The story that follows is Peter's story, but it is also a story about new visions of assessment embedded in collaborative teaching and multiple ways of knowing curriculum. This new view of assessment is predicated on an aesthetic view of literacy, a view that embraces the notion that literacy develops as individuals make sense of their lived experience using the full range of human meaning-making systems. From this perspective, print literacy is not a separate strand of knowing but rather a communicative skill that develops simultaneously with other knowledge and skills. Reading is thought of as a larger process than just making meaning of print. It is a process that also goes on when an individual interprets a piece of art, watches a drama, or views a film (Berghoff, 1998).

But I am getting ahead of the story. Let me back up and start again by saying that Peter's story comes from the most powerful experience I have had as an elementary teacher. Like many special educators, I was invited to collaborate with a general education classroom teacher, Susan Hamilton. Susan and I had met in a college class that challenged us to read and synthesize current research and to rethink some of our basic assumptions about literacy and curriculum. A few months after that experience, we decided to spend a year working together in Susan's urban first-grade classroom to develop curriculum that reflected the new ideas developing in the language education field and to experiment with new ways of thinking about assessment. It is that year that I am writing about.

Working collaboratively really stretched Susan and me as teachers. Being half of a team forced both of us to articulate what was on our minds and to be open to questions that challenged our tentative notions of what we were trying to accomplish. We learned to talk about our personal theories and to explain the assumptions underlying our actions. We learned that we did not always see the same things happening, that we sometimes had different lenses for viewing classroom life. We found that we could learn more about what was happening with the children if we assumed responsibility for different roles. When one of us focused on teaching small groups, the other floated around the classroom and conversed with children at work, gathering information about what they could do in a group with peers, what they chose to do on their own, and how they used literacy to interact with their peers and to learn. We benefited from having the input of our two unique perspectives when we sat down to plan curriculum or assess how the learners were doing. As with other learning processes, creating curriculum and conducting assessment became experiences with more depth and dimension when they were done collaboratively.

Susan and I agreed that the basic goals of the school curriculum should remain intact in our classroom. We wanted each child in this urban class to learn to read and write, to think mathematically, and to be successful on the measures of learning used by the school district. We wanted to introduce the concepts and knowledge identified in the science and social studies guides for first grade. In addition, however, we wanted the learners to be able to use a wide variety of sign systems to learn from experiences that evolved from their questions and interests. For this to happen, we had to significantly change the ways we set out to accomplish our goals, the "how" of the curriculum, as well as the ways we assessed the children's learning and development of literacy. We decided to build our curriculum around the following three assumptions:

▶ Literacy develops via multiple sign systems.
▶ Literacy supports the process of inquiry.
▶ Literacy is shaped by the learner's theories about learning and literacy.

We also decided to attempt to conduct assessment from an "aesthetic" stance.

"Aesthetic," as we were using the term, represents a concept borrowed from reading theorist Louise Rosenblatt (1978), who described reading as a continuum of possibilities that depends on one's purpose and stance toward reading. She described an aesthetic stance as one in which the reader transacts with a text to have a "lived-through" experience. The reader expects to create an imaginary world where he or she can anticipate and vicariously experience sensual pleasures or the tragedies of life. A reader taking an aesthetic stance reads a text to gather information that adds to the richness of the experience and yields more complexity to his or her understanding of events and characters. In contrast, Rosenblatt described an efferent reading stance. An efferent reader reads for the information needed to accomplish a task. The efferent reader is more interested in the efficient retrieval of information than in having a human experience.

Similarly, when we, as educators, conduct assessment in schools, we also have a range of purposes. Some assessment is meant to provide efficient accountability information. For example, a benchmark assessment may provide information about what a child can or cannot do. Another type of assessment requires that we enter the world of the child and imagine what it is like to be the child. When this kind of assessment is done, the evaluator is taking an aesthetic stance toward assessment. The purpose is to understand how the students lives and thinks; how the student likes to spend his or her time; how experiences contribute to his or her development and understanding; and what the child is likely to learn next. When an aesthetic stance is taken, the purpose is to know the lived experience of the child, not to check skills off a list as they are mastered. The evaluator creates his or her own story of the child and continually gathers more information to check predictions and deepen understanding.

Susan and I were beginners in this regard. We laid the path as we walked down it together. This worked well for us because we had each other and because we were clear about the assumptions we wanted to serve as the framework for our curriculum and assessment. These assumptions are explained in greater detail in the next section of this chapter, and examples are provided to show how we translated these assumptions into classroom practice in our first grade.

Our class was made up of a diverse group of children. Some came from the low-income neighborhood around the school; others rode the bus from an outlying working-class neighborhood. There were 10 girls and 8 boys—6 African-American, 1 Asian, and 11 Caucasian. All of these children made good progress toward the goals of the curriculum except Peter. He struggled with print literacy. Unlike the other children who were eager to unravel the complexities of written language, Peter was reluctant to read and write. His development was painfully slow and confusing. Fortunately, we had new kinds of learning experiences happening in the classroom, and these changed what we were able to see. We were able to step back and observe Peter in an aesthetic way, seeing how he used systems other than language, and we were able to piece together his lived experience in the classroom. The second half of this chapter tells Peter's story and shows what we learned about Peter in our first attempts to take an aesthetic stance toward assessment.

Assumptions Behind an Aesthetic Stance Toward Literacy

Literacy Develops Via Multiple Sign Systems

Many educators are not familiar with the term *sign system* because education has been almost solely focused on the single sign system of language. In part, the focus on a single sign system is historical. When the Committee of Fifteen designed elementary curriculum for public schools in 1895 (Shannon, 1990), written language was the major form of mass communication. Much has changed in the past 100 years. Today, our information comes in a rich variety of signs—think of the visual images on the Internet, the musical scores of films, the hip-hop dance of rappers on MTV, the rich variety of clothing at the shopping mall. We are no longer limited to paper and ink, yet our schools are slow to acknowledge that literacy involves more than language. We include art, music, and physical education in the curriculum, but they are often not equal partners to language and math.

The term *sign system* originates from the discipline of semiotics, the science of human meaning making. Sign systems like art, music, drama, mathematics, and language are communication systems. We use them to construct and express meaning. They comprise different elements and rules for combining these elements to make meaning. For example, painting uses the elements of color, line, and shape presented simultaneously to the viewer, and songs use tempo, pitch, and rhythms unfolding across time. We have multiple sign systems in our cultures because each sign system is effective in communicating certain kinds of messages. Music can express feelings that are not easily put into words; language is a better medium for humor than math; yet math can represent concepts that are not easily represented in art.

A growing body of research supports the inclusion of multiple sign systems in school curriculum. Harvard's Project Zero (Csikszentmihalyi, 1996) has demonstrated that students learn at higher cognitive levels when art and music are incorporated into learning experiences than when they are not. John-Steiner (1985) also asserted that intellectual work is richer when an individual can work with a combination of "languages of the mind." When she interviewed or corresponded with more than 100 highly creative and successful adults in such fields as mathematics, science, music, choreography, writing, and art, she discovered that these individuals do not rely solely on language to do their thinking. Rather, they work in multiple sign systems simultaneously, like British writer Margaret Drabble, who explained that, for her, writing a novel was not a matter of putting words on paper but was rather a process of listening to her dramatic inner voice and capturing the visual images of her imagination.

In the language education field, the realization that children use sign systems in flexible ways was first documented by Harste, Woodward, and Burke's study summarized in *Language Stories and Literacy Lessons* (1984). These researchers studied preschoolers' literacy development by asking them to write for different purposes. They observed that the children moved freely between art and writing, seeing both as valid ways of communicating their meaning. Later, Hubbard (1989) analyzed the ways in which first graders combined the use of art and writing in their work. She pointed out how thoughtfully the children allocated information between the two systems. For example, a child writing a story about a bird might provide the problem and solution in writing but then describe the features of the bird and the bird's motion in drawing.

Anyone who teaches in an early childhood setting knows that children are happiest when they can use a full repertoire of communicative systems, including dramatic play, drawing, dancing, singing, and writing. Children do what Newkirk (1989) described as "symbol weaving"; they sing while they paint and dance as they reenact a story. They use sign systems in flexible and intertwining ways to explore the world and make meaning.

In the school where Susan and I worked, first grade was the place where symbol weaving stopped being appropriate. In the first-grade classrooms, children were trained to work quietly on paper and pencil activities. The classroom lessons focused largely on language and numeracy, while art, music, and movement were studied in special classes for 30 minutes once or twice a week. As in school systems all over the country, this school system put a premium on language arts and mathematics test scores, and the teachers believed this narrowing of the curriculum was necessary if the children were going to become proficient users of language and numbers.

While we knew it was somewhat counterintuitive, Susan and I had been convinced by our reading and discussions that it would actually be better for first graders to be immersed in multiple sign systems than to be limited to language and math. We wanted to foster children's use of a rich blend of sign systems to learn. To do that, we believed we had to support the children in becoming more sophisticated users of multiple sign systems and make multiple sign systems available as tools for learning. So we demonstrated how sign systems were used in the culture to communicate particular kinds of meanings, and we provided engagements that invited the children to explore their own questions and interests using a variety of sign systems.

For example, when we were studying Colonial America, an art teacher suggested that we introduce the children to the portrait painting typical of the era. She helped us find a packet of art print portraits that the children could examine and showed us how she often taught children to sketch faces. To give the kids a sense of the historical setting that made portrait painting an important art form, I dressed up like an itinerant painter of the mid-1700s and stopped in to see if the class would be interested in having any portraits drawn. Susan reminded the class that I was coming from a time before cameras had been invented for taking family pictures. I showed the children my portfolio of portraits from the era, and their observations about the portraits led to a discussion about the lives of children in colonial times. Once their questions had been answered, I asked for a volunteer to sit for a portrait. I set up my easel, and as I drew and colored the portrait of the child I taught the art lesson (shared by the art teacher) about sketching faces.

Demonstrations like this provided the students with information about different sign systems by providing examples of past or present use of the sign systems and information about the elements used to create meaning by each sign system. We reasoned that these demonstrations were important because they broadened the students' sense of what different sign systems did most effectively and what elements were essential to communication.

As noted earlier, we also provided engagements that invited the children to explore sign systems as a means for communicating and expressing themselves. We provided the time and materials for students to think via multiple sign systems by setting up a number of activity centers with various media and artifacts—or "invitations," as we called them—from which the children could choose each day. One invitation was called the Portrait Center. After introducing the art prints and portrait drawing to the students, for example, we set up a gallery where students could study the portraits, and we set up an easel with pastel crayons so they could draw one another. In addition to this drawing invitation, we also extended invitations on a daily basis for the students to use drama, writing, math, music, science, movement, and art to reflect on and express ideas. During their 40 to 60 minutes of daily "invitation time," the children were free to choose "invitations," or activity centers, where they wanted to work. The demonstrations we conducted in class gave them ideas about what was possible at each invitation, but they were free to go where the media and materials led them as well. The invitations were kept intact as long as students were actively using them. When the interest in an invitation diminished, we invented a new demonstration and invitation to take its place.

Literacy Supports the Process of Inquiry

> Inquiry isn't just asking and answering a question. It involves searching for significant questions and figuring out how to explore those questions from many perspectives.
> —Short, Schroeder, Laird, Ferguson, & Crawford, 1996, p. 9

The whole language movement has taught educators that children do much more than just learn to use language. They learn to use language to accomplish their own purposes as learners and to participate in the social life that surrounds them. As teachers, we have a choice. We can support and guide the children's personal use of language for inquiry and social participation or we can teach some systematic language program that disconnects language learning from the children's personal questions and purposes.

Many teachers now teach in "inquiry-based" ways (Mills & Clyde, 1990; Short et al., 1996). They appreciate that inquiry is a process of coming to know rather than a skill or step-by-step procedure. They understand that inquiry involves interests, active explorations, tensions, posing questions, hypothesizing, investigating, and constructing new understandings and new questions. They realize that the inquiry process is dependent on many smaller processes, such as reading, authoring, transmediating (taking meaning from one sign system to another), conversation, and reflection. They know that children's literacy develops as children engage in these communicative processes for the purposes of answering their own questions and those of their peers (Berghoff, 1994).

In the view of many educators today, inquiry is a better vehicle for organizing curriculum than the discipline blocks of language arts, mathematics, science, and social studies, because it encourages the kind of symbol weaving that happens when children are using a full range of sign systems. Good questions cut across disciplinary boundaries and encourage students to construct knowledge that incorporates multiple perspectives.

To set up a classroom where literacy supported inquiry, Susan and I planned units around big conceptual questions that we knew were puzzling to the children, such as: *What are predictable books? What was it like to live in Colonial America? What is winter? What is Africa? What is real?/What is make-believe?* Each of these units lasted several weeks and involved the children in shared experiences and invitations that provided them with a great deal of information to explore and synthesize. They read, wrote, made artifacts, conversed, and reflected using all of the sign systems, not just language. Then we encouraged the children to formulate personal inquiry questions, to conduct personal explorations, and to share their new understandings with the class.

Across the span of the year, we saw the students internalize the inquiry process and make it their own. They began to identify books and engagements that would add to their knowledge. They watched one another and borrowed ways of organizing and representing their knowledge. They eagerly discussed their ideas and asked new questions. They grew very patient with one another, really listening to others and asking good questions.

Literacy Is Shaped by the Learner's Theories

One difficulty we faced as we changed our teaching to demonstrate our new beliefs about learning and literacy was that the children did not automatically share our assumptions. They came to the curriculum with assumptions of their own about how school and literacy learning were supposed to happen. Their theories were often not easy to discern because the children were not very articulate about their theories; often we had to infer their beliefs from what we saw the children do and heard them say.

We intentionally gathered data from the classroom that would allow us to sort out these different theories. For example, we watched the children, keeping in mind a study done by Dahl and Freppon (1991) in several low-socioeconomic, whole language and skills-based kindergarten classrooms. In that study, Dahl and Freppon observed kindergartners' responses to literacy engagements and identified three learning stances: Stance A, Stance B, and Stance C. Children exhibiting Stance A displayed a dependency on the teacher's instruction and a cautious or negative attitude toward literacy activities. Children exhibiting Stance B showed attentive engagement with written language but a reluctance to try new or unfamiliar tasks without support. And Stance C children enjoyed intense engagement with literate activity and had a personal agenda for learning about reading and writing.

It is not surprising that at the end of the kindergarten year the Stance C children were beginning readers and writers while the Stance A children were just understanding the intentionality of written language. The Stance A children were writing strings of letters and assigning meaning to their writing but were not yet using the alphabetic principles of writing independently. When the Stance A children of the whole language classrooms were compared to Stance A children in a skills-based classroom, the researchers found that the children's development reflected the assumptions of the instruction. The whole language students were aware that print carries meaning and can be used to get things done, whereas their counterparts in skills-based classrooms were focused on letters and standards of correctness or accuracy. They were more interested in the details of written language than the function.

While the difference between these two endpoints of kindergarten curricula is subtle, we believed that the whole language endpoint was much more educative than the skills-based endpoint. Newer views of literacy helped us to understand that literacy is functional. It is our primary tool for knowing and acting on the world, yet schools have treated literacy as a skill to be learned separate from function, as a set of skills to be mastered in the context of school and then applied in the world outside. The problem with this old view of literacy, which is still prevalent in the culture at large, is that children mislearn what literacy is. The kindergartners in the skills-based classroom, in keeping with a traditional view of literacy, learned that letters and accuracy are the most important aspects of literacy. Without meaning to, perhaps, the teachers instilled in these students the idea that literacy is about manipulating abstract symbols according to a set of rules. Although this insight is important, it presents literacy as separate and disconnected from life rather than essential to living and knowing the world.

Rosenblatt's contention that our purposes for reading shape the experience (Rosenblatt, 1978) has not been translated equitably into curriculum. Students like the Stance C kindergartners are apt to discover, either in school or on their own, that reading can be aesthetic. In a study of "good" readers, Langer (1989) found that her subjects created a "personal text-world" that incorporated their assumptions and things imagined on the basis of the text. She noted that this world stayed with the readers even after the reading was completed and could be discussed and critiqued. In a similar study of "poor" readers, Purcell-Gates (1991) found that poor readers did not create a text world. Rather, they read literary text from an efferent stance, using their energy to gather information and reacting to the text as if it were bits of isolated information. Each idea they read was like a stepping stone along the way rather than a connected idea that further illuminated the whole.

In other words, if we are not careful, we teach students with differences different things about literacy without meaning to do so. School curriculum that is focused on teaching students to accurately encode and decode written language and to answer the teachers' questions about texts does not provide poorer students with access to the full range of literacy's potential. They may learn to produce and process written language, but they also develop personal theories of how reading and writing work that diminish their ability to use literacy to make sense of the world.

To ensure that the students in our first-grade classroom were developing functional views of literacy, we talked often with them about their beliefs and values in relation to reading and writing and using other sign systems. We also did things to demonstrate our own beliefs. For example, we demonstrated writing for many purposes and reflected on our own aesthetic experiences with shared books. We built reflective writing into the classroom routine at both the beginning and the end of the day, starting with morning journals and ending with learning logs, so that the children saw writing as a means of knowing more about themselves and one another and as a way of consolidating learning. We also integrated writing into the life of the classroom. We asked the students to write throughout the day, recording their problem-solving processes, doing research, and writing stories. We offered an invitation we called Photo Reflection (Burke, 1990). To create this invitation, we kept a camera in the classroom and snapped photos of the children engaged in different learning activities. Then we simply placed a stack of these photos on a table and invited the children to choose pictures of themselves, to tape a picture to a piece of paper, and to write about what they were doing in the photo and why they were doing it. The children's responses provided a wonderful window onto their notions of learning and the role of literacy.

Peter's Story

Our assumptions about literacy allowed us to design our curriculum so that multiple sign systems were introduced and available for use, so that the children's inquiry questions were central to the work of the classroom, and so that we heard the theories and thinking of the children as they worked. Our assumptions also provided us with new lenses for assessing how the children were learning. We watched to see how the children worked with various sign systems. We were always assessing their language literacy development, but we were also watching how the other sign systems supported that development or supported other kinds of thinking and growth. We watched to see what questions and interests sparked each student and how inquiries unfolded and added to students' knowledge. We also tried to understand what the students believed and understood about literacy and learning. We were interested in their personal theories of the world and their role in it.

The story that follows is Peter's story. Most of the children in the class were fairly predictable. They liked the engagements we offered and showed steady growth in all areas of the curriculum. Peter, however, was a puzzling child. Susan and I worried about Peter. We could see that he was learning, but even at the end of the school year he did not have reading and writing fully under control. We made it a point to collect work from Peter and to systematically study his artifacts, videotapes of him at work, and recorded conversations. We learned a great deal about Peter and about our teaching by doing this. His unique development is shared here in three "snapshots," each representing an interval of about a month of time.

September/October

During the first few weeks of school, Peter appeared to have some important strengths. His early attempts at writing were fairly successful. He was aware of environmental print and could copy off the board. He knew how to write all of the letters in the alphabet, even though he didn't always know the letter names. His September 13 journal entry, in which he wrote the single word "Dad," was typical of this time period. In most of his journal entries he would write just one word, often one he had in his word bank or one of the few he knew by memory. He had to be encouraged to write anything more, but with help he could work out letter/sound correspondences. If we said a word slowly for him and stopped after each consonant, he could often recognize and write the letter, as he did when writing DATBIK for "dirtbike" (Figure 9.1).

As time progressed, however, it became clear that Peter had some negative feelings toward language activities. He continued to limit his writing to single word efforts, and when a guest playing the part of the "Pilgrim Lady" asked the children sitting at her feet if they would like to hear a story, Peter emphatically answered, "No!" While most of the children soaked up details and information from the nonfiction texts Susan read to them about the Pilgrims and Native Americans, Peter seemed to let the texts wash over him. He knew, for example, that corn was mentioned in the stories, but he had no recollection after hearing the stories of who taught the Pilgrims to plant corn or why it was important.

FIGURE 9.1

On October 8, as Peter and I were walking down the hall, he confided, "I didn't want to come to school today because I can't read." I assured Peter that he *was* a beginning *reader* and pointed out a couple of things in the hallway that he could read—the signs on the bathroom doors, the exit signs, and the word "rainbow" on a bulletin board. But my message and the model of literacy we promoted in the classroom did not align with messages he was getting at home and elsewhere in the school. At Back-to-School Night, Peter's father looked at his journal and asked why Peter's invented spelling had not been marked wrong or corrected. Both of Peter's parents were concerned that Peter could not read the words in the predictable books that he brought home. In spite of Susan's encouragement to keep supporting Peter's reading and to watch for development in his writing, his parents began to make Peter study a set of 10 words each week. He had to practice spelling the words correctly and was either grounded or allowed to play with his friends based on what happened when his father tested him each Friday. In addition, Peter's kindergarten test scores earmarked him for Title I services, and he was being pulled out of the classroom every day for half an hour to work with a special tutor who insisted on drilling him on letters and sounds.

It was not hard to understand why Peter was unsure of himself. He was getting many mixed messages from the adults in his life, and Susan and I were not having much success in changing any of that. We knew that we could not let Peter give up on himself. In fact, we pushed him a little harder and gave him a little more support than the other children when we were reading and writing, and he did maintain a willingness to try. He liked the social aspects of the literacy rituals in our classroom. For example, he loved to share his journal with the class because he was expected to make eye contact with his peers and wait for their attention before beginning to read. He could stretch this into a long, dramatic process of looking one by one into the faces of his classmates, and someone almost always had to encourage him to get on with his sharing. While his journal entries were often only single words, this preliminary bid for attention often made his turn at sharing seem just as substantial as the sharing done by children who had written longer texts.

Our multiple sign systems learning environment included a Reflection Center. It consisted of a shelf full of scrap paper, yarn, glue, crayons, a stapler, scissors, and so forth, a table to work on, and a bulletin board for displaying finished work. During "invitation time, " or choice time, each day, Peter would mainly work at this Reflection Center. The invitation was simply to use the tools and media at the center to reflect on the current literature study or the inquiry in process. Peter seemed to understand the purpose of the center, as he explained that "you go there to think about what you are doing."

At the Reflection Center, Peter created three-dimensional artifacts that mirrored their concrete counterparts. For example, he made a "pocket" by stapling two papers together. His creations suggested that Peter was focused on an important literacy concept that Howard (1992) described as "showing forth" and Dyson (1991) described as "establishing equivalences." He was focused on the ways signs are connected to the real world. Using the paper and staples, he created what he designated as a sign for "pocketness." Dyson said this is a first step in discovering how to transform the experienced world into an imagined one. It amounts to realizing that a visible sign can represent invisible prior experiences or, in this case, the invisible concept of pocketness.

At the Reflection Center, Peter made things like a quiver full of paper arrows, three-dimensional numbers, and a replica of a wigwam. While his written language productions were minimal, the works he created at the Reflection Center were often fairly complex and required a great deal of concentration. What he was not able to do with language, he was able to do with drawing and three-dimensional paper sculpting. He could concentrate and reflect in depth. He could make things mean what he wanted them to mean, and he could connect what he was thinking to events in the curriculum. As I reviewed video footage recorded in the classroom during September and October, I noticed that Peter seldom talked during writing or reading activities. Yet, he carried on active conversations with those around him when he was at the Reflection Center or creating a drama or doing anything of a physical nature. He especially came alive during recess and joined any kind of ball game he could find.

November

By November, Peter was able to move into his zone of proximal development (Vygotsky, 1978) in experiences that involved sign systems other than language, but he was not doing so with his reading choices. Each week, Susan offered the children a choice of four or five literature study books. She provided time for the children to browse through the books and expected them to choose the one they wanted to read and discuss. The selections ranged from extremely predictable books to ones with fairly complex text structures. Most of the children gave their choice considerable deliberation, reading pages of each book to see if the text was manageable, flipping through the books to look at pictures, and comparing the length of books. We noticed that Peter, however, chose the first book he flipped through. He showed no curiosity about the books and devoted no energy to finding a book that was suited to his own literacy development.

Peter's writing development was also behind that of his peers during this time period. He persisted in doing as little writing as possible. Susan finally insisted that he write sentences instead of single words in his journal, so he began every entry with "I like." Initially, he would look up the word "like" in his deck of word cards and spell it from the card, but then he began experimenting with the spelling—LKIE, LIKEE, KLE, and KLIE (Figure 9.2). At one point, Peter and I spent 30 minutes talking about the word "like," reviewing the relationship of the sounds and the spelling, writing it on the board repeatedly, and spelling it out loud. I was sure this concentrated practice would enable him to write the word successfully in the future, but the very next day he seemed absolutely clueless about the word. His memory did not hold the orthographic pattern of the letters. Spelling a word correctly one day did not lead to spelling it correctly the next. A note from his mother, returned with his

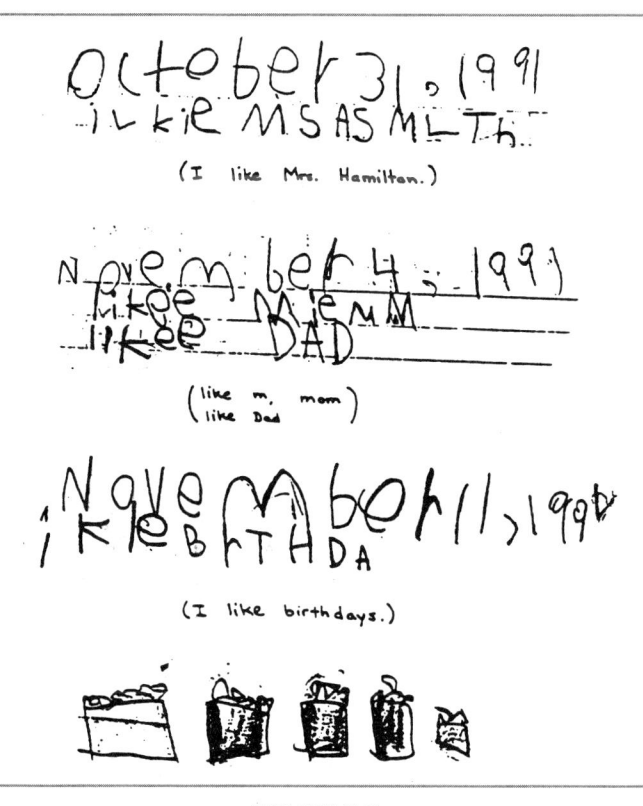

FIGURE 9.2

Colonial America portfolio, echoed a similar frustration. She wrote: "I wish that when I worked with Peter at home that I could make him comprehend the basics of reading and writing and that I had more patience. (We could probably get more accomplished.)"

In a conversation with Peter, I asked him how he thought a person might become a better reader and writer. Peter explained that learning in school depended on "doing what the teacher says to do." This stance echoed the first stance described by Dahl and Freppon (1991) in their study of kindergartner's literacy learning—a dependency on the teacher's instruction and a cautious or negative attitude toward literacy activities. While Susan and I were not aware of how this way of thinking played out for Peter at the time, we observed later, as we watched videotapes from this time period, that Peter was learning to *act* literate even if he wasn't learning to read and write. He was living his theory that he needed to do what the teacher said to do. He was trying very hard. He sat attentively for stories. He labored long and hard over single word entries in his learning log, timing his finish to coincide with those students who wrote several sentences. In reading groups, the children often read predictable books out loud in unison. Peter went through all the motions in these readings, trailing his finger across the page and mouthing the words with the group, but he never made a prediction if the group got stuck. Nor did he ask questions or answer any. He learned how to watch the others when he was reading and to turn the pages at the same time they did. In fact, in the videos, we could see that he consistently did what the other children did, just a split second after them. When raising his hand to answer a question, when following a direction, or when reading in unison, he was always a beat behind, cueing off the others.

During choice time, Peter avoided invitations that involved reading and writing, but he began to try more complex tasks, such as sorting the artifacts in the Colonial America museum in Venn diagram fashion, using mathematics manipulatives to create and solve problems, and drawing portraits of himself. In these settings, he was a constructive learner. He talked his way through the tasks and recognized and solved problems. He often asked those around him for help with questions like "What is this?" and "What numbers do I write?" and "How do you draw the eyes?"

Peter's focus on the procedural aspects of becoming literate and his passive approach to written language were also apparent in his learning log. At the end of each day, when the class spent 15 minutes recording their thoughts about what they had learned in their learning logs, Peter typically wrote a single word and illustrated it with a simple picture. Figure 9.3 shows Peter's learning log entries for two different days. One entry says "Mit," and he has drawn mittens; the other says "Itentes," and he has drawn an Indian. It was not uncommon for Peter to record things that had no obvious link to the concepts we were trying to develop through the curriculum.

FIGURE 9.3

He didn't seem to grasp the concept that the learning log was a place to gather the threads of the curriculum; instead, he treated it as an isolated task.

Peter adhered to this stance of doing his work for the teacher until the day Susan read an informational book about the Plains Indians. Peter was finally compelled to record information for himself. That day, instead of writing his usual one-word entry in his learning log, he wrote a complete sentence: "I like Indians because they shoot buffaloes" (Figure 9.4). This particular bit of information kept him occupied for the next 2 weeks. As an inquiry question, he asked, "How did the Indians shoot buffalo?" He took this question and a book about Indians home to get help from his family. They helped him write about the weapons and the skinning of the buffaloes. He joined a poetry group whose members were memorizing a poem about buffaloes. He made arrows and knives at the Reflection Center and continued to write sentences about Indians and buffaloes for days in his learning log.

May/June

Throughout the school year, drama was one of the sign systems Peter used with regularity. He especially liked the performance aspects of drama. Although he was visibly nervous when he was in front of the group early in the year, he continued to accept parts. He almost never initiated ideas in the planning and was usually told by other, more assertive youngsters what his part would be. But as the year went on, the props he made became more elaborate, and he began to act like his character in the plays.

In the last month of the school year, Peter accepted the lead in a play for the first time. He volunteered to be the Gingerbread Man. Susan had worked with the children

FIGURE 9.4

as a class to write the script on large chart paper, and to save time, she had not written out all of the Gingerbread Man's repeated lines. Practicing for the play, Peter and a few other children were reading the script together, and the children were feeding him all of his lines because he could not remember the sequence of characters that he was to add cumulatively to his list ("I've run away from the Little Old Woman and the Little Old Man" . . . and the cow and the horse and the mowers and so on).

When Susan suggested that the children start to act out the parts, they set the stage so that Peter would run in a circle, and each time he came around he would meet a new character. Once the Little Old Woman and the Little Old Man had chased Peter, they stood at the edge of the circle where Peter could see them and remember to include them in his monologue. It was by doing this physical circling past characters that Peter finally grasped the structure of this cumulative tale. He had been reading cumulative tales all year with little understanding, yet he could act this one out because he figured out the underlying structure.

Kress (1998) described drama as a system that involves "acting with one's whole (social and physical) body in spatial relations to other social and physical bodies" (p. 9). This kind of learning was more powerful than print literacy in Peter's life. The power of the physical realm showed up again in a picture Peter drew of a baseball game. Shown in Figure 9.5, the picture reflected a new sense of structure and the relatedness of events. When Peter shared this picture, it helped us to understand that Peter's favored learning realm was physical and social. As he made discoveries in this physical realm, new things made sense to him in the realm of reading and writing.

Peter began to show persistence as a writer. The page of "I likes" shown in Figure 9.6 illustrates the kind of writing Peter did of his own free will. He was using what he finally controlled ("I like") to set up opportunities to work at the edge of his knowing. This is what he had been doing for months at the Reflection Center, and finally he was doing it in writing as well.

Peter's writing began to give more insight into his conceptual frameworks. After a field trip to a local park with a small reservoir, Peter wrote, "Today I went to Eagle Creek and I saw the ocean" (Figure 9.7). This sentence told us that the experience of making a papier-mâché globe and painting on the oceans and continents had some impact on Peter and that he was making connections. It also told us that unlike many of his peers who could name the oceans and understand the abstraction of a globe, Peter could not yet extend his learning beyond his concrete experiences.

Clearly, Peter was not reading and writing up to the benchmark standards of the school, and his peers still found much of his written communication unintelligible. But Peter's sense of what he was doing, his personal theory about print literacy, had changed dramatically. During the last few weeks of school, Peter frequently visited the invitation called Photo Reflections. He finally understood the importance of explaining his learning processes to himself. He valued answering the two questions about himself as a learner: What are you doing in the picture? Why are you doing it? First, he wrote about himself making props for a play. Next, he picked a picture of himself reading and wrote, "I am reading because I can learn to read *Pumpkin,*

BASBL IZ FUN BKS
V IT IT O HIT AND KSh
   IT
BAeBL

FIGURE 9.5

Pumpkin." Finally, he chose a picture of himself writing and wrote: "I am writing because I am learning" (Figure 9.8).

Finally Peter understood that reading and writing are ways to learn. His stance had changed from Stance A to Stance C as described by Dahl and Freppon (1991).

He was initiating engagements with written language and had a personal agenda for learning about reading and writing. He was no longer dependent on the teacher's directives or reluctant to read and write.

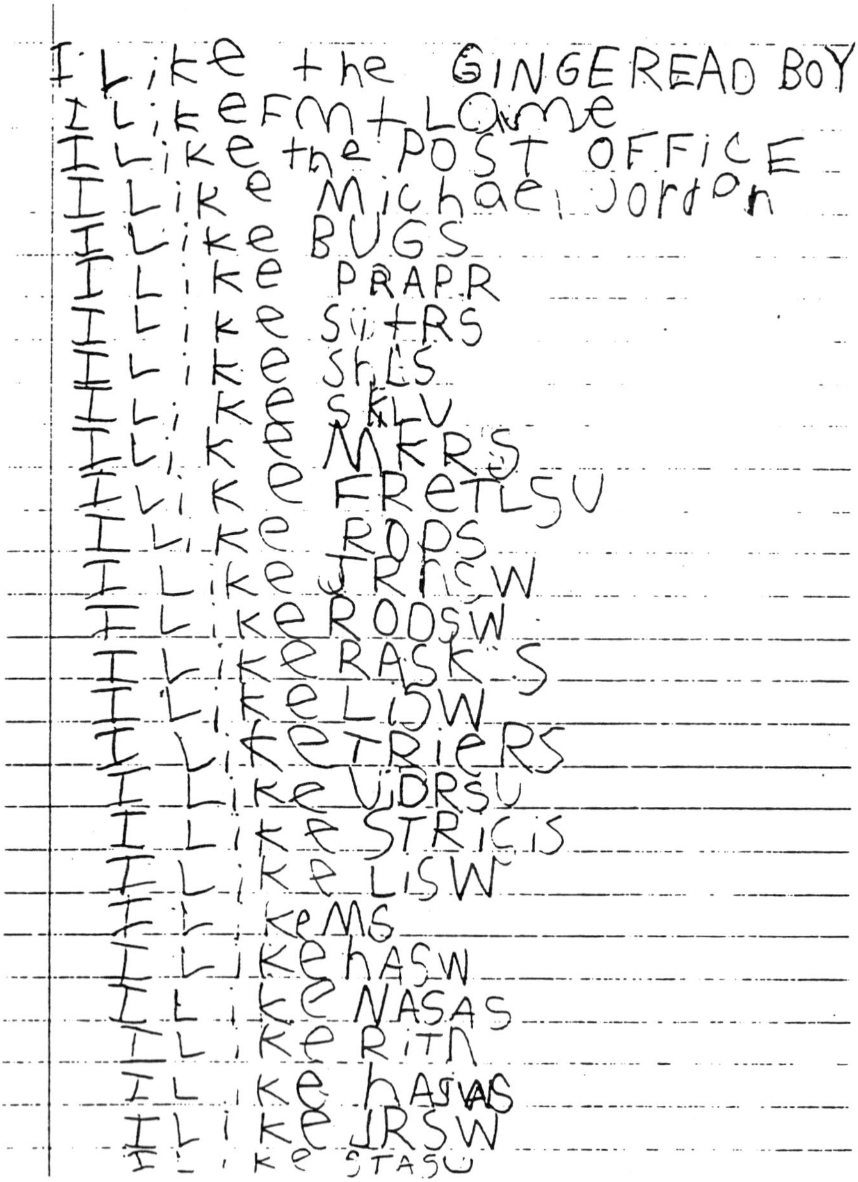

I Like the GINGEREAD BOY
I Like FM t LQme
I Like the POST OFFICE
I Like Michael Jordon
I Like BUGS
I Like PRAPR
I Like SitRS
I Like ShLS
I Like SKLV
I Like MKRS
I Like FReTLSU
I Like RDPS
I Like JRSW
I Like RODSW
I Like RASKS
I Like LSW
I Like TRieRS
I Like VDRSU
I Like STRiCiS
I Like LiSW
I L keMS
I Like hASW
I Like NASAS
I Like RiTN
I Like hASWAS
I Like JRSW
I Like STASU

FIGURE 9.6

> ISTA We Ut
> OT eGLCRek
> AnD I SL the
> oshin.

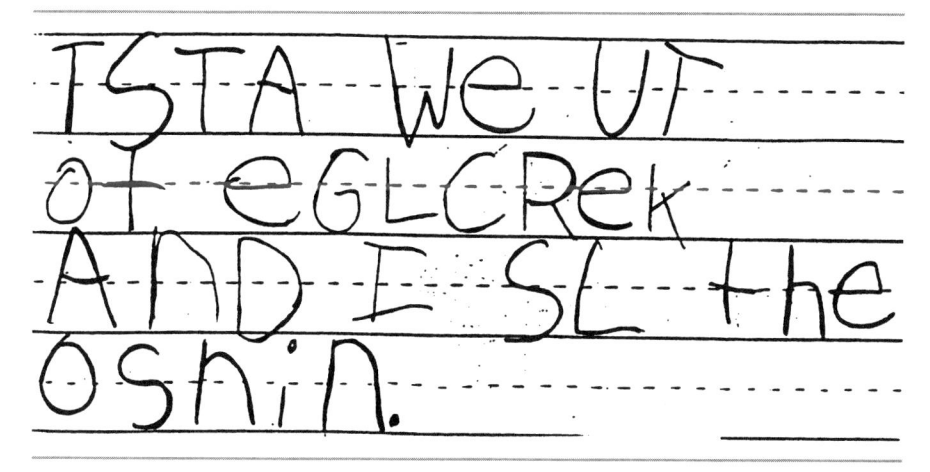

FIGURE 9.7

> I am riTen
> Because I
> am learning

FIGURE 9.8

Summary

It is not possible to know how learning might have proceeded for Peter if he had been in one of the other first grades in our school where there were no reflection centers, museums, easels, or drama corners. In the early months of the school year, these were clearly his favorite places for learning. He sought out sign systems other than language, and these systems supported his social interaction. Whereas he was passive and quiet when there was a language activity going on, he was engaged and talkative at the centers, where he was cutting and stapling, sorting and organizing, or playing a part. These interactions kept him from being marginalized in the class. He was able to maintain social status because he was an interactive learner in these settings. He formed friendships and demonstrated that he was a worthy work partner.

Like many other children, Peter's belief system about learning in school was focused on doing what the teacher told him to do. Few teachers or adults would argue against the value of this belief. Children are expected to do what they are asked to do. But this is a very limited and partial understanding of school learning. It is like understanding efferent reading (reading to accomplish a task) but not aesthetic reading (reading to live vicariously). Once Peter stumbled onto the excitement of his own deep interest, he began to use print literacy to get answers to his own questions and to create texts of significance to himself. Then he had a more complete sense of what was possible. He realized that there was more to school and learning than the procedural layer of doing the task required.

In some ways, Susan and I learned the same lesson during this experience. By making a strong commitment to our own interests and questions, we also developed a deeper sense of what was possible. We began to understand that Peter might well be making important conceptual gains even though he was passive and threatened by written language. To find out if this was the case, we had to interpret what we saw Peter do. We had to gather information from many aspects of his life in the classroom. We watched him live and learn alongside his peers. We pondered his willingness to perform and his penchant for a 3-D world. And we were patient, because it took time for the story to unfold. It was not always clear whether our interpretations were valid or how the larger pattern of Peter's development would evolve.

We started using the notion of aesthetic to talk about our experience of coming to know Peter as a learner because it captured the essence of our experience. We were comparing our interpretations and continually gathering information to make Peter more predictable to us. We found ourselves generating questions like the following to guide our observations: What sign systems does he favor? What does he understand about using those sign systems? What interests and questions are compelling to him? What are his theories about literacy, school, and the world?

By taking an aesthetic stance toward the assessment of Peter's learning, we realized that we could do a better job of teaching Peter. Our strategy of providing choice time each day during which students could work at things their own way was a good one for Peter. But we also did a great deal of instruction that did not connect well to Peter. We were teaching about globes and corn and history before Peter had the schema to use this information. We needed to keep in mind that he was at a different phase of development than the other students and needed more concrete support. It was not enough to mention corn. We needed to bring in the stalks of corn and husk the ears. We needed to do lessons with the children that worked at many levels. Peter needed to put his hands on the corn, to smell it, to taste it, and to dissect it, while other children were ready to graph the number of sheaves in a husk and to study corn's Native American origins.

As we organized our observations and data from the classroom to write Peter's story, we found support for the assumptions about literacy that we were using to frame our curriculum. We saw turning points in Peter's literacy development that originated in sign systems other than language. For example, we saw that he worked out the concept of equivalency by constructing 3-D models of things in the real world. If a paper sculpture could stand for a real-world object, so then could a word. He also learned about story structure through drama. The physical act of running in circles helped Peter understand the nature of a cumulative story. He transferred this realization to reading and began to read predictable books that had a cumulative structure with more assurance.

Peter demonstrated that literacy supports inquiry when he started to pursue his question about how Native Americans killed buffaloes. He discovered that many of the things people have learned are written down. If he could locate and reconstruct the information from a text, or if he could find someone to read the information to him, he could know important things in detail, like the length of the knives used to kill buffaloes or the Native American's tricks for getting close to the buffalo. It was another turning point when Peter learned that he could use literacy to support his personal inquiry.

Finally, we saw our assumption that literacy is shaped by theories illustrated in Peter's story as well. In the beginning of the year, Peter was a victim of conflicting theories. On the one hand, he was learning that spelling was the most important aspect of literate work; on the other hand, he was encouraged to invent spelling and to write for meaning. It is little wonder that he took up the stance of least resistance—do what the teacher tells you to do, leave it to the teachers to know what is best. Fortunately, he moved beyond this dependency, and by the end of the year, he believed that he could establish his own learning challenges. He even explained in an interview at the end of the year that we should help the next group of first graders understand that they could learn to read and write by reading and writing and *being artists.*

Looking back, we can see that we missed some potential learning opportunities with Peter. He was learning all kinds of things from playing ball, but we were not tuned in. In fact, our learning environment made little provision for knowing the children in terms of movement and physical activity. As we think about Peter and some of the other boys in the room, we realize that kinesthetic knowing might well be their most cogent mode of knowing. So we have new questions about how to set up the learning environment and where we should go to watch our children learn.

When we took an aesthetic stance toward literacy, curriculum, and assessment, we made lived experience central to our thinking and thereby changed the texture and quality of our work. We liked the change. We were in control, interacting to clarify our own thinking and following our own interests and questions. We put ourselves in a position to see learning in multiple ways and to learn about learning by watching the children. We were alive and thinking in the classroom, not just doing the tasks expected of us. Like Peter, we came to understand the possibilities of school differently. We discovered that we could know our children so well that we could teach to their strengths and talk with them about their theories of learning and literacy. We think this is exactly the kind of teaching and assessment that serves *all* children well.

References

Berghoff, B. (1994). Multiple dimensions of literacy: A semiotic case study of a first-grade nonreader. In C. Kinzer & D. Leu (Eds.), *Multidimensional aspects of literacy research, theory, and practice* (pp. 200–208). Chicago: The National Reading Conference.

Berghoff, B. (1998). Multiple sign systems and reading. *The Reading Teacher, 51,* 520–523.

Burke, C. (1990, Fall). Seminar in curriculum and instruction, Indiana University, Bloomington.

Csikszentmihalyi, M. (1996, Summer). How to measure learning. *The Institute View.* Los Angeles, CA: The Paul Getty Center for Education in the Arts.

Dahl, K., & Freppon, P. (1991). Literacy learning in whole-language classrooms: An analysis of low socioeconomic urban children learning to read and write in kindergarten. In S. McCormick & J. Zutell (Eds.), *Learner factors/teacher factors: Issues in literacy research and instruction* (pp. 149–159). Chicago: The National Reading Conference.

Dyson, A. H. (1991). Viewpoints: The word and the world—reconceptualizing written language development or do rainbows mean a lot to little girls? *Research in the Teaching of English, 25,* 97–123.

Harste, J., Woodward, V., & Burke, C. (1984). *Language stories and literacy lessons.* Portsmouth, NH: Heinemann.

Howard, V. A. (1992). *Learning by all means: Lessons from the arts.* New York: Peter Lang.

Hubbard, R. (1989). *Authors of pictures, draughtsmen of words.* Portsmouth, NH: Heinemann.

John-Steiner, V. (1985). *Notebooks of the mind: Explorations of thinking.* Albuquerque: University of New Mexico Press.

Kress, G. (1998). *"You just got to learn how to see": Curriculum subjects, young people, and schooled engagement with the world.* Unpublished manuscript.

Langer, J. (1989). *The process of understanding literature* (Report Series 2.1). Albany, NY: State University of New York, Center for the Learning and Teaching of Literature.

Mills, H., & Clyde, J. (Eds). (1990). *Portraits of whole language classrooms.* Portsmouth, NH: Heinemann.

Newkirk, T. (1989). *More than stories: The range of children's writing.* Portsmouth, NH: Heinemann.

Purcell-Gates, V. (1991). On the outside looking in: A study of remedial readers' meaning-making while reading literature. *Journal of Reading Behavior, 23,* 235–253.

Rosenblatt, L. (1978). *The reader, the text, the poem.* Carbondale: Southern Illinois University Press.

Shannon, P. (1990). *The struggle to continue: Progressive reading instruction in the United States.* Portsmouth, NH: Heinemann.

Short, K., Schroeder, J., Laird, J., Ferguson, M., & Crawford, K. (1996). *Learning together through inquiry: From Columbus to integrated curriculum.* York, ME: Stenhouse.

Vygotsky, L. (1978). *Mind and society: The development of higher psychological processes.* In M. Cole, V. John-Steiner, S. Scribner, & E. Souberman (Eds.), Cambridge, MA: Harvard University Press.

10

Successful Teacher Strategies in a Multicultural Language Arts Classroom: Organization, Techniques, and Discipline

Angela E. Rickford

This chapter describes elements of teacher practice that supported learning and growth in a multicultural language arts classroom of lower socioeconomic status inner-city students. The reading achievement level of the students in the class was quite low. Some of the students had identified learning disabilities, and almost all of them had scored at or below the 12th percentile on their most recent standardized test—the Spring 1990 California Test of Basic Skills (CTBS). Their teacher, Mr. Peters, was an African-American man who dressed formally in long sleeves and a tie. A self-described "humble farm boy from the South," he was a veteran teacher of over 20 years. The 25 students in the class were at the middle-school level in a seventh-grade classroom at a K–8 elementary school in northern California. The students were predominantly African-American, but the group also included Samoan, Fijian, Tongan, and Latino students. With five different ethnicities present, Room 27 was the epitome of ethnic diversity and cultural heterogeneity. Still, Mr. Peters managed to effect a strong sense of cultural unity in the classroom and to use this potential strength together with culture-based techniques and strategies as the framework for teaching reading and language arts and for maintaining order and discipline among his challenging preadolescent students.

I report here on information and insights gleaned over the period of 2 years (1993–1995) that I spent as a participant-observer in the students' language arts classroom. My primary focus is on observations of their seventh-grade year during Mr. Peters's tenure. I was also a regular volunteer in their previous sixth-grade language arts classroom during the 1993–1994 academic year, when the students had another teacher, but that year was marked by classroom chaos, a lack of discipline, and minimal student engagement. My interest in writing this chapter was spurred by the marked improvement I saw in the students' behavior and interest level with Mr. Peters as their teacher and also by the students' improvement in reading comprehension under Mr. Peters's guidance. These developments were documented by a reading comprehension research project I conducted that year. My analysis of Mr. Peters's teaching strategies is therefore based on the observations and reflections that I made during my research in his classroom and draws on the results of my work there.

Background and Profile of Students

The students in the class were a challenging bunch of youngsters. On the threshold of adolescence, they were filled simultaneously with youthful exuberance and gnawing self-doubt. To make matters worse, the community in which they lived afforded them little opportunity to channel their burgeoning energy constructively. Teenage pregnancy, the drug trade, alcoholism, and unemployment plagued the community and threatened to derail its youth. A few students came from traditional two-parent families, but most lived in very challenging circumstances. Some came from single-parent homes where a mother (or father) worked for long hours and the children were left to fend for themselves. For example, one of the students lived in a small apartment with a dozen or more relatives. Another student was a youngster whose mother had been institutionalized because of drug abuse; in yet another case, a young man's father had been recently incarcerated. Some of the youngsters had already begun to form gang affiliations, and behavioral problems abounded. Everyone qualified for free meals at school.

As noted earlier, the students were not achieving academically in the areas of reading and writing, as demonstrated by both standardized scores and informal direct observation. Another measure, the 1989–1990 California Assessment Program scores for their school district placed eighth graders on the second percentile in reading and sixth graders on the third percentile in writing. Scores from the more recent 1994 California Learning Assessment System (CLAS), despite its modified assessment approaches, marked no real improvement in the situation. The results placed the upper graders at or below the level of 3 on the 6-point evaluation scale, a rubric that states that students ["make superficial connections . . . (are) unwilling to take risks . . . but also demonstrate confused, superficial or illogical thinking in (their) writing"] (*San Jose Mercury News,* p. 12 A). But although these students faced enormous challenges and responsibilities in their personal lives, and despite the problems in their academic lives to which their low reading scores attested, Mr. Peters was consistently able to motivate and engage them in reading, writing, and language arts activities. He achieved this considerable measure of success by the skillful manipulation of classroom dynamics and by incorporating various dimensions of the students' culture into his innovative instructional techniques and tough-love discipline strategies.

In the sections that follow, I discuss the strategies Mr. Peters used to design a multicultural classroom and to create an environment of cultural diversity and tolerance. I then discuss the strategies he used to inspire and challenge his students. Also covered are his innovative instructional techniques, with a focus on curriculum choices, narrative comprehension questioning strategies, strategies for teaching writing, and his incorporation of church-based discipline techniques into the classroom. Following this discussion, I draw out the implications of my findings and make recommendations for improved teacher practice in classrooms of students who are at risk for academic failure.

Strategies Used to Design a Multicultural Classroom

Mr. Peters created a model of multiculturalism in his classroom. He took a situation that had the potential for conflict and divisiveness and forged an environment that represented tolerance, sensitivity, acceptance, and appreciation among students of diverse ethnic minority backgrounds. On one of my early visits to his classroom, I noticed that the seating arrangement was dramatically different from that in the students' classroom the previous year. In their sixth-grade class, the students had been responsible for their own seating arrangements and generally chose to sit together according to ethnicity and gender. There were pockets of males and females and three- and four-person desk groups of same-ethnicity students sprinkled throughout the room. This arrangement seemed to encourage animosity between groups that became almost palpable at times. On one occasion during that year, members of one group publicly accused the teacher of having favorites in the class and of curry favor because she tended to choose her class volunteers and monitors from the same group of students.

The situation was now very different in Room 27. Students were noticeably intermixed, and a visitor to the classroom could immediately perceive a measure of harmony among the students. Undoubtedly, the path to this outcome was not without difficult moments, but Mr. Peters was able to build on the similarities among the diverse groups of students in order to celebrate and appreciate the differences among them and guide them to do the same. The fact that they were all poor, ethnic minority students growing up in the same marginalized community and working toward the same ultimate life goals seemed to form the foundation of their unity. This factor was the common denominator that combined with a firm but sympathetic and amiable teacher-leader to fashion an emerging sense of togetherness among all of the students in the classroom.

I asked Mr. Peters about the seating arrangements in his class during an interview. He explained that he actively discouraged his students from sitting along same-gender or same-ethnicity lines because this approach, though "natural," contravened his philosophy as a teacher. He believed in and modeled inclusiveness. He showed respect for each student in his classroom and each culture represented there, and he encouraged his students to do the same. He believed that a prerequisite to learning was a strong sense of self, which grew out of respect for both oneself and others. This sense of self is what educational psychologists have labeled as positive self-construct and self-efficacy (Bandura, 1977). Mr. Peters explained that his "vegetable soup" seating technique laid the groundwork psychologically for students to stretch toward these achievements in his classroom. He explained his technique as follows:

> I broke them up. Absolutely. The first day of school I would have them all to stand around a wall, and I would put everybody together [and] say, "We're just gonna have a nice vegetable soup. I want everybody mixing together in this classroom. Let me see, I want a carrot over here. You're a carrot. I say, I want some potatoes now. Potato, you go over to that group now. And I want a little broccoli here." I don't let them sit together, see. 'Cause that will work against you.

This unique approach to heterogeneous grouping seemed to have a sanguine effect on the members of the class. Despite their initial resistance, students learned respect for one another and for diversity and difference. They developed a willingness to be open to others' cultures and ethnicities and to interact with and learn from one another. This unabashed celebration of ethnicity had other positive outcomes as well. Students were encouraged, and felt comfortable enough, to speak their natural language (African-American Vernacular English dialect) or their second language (Spanish or Hindi or Samoan or Tongan) in the classroom during non-class time, although not to the exclusion or embarrassment of nonnative speakers. There was no diminution of dialect or "other" language in this classroom. Yet Mr. Peters constantly modeled the use of standard English, which he promoted and required during class, as the vehicle for success and advancement both in school and in the larger society.

An added benefit of this culture-sensitive classroom environment was that the students formed and nurtured strong friendships and relationships across ethnic boundaries. Other scholars have also observed this dynamic in successful multicultural classrooms (Heath, 1995), and, indeed, mutual respect among diverse cultures is a goal that proponents of multiculturalism espouse. Mr. Peters seemed to have achieved it. Whether they were working in the classroom or socializing on the playground, Mr. Peters was coaching his students into creating an environment that was conducive to their acquisition of "the knowledge, skills, and attitudes needed to function effectively in a culturally and ethnically diverse nation and world" (Banks, 1993, p. 27).

Strategies Used to Inspire and Challenge Students

Mr. Peters endeavored to inspire his students in many ways. He wanted to encourage them to value academic achievement in general and reading and writing in particular (language arts was his primary subject), since like most marginalized youth, they showed a general indifference to the academic pursuit. He considered teacher expectations, a well-established factor in student performance (Rosenthal & Jacobson, 1968), as critical to the achievement of his students. He therefore held high expectations for them, articulated those expectations clearly, and used every available avenue of space and time to motivate his students. By demanding more of his students, he received more from them.

The power of the word in the African-American culture has a long and significant history by way of the Black Church (a point I develop later in this chapter), and the oral culture tradition. Contemporarily, it is manifested in ritualized wordplay, music, and pop culture. Since the ethos of the classroom supported ethnic intermixing and acceptance, and since he and the large majority of the students were of African-American descent, Mr. Peters was able to summon the underlying cultural power and authority of words to inspire and challenge his students. Words were the catalyst that transformed the physical environment from a classroom that the students inhabited daily to a rendezvous where they encountered expectations, principles, ideals, and rules. The walls and additional poster boards contained reminders of elements of good practice for the students. In addition to the usual kind of academic materials and information that adorn the walls of the average mainstream classroom, the walls in Room 27 communicated the scope of acceptable performance in the classroom and focused on behavior modification and on setting limits. There were classroom rules, arrival procedures, lifelong guidelines, life skills, departure procedures, and more (Figure 10.1).

The walls also bore admonitions to support academic achievement and motivational sayings to build the students' spirit and buttress them against the challenges of their difficult life circumstances (Figure 10.2). Other affirmational rhymes and verses, some of which Mr. Peters led the students in rehearsing in the mode of a song, occasionally composed extemporaneously, were standard texts in the classroom. These affirmations were an inherent part of the students' workday, and time was therefore devoted to reciting and repeating them. In addition, Mr. Peters read the affirmations aloud several times each day as a constant reminder to the students that they were capable achievers.

This strategy is not uncommon among teachers of diversity. For example, parallels exist to the recent work of Folásadé Oládélé with her eighth and ninth graders at a junior high school in Oakland, California. "I taught my students affirmations to help them cope with life and to build their self-esteem," she wrote in characterizing the ways in which she "passed down the spirit" of all the lessons she herself had learned at home about the meaning of education (Oládélé, 1999).

Throughout the class, Mr. Peters used language with a flair that connoted the black artful style (Foster, 1992) and that typically incorporated features that signaled

Classroom Rules	Be in your assigned seat ready to work when the tardy bell rings.
Arrival Procedure	Enter quietly, greet teacher, place homework in paper tray. Get a book and read for 10 minutes.
Departure Procedure	Get homework assignment. Clean up. Wait for teacher to dismiss you.
Lifelong Guidelines and Life Skills	Truth, Trust, No Put-Downs, Active Listening, Personal Best. Integrity, Initiative, Flexibility, Perseverance, Organization, Sense of Humor, Effort, Responsibility, Cooperation, Caring.
Academic Prompts	A metaphor describes a thing or situation. A verb is an action word.

FIGURE 10.1

Some Reminders of Good Practice Adorning the Walls in Mr. Peters's Classroom

an ethnocultural mode of communication. These strategies were designed to connect with and reach his adolescent students, for whom language was increasingly becoming an avenue for self-identity and self-expression. His speech included oral embellishments, variations in pitch, tone, and tempo, and the use of "poetic devices" such as rhyme, rhythm, repetition, and alliteration—features that grabbed the attention of the students, drew them in, and seemed to inspire their learning. He often used catch phrases such as "Wonderful Wednesday" and "Tremendous Thursday" when greeting students. His classroom "speeches" included reflections such as the following: "Time wasted is forever lost/Lost to me as a teacher/And lost to you as a student."

Such an emphasis on extra-academic pursuits might seem puzzling and off-balance to the casual observer. Similarly, the military-like repetitions and directives might seem reactionary in the face of postmodern concepts and educational ideologies. One might also be concerned that there were too many informal measures of control and not enough opportunities for self-discipline among the students. But to an insider, one who had witnessed the disciplinary and achievement problems that plagued the students' previous year, the emphasis was understandable. No work could be done in the chaos and indiscipline that characterized the students' former classroom. Mr. Peters's aim was, therefore, to provide a vital framework within which his students could perform and to embed it in a warm and inviting environment while yet maintaining balance in discipline.

Mr. Peters viewed the use of space, time, and language in his classroom as the icons of structure and organization. As he explained, his imposed routines added an

Admonitions for Academic Achievement	Pledge of Allegiance to Me	Motivational Sayings
Use your cerebrum and your triune brain. Expand on your work. Give your point of view. No short answers allowed.	By doing the best In everything I do And taking pride In who I am, my faith Will see me through.	Society will draw a circle that shuts me out. But my superior thoughts will draw me in (from the Marva Collins Creed).
Our work must always be: Correct, Neat, Comprehensive, Complete.	I believe I can learn I can learn I will learn	No one is good At doing everything. But everyone is good At doing something.

FIGURE 10.2

Achievement Boosters in Mr. Peters's Classroom

important dimension of stability and predictability to his students' lives. The students came to know what class work and activities marked different days, and certain phrases became a stimulus for preparation to do specific kinds of activities. The "tough" students seemed somewhat constrained by the rules and regulations and conformed to them only reluctantly at times. But the rules and regulations provided a standard of behavior and performance to which Mr. Peters could hold the students, and generally they responded. He articulated his approach thus:

> I stress organization, a lot of good organization. That's very important to these children. They have to organize to survive. That's so important, to be organized. Yeah, I'm adamant about that. . . . Another thing we do is in the morning time we have a little routine we go through [referring to the "Pledge of Allegiance to Me" and "Motivational Sayings"], 'cause they need structure.

Innovative Instructional Techniques

In this section I draw on Mr. Peters's involvement during the planning and execution of my field-based research project to analyze his ideas and techniques for incorporating meaningful approaches into language arts instruction. I digress momentarily to fill the reader in on the thrust and substance of the project, since it is the backdrop against which I analyze his ideas and practice.

My study investigated whether students at risk for academic failure would become engaged with and interested in ethnic folktales and stories with which they could identify and in which they saw themselves reflected. The study also examined the effect of asking students to answer comprehension questions strategically constructed to expose students not only to the traditional literal and memory-type questions, but also to questions which were contextual and which required higher levels of thinking, analysis and interpretation. Mr. Peters's insights into the interface between culture and learning made him a good match for my study and in some ways helped to shape it. In the following sections, the philosophy that undergirded his teaching is analyzed from the perspective of three themes that emerged from my work in his classroom—curriculum choices, narrative comprehension questioning techniques, and strategies for teaching writing.

Curriculum Choices

Mr. Peters had been strongly recommended to me by the school principal as a teacher who was committed to exploring the cultural strengths of his students as the bedrock for learning and literacy and whose philosophy of teaching would be consonant with the thrust of my research. I discussed the details of the project with Mr. Peters and explained that one aim of my study was to examine the efficacy of using African-American folktales and contemporary black narratives as motivational materials in teaching narrative comprehension to ethnically diverse students (see Rickford, 1999, for a complete report and analysis of this research project). Mr. Peters was immediately receptive to incorporating my research study into his curriculum and to establishing a teacher-researcher relationship with me. He explained the reason for his receptivity to the project with these words:

> I agree with the whole idea of giving them black literature because they read it better; they can relate to it better. They can identify with the feelings, the empathy. Even the choice of words that is in the flow. Yes, I absolutely like it, doing black literature. Stories about their culture they really enjoy. Even the Polynesian and the Indian kids enjoy stories about blacks. And those kids enjoy stories about <u>them</u>. That's so.

Mr. Peters went on to explain that he tried to promote the use of literature from all of the cultural backgrounds that were represented by students in his classroom. He explained his intuitions about the potential of ethnocultural literature to connect with students, to lift their spirits, and to imbue them with a positive sense of self.

Mr. Peters's philosophy resonates with emerging theories of "cultural congruence" as articulated by Ladson-Billings (1995), of "culture-centered knowledge" as articulated by King (1995), and of "socio-culturally relevant text selection techniques" as I have articulated elsewhere (Rickford, 1999). Mr. Peters's perspective on the significance of culture in facilitating learning was also validated by students who participated in the study. As I have explained elsewhere, (Rickford, 1999), students identified with both the "deep-structure" and the "surface-structure" elements of the texts. By "deep-structure" elements, I allude to the themes, issues, characters, situations, and perspectives portrayed in the stories and in which the students saw themselves reflected. "The surface-structure" elements include the dialect and ethnic minority illustrations, which captured the students' interest and enhanced their feelings of dignity and self-worth. Their comments about the dialect used in the texts were sharp and strong and were expressed and recorded across ethnicities. For example, an African-American male student reported: "I like it because it is like I am in the story. It helps the story a lot because it makes the story younik [= unique] in its own way; people have to hear there own way of talking." A Latino male student wrote: "I like it because dialect made the story more interesting. Yes, because it helps the story sound like real people are talking." And a Fijian female student commented: "I like the dialect because it puts a lot of feelings in it." Referring to the ethnic illustrations, an African-American female student wrote, "I like the way they are made and everything. AND THERE ARE BLACK PEOPLE" (student's emphasis). A Tongan female student reported that the illustrations "brought out some thought out of the story."

A few caveats are in order. First, these testimonials need to be interpreted with sensitivity to the needs of ethnic minority students who live on the periphery of the dominant group and who often feel marginalized and alienated. Second, the concept of cultural congruence does not, de facto, exclude works from the traditional literary canon. The works of Shakespeare, Dickens, Austen, Faulkner, and so forth—"the classics"—represent literary qualities that should be held in high esteem, valued, taught, and related to students' experiences, conflicts, and aspirations where possible. Third, standard English should always be valued and taught, as Mr. Peters demonstrated unequivocally. However, paying attention to issues of cultural congruence in the language arts classroom stimulates deeper emotional and cognitive involvement among students and better preparation for the sociocultural milieu of the country and world today.

Current textbook adoptions and basal readers are themselves attending to these issues. They include ethnic folktales, and there are increasing numbers of catalogs and other sources with an emphasis on multiculturalism. For example, the 1999 Puffin Books catalog includes stories from Native American, Haitian, Irish, Mexican, Finnish, Chinese, Japanese, African, Peruvian, Colombian, Middle Eastern, African-American, Hungarian, Chinese-American, and South African cultures. Teachers can take advantage of such texts and harness them for use in their classrooms. Not only do folktales represent the kind of high-interest, low–readability level texts that teachers crave for poor readers in middle school grades, but they have the additional benefit of encapsulating some of the great ideals, values, mores, and customs of a people, which can be passed down to the younger generation to good advantage for their edification and guidance. They can also be chosen to represent the specific cultures of the classroom and are usually available in local libraries and bookstores. The following testimony of Amy Tan, author of *The Joy Luck Club,* attests to the empowering effect of ethnocultural literature in which students can see themselves reflected. Of her first exposure to an Asian American writer, she noted: "It was the first time that I had read anything by anybody who was not white, and it was so nourishing and affirming to be able to see a character like myself in art, and to see that I am worthy of art, and that I could produce art" (Meier 20–21, 1997).

Narrative Comprehension Questioning Techniques

The kinds of understandings and teachings that remain with students following narrative reading are largely influenced by the thrust of teacher questioning that accompanies such reading (Kirby, 1996). To help his students learn valuable lessons from narrative text, Mr. Peters posed questions to them that were engaging, authentic, and purposeful. His questions more often encouraged the students to think, argue, claim, doubt, speculate, and infer than required them to recall a single item of fact or one right answer from a text. When I inquired about this practice, he explained that "those higher order kinds of questions are very important; and they like them better."

Mr. Peters's perspective on the value and appeal of higher order questions is borne out in research, yet educators have observed this type of questioning to be largely missing in classrooms heavily populated by low socioeconomic status and ethnic minority students (Darling-Hammond, 1985; Harris, 1995). It is an orientation to interacting with and interpreting texts that tends to be reserved for the high-achieving student but that teachers ought to adopt for the low-achieving student also. Darling-Hammond (1985) urged that the entrenched "minimal skills" approach to teaching low-achieving students be replaced with questions that embrace "inferential and critical problem-solving." Calfee and Patrick (1995) similarly recommended that teachers design questions that help provoke students' thought and not merely force them to recall data. It is not that one-word memory-type questions, the so-called lower order questions, are unimportant, but that they are less authentic and purposeful and therefore less appealing to students who tend to be indifferent to school. As Calfee and Patrick (1995) sagely pointed out, the world is complex—more like an essay-type question than a one-word multiple-choice test.

Other researchers have also suggested that practitioners encourage students to think more critically and to make their literary experiences relevant and meaningful to their own backgrounds and personal experiences. For instance, Rosenblatt (1991) recommended "aesthetic" questions, or the more personal and private perspective, over "efferent" ones, or the more public stance; Beck (1997) recommended that students take an approach of "questioning the author" rather than being questioned (by the teacher); Ruddell (1999) characterized "influential" versus "noninfluential" teachers in terms of the balance they establish between lower order and higher order thinking questions; and elsewhere I recommended that teachers embed narrative comprehension questions in the essential structure of stories, an approach that leads naturally to higher levels of questioning and interaction with text than students are normally exposed to (Rickford, 1999).

Some researchers have pushed this line of argument even further. Heath (1983), for example, contended that low socioeconomic status African-American students (and, by implication, other ethnic minority students also) are better prepared culturally to engage with narrative text at high levels of argumentation, inference, and problem solving than at low levels of memory and recall because these students are able to use their powers of imagination in remarkable ways. She argued that students of diversity can manipulate textual features in shaping their ideas and opinions, and can forge links with seemingly disparate narrative units, because of the cultural propensities of the discourse communities in which they are immersed outside of their formal schooling. Heath noted that these well-honed abilities for contextualization prepare them for engagement with higher order kinds of questions, and the school's consequent inability to build on these ingrained skills in the elementary years causes these students to lose interest in school. A classroom that "depends on responses based on lifting items and events out of context is a shock" to them (p. 353), she argued, one that causes a loss of interest in school, and one of the factors that ultimately contributes to their high drop-out rate.

Beyond this, teachers should recognize that poor readers are not de facto poor thinkers. In fact, the more we learn about the functionings of the brain in the case of low- achieving readers with disabilities such as dyslexia, the more we are coming to understand that it is an inefficient "phonological module" that impairs the ability of these students to receive and process the sounds of words. The higher language processes of reasoning and concept formation, of meaning and discourse, and general intelligence tend, in fact, to be intact and fully functioning (Shaywitz, 1996). But the reality is that these students are usually subjected to effete kinds of questions, partly because their teachers are of the opinion that those questions are easier for the students to handle. For all of the reasons laid out here, Mr. Peters's students and others who are at risk for reading failure stand to benefit from questions that tap into their higher order thinking processes.

The outcomes of the comprehension and cognition study that I conducted with Mr. Peters's students fully support this argument. In the study, the students gained their highest scores (approximately 80% of the maximum total points possible) on the interpretive reading and critical evaluation questions and their second highest scores (approximately 75%) on creative reading questions (Rickford, 1999). Under the former category were questions requiring moral reasoning and judgments, questions about their favorite character in the stories and reasons for their preference, questions about the feelings and qualities of characters facing stressful situations in the texts, and other inferential questions. Under the latter category were questions requiring problem solving and creative reading questions requiring that students construct different endings to the stories they read. The students gained their lowest scores (59% of the maximum total points possible) on the literal meaning category of questions, which required memory and literal recall. The words of a Yale professor reflect the propriety of higher order over lower order thinking strategies: "Never once in my career have I had to memorize a book or lecture, but I have continually needed to think analytically, creatively, and practically in my teaching, writing, and research" (Sternberg, 1997, p. 23).

In addition to involving his students in authentic comprehension questioning techniques, Mr. Peters also explored other ways to help them develop a spirit of inquiry. He constantly encouraged them to be active learners and to take control of their learning. He articulated the desired intellectual approach and then empowered them, with words like the following, to be confident and self-assured enough to adopt it:

> Be curious about things. Don't just accept everything that someone says to you. Go to the library, ask your friends about it [the matter at issue], be curious about it. . . . I don't want you to be passive. I want you to challenge the teacher. Let them know that you are the best that there is. Say, "I don't understand. Will you please explain it?" Exactly right.

Strategies for Teaching Writing

Writing is a difficult task for many students at all levels of schooling, but it is particularly challenging for students who are at risk for academic failure. Thus, in addition to the typical writing assignments of journal entries and spelling sentences, Mr. Peters applied his philosophy of building on his students' cultural strengths to the area of writing instruction also. Building on his students' verbal skills of wordplay, developed especially by the boys in their in-group rappin' and playin' the dozens activities, he included authoring assignments such as poetry writing, rhyming, and rapping activities in the writing component of the language arts curriculum. He was pleased that one of the questions in my research study required the students to write a rhyming verse "because children learn in various modalities." Some were good at (conventional) writing, he explained, and some were good at rhyming and rapping.

Church-Based Discipline

Aware of the common foundation of the Black Church experience that he shared with the majority of his students, Mr. Peters explored incorporating church-based discipline routines into the classroom. Two examples of the tough-love discipline strategies he incorporated that were influenced by church culture—classroom seating procedures and discourse techniques—are described in the following sections.

Classroom Seating Procedures

Under the leadership of a designated class monitor, the class practiced a complex entry and exit routine on designated days and on assembly days. In the routine, the appointed class monitor for the day took his or her position of leadership at the head of the class and directed the group to sit or stand in unison or to exit in single file. The students performed each action in response to the leader's direction. To signal the class to sit, the class monitor stood with arms outstretched, palms facing downward, and slowly moved his or her arms toward the floor and back to his or her sides. Similarly, to signal the class to stand, the monitor stood with arms outstretched, palms facing upward, and slowly moved his or her arms toward the ceiling. The signal to exit the classroom was given by putting the left hand behind the back and holding it there while pointing to the door with the right hand, palm up, fingers held together, and body slightly angled. Everyone responded (in silence) by sitting, standing, or exiting the room row by row according to the monitor's instructions. These movements were directly borrowed from the role of the usher and/or choir director of the Black Church. The students responded with an appropriate measure of respect, and the calming effect of the routine on class discipline was noticeable. Because of the environment of cultural sharing and acceptance that Mr. Peters led his students in creating in the classroom, all of the students participated in the routines established regardless of ethnicity.

Classroom Discourse Techniques

Previous scholars who have examined African-American culture-based strategies for successful classroom communication have referred to the use of the language of power (Delpit, 1991) or the language of control (Foster, 1995). With these strategies, the asymmetry of the teacher-student relationship is emphasized, and the potential for an inflammatory situation is strong. The teacher's skill and sensitivity are of paramount importance in achieving whatever ends he or she has in mind while maintaining the students' dignity and integrity. Mr. Peters achieved this delicate balance by alternating between rebuke and praise in verbal interactions with his students. Whether he was acting in the mode of preacher or parent, he alternated between chastisement and a declaration of unconditional love. This dynamism characterized Mr. Peters's classroom communication style. The technique helped his students translate the importance of his message and helped Mr. Peters maintain discipline in the classroom.

On one occasion, I recorded the following exchange between Mr. Peters and Damion, a student who was misbehaving:

> You'd better take that attitude and throw it in the wastebasket. Damion is good; he helps set up the computer center, pass out the papers. . . . But he's got an attitude problem. If we could fix that, he'll be a good student. And I'll have to give him that trophy by the end of the year. We're working on it.

In his communication with his students, Mr. Peters's outbursts of praise and trust matched his sanctions in intensity and sincerity. One day, when things were going well with work and behavior, he remarked:

> See, I like the class when they are sitting up straight. Your body language tells me a lot about the way you feel, your attitude. And I want that to be right. I'm going to have to let these children out early for recess today, they're behaving so well.

The parental overtones evident in these excerpts were revealed even more candidly in the theme of trust and love that kept recurring in our interviews. Mr. Peters's classroom exemplified the caring and concern typically found more in the family unit than in school. It is not surprising that this profile is characteristic of schools that have been identified as successful in teaching ethnic minority schoolchildren

(Willis, 1995). Mr. Peters constantly let his students know that he cared about them, an important theme in the successful schooling of children (Noddings, 1995). As he told me:

> I let them know that they're special, and I love them. I respect them. I do so respect them. Then they give it back to me. And I think that's the main thing. And I tell them that constantly. It goes right back to that love, that deep concern. And you can't get that in a university. It's just something to that, to care for them.

It became obvious early in the year that the feelings were reciprocal. One student seemed to speak on behalf of the whole class when he said to me: "Well, I like Mr. Peters because he like us too. And we know he like us, so . . ."

Implications and Summary

In this chapter, I discussed the teaching practices of Mr. Peters, a successful middle-school language arts teacher of ethnically diverse, academically at-risk students. I examined his behavior and classroom management strategies as well as his instructional techniques. I demonstrated ways in which Mr. Peters was able to draw that delicate but crucial line between a teacher who is too permissive and one who is too restrictive, and I showed the potential for success that emerges in a classroom where that line is carefully drawn. When the 1995 CTBS Reading comprehension scores were published, the scores of Mr. Peters' students had increased by 13%, 17%, 10%, 3%, and 6% in the sub-areas of stated information, passage analysis, central thought, technique in written forms, and critical assessment respectively, a modest improvement but one worthy of mention. All teachers, whether or not they work with students with learning disabilities or at-risk students could benefit from following the lead of teachers like Mr. Peters, Folásadé Oládélé, and Jaime Escalante in holding high expectations for their students and in shaping a classroom environment that facilitates culture, learning, and achievement.

References

Bandura, A. (1977). Toward a unifying theory of behavioral change. *Psychological Review, 84,* 191–215.

Banks, J. A. (1993). Multicultural education: Development, dimensions and challenges. *Phi Delta Kappan, 75,* 22–28.

Beck, I., McKeown, L., Hamilton, R., & Kucan, L. (1997). *Questioning the author: An approach for enhancing student engagement with text.* Newark, Delaware: International Reading Association.

Calfee, R. C. & Patrick, C. L. (1995). *Teach our children well* (Portable Stanford Book Series). Stanford, CA: Stanford University.

Darling-Hammond, L. (1985). *Equality and excellence: The educational status of black Americans.* New York: College Board.

Delpit, L. D. (1991). The silenced dialogue: Power and pedagogy in educating other people's children. In M. Minami, & B. P. Kennedy (Eds.), *Language issues in literacy and bilingual/multi-cultural education* (pp. 483–502). Cambridge, MA: Harvard Educational Review, Reprint Series #22.

Foster, M. (1992). Sociolinguistics and the African American community: Implications for literacy. *Theory Into Practice, 31,* 303–311.

Foster, M. (1995). Talking that talk: The language of control, curriculum, and critique. *Linguistics and Education, 7,* 129–150.

Harris, V. J. (1995). Using African American literature in the classroom. In V. L. Gadsden & D. A. Wagner (Eds.), *Literacy among African American youth* (pp. 229–259). Cresskil, NJ: Hampton Press.

Heath, S. B. (1983). *Ways with words: Language, life and work in communities and classrooms.* Cambridge: Cambridge University Press.

Heath, S. B. (1995). Race, ethnicity, and the defiance of categories. In W. D. Hawley & A. W. Jackson (Eds.), *Toward a common destiny: Improving race and ethnic relations in America* (pp. 39–70). San Francisco: Jossey-Bass.

Kirby, P. (1996). Teacher questions during story-book readings: Who's building whose building? *Reading, 30*(1), 8–14.

Ladson-Billings, G. (1995). Toward a theory of culturally relevant pedagogy. *American Educational Research Journal, 32,* 465–492.

Meier, T. (1997). Kitchen poets and classroom books: Literature from children's roots. *Rethinking Schools, 12*(1): 20–21.

Noddings, N. (1995). Teaching themes of care. *Phi Delta Kappan, 76,* 675–679.

Oládélé, F. (1999). Passing down the spirit. *Educational Leadership, 56 (4),* 62–65.

Rickford, A. M. (1999). *I can fly: Teaching reading and narrative comprehension to African American and other ethnic minority students.* Lanham, MD: University Press of America.

Rosenblatt, L. (1991). The reading transaction: what for? In B. M. Power & R. Hubbard. (Eds.), *Literacy in process.* New Hampshire: Heinemann.

Rosenthal, R. & Jacobson, L. (1968). Pygmalion in the classroom: Teacher expectations and pupils' intellectual development. New York: Holt.

Ruddell, R. B. (1999). *Teaching children to read and write: Becoming an influential teacher.* Cambridge, Massachusetts: Allyn & Bacon.

San Jose Mercury News, 1994. March 9, p. 12A.

Shaywitz, S. (1996, November). Dyslexia. *Scientific American,* 98–104.

Sternberg, R. J. (1997). What does it mean to be smart? *Educational Leadership, 54*(6), 20–24.

Willis, M. G. (1995). *We're family: Creating success in an African American public elementary school.* Unpublished doctoral dissertation, Georgia State University, Atlanta.

Section 3

Student-Centered Curriculum Approaches

This section focuses on curriculum and how the practices of teachers of students identified as learning disabled change as they adopt a constructivist orientation toward teaching and learning. Special education has a history of focusing on basic skill instruction that students might eventually master. However, such a curriculum does not prepare students for the demands of today's world. The thought piece for this section promotes the necessity of having new types of conversations about teaching and learning that will provide a theoretical basis for shifting what educators do on a day-to-day basis with students identified as learning disabled. The entire section promotes changing from a "specialized" curriculum that usually focuses on using a menu of strategies that oversimplify the teaching/learning process to a curriculum that focuses on the individual learners, what they need, and their patterns of learning. This section promotes an enhanced understanding of the learning process itself and making curriculum changes based on what is now known about how children learn.

The accompanying chapters afford readers the opportunity to "see" classrooms in which students are successfully learning. Readers are given a number of curricular strategies and activities that can be easily adapted and used in their classrooms so that the theory is also understood from a practical basis. The curricular discussions reflect content standards that have been developed by national organizations for nondisabled learners. We believe that students with learning disabilities deserve to have access to a rich, broad-based curriculum.

11

Necessary Conversations: Reframing Support in General Education Classrooms for Students With Learning Disabilities

Elizabeth Althardt

Recently, after a summer lunch with my friend Jennifer, a general education teacher, we sat talking in my car. Several years ago, we had been co-teachers in an inclusionary language arts class. That we were still able to maintain a friendship throughout an absolutely hellish year of inclusion was a testament to our collective determination to try to make inclusion work.

The year had not gone well. I was a special education teacher; she was a general educator. We had individual agendas for our kids, and they didn't seem to fit well together. There was absolutely no direction given to us. Nor was there a schoolwide inclusionary framework or operating guidelines to help us organize ourselves. I was angry; she was angry. I thought that she moved too quickly through the curriculum guidelines. She thought that I coddled the kids.

The students suffered the brunt of our frustration. Though they were in a general education classroom, they had two separate teachers with two separate sets of expectations. Jennifer taught her kids, and I taught mine. The class degenerated into two classes within one, exactly what all my college textbooks stated was the quintessential "no-no" regarding inclusionary practices. When my department chair graciously asked me to write down my teaching preferences for the following year, the only thing that I wrote, using bold, highlighted, and italicized letters, was, "I do not want to co-teach in an inclusionary classroom." In many ways, it had been a frustrating and unproductive year.

Frustration is not new to me. As a special education teacher, I offer my middle school students a unique perspective: Not only do I teach students with learning disabilities, but I, too, have a learning disability. I was diagnosed with dyslexia at the age of 13. My perplexed parents finally had an answer to why their oldest daughter preferred writing upside down and backward, still couldn't tell the time in eighth grade, and wore her shoes on the wrong feet. My dyslexia, in retrospect, has been my greatest teacher and has allowed me to deepen my sense of empathy for students who struggle academically and socially in school.

Although the memories of my classmates snickering still mortify me, I am the one who is truly enjoying the last laugh. On the first day of each semester, I announce to my new students, "Everyone in here has been diagnosed with some sort of learning disability, including me." Eyebrows lift. On their blasé faces, I observe a flicker of masked curiosity. As I confess that I didn't know my right from my left until I was a teenager, smiles emerge, and an occasional "Me, either!" punctuates the air. By the time I write upside down and backward for them, shouts of "That's wild!" and "Hey, Mrs. A's LD [learning disabled], too!" reverberate throughout the room. The process of connecting has begun. I tell my kids that no mistake on their part will shock me, because I've probably made the same mistake myself. Suddenly an implicit bond is formed. We aren't learning disabled; we all simply share special talents and learn differently. I also tell them that the road to success will not be easy and will sometimes be extremely lonely, especially since other kids and teachers will view them as less capable.

Though new federal legislation has created opportunities for students with learning disabilities to participate in meaningful ways in general education environments, negative attitudes persist as to the viability of inclusionary approaches. Moreover, these pejorative attitudes can be exacerbated when instructional conditions do not support a collaborative teaching format. My first experience trying to teach with my general education partner, Jennifer, is a testament to how difficult a collaborative teaching format can be and how that difficulty can translate into misperceptions and, potentially, the demise of this potentially powerful methodology.

I have learned a great deal since my first inclusion class with Jennifer. In this chapter, I seek to eliminate some of the miscommunication that too often results in poor organizational and instructional practices in inclusive classrooms. It is my hope that the chapter will help teachers to sidestep some of the issues that deflated Jennifer and me in our most difficult year of co-teaching together.

A Context for Change

Philosophically, inclusion means that educators are committed to educating students in general education classrooms as much as possible. However, without a clear foundation in co-teaching models, alternative assessment, and powerful teaching strategies, inclusionary efforts can flounder on the shoals of good intention.

Though general education classes are burgeoning with students who are at risk for school failure and who have special needs, current schoolwide principles, policies, and procedures do not create an environment wherein two teachers can effectively plan and work together. I have, for example, taught in inclusionary classrooms where, due to administrative fiat, one half of the class was made up of learners with cognitive and behavioral disabilities. This is not inclusion; it is an instructional nightmare for both students and teachers alike. For inclusionary practices to become a mainstay on public school campuses, program coordination issues, such as administrative support, planning time, and equitable distribution of students must be addressed in a forthright manner, rather than as an afterthought.

Moreover, there is a lack of good teacher training in college courses regarding how to bridge the gap between special and general education through collaborative efforts by classroom teachers. In the classroom, teachers are "thrown" together haphazardly with no common preparation time or insight into how to work side by side. This places an undue burden on both the general and special education teacher.

So, how do we reduce the burdens and barriers associated with inclusion? An initial and fundamental step is to make certain that teachers choose to work together. Once that happens, they must agree on parameters, ranging from discipline to grading, prior to beginning this ambitious undertaking. Often the simple act of sharing ideas about room setup, duties, and responsibilities can offset potential conflicts of interest.

Further, the special education teacher must be familiar with and able to articulate to the general education teacher how and why a particular learner can profit from special education. The teachers should be able to discuss testing and portfolio results, learner strengths, and areas in need of improvement. More important, the special education teacher should be able to explain how a student's individualized education program (IEP) goals and objectives fit with the core curriculum of study. If special educators are informed, can speak cogently and persuasively regarding a child's particular goals and objectives, and have a variety of instructional strategies to help all students in a general education class, then they can truly be seen as professional equals, not as teacher aides—a common misperception among unaware students and teachers.

In addition, the general education teacher should be familiar with and able to articulate to the special educator the general education course requirements. The general education teacher should explain how those requirements will be taught on a daily, weekly, and monthly basis. If the special education teacher is cognizant of what areas of the curriculum will be addressed during the week, he or she can make the necessary modifications pursuant to each student's IEP. By specifying guidelines, both teachers will be able to focus on key instructional areas. Such guidelines will help to prevent such common complaints as special education teachers move too slowly, wanting mastery of the subject, while general education teachers move too quickly, regardless of student comprehension.

When teachers choose to work together, it is essential that they maintain a flexible and open attitude. Initial planning sessions can center on sharing academic strengths and weaknesses with each other. By sharing personal competencies, a dual sense of classroom ownership emerges. What appear at first to be major differences of opinion often disappear.

Discussing and agreeing upon the following questions is the first step in the process of building an instructional framework to serve all students in the general education classroom and an important step in pushing for schoolwide collaboration between special and general education teachers. These questions should be revisited periodically during a collaborative arrangement.

Important Questions for Special and General Educators to Discuss Prior to and During a Collaborative Arrangement

What Are the Goals That We as Teachers Have for Our Students?

As a special educator, I want my students with learning disabilities to build upon their current strengths and skills. For instance, standard language arts curricula are fraught with details and distractions, creating innumerable problems for students with learning disabilities. Often students with learning disabilities have difficulty sifting through large amounts of information and discerning what is truly important. My job as a special educator is to sort classroom information into what is conceptually essential and nonessential. I base my decisions on three points: (a) the student's level of academic functioning, (b) my school district's directives, and (c) what I use every day as a working adult. Since my orientation is student centered rather than grade-level-curriculum oriented, initial conversations with my co-teachers can be a bit tense as we begin to define our roles and establish unified goals. Patience is a virtue when teachers begin to share turf and philosophies.

How Can We Combine Our Individual Wants Into a Cohesive Co-Teaching Goal?

As a result of the amendments to the Individuals With Disabilities Education Act passed in 1997, all students in special education must participate in the general education curriculum. Further, the law affords general and special educators the opportunity to combine instructional interests and talents. Since many school districts have written curriculum guidelines and a listing of competencies that each student should be able to demonstrate before moving to the next grade or level, it makes prudent sense to share expertise. I concentrate my efforts on areas of the curriculum that my students will need to know after their formal schooling has been completed. I do this without watering down the curriculum or tracking my students into a lower level. In fact, since I am an advocate of co-teaching, and enjoy this instructional arrangement, my students participate in general education across the board. Pullout from the mainstream is temporary and used for skill-building purposes.

How Do We Make Modifications to the Curriculum to Ensure that IEP Goals and Objectives Are Met?

By taking the time to plan as well as by ensuring that the students grasp the curriculum, both teachers can make the necessary instructional modifications to help students with learning disabilities meet their goals and objectives. The bottom line for me is that, as a special education teacher, I am responsible for IEP compliance and for ensuring that each one of my students receives the services mandated by law. The general education teacher is responsible for making sure that all students meet grade-level expectations. By combining our special talents and knowledge, we help students gain a better understanding of what is expected of them academically.

What Is Our System of Assessment, and Is It Different for Students With Learning Disabilities?

I believe in keeping my students' assessments as close to those of their general education peers as possible. Unless a modification is necessary for a reason specified in a student's IEP, my students take the same tests and quizzes and write the same papers as their classmates. When curricular modifications become necessary, my co-teacher and I meet individually with the student and ask for input to ascertain what he or she believes would be an accurate reflection of his or her knowledge and ability. We either agree with the student's self-evaluation or offer other suggestions. With this arrangement, the student begins to see that his or her input is valued and prized and that minor accommodations can often increase the likelihood for success.

Which of Us Is in Charge of Which Activities?

Once again, planning is essential. An effective way for the special and general education teachers to divide the daily, weekly, and course teaching tasks is to capitalize on their individual strengths and weaknesses. For example, if one teacher likes to give the weekly vocabulary and the other doesn't, the teacher who enjoys that activity should be responsible for it. Basic instructional tasks and classroom management can be accounted for in this commonsense manner, which frees the teacher not conducting the activity to spend more intensive time with students. I suggest that teachers check with each other periodically to ensure that the workload is equitable. What sounds short or easy in theory may be longer and more difficult in reality. For tasks that both teachers consider undesirable, the work can be divided according to the demands of each teacher's work schedule.

How Do We Approach Classroom Discipline?

When working together, teachers need to negotiate and agree upon a consistent response to problem behaviors in the classroom. Which behaviors require disciplinary measures? What consequences will be applied for which behaviors? These questions are important to answer, because behaviors that truly irritate one teacher may not faze the other teacher at all.

Discipline and classroom management are difficult enough for one teacher. With two teachers, the potential difficulties multiply. Therefore, when collaborating, it is important for the teachers to write down their collective classroom expectations, procedures, and policies. Since special education often requires additional documentation for students with behavioral problems, the general education teachers should be apprised of any such requirements. A question to start the conversation about discipline and classroom management might be, How do we want to setup rules and expectations in the classroom? Along those lines, student input should be solicited. Once behavioral expectations are clear, the discipline policy should be posted where everyone in the classroom can see it. A copy should be given to each student and sent home or shared at open house. Friction and guesswork are eliminated when everyone—students, parents, and teachers—is cognizant of classroom expectations.

How Do We Decide Which of Us Will Be the "Point Person" in Problematic Interactions?

Despite the best efforts to eliminate academic and behavioral difficulties, problems do occur. Parents become angry, administrators override teachers' decisions, kids give teachers trouble. When dealing with such problem areas, one teacher could be appointed as the spokesperson and the other as the "quiet supporter." In the case of upset parents or angry administrators, the two teachers need to decide what their united-front response will be. This will reduce the "he said/she said" manipulations, third-party information, and political struggles that characterize some schools. Once the point person has been designated, that teacher should explain the agreed upon position, and the other teacher should silently support him or her.

Summary

There is no magic formula for developing good working relationships between co-teachers. Each co-teaching situation is different and requires different responses. However, the key to unlocking the power of co-teaching revolves around answering the questions posed in this chapter and myriad other questions that will arise throughout the process. If co-teachers agree on individual goals, interests, strengths, and "pet peeves" as well as provide a forum for ongoing conversations to take place, they will have paved the way for powerful learning experiences for all students.

12

"Traigan sus vidas, yo traigo la mía"[1]: Shared Reading for Older Emergent Readers in Bilingual Classrooms

Tomás Enguídanos and Nadeen T. Ruiz

Historically, and continuing to the present, children in the primary grades receive the lion's share of attention and resources in learning to read. This makes sense: Young, early readers have a head start in achieving well not only in literacy skills but in school in general. However, as inner-city, middle-grade teachers will readily attest, emergent readers make up a part of their intermediate classrooms as well. The challenge, then, becomes providing effective early reading instruction to older students whose interests and motivation often differ widely from those of 5- and 6-year-olds.

We do not expect any of this to be news to special education teachers. Part of the charge of special educators has always been to work with older, struggling readers to help them become strategic, effective, and enthusiastic readers. The data on how well this goal has been accomplished are disheartening, however. Though there have been successes with individual students, the aggregated data do not show widespread improvement in reading and writing achievement of students in special education (Skrtic, 1991). The picture for special education students from culturally and linguistically diverse (CLD) backgrounds is even worse in terms of reading and writing test scores (Figueroa, 1992).

---
[1] "Bring Your Life [experiences], I'll Bring Mine"

We focus our work as educators precisely in this area of literacy instruction for CLD students in general and special education. Both of us are associated with a literacy program called the Optimal Learning Environment (OLE) Project (Ruiz, Garcia, & Figueroa, 1996; Ruiz & Figueroa, 1995). Tomás teaches students with learning disabilities in a special day class and is a teacher leader with the OLE Project. Nadeen was involved in the OLE Project's inception in 1989 and has directed the project since 1994 (Ruiz, 1989, 1995a, 1995b). Together, we have trained many special and general education teachers throughout the southwest and in Mexico on how to provide CLD students with an optimal learning environment. We have also written together for our field. For example, we collaborated on an article about Arturo, Tomás's student, who at 9 years of age, began the year at the scribbling stage of writing and progressed within a few months under the OLE Project, to become a prolific writer of various genres, including poetry fashioned after the odes of Pablo Neruda (Ruiz & Enguídanos, 1997).

In this chapter we share with you another product of our collaboration, an instructional strategy called Shared Reading for Older Emergent Readers (also known simply as Shared Reading). This strategy is one of a number of powerful techniques that we have found helps to move older emergent readers to fluency, comprehension, and enthusiasm and confidence as readers.

Nadeen begins the chapter by contextualizing Shared Reading within the research base underlying the OLE literacy program. She also points out that Shared Reading is only one of a number of instructional strategies associated with increased reading and writing achievement among students in OLE classrooms and should be used in conjunction with the other techniques to the greatest extent possible.

Tomás then shares, teacher-to-teacher, his classroom approach to using Shared Reading as he has developed it with the inner-city, Spanish-English bilingual students in his special day class. He begins by telling of his initial doubt regarding the appropriateness for his intermediate students of Shared Reading—an instructional strategy typically used with preschool and primary grade children. Tomás follows this with a classroom literacy story of reflection and change. Staying true to the theory and research behind using Shared Reading with emergent readers, Tomás has made the strategy an integral part of how he helps his older, struggling readers "break the code." Tomás details the procedures he uses so that others may implement this strategy in their own classrooms.

Research on Effective Literacy Instruction for Linguistically Diverse Students in Special Education

In a number of recent publications I (Nadeen) have extensively reviewed the research base for literacy instruction for bilingual students in special education classrooms (Ruiz, 1995b, Ruiz, 1999). In all of these reviews, I noted the growing body of naturalistic studies, ones in which researchers have spent extensive time in classrooms looking for co-occurrence relationships between bilingual students' language and literacy performance and instructional contexts. Although the research has taken place in several different states, the convergence of findings is striking.

In my most recent analysis of this research (Ruiz, 1999), I found that four overarching principles have arisen from the classroom studies of bilingual students in special education that can guide us toward optimal instruction. In the following sections, I briefly explain these principles, linking them to the research base in both bilingual special education and second language education.

Principle 1: Connect Students' Background Knowledge and Personal Experiences With Literacy Lessons

Many studies of bilingual students in special education have noted that students improve their language and literacy performance when lessons tap into and build on their experiences and background knowledge (Echevarría & McDonough, 1995; Flores, Rueda, & Porter, 1986; Goldman & Rueda, 1988; Graves, Valles, & Rueda, 2000; López-Reyna, 1996; Rueda & Mehan, 1986; Ruiz, 1995a, 1995b; Willig & Swedo, 1987). That this finding has been validated many times over is not surprising, especially when it is viewed from a second language acquisition (SLA) perspective. Research on SLA has documented consistently that second language learners improve various aspects of their reading performance when their background knowledge is elicited or built up before they approach a text (Au, 1993; Barnitz, 1986).

Principle 2: Foster the Use of Students' Primary Language (L1) in Literacy Lessons

The rationale for using students' primary language for instruction is buttressed by studies in both bilingual special education (Echevarría & McDonough, 1995; Flores et al., 1986; Goldman & Rueda, 1988; Graves, Valles, & Rueda, 2000; López-Reyna, 1996; Rueda & Mehan, 1986; Ruiz, 1995a, 1995b; Viera, 1986; Willig & Swedo, 1987) and bilingual general education (Greene, 1998; Ramírez, Pasta, Yuen, Billings, & Ramey, 1991; Thomas & Collier, 1996). In short, when instructed in their native language, bilingual students show improved language and literacy skills. Further, as shown by the bilingual general education studies just cited, these language and literacy skills transfer to the students' second language.

Principle 3: Create Opportunities for Students to Meaningfully and Authentically Apply Their Developing Oral Language and Literacy Skills

The research in both bilingual special education (Echevarría & McDonough, 1995; Flores et al., 1986; Goldman & Rueda, 1988; Graves, Valles, & Rueda, 2000; López-Reyna, 1996; Rueda & Mehan, 1986; Ruiz, 1995a, 1995b; Viera, 1986; Willig & Swedo, 1987) and second language education (see reviews in Chaudron, 1988, and Tharp, 1997) has made an exceedingly strong case that language and literacy instruction for second language learners must begin in a meaningful context. Simply put, second language learners do poorer in instructional contexts in which oral language, reading, and writing are removed from any real communicative intent and in which reading and writing are formatted into drills and worksheets. Second language researchers and teachers have known this anecdotally since the failure of the drill-oriented second language methods of the 1960s and 1970s, and empirically since the late 1980s (Chaudron, 1988). The bilingual special education studies cited earlier have also validated this for second language learners in research beginning in the 1980s and continuing to the present.

This principle is an extremely important one in the face of current literacy instruction trends. National media have pushed a reading instruction agenda that highlights decontextualized phonics as a way of reversing underachievement in reading. They repeatedly cite an unpublished manuscript by Foorman and colleagues (SRA McGraw-Hill, 1996) which purportedly showed that for an ethnically diverse group of general education students a decontextualized, systematic phonics program worked best in terms of their reading achievement. The Foorman study, however, is so flawed that drawing any strong conclusions from it is suspect. (See Taylor, 1998, for a thorough analysis of the Foorman study.) Most important, because of its flaws, it does nothing to counter the research from bilingual special and general education. Unlike the researchers listed earlier, Foorman did not identify which of her Hispanic subjects were Spanish speakers, nor did she provide information on their place of birth, age on arrival to the United States, languages spoken at home, or language proficiency in English and Spanish. Even the most rudimentary study of bilingual students includes this sort of information, given its impact on language and literacy achievement. Consequently, the research base for a meaning-driven literacy curriculum for second language learners in both special and general education remains uncontested.

Principle 4: Foster Increased Levels of Interaction (Oral Language, Reading, and Writing) Among Students and Teachers

Many studies in the bilingual special education area have explored what happens when teachers reverse the patterns of student passivity typical of remedial classrooms and instead organize their classrooms into highly interactive language and literacy settings (Echevarría & McDonough, 1995; Flores et al., 1986; Goldman & Rueda, 1988; Graves, Valles, & Rueda, 2000; Gutiérrez & Stone, 1997; López-Reyna, 1996; Ruiz, 1995a, 1995b; Willig & Swedo, 1987). All of these studies share a common conclusion: Students experience greater growth in language and literacy skills when they can actively initiate extended turns of oral language, reading, or writing or when they can collaborate with others in classroom literacy events. The literature from second language instruction validates this principle, with multiple studies showing the advantage of collaborative contexts for language and literacy as opposed to teacher-dominated, student-passive contexts (TESOL, 1997).

Special educators looking to reverse the underachievement trends among bilingual students would do well to incorporate these overarching principles in designing effective literacy programs for their students. A few literacy projects have already heeded this research base, such as AIM for the BEST, developed at the University of Texas at Austin (Ortiz, Wilkinson, Robertson-Courtney, & Kusher, 1991). In the following section I describe another such project—the Optimal Learning Environment Project located at California State University Sacramento—which provided the context for Tomás's and my collaboration.

Research-Based, Effective Literacy Instruction: The OLE Project

The OLE Project is a program of balanced literacy instruction for culturally and linguistically diverse students in general and special education (Ruiz, García, & Figueroa, 1996). The project began in 1988, when the California State Department of Education asked a team of researchers to address the underachievement of Latino students in special education (Figueroa, Ruiz, & Rueda, 1988). Using the four principles described earlier, as well as others derived from the areas of bilingual education and second language education, the project identified 12 optimal conditions for effective literacy instruction of bilingual students (Table 12.1). The project then identified instructional strategies that helped to create those optimal conditions in classrooms. Subsequently, the OLE Project was further encouraged to include general educators in its trainings, given the finding that special education students sometimes returned from an accelerated, enriched, OLE special education classroom to a very remedial, instructionally poor, general education classroom (Ruiz & Figueroa, 1995).

The instructional strategies that the OLE Project currently emphasizes in its trainings are the following: Interactive Journals, Roll-Call Variation (phonemic awareness and early phonics activities), ABC Wall Charts, Shared Reading, Guided Reading, Literature Study Circles, Drop Everything and Read Time, Shared Writing, Creating Text With Wordless Books, and Writers' Workshop. However, this list is very dynamic. At the core of the OLE Project are the research-derived optimal conditions. As long as a proposed instructional strategy helps to create most of the conditions in the classroom, we consider its use with our students.

To make clear the OLE Project's strong link between theory and practice, I now describe generally the instructional strategy Shared Reading, the focus of this chapter, and show how it helps to create optimal conditions for bilingual students' literacy learning.

Shared Reading as a Link Between Classroom Research and Practice

In 1979, Don Holdaway, a literacy researcher from New Zealand, coined the term *Shared Reading*. He had spent months observing primary teachers approximate in their classrooms what has been called the "bedtime story routine," that is, the routine in which a parent and child interactively read and talk through a book. The

TABLE 12.1
Shared Reading as Part of an Optimal Learning Environment

Optimal Conditions for Learning	How Shared Reading in Tomas's Class Creates Optimal Conditions
1. Student Choice Students exercise choice in their learning when possible, such as by selecting writing topics, books, research projects, and thematic cycles.	Students negotiate the choice of poems that they will work with during Shared Reading. They select sections of poems that they connect with and want to discuss. They choose how and what to write in, for example, their reflection journals.
2. Student-Centered Instruction Lessons begin with and revolve around students' personal experiences, background knowledge, and interests.	Tomás often introduces the poems by eliciting or building up relevant background knowledge. Students immediately make personal connections with lines of the poems.
3. Whole-Part-Whole Approach Lessons begin with whole texts (e.g., books, poems, newspaper articles) to maximize the construction of understanding, then move to the analysis of smaller units of language forms (e.g., phonics, spelling, punctuation), and then return to the text as a whole.	Poems and songs constitute the primary texts for Shared Reading. Once students understand them, Tomás "decontextualizes" the texts by separating them into smaller units of language—words, phonemes, graphemes, onset/rimes, affixes, etc.—and uses smaller units to teach word recognition and spelling skills.
4. Active Participation Students actively engage in lessons with frequent and long turns of talk.	Students must explain their choices, personal connections to, and opinions about the texts to the learning community. They chorally reread the text many times.
5. Meaning First, Followed by Form Students construct meaning from (reading) or through (writing) text first, then move to a focus on correct forms of language such as spelling and grammar.	Tomás first works on comprehension of the poems and the students' personal responses to them. Then he emphasizes the decoding and spelling aspects of texts, working on sound-symbol correspondences, onset and rime patterns, spelling, etc.
6. Authentic Purpose The end products of lessons have a real-life function that often extends beyond the classroom; There are real audiences and real purposes.	Tomás and his students may create an innovation on the poem or song's pattern, their own class book, or a performance to be shared with people outside of the classroom.
7. Approximations Students are encouraged to take risks and successively approximate language and literacy skills (following a developmental course).	In their reflection journals or in creating their own poems, students write at their own developmental level (e.g., prephonetic, transitional, etc.). Tomás selects developmentally appropriate reading skills as his focus in skill lessons with the texts.

TABLE 12.1
(Continued)

Optimal Conditions for Learning	How Shared Reading in Tomas's Class Creates Optimal Conditions
8. Immersion in Language and Print The classroom is saturated with different print forms and functions and with opportunities to hear and use language for a wide range of purposes.	From the initial stage of selecting the poems from the classroom walls, students see writing, often their own, posted throughout their room. This writing includes evidence of systematic phonics instruction.
9. Demonstrations Teachers demonstrate their own reading and writing and share their ongoing efforts with students.	Tomás explains to his students how he initially selects many of the texts through his own extensive reading of poetry. He also shares his own poetry writing.
10. Response Students receive timely responses to their oral and written texts that go beyond letter grades to personalized and thoughtful acknowledgements of their ideas, experiences, and efforts.	During Shared Reading, Tomás and his students come together daily to share and discuss their reading and writing. The students organize a special evening where they demonstrate Shared Reading for their parents.
11. Community Students, parents, and teachers form a community of readers, writers, and learners who explore a range of questions relevant to them.	Throughout all phases of Shared Reading, students receive immediate feedback to their orally-expressed ideas and written reflections. These responses constantly push the students toward more advanced language mechanics and deeper content.
12. High Expectations Teachers, parents, and the students themselves expect that the students will become proficient and independent speakers, readers, and writers.	Tomás expects that all of his students will learn to decode and comprehend the different texts used for Shared Reading and will transfer those skills to other literacy events.

teachers in Holdaway's teacher study group had developed a way of modifying this typically one-on-one routine to accommodate their classrooms full of children (Holdaway, 1982). One especially helpful modification was to use enlarged texts so that all children could see both the print and the pictures as the teacher and children co-constructed meaning from the text. The current proliferation of Big Books in primary classrooms is a direct result of Holdaway's work with teachers.

Researchers established years ago the relationship between a bedtime story routine and early development of literacy. In such a literacy event, children build up their knowledge of story structure, "booklike" talk, connections between texts and the world, concepts about the way print works, phonemic awareness, and even early word recognition skills—all important precursors to independent reading. Primary teachers can quickly pick out those students who have been read to frequently and intensively. But it is equally clear that not all children have had the same access to books and literacy events, making Shared Reading critically important to establish as a classroom routine.

The *OLE Curriculum Guide* (Ruiz, García, & Figueroa, 1996), as well as almost every current reading methods textbook, contains a section describing traditional Shared Reading procedures. Briefly, the teacher introduces a book by conducting discussions about the cover's pictures and title and inviting the students to predict the story's content. In this introductory phase, the teacher also attempts to have students personally connect to the book. For example, in introducing a story about a lost duckling, a teacher may say, "Before we begin to read this story, let me ask whether any of you have ever been lost. How did that feel? What did you do?" The teacher then begins to read the book to the students, continuing to elicit predictions and personal connections throughout. At the end of the first reading, the teacher and students discuss their reactions to the book. Then, rather than shelving the book, the teacher rereads it on subsequent days, following the readings with developmentally appropriate lessons on literacy skills and strategies. These lessons can focus on phonemic awareness, phonics, punctuation, sight words, and so on. To make these rereadings attractive, teachers seek out books with texts that are conducive to choral rereadings, such as rhyming texts and texts with repetitive patterns that are fun to read aloud.

In a nutshell, Shared Reading creates the opportunity for all students to develop key early literacy skills listed above in a highly interactive context with the support of more expert readers such as the teacher and, often, other students. It is a very "dense" literacy strategy given both the long list of skills that it teaches (it is difficult to call to mind a prepackaged, remedial reading kit that could promise the same) and its connections to literacy acquisition theory (e.g., Vygotsky's observations (Moll, 1992) that language and literacy development occur first on the interpersonal plane, with assistance from a more expert person, and then on the intrapersonal or independent level of performance).

The OLE Project selected Shared Reading as one of its key literacy strategies based on how it has helped teachers to create the 12 optimal conditions the project identified for effective literacy instruction of bilingual students. The ways in which Shared Reading facilitates these conditions are described in Table 12.1. The table also describes Tomás's application of Shared Reading with his older emergent students in special education as a means of both explicating the link between classroom research and practice, and previewing Tomás's description of his modification of traditional Shared Reading.

Implementing Shared Reading for Older Emergent Readers

Why implement Shared Reading with poetry? A teacher recently told me (Tomás), "I don't think I even like reading poetry myself." For many people, experience with poetry in school has not been particularly positive. We are given poems to read from a textbook and we answer the questions at the end of the selection without connecting to the poem. In most cases, there is little choice of material to read. And after we read the poem and answer the questions, the well-meaning teacher or professor begins to interpret the poem's meaning according to literary criticism. I think that poets likely find this humorous or preposterous. As a student, I always had my own interpretation that I tried to defend, but my reaction or what I brought to the poem as the reader was often considered less than valuable. I always found this mysterious and frustrating.

When I began working with the OLE Project, I avoided the strategy of Shared Reading, because the predictable texts that were traditionally used with this strategy were written for emergent readers in early elementary grades. I worked with older emergent readers in upper elementary and felt that the predictable texts were belittling to my students. I didn't want to talk down to them. Nadeen challenged me to find texts that were appropriate for my students, because she felt they really needed the balanced approach to reading skills and reading strategies that shared reading offered. One day in a workshop, she began a Shared Reading talk with Maya Angelo's "Life Doesn't Frighten Me." Nadeen introduced the poem with an incredibly frightening and moving story of a time when she and her family witnessed an armed robbery in a convenience store. Maya Anglelo's chilling poem further made my hair stand up on the back of my neck. I saw that the poem is predictable with rhyming and repetitive text yet has a theme to which my students could connect, because of all they see and have become accustomed to as inner-city youth. I was inspired (as I so often am by my colleagues in OLE) to try the poem out on them. Here was a predictable text that I could bring to life in Shared Reading. The strategy that I now use in my classroom began with and evolved from working with this poem.

As I dove into poetry, inspired by Nadeen's workshop I began to see the poetry in everyday life. I realized that it existed in the moment when Nadeen witnessed the robbery. I saw that the street has a rhythm as I walk to lunch each day. The sights, the sounds, the smell, the textures, all of these come together in poetic elements, images, and moments. As I began to view the images that were present in the moments in my life, I realized that these were symbols of all that I must learn. They were symbols or signs that life had placed before me. The images of daily life for the poet are the potter's clay, the carpenter's wood (see "Poetic elements" later in this chapter).

We all have poetry in our lives. It is in the symbols placed before us that to each of us have a unique set of meanings and connections, if we open our eyes, ears, and hearts. We are touched. This is the muse, or inspiration.

Octavio Paz, in a book titled *El Arco y la Lira,* discussed the confusion that exists between poetry and poems. He wrote that there is poetry without poems; a landscape, people, and occurrences can be poetic. They are poetry without being poems. When poetry is seen as a condensation of chance or a crystallization of forces and circumstances independent of the will of the poet, we encounter the poetic moment. When, either passively or actively, awake or dreaming, the poet is the conductive wire and transformer of the poetic current, we are in the presence of something entirely different: a poetic work. For these reasons Paz stated that a poem is not a literary form but rather the encounter between "man" and the poetic moment.

We all encounter poetic moments in our lives. Bringing poetry into the classroom and sharing its vivid language with our students gives voice to the poetic moments each of us has experienced. The poet's voice models precise language for describing the students' own experience. I use these texts because they are age-appropriate—and motivational.

Management

In a typical week in my classroom Shared Reading fits into two parts of our daily classroom management routine. First we begin each day with our morning community circle in which poems or songs are introduced to the students. This daily celebration of the language of poets and song-writers sets a tone for creative use of language and leads to the selection on Friday of one poem or song for the following week's in-depth study in the Shared Reading with Poetry literacy center. The poem which students help to select is studied in the literacy center for five days. Figure 12.1 shows where in the daily class schedule the teacher might fit both Circle Time and Literacy Center rotations. The Shared Reading with Poetry Literacy Center weekly plan is detailed in figure 12.2 (p. 210). A center activity typically lasts for 40–50 minutes. Our centers have included Shared Reading with Poetry, Interactive Journals, and Writer's Workshop rotating with Drop Everything and Read (independent reading) or literature studies extension activities.

Figure 12.1 provides a general view of our week. Depending on the time of year and where our studies have led us, we might put more emphasis on literature studies and Writer's Workshop and less on Shared Reading of Poetry and Interactive Journals.

Selecting Poems, Songs and Poets

If Shared Reading with Poetry and Song is to be implemented there need to be some structures in the classroom for selecting poems and songs, having students react to them, and for in-depth study of the selected pieces. The following list illustrates structures I have used during circle time to select poems for later in-depth study in the "Shared Reading with Poetry" Literacy Center. These structures are described in detail in the following sections. The structures include:

1. Circle Time Read Aloud
2. Round-Robin Read
3. Sing Along
4. Drop Everything and Read (DEAR Time)/Poetry Dig with poetry mini-lesson

CIRCLE TIME READ ALOUD

It is important to make the language of poetry a regular part of your day with your students. In my class, I try out new poems and songs in the morning during circle

FIGURE 12.1
Daily Class Schedule

Time	Monday	Tuesday	Wednesday	Thursday	Friday
8:40– 9:00	Community circle/poem or song	Community circle/poem or song	Community circle/poem or song	Community circle/poem or song	Community circle/poem or song selection
9:00– 9:20	Daily news/ shared writing/ mini-lessons	Daily news/ shared writing/ mini-lessons	Daily news/ shared writing/ mini-lessons	Daily news/ shared writing/ mini-lessons	Library
9:20–10:00	Rotation 1 literacy centers	Rotation 1 literacy centers	Rotation 1 literacy centers	Rotation 1 literacy centers	Rotation 1 literacy centers
10:00–10:40	Rotation 2 literacy centers	Rotation 2 literacy centers	Rotation 2 literacy centers	Rotation 2 literacy centers	Rotation 2 literacy centers
11:00–11:40	Rotation 3 literacy centers	Rotation 3 literacy centers	Rotation 3 literacy centers	Rotation 3 literacy centers	Rotation 3 literacy centers
11:40–12:10	Literature studies	Literature studies	Writer's Workshop	Writer's Workshop	Computer lab scanning
12:10–12:50	Lunch	Lunch	Lunch	Lunch	Lunch
12:55– 1:10	Read aloud	Read aloud	Read aloud	Read aloud	Read aloud
1:10– 1:50	Math	Math	Math	Math	Math
1:50– 2:30	Science	Social studies	Science	Social studies	Science

time, introducing at least one a day. The circle is an intimate place in our classroom, where the students and I share the ups and downs of our lives. We may bring in favorite books, poems, and songs to share, including works in progress of our own creation. It has become a ritual that we always do the first thing in the morning. Sometimes we call an impromptu circle at other times of the day as well. *The important thing is to have a predictable time to celebrate the unpredictable language of poetry time to bring our voices and hearts together in a song.*

ROUND-ROBIN READ

Another effective means of sharing poetry is to invite two or three other adults into the circle to join you in reading poems to the children. You and the other adults are each armed with two or three poetry books, and you trade off reading, one person at a time. If you and the other adults aren't prepared ahead of time, just prior to circle time you can all skim through the books and mark several that you wish to try. Then

Time	Monday	Tuesday	Wednesday	Thursday	Friday
5–10 min.	Mark the line that moved you	Warm-up activity	Warm-up activity	Warm-up activity	Warm-up activity
10–20 min.	You bring your life, I'll bring mine	Lit. conversation	Poetic elements skill work	Poetic elements skill work	Las Vegas
10–30 min.	Written reflection	Director's chair	Extension activity I	Extension activity II	Performance/ presentation

FIGURE 12.2

A Week in the Shared Reading with Poetry Literacy Center

you can simply give them a go off-the-cuff. It's a fast paced whirlwind of poetry that is contagious. The students get caught up in listening and responding. You can really tell which poems grab them and which fall flat. It helps if the adults are comfortable reading poetry and read with expression. Some people prefer more rehearsal time. I know that I sometimes get nervous reading in front of the other adults. I try to overcome this by diving into the poem and feeling the words and rhythm.

SING ALONG

I've been a musician for years, but until we started working with Shared Reading I hadn't tapped into the power of songs for teaching reading. Music is a natural way to learn language in a soothing or an exciting and rhythmic, way. By sharing your own musical tastes or talents (e.g., your favorite compact disks or tapes), you open the door to a rich poetic form for Shared Reading. You can invite local musicians to join you and collaborate. You and the students can transcribe the lyrics and study what songwriters have to say. You can engage the class in singing: It's a great way to center your class in times of stress, to celebrate the "dance of joy" of life, and to teach reading on the sly.

There are many wonderful songs that can be used with shared reading strategy. Children love to sing, and singing helps them to memorize words. Once memorized, the words can be worked with out of context, focusing on word recognition and other skills. In Latin music it is not unusual to find songs that come directly from the words or inspiration of Latin poets. Indeed, many poems (including those in English) have a rhythm that can be sung naturally. We sometimes sing, chant, or rap poems to practice reading them.

There are many web sites dedicated to song lyrics. Here are a few of my favorites:

http://www.lyrics.ch/
http://condorito.metro.msus.edu/artistas.html
http://www.uclm.es/~jaiglesi/

http://www.geocities.com/CapitolHill/6590/index.html
http://spin.com.mx/~luisg/Pablo/
http://planetx.bloomu.edu/%7Egmalbert/songlyrics/
http://tinpan.fortunecity.com/petebest/10/lyrics.html
http://www.deltablues.com/blues.htm
http://www.superior.net/~jimligon/lyrics/Rhythm_and_Blues/
http://www.fiftiesweb.com/lyrics/lyrics.htm

Rap musicians are the poets of today's youth. I personally like rap, although I have trouble reconciling the feelings many of the songs evoke. I know of family members of students, current and former, who have been gunned down by the violence of the streets. Rap music often glorifies this violence, but I believe it also lays bare what is happening to many young people. I ask my students to bring in music that they would like to study. Sometimes we get into conflicts about the lyrics. My ground rules are that the songs cannot disrespect women, disrespect people's lives, or promote violence. I also rule out songs that contain language that is inappropriate for school. My students, however, have struggled with these limitations. They feel the songs I've ruled out tell the truth, and they like them. They tell me that I said they could bring in their favorites. They feel I am censoring. We have good discussions about these issues. I can honestly say that I haven't resolved them for myself. Nor have I explored the genre to its fullest extent. The following is a link to hip-hop lyrics: http://www.ohhla.com/index.htm.

DEAR TIME WITH MINI-LESSON/POETRY DIG

Drop Everything and Read (DEAR Time) mini-lessons are short, 3–15 minute lessons that help guide students toward becoming excellent independent readers. The lesson can come at the beginning of DEAR Time, which is an independent reading period of about 15–20 minutes. The lesson can be on a specific type of poem, a poetic theme, a poetic element, or a poet. In the lesson you may model how it is that you find poets and poems that are meaningful to you as a reader. You can focus on how you read poetry, on what makes a particular poet your favorite, on what you would like to see the students doing with a partner or a group of friends as they immerse themselves in this genre. You can read poetry or compare and contrast poets and their poetic works.

Another strategy I use to get students immersed in poetry is the Poetry Dig. I have found that students are most eager to explore poetry books when the books and poems are arranged in an inviting way. I have a poetry section in our classroom library. But when I want to focus the children specifically on poetry, I arrange the poetry books in the library in tubs or on tables. I also provide access to poems previously studied through pocket chart versions (described later in this chapter) and through having available a large box of poems written on butcher paper.

GALLERY WALK

A fun way to immerse students in poetry (poems) and at the same time form working groups for in-depth poetry study is to conduct a Gallery Walk. In a Gallery Walk, the class peruses poetry on the classroom wall just as they would enjoy art in an art gallery.

There are many options for choosing the poems the students will read and discuss during the Gallery Walk. One option is to select poems that the students have heard and responded favorably to but have not yet studied in an in-depth way. Another option is to introduce new poems of a favorite poet students have already enjoyed. Because my students have needed help with reading the poems, I have had an adult or strong student reader stand at each poem to help the students enjoy them.

After the students have read all of the poems, I instruct them to group around the poem that most affected them, their favorite, or the one they would most like to study. The rule is that no more than four to six students can gather in front of any one poem. Although it is possible to use a different number of students, I have found that groups of four to six students are most effective, as they promote equitable and active participation for each student. My students have respected this limit without much grumbling, although sometimes we have to negotiate. It is most important that the students understand that they are selecting a poem for in-depth study and that each student must be prepared to contribute.

I instruct my students to attach a Post-it to the poem, indicating their name and the part of the poem that attracted them or made them react. Their comments on the Post-it will later help guide their written reflection and literature conversation, and the names listed help me keep track of who is working on each poem.

The groups of students then meet to discuss why they chose their particular poem. This is a form of an inclusion activity, since the students form affinity groups around a piece of good literature. They also tend to have deep conversations that lead to a deepening sense of community. In addition, it is a natural language lesson, because the students must put their feelings into words. In doing so, they act as models for one another. I have had an adult at each poem to facilitate the discussion and model the type of introspective response to the poem that I am looking for (i.e., "You bring your life, I'll bring mine"). However, I have found that once the students have learned the type of response I am after, they tend to want to facilitate their own discussion. This is good. When all have had a chance to share, the group members are instructed to go off individually to write, draw, and reflect in their poetry journals. These written reflections are enriched by the discussion they have had and are used for later activities, conversations, and creativity (writing, dramatizing, artwork, movement, etc.).

Following their reflection, we ask the students to go back to the poem and talk about what made the poem work for them (stylistic elements, imagery, rhythm, sound elements etc.).

Eliciting Personal Reaction/Constructing Meaning

What the reader brings to a poem is an essential part of the life of the poem. One's initial reaction leads to the discovery of poetic moments in one's own life. These moments are the source of inspiration for in-depth poetry study. They also inspire the emerging reader to take risks as a reader and writer.

Marking the Part of the Poem That Moves You: "You Bring Your Life, I'll Bring Mine" (MONDAY 5-10 MINUTES)

As just noted, each of us brings to a poem a poetic moment that connects with that of the poet. In Shared Reading, the teacher and other adults serve as facilitators or guides to the search for that moment, a moment in each student's life that he or she connects with the poem. I ask my students questions to elicit what they felt when hearing the poem as well as what they felt in their own poetic moment. I ask for examples from their lives that will help me and the class feel what they felt as a reader. Responding is at first difficult for some. But with practice, my students have learned to dive into both the poem and their lives. They stretch their vocabulary to try to put into words what they experienced and felt. They use the text as a fountain from which to draw fluid language, and they begin to approximate the language of the poet to describe poetic moments in their own lives.

Lauren O'Leary, a speech and language specialist who has collaborated with me during Shared Reading, was amazed at the depth of language she observed my students in a bilingual third- to fifth-grade Spanish bilingual class use during these discussions. As a result, she encouraged the deaf education teacher, Bea Worthen, to try the strategy with her deaf students. She related the following to me about how she and Bea conducted Shared Reading with poetry with these students:

> Bea and I talked [with the students] about what the overall poem meant to us (surprise, surprise, totally different interpretations), then picked our favorite lines, explained why, then requested the students do the same. I expected that the one fifth-grade student, Jasmine, would probably be able to make some kind of response that made sense but was not expecting anything too deep. With the other students, I was expecting off-the-wall responses, and that we would have to do pretty heavy-duty scaffolding with them to get a response that made some kind of sense. Then, much to our shock, as each student got up and made a response, not only did the responses make sense; they were beautiful and moving. The last student to get up was Nina (a student labeled with severe learning disabilities, attention deficit disorder, cerebral palsy, and deafness). She walked up to the chart, pointed to the word "green," and signed "green." She was very happy with herself. Bea and I congratulated her on knowing the word, and she went back to her seat. Jasmine was irate! She said to us, "That's not right. She's supposed to tell why she liked that line, not just read a word." We said something back to her to the effect that it was all right for Nina to just read the word, but Jasmine refused to accept that. Jasmine then started scaffolding for Nina, saying "Why did you pick that word? Is it because you like grass, and grass is green? Or is it because you don't like green things? Or why?" Nina then signed back, "No, favorite." Later, checking back with Pat (Nina's mother), it turned out that green was her favorite color. That was a turning point for me, because prior to that lesson, I was not certain of the student's capacity for higher order thinking. After that, both Bea and I realized that although they had a lot of syntactic difficulties and limited vocabulary in signing, there was a lot going on inside their minds that we had not been giving them the opportunity to express. It was a revelation. (from an e-mail correspondence from Lauren O'Leary)

Written Reflection (MONDAY 10-30 MINUTES)

After this initial discussion of the poem, everyone writes a reflection. Students and teachers can go deep into the thought and feelings, the memories, that the poem evoked in this reflection. I believe that this type of reflection is a tool we use to find our own voice as writers. With the help of expert writers, we dive into the important themes in our life and see what we uniquely have to say. Often, the students begin to approximate the language of the poet. Often, they go deeper than we imagined they could go. We just need to set up the proper conditions for this to occur.

Conversation/Literature Circle (TUESDAY 10-20 MINUTES)

The written reflections help the students to deepen their conversation about the poem. So, as a next step, I have the students take turns sharing where their reflections have taken them. The conversation is similar to other Literature Study Circle conversations (see the *OLE Curriculum Guide* [Ruiz et al., 1996] or Harvey Daniel's, 1994 *Literature Circles*). As each student takes a turn, the other students are to actively listen, question the speaker, and make connections to their lives and to other literature. After all the students have shared, I facilitate another look at the poem, helping the students to find a direction for further work with the poem. If, for example, one student's connection to a poem is particularly strong, with vivid images from a moment in his or her life, then I might ask that student to be the director in Director's Chair (see next section).

Director's Chair With
Response From an Audience (TUESDAY 10-30 MINUTES)

Some student responses to poetry and songs are so vivid and moving that they easily lend themselves to dramatization. The moment of feeling and inspiration that a poem evoked in a reader, the poetic moment for that reader, serves as a starting place for dramatizing the feeling of the poem. I have the student who seems most connected to the feeling of the poem, or the most inspired, lead the way. This student becomes the director of the activity (I am the executive producer). The student, using his or her written reflection or the part of the poem he or she selected as a prompt, initiates a casting call. The student tells the other students how many actors are needed and asks for volunteers for each role. It's the director's vision of the poem that will be brought to life, so he or she has to be able to describe to each character how to play the part.

In this activity, the audience plays an active role in helping the actors and the director to improve their performance. The audience members keep notes on strengths and areas that need improvement in the performance, and after the director gives the actors feedback, the audience is invited to share their notes with the actors. We use visual prompts to guide these comments—visual gauges with scales of 1–10 to help give actors feedback (see Figure 12.3). If, for example, our focus is on clarity of expression, the students give feedback in terms of the actor's performance volume, pitch, tension, and timing. A similar structure can be used for feedback

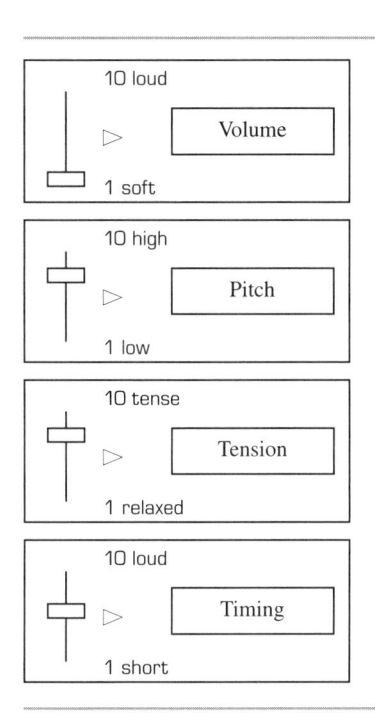

Volume, pitch, tension, and timing are important frames of reference for performers, whether speaking, singing, moving, or making sound effects. With a visual poster of adjustment knob settings, students can easily direct one another with immediate feedback. The settings can range from 1–10.

- ▶ At times, students are either too loud or too soft in their presentation. The class can suggest raising or lowering the volume.
- ▶ In adopting voices for presentations, students often change the tone or pitch of their voice. The class can suggest deepening or lowering the pitch.
- ▶ Tension refers to either body tension or mood of expression. At times, students speak in a calm voice when the words actually call for rage, sadness, or passion.
- ▶ Timing can refer to movement or to the speed in which a student speaks or reads a passage.

FIGURE 12.3

Scaffolding for Group Feedback in Director's Chair and in Other Performances (Tuesday)

on any type of class presentation or performance. The teacher can elicit from the class criteria for excellence in performing, and the students can then hold one another to those standards.

Skill Work: Daily Practice (5–10 MINUTES)

Warm-Ups

After having immersed ourselves in a poem and reacted to it according to our personal experiences, we play games with the words and phrases in the poem. These games include "find a word" games and reading games that encourage the students to read phrases in the poem aloud with varying interpretations of the feelings the words convey. These games are described in the following sections.

INITIAL AND FINAL SOUNDS/BLENDS. (WARM-UP ACTIVITY)

In daily warm-ups and later in pocket chart reading (described in a later section), I begin by asking the students to point to certain words of the poem and read them.

It's good to have Post-its for the large chart on which the poem is written and pieces of oak tag for the pocket chart, so that you can isolate certain parts of the word and encourage the students to sound them out. In Shared Reading, we work whole-part-whole (see Table 12.1, Condition 3), and now is when I jump into the fragments of the poem.

FIND A WORD (WARM-UP ACTIVITY)

Children seem to enjoy the challenge of finding words within a body of text. Depending on the developmental level of the student, the game may focus on beginning and ending sounds, words that have combinations of sounds (word families), or grammatical categories of nouns, verbs, adjectives, and so forth. In some cases, I give a definition of a word for a word search, so the students can develop their vocabulary while playing Find a Word.

With these games, the students overcome their fear of the written word and use a variety of cues to find the word you are asking for. Some rely mostly on visual cues, while others "read" the whole piece by memory, stopping at the correct word. Still others use the context to find the part of the poem in which they remember hearing the word used and thus narrow their search. Then they switch to visual cues. I make these cues explicit by celebrating the strength of each attempt, similar to the way I discuss solving math problems. This activity is quite revealing in showing the students' strengths as readers.

PHRASE MIRRORING (WARM-UP ACTIVITY)

Linda Carr, choreographer and dancer for the Performance Arts Workshop in San Francisco, helped us to focus on our reading of a poem. Knowing that the tone with which we read a poem affects our ability to reach an audience, she helped the students practice reading poetry by showing them a mirroring game involving partners. One partner faced the poem and read a line of the poem while the second partner, standing with his or her back to the poem, faced the reader and mirrored or repeated the performance of the line. If the reader felt that he or she had been mirrored precisely, then they would switch places and start the game again. We found that this game increased reading fluency. As students got into their interpretive reading they forgot their fear of reading aloud. They also became more expressive readers.

DANCING/CHOREOGRAPHY/MOVEMENT

Also with the support of Linda Carr, we found that words and phrases or sections of poems could be expressed nonverbally through movement. She took us through the warm-up activities that are usually associated with dance and theater and connected these to our study of literature, especially poetry. This required daily practice and discipline on the part of all of us. Linda celebrated when one of the students captured a poetic moment with clarity. These warm-ups led to students choreographing performance art with poetry.

LAS VEGAS (RECONSTRUCTING THE POEM IN THE POCKET CHART). (FRIDAY)

"Las Vegas" is a name I have given to a game involving pocket chart reading (see *OLE Curriculum Guide* [Ruiz et al., 1996]). I write the words of the poem on oak-tag strips, cut them apart, and place one line of words per pocket. I tend to work with one verse at a time; however, I attempt to provide one line per child. That is, I ask each student to be responsible for facilitating the reconstruction of one of the lines. To begin the game, I deal the words for one line to the students, who are sitting around the table like they are playing a card game. The student-facilitator for the line says the words of the line, one at a time, and asks the participants to look at their cards to see if they can find the word. The student who has the word comes to the chart and places it in the appropriate pocket. Only one student may come to the chart at a time. Student errors are viewed as teachable moments. I refer the student who made the error to the initial and ending sounds of both the word on the card he or she placed in the chart and the word we were looking for.

A different student facilitates each line, and students must correctly place punctuation on the cards and place the words in correct order. Mini-lessons come up around capital letters, consonant blends, diphthongs, word families, and vocabulary. The students continue until they have reconstructed the entire verse correctly.

Vocabulary. I personally don't believe in reviewing vocabulary before students have enjoyed a poem. I do, however, want my students to learn the words that are unfamiliar to them. Generally, our work with vocabulary comes after our initial conversations, but if a student asks what a word means, during an initial conversation, we discuss the meaning then.

After we have dealt with our initial reactions to the poem, we start to pick it apart day by day. During daily warm-ups, when I ask the students to point to a word, I sometimes ask them what the poet meant by that word. I may ask for examples, similes, or definitions. Sometimes I pull the vocabulary words out of the pocket chart, mix them up, and deal them out so that the students must place the right word in the right space in the poem.

Sentence/Grammatical Structure. When teachers isolate words by pulling them from pocket chart and then have the students place them back, the students naturally use syntactical or semantic cues to assist them in their effort. Watching the individual differences between students in determining how to reconstruct the poem or phrase is informative. Each student relies on the skill or cueing system that he or she has most developed. Some students are quite anxious when asked to reconstruct a part of the poem in the pocket chart. They feel that their status among their peers is on the line. They don't want to fail. A certain amount of this tension is, I believe, good for motivation, but I am, at the same time, trying to create an atmosphere where no one can fail because it is everyone's responsibility that everyone succeed. Thus, I insist that the students help one another. "We are all students, and we are all teachers." I tell them. I explain that they shouldn't feel ashamed if they don't know something, but they should feel ashamed if they have useful knowledge that they haven't shared with the other members of their community. They shouldn't feel badly if they try, only if they don't.

Once this ethic of collaboration is in place, students are free to be creative in how they solve the problem of learning to read. They begin to develop each of the cueing systems, because I as a teacher have set up their peers as models and teachers. Each of them has a strength or bag of tricks. I try to help them become aware of how it is that they are reading and what they can try when that doesn't work. When they become aware of their strengths, they naturally want to share them. They become the experts, and their status is raised to a new, more exciting level among their peers. I'm like that, too. I want to feel competent, and I want you to feel that way, too.

Performance and Extension (Going Public)

My students have a monthly audience for their work, the people who come to the monthly family meeting. I also try to set up other authentic opportunities for my students to present their hard work. I feel that an incentive to do work that is difficult is knowing that you will have an audience. Thus, we have school performances, we have poetry readings in the school or in bookstores or cafés, we set up displays, we perform for other classes, we invite important people to see our work (actually anyone who walks in the door is fair game). It's fun.

Getting Started Writing Poetry

If we make the rich language of poetry a viable part of our students' lives as readers in the classroom, then we will begin to see the students incorporating poetic elements into their own writing. In early literacy programs, teachers use the patterns of predictable text to create class books with innovations on the pattern. Picasso loved Velázquez' painting "Las Meninas." It was reportedly his favorite painting of all time. He spent an entire year painting innovations on this great work. If we want our students to become great writers, we must allow them to innovate on the works of their favorite writers as well.

Poetic Elements (Sound, Rhythm/Line, Imagery, Diction/Tone/Voice)

Poetic elements are the tools that the poet uses to connect to the poetic moment. In the moment of inspiration, the poet pulls out the tools that fit with his or her experience. For example, this morning I awoke realizing that all migratory birds don't fly south during the winter. The seeds of this realization originally came to me last year when I was in Brazil talking with a colleague about the weather, but the image about the birds came to me in a dream last night. I had been in São Paulo with some Brazilian teachers and asked one of them if it was warmer in Rio de Janeiro. My colleague politely explained that my way of viewing the world now must change because I am south of the equator. The further south you go, the colder it gets. From my dream, which was inspired by this conversation, I realized that if I write a poem about migratory birds from this new point of view, the migration would, at the very least, have a very different rhythm. It would be more like a pulse than north-south, south-north. It would be a pulse from equator to poles and back, as if the planet were exhaling and inhaling birds. It's a strong image that to me makes more sense than the way

I was taught that birds fly south. This is a very different image than one I might create based on the idea that birds only fly south in the winter, and I think the tone and the rhythm would be different as well. I now imagine the reunion of birds at the equator as a much bigger and more exciting event!

How a poet interprets an inspiration such as this depends on his or her style and the tools he or she knows how to use. In the hands of each poet, the moment is given a different treatment and is unique. The treatment is based on the poet's craft, skill, and life experience. One thing I know is that poems have existed regardless of culture or geographic location as long as poetic moments have coexisted with the poetic elements of sound, rhythm, imagery, and independent thought and style, or voice, and the poet.

The crafting of a poem is similar to the deconstruction of a poem in Shared Reading in that each poem is different. Each one has a different set of poetic elements to play with, to bring forth, and to study. I refer you to Georgia Heard (1989) and Mary Oliver (1994). By studying what they have to say about how poets use the poetic elements, you can better help your students learn from the poets they study.

Author Studies: Diction/Tone/Voice/Style

Over time we begin to recognize our favorite poets' style of writing. We try to make explicit what makes a poem special, what sets it apart in diction, tone, voice, and style.

Follow-up

At the end of the study of a poem, it is helpful to store the poem in a way that allows for easy access by both the students and the teacher. Teacher Rosina Tong laminates posters that she makes of the poems so that they can be hung like shirts in a clothing store. Her students use the laminated poems during DEAR Time. Teacher Dana Romo places completed poems in manila envelopes along with center activities for independent study. Teacher Margie Pollock makes poster-size versions of favorite (keystone) poems and puts them in a huge box that she makes available to the class. She also has these poems available on sentence strips for independent pocket-chart reading during DEAR Time or in literacy centers.

Summary

This chapter addresses the challenge of providing early reading instruction to older students whose interests and motivation often differ widely from those of 5 and 6 year olds. We have focused on the use of Shared Reading of poetry and song as appropriatae texts for 3rd–5th grade students. Of course students of this age will also greatly benefit from shared reading or guided reading with narrative, informational and expository texts, since they will need to develop comprehension strategies across a wide variety of texts to be successful in secondary school and later in college.

Shared reading with Older Emergent Students is one of a group of key literacy strategies used by the Optimal Learning Environment project (OLE) that helps teachers create optimal learning conditions through highly interactive activities which tap into the linguistic and cultural intelligence of each student. It is recommended that this strategy be used with other complementary literacy strategies to provide a complete balanced literacy program.

References

Au, K. H. (1993). *Literacy instruction in multicultural settings.* Orlando, FL: Harcourt, Brace, Jovanovich Publishers.

Barnitz, J. G. (1986). Toward understanding the effects of cross-cultural schemata and discourse structure on second language reading comprehension. *Journal of Reading Behavior,* 18, 95–113.

Chaudron, C. (1988). *Interactive language teaching.* Cambridge: Cambridge University Press.

Daniels, H. (1994). *Literature Circles. Voice and Choice in the Student-Centered Classroom.* York. Stenhouse Publishers.

Echevarría, J., & McDonough, R. (1995). An alternative reading approach: Instructional conversations in a bilingual special education setting. *LD Research and Practice, 10,* 108–119

Figueroa, R. A. (1992). *The failure of the special education reductionist paradigm: The unique case of California's resource specialist program.* Unpublished manuscript, California State University Sacramento, The OLE Project.

Figueroa, R. A. & Ruiz, N. T. (1993). Bilingual pupils and special education: A reconceptualization. In R. C. Eaves & P. J. McLaughlin (eds.) *Recent advances in special education and rehabilitation.* New York: Andover Medical Publishers, 73–87.

Figueroa, R. A., Ruiz, N. T., & Rueda, R. (1988). *Special education/demonstration project for Hispanic pupils: The OLE model.* Research Proposal University of California at Davis.

Flores, B., Rueda, R., & Porter, B. (1986). Examining assumptions and instructional practices related to the acquisition of literacy with bilingual special education students. In A. C. Willig & H. F. Greenburg (Eds.), *Bilingualism and learning disabilities* (pp. 149–165). New York: American Library.

Goldman, S., & Rueda, R. (1988). Developing writing skills in bilingual exceptional children. *Exceptional Children, 54,* 543–551.

Graves, A. W., Valles, E. C., & Rueda, R. (2000). Variations in writing instruction: A study in four bilingual special education settings. Learning Disabilities Research, 15(1), 1–9.

Greene, J. P. (1998). *A meta-analysis of the effectiveness of bilingual education.* Manuscript sponsored by the Thomás Rivera Policy Institute, University of Texas at Austin.

Gutiérrez, K., & Stone, L. D. (1997). A cultural-historical view of learning and learning disabilities: Participating in a community of learners. *LD Research and Practice, 12,* 123–131.

Heard, G. (1989). *For the Good of the Earth and Sun. Teaching Poetry.* Portmouth, N.H. Heinemann.

Holdaway, D. (1982). Shared book experience: Teaching reading using favorite books. *Theory Into Practice,* 21(4), p. 293–300.

López-Reyna, N. (1996). The importance of meaningful contests in bilingual special education: Moving to whole language. *LD Research and Practice, 11,* 120–131.

Moll, L. C. (1992). *Vygotsky and Education: Instructional Implications and Applications in Sociohistorical Psychology.* Cambridge, N.Y.: Cambridge University Press.

Oliver, M. (1994). *A Poetry Handbook.* San Diego. Harcourt Brace & Co.

Ortiz, A., Wilkinson, C. Y., Robertson-Courtney, P., & Kushner, M. I. (1991). *Aim for the BEST: Assessment and intervention model for the bilingual exceptional student.* Arlington, VA: Development Associates, Inc.

Ramirez, J. D., Pasta, D. J., Yuen, S., Billings, D. K., & Ramey, D. R. (1991). *Final Report: Longitudinal study of structural immersion strategy, early-exit, and late-exit transitional bilingual education programs for language-minority children.* Aguirre International Report to the U.S. Department of education, San mateo, California.

Rueda, R., & Mehan, H. (1986). Metacognition and passing: Strategic interaction in the lives of students with learning disabilities. *Anthropology and Education Quarterly,* 17, 145–165.

Ruiz, N. T. (1989). An optimal learning environment for Rosemary. *Exceptional Children, 56,* 130–144.

Ruiz, N. T. (1995a). The social construction of ability and disability: I. Profile types of Latino children identified as language learning disabled. *Journal of Learning Disabilities,* 28(8), 476–490.

Ruiz, N. T. (1995b). The social construction of ability and disability: II. Optimal and at-risk lessons in a bilingual special education classroom. *Journal of Learning Disabilities,* 28(8), 491–502.

Ruiz, N. T., & Enguídanos, T. (1997). Authenticity and advocacy in assessment: Bilingual students in special education. *Primary Voices, 5*(3), 35–46.

Ruiz, N. T., & Figueroa, R. A. (1995). Learning-handicapped classroom with Latino students the optimal learning environment. *Education and Urban Society, 27*(4), 463–483.

Ruiz, N. T., García, E., & Figueroa, R. A. (1996). *The OLE curriculum guide.* Sacramento: California State Bureau of Publications.

Ruiz, N. T. (1999). Effective literacy instruction for Latino students receiving special education services: A review of classroom research. In T. V. Fletcher & C. S. Bos (eds.), *Helping individuals with disabilities and their families: Mexican and U.S. perspectives.* Tempe AZ: Bilingual Review/Press, pp. 161–174.

Ruiz, N. T., Vargas, E., & Beltrán, A. (in press). Literacy research practice and a few questions from bilingual special education. In M. Reyes & J. Falcón (Eds.), *The best for our children: Latino/a voices in literacy.* New York: Teachers College Press.

Skrtic, T. (1991). The special education paradox: Equity as the way to excellence. *Harvard Educational Review, 61,* 148–206.

Snow, C. E., Burns, M. S., & Griffin, P. (1998). *Preventing reading difficulties in young children.* Newark, DE: International Reading Association.

SRA/McGraw-Hill. (1996). *Open Court school-based results.* Unpublished manuscript.

Taylor, D. (1998). *Beginning to read and the spin doctors of science.* Urbana, IL: National Council of Teachers of English.

TESOL. (1997). *ESL standards for Pre-K–12 students.* Alexandria, VA: Teachers of English to Speakers of Other Languages.

Tharp, R. (1997). *From at-risk to excellence: Research, theory, and principles for practice.* Washington, D.C.: Center for Research on Education, Diversity & Excellence, Center for Applied Linguistics.

Thomas, W. & Collier, V. (1996). *Language minority student achievement and program effectiveness.* Unpublished manuscript, George Mason University.

Viera, P. (1986). Remediating reading problems in a Hispanic learning disabled child from a psycholinguistic perspective: A case study. In A. C. Willin & H. F. Greenburg (Eds.), Bilingualism and learning disabilities (pp. 81–92). New York: American Library.

Willig, A., & Swedo, J. (April, 1987). *Improving teaching strategies for exceptional Hispanic limited English proficient students: An exploratory study of task engagement and teaching strategies.* Paper presented at the annual meeting of the American Educational Research Association, Washington, DC.

13

Tools for Reconceptualizing the Inclusive Classroom: Computers and Cooperative Learning

Mary Male

"What I like about using computers," said one computer "nerd" to his friend as they passed down the bustling college classroom hallway, "is you have all the interactions of a relationship but none of the problems!" This brief vignette illustrates the mind-set that has historically separated the group of educators who are passionate about social development through human interaction, carefully structured to promote the acceptance of diversity, and the group of educators who are passionate about the capacity of technology to enhance learning and productivity. A small but growing group of educators has chosen to investigate the power of combining these two passions into a synergistic classroom where computers are used as catalysts for human interaction and lessons using computers are carefully structured to promote communication and sharing with groups of two or three students working together (Parr, 1995; Signer, 1992). In such classrooms, the differences between students with and without learning disabilities become blurred, and all students become more powerful and productive both academically and socially. The purpose of this chapter is to equip all educators with the skills and confidence to take advantage of two of the most powerful classroom tools—computers and cooperative learning—to enhance the ability of classrooms to accommodate a wide range of learning needs.

Because of the scarcity of computers in schools, many teachers have put students in groups at the computer but without knowing or using the same principles of cooperative learning that apply to noncomputer lessons. Cooperative learning, is not simply placing students in group activities. Cooperative learning is defined as a way of structuring student interaction so that the following conditions are met:

- Students know that they can be successful only if their group is successful.
- Students are accountable for their individual understanding and mastery of whatever is being taught.
- Students are given specific instruction in the social skills necessary for the group to be successful.
- Students are given the opportunity to discuss how well their group is working and receive feedback to improve future performance (D. Johnson & B. Johnson, 1994; Kagan, 1997).

Cooperative Learning Groups Versus Traditional Learning Groups

A summary of the differences between cooperative and traditional learning groups is provided in Table 13.1. A clear understanding of these differences will help you understand how to incorporate cooperative learning into your students' computer experiences (Hooper, 1992; Male, Johnson, Johnson, & Anderson, 1986; Polin, 1992).

As indicated in Table 13.1, cooperative learning groups are based on positive interdependence among group members; goals are structured so that students need to be concerned about the performance of all group members as well as their own. In order for a situation to be cooperative, students must perceive that they are positively interdependent with other members of their learning group. This understanding may be facilitated in a number of ways, including incorporating mutual goals

TABLE 13.1
A Comparison of Cooperative and Traditional Learning Groups

Cooperative Learning	Traditional Learning
Positive interdependence	No interdependence
Individual accountability	No individual accountability
Heterogeneous	Homogeneous
Shared leadership	One appointed leader
Shared responsibility for one another	Responsibility for self
Task and maintenance emphasized	Only task emphasized
Social skills directly taught	Social skills assumed
Teacher observes and intervenes	Teacher ignores group functioning
Groups process their effectiveness	No group processing

(goal interdependence); dividing the work task (task interdependence); dividing materials, resources, or information among group members (resource interdependence); assigning students differing roles (role interdependence); and giving joint rewards (reward interdependence).

In addition, the students' mastery of the assigned material must be assessed to ensure individual accountability. Each student should be given feedback on his or her progress, and the group should be given feedback on how each member is progressing so that the other group members will know whom to assist and encourage. All group members in cooperative learning groups are accountable for mastering the assigned material. In traditional learning groups, individual students are often not held accountable for providing their share of the group's work, and occasionally students will "hitchhike" on the work of others. Further, cooperative learning groups are typically heterogeneous in ability levels and personal characteristics, whereas traditional learning groups are often homogeneous in membership. All members in cooperative learning groups share responsibility for performing leadership functions in the group, whereas traditional learning groups frequently have a leader assigned to be in charge.

In cooperative groups, students also share responsibility for one another's learning. They are expected to provide help and encouragement to one another to ensure that all members do the assigned work. In traditional learning groups, in contrast, members are seldom held accountable for one another's learning. Another difference is that the goals of cooperative learning groups focus on both bringing each member's learning to the maximum and helping the students to maintain good working relationships. Traditional learning groups focus primarily on completing the assignment.

Finally, cooperative learning groups present an opportunity for the teacher to observe the groups and give feedback to students on how effectively they are working and for the students, themselves, to process their effectiveness. Students are given the time and procedures to process how effectively they are working together. Students need to have a chance to analyze how well their learning groups are functioning and the extent to which they are using their collaborative skills to promote the learning of all group members and to maintain effective working relationships within the group. Students may then plan how to work with one another more effectively the next day and in the future (D. Johnson, R. Johnson, Holubec, & Roy, 1984).

In summary the teacher must teach needed social skills instead of assuming that students will bring these skills to their groups.

Synergy of Cooperative Learning and Computer Activities

When cooperative learning and the computer are combined for instruction, the computer, depending on the software, may be used for one or more of the following functions:

▶ Presenting the learning task

- Providing strategy instructions
- Controlling the flow of activity (e.g., signaling when a new task should be initiated)
- Monitoring learning activities in an objective and efficient manner
- Providing reinforcing messages for good performance on all aspects of the task
- Keeping track of students' responses for future analysis
- Tailoring learning activities to the students based on pretraining measures and on responses to tasks within the learning sequence
- Providing tests on the training materials and, based on students' responses, branches to further strategy instructions
- Performing computation to free the cooperative group from lengthy calculations, allowing members to spend more energy on problem solving and conceptual learning
- Providing expert content

As noted earlier, cooperative learning groups allow students to serve as models for one another. Students assist one another in analyzing and diagnosing the problems being addressed, explain to one another the material being learned, teach relevant concepts and procedures to one another, keep one another on task, and share their satisfaction and sense of accomplishment with one another. Two studies have compared computer use in cooperative, competitive, and individualistic learning (R. Johnson, Johnson, & Stanne, 1986a, 1986b). The results of these studies indicate that computer use in cooperative learning promoted a greater quantity and quality of daily achievement, more successful problem solving, and higher performance on factual recognition, application, and problem-solving test items than did computer use in competitive and individualistic learning. The combination of cooperative learning and computer activities had an especially positive impact on female students' attitudes toward computers. The combination of competition and computer activities had an especially negative impact on female students' achievement, achievement motivation, confidence in their ability to work with computers, attitudes toward computers, and attitudes toward the subject being studied.

Essential Components of Cooperative Computer Lessons

Although differences exist in the ways in which researchers have identified the essentials of cooperative learning, some basic principles are common among most of the formal cooperative learning strategies being used by teachers. The following description of the essential components of cooperative computer lessons is designed to assist you in structuring your own version of cooperative learning involving computer activities.

Assignment to Teams and Team Preparation

The purpose of team assignment in cooperative learning is to assure a good heterogeneous mix of students that takes into account gender, race, cultural and language differences, problematic behaviors, and past performance (achievement and communication skills). In the past, schools have made every effort to group students homogeneously by age, ability, and the like, with limited success. Cooperative learning offers teachers an opportunity to capitalize on the benefits of heterogeneous groups. These strategies work particularly well in mainstreaming and inclusive classroom situations.

Some teachers choose to randomly assign students to teams, as random assignment allows for a heterogeneous mix while keeping team assignment simple and demonstrating to students that they are expected to work together in groups no matter where they are assigned. Assignment to teams can be as simple as having students count off or dealing a deck of cards and having students gather in groups of four.

The purpose of team preparation activities is to build a sense of team identity and spirit as well as trust among team members. Teachers may ask students to select a name for their team and display it on a class bulletin board. Getting-acquainted activities or values-clarification activities that are tied into computer use may be conducted as team members are developing working relationships (Anderson, 1989; Mevarech & Light, 1992).

Creating Positive Interdependence Among Students

Positive interdependence is the feeling among team members that no one is successful unless everyone is successful. The following are sample statements that can be used to foster each of the types of interdependence associated with cooperative learning groups:

- ▶ Goal Interdependence: "You're not finished until everyone in the group can explain the pattern for sorting."
- ▶ Task Interdependence: "Each of you will be an expert on a different aspect of the story—one on the setting, one on the characters, one on the plot. You must agree on how to put your story together."
- ▶ Resource Interdependence: "I will give only one worksheet to the group. You must record your group's prediction of what the product will look like on the worksheet."
- ▶ Role Interdependence: "Each of you will play a crucial role in discovering the solution to the mystery. The jobs are taxonomist, ecologist, ethnobotanist, and plant chemist. Each of you has information the others do not, and you must share your information to solve the mystery successfully."
- ▶ Reward Interdependence: "Your grade will be made up of the sum of the individual grades on the test."

Most students with disabilities have had much experience with competitive classroom goal structures (and many have failed in such settings) and some have had experience in individualized special education classrooms; few have had practice in positive interdependence. Therefore, positive interdependence needs to be concretely and clearly communicated, especially when first presented. Otherwise, students may use their usual ways of working to get the job done, and the group will experience problems. For example, before having students start their group work, it is important to establish the benefits of working together. Helpful statements include, "You will want to work closely with one another so that your group grade will go up," "You will receive bonus points for your grade for every student who makes 100 percent in the group," and " If your group does all of its work correctly, you can earn the opportunity to be a computer tutor in the kindergarten class."

Individual Accountability

Most teachers who have experienced working in traditional groups or who have tried using traditional learning groups in their classrooms find that the addition of individual accountability ensures that each student contributes to the group. Further, it helps the teacher to monitor exactly how much each student has contributed and to determine the student's level of mastery of the target skills. For example, in a cooperative computer activity, each student must be able to explain the activity, produce a printout, or score at a certain level on a quiz. All students must know in advance that they will be responsible individually for demonstrating mastery.

Direct Teaching of Social Skills

Teachers who use cooperative learning computer activities successfully place as much importance on the mastery of key social skills as they do on the mastery of the use of the computer for instructional tasks. Most teachers begin by teaching one particular social skill, such as praising: They provide examples of praising, solicit examples from students, and frequently list behaviors and words that characterize praising. In addition to providing systematic instruction in the targeted social skill, teachers monitor the groups, using an observation sheet, and award all group members with bonus points or a portion of their grade based on their use of the social skill. A sample list of social skills on which teachers can focus is provided in Table 13.2.

Processing

In addition to observing the collaborative skills within the groups, the teacher provides structured opportunities for students to discuss and process what happened within their group. The best way to ensure that the effectiveness of the groups continues to improve is to provide time for students to share what they contributed to their group, how the group helped each student learn, problems that the group was able to solve, and problems with which the group would like help. In this way, the teacher creates a feeling that everyone is in this together, sink or swim.

TABLE 13.2
Social Skills at Various Grade Levels

Grade Level	Task Skills	Maintenance Skills
Lower Elementary	Check others' understanding Give ideas Talk about work Get group back to work Repeat what has been said Ask questions Follow directions Stay in seat	Encourage Use names Invite others to talk Respond to ideas Look at others Say "thank-you" Share feelings Disagree in a friendly way
Upper Elementary	Check others' understanding Contribute ideas Stay on task Get group back to work Paraphrase Follow directions Stay in own space	Encourage Use names Encourage others to talk Respond to ideas Use eye contact Show appreciation Disagree in a friendly way
Junior/Senior High/Adult	Check others' understanding Give information and opinions Stay on task Get group back to work Paraphrase Seek information and opinions Follow directions Disagree in a friendly way Practice active listening	Encourage Use names Acknowledge contributions Encourage others to talk Use eye contact Express appreciation Share feelings

Source: Adapted from *A Guidebook for Cooperative Learning* by D. Dishon and P. W. O'Leary (Holmes Beach, FL: Learning Publications, 1984).

Learning Together: A Cooperative Learning Strategy

Learning Together is a cooperative strategy that illustrates the use of the essential components of cooperative learning (D. Johnson, Johnson, & Holubec, 1993). In a lesson with computers, the teacher would do the following:

1. Assign students to heterogeneous teams and do team building as necessary to establish trust and friendship.
2. Present the group goal (the payoff for working together).
3. Review the group skill to be emphasized (checking, praising, summarizing, etc.).
4. Make sure that at least one student in each group can operate the software program.

5. Explain how each student's understanding of or contribution to the team effort will be evaluated.
6. Observe the group working both at the computer and at a table as the members plan their strategies and complete their assignment at the computer.
7. Keep records (or observe) on who should receive special recognition points for social skill mastery and on problems that should be discussed during the processing phase.
8. Review the group product.
9. Check for individual participation, understanding, and contribution.
10. Recognize outstanding group performance.
11. Lead the processing discussion.

Two sample lessons incorporating the Learning Together strategy are provided in Figures 13.1 and 13.2.

The Computer Lab

The computer lab is the ideal place for students to complete drafts of a composition, edit earlier work, and print final copies (Broad, 1991). However, most computer labs are not set up for small groups to share their work or even for teachers to conduct discussions with the whole class about discoveries, challenges, or strategies that are working or not working. In some schools, the computer lab is run by a computer specialist, who may or may not be involved in integrating computer activities into classroom curriculum. In other words, in the computer lab, the advantage of having one computer for each student may be far outweighed by the disadvantages. Do not assume that the computer lab is the ideal place for a computer lesson. If you need your class to use the lab to complete a lesson, think about ways the class can fit into the way the computer lab typically operates.

Classroom Designs to Promote Social Development

The Center for Special Education Technology (1991) described the following three scenarios of classrooms where computer use promotes social as well as academic development. Though introduced in 1991, they are still applicable and useful today.

Scenario 1

Students are clustered around a computer using word processing. They are in the prewriting stage and are making a vocabulary list about a topic. Each student gives an idea, which is added to the list on the screen. If someone doesn't know what to say, others give suggestions. When the list is complete, it may be printed out, and students can go to their desks to write their story or the group may continue working together to create a group story.

Grade Level: 8–12
Subject: Geography
Length: Five 40-minute class periods

Lesson Description:
In this lesson, student groups make a software program that plans a trip and gives information about a place they would like to visit.

Preparatory Information:
Group Size: 2–3 students
Group Assignment: Students select groups according to places they would like to visit.
Materials Needed: HyperStudio, HyperCard, or LinkWay; encyclopedias/references.
Task to Be Assigned: Keyboarder (rotates) who listens to group ideas and responds to suggestions as he or she uses the keyboard and mouse. Decision making to be shared by all team members.

Step 1: Setting the Lesson:
Task: The teacher introduces the topic of places in the world by asking students the place they have visited that is farthest away from where they live now. The teacher explains that students will be working in teams who will visit, by way of computer, some place in the world.

Students are instructed to think about the continent in the world they would like to visit. They are then directed to parts of the room according to the continent they have selected. When they find one to two other people with similar interest, they are to sit in a group and agree on a specific destination for their simulated visit.

The entire class brainstorms some of the things that are done when planning a trip: buying tickets, finding out about the country (its weather, historical sites, national heroes, monuments, animals, parks), setting an itinerary.

The teacher directs the class as they create a hypermedia about their destination. Cards, buttons, and fields are created for the stack.

Positive Interdependence: Each group member contributes ideas and helps to plan and make the program. Each group member helps the group make decisions.
Individual Accountability: Each group member creates at least one card of the stack and does special research focusing on one topic related to the group's destination.
Criterion for Success: a completed stack
Specific Behaviors Expected: contributing ideas, listening to others' ideas, sharing the keyboarding work, helping the group come to consensus

Step 2: Monitoring and Processing
Evidence of Expected Behaviors: students reading about the destinations, discussing and sharing ideas, planning and creating the stack
Plans for Processing: All groups will have a chance to use other groups' stacks. There will be a session to reflect on what each group learned about their destination and about the group process of listening to one anothers' ideas and making decisions.

Step 3: Evaluate Outcomes
Task achievement
Group functioning
Notes on individuals
Suggestions for next time:

FIGURE 13.1

HyperStudio Vacation Lesson Plan (Anderson, 1995)

Students are detectives using clues to catch a thief who is hiding in one of 30 cities. The *World Almanac and Book of Facts* helps in exploring cities and countries.

Subject Areas: Problem solving and logical thinking, geography
Grade Level: 5th grade and up

I. Objectives:
   A. Students will be able to use problem solving and logical thinking skills while working with clues to solve a mystery.
   B. Students will be able to use the dictionary and *World Almanac* as reference tools.
   C. Students will gain information to enlarge their understanding of geography.
   D. Students will be able to ask other team members why they are advocating an action and will be able to listen for the response.
II. Materials Needed: "Where in the World Is Carmen Sandiego?" manual and software, *World Almanac,* dictionary, police dossiers in software booklet, paper and pencil, marbles, jar, job cards, evaluation forms
III. Time Required: One class period per activity
IV. Procedures
   A. Preparation
      1. Assemble needed materials.
      2. Practice using "Where in the World Is Carmen Sandiego?" software; solve several cases.
   B. Setting the Lesson
      1. Ask students what mystery programs they have seen on TV. Ask what the role of the detective is.
      2. Tell students: "James Bond always started with an assignment. Today you have an assignment to catch a thief. You will use clues about Carmen Sandiego's gang and clues about cities and countries to solve the mystery. Your team will work together in the investigation."
   C. Teacher Input
      1. As a total class activity, use the program "Where in the World Is Carmen Sandiego?" to solve a case. Randomly select three random students to decide on a menu option. Then select another three students to choose the next option.
      2. Ask three students what to do next; ask each for their reason for their decision, and listen to the response. Get agreement on their next action for the case. Repeat with additional decisions and additional ideas from three students.
      3. Assign students to heterogeneous teams.
      4. Explain the group goal: "Your team will work together on a case assignment today to catch a thief. You may use the almanac, the dictionary, the police dossiers in the manual, and the hints that you get as you run the

(continued)

FIGURE 13.2

Learning Together (Where in the World Is Carmen Sandiego?) Lesson Plan

program. As you decide what to do next, you are to ask each member for his or her idea and then listen carefully to the response. Then you are to agree on your course of action."
   5. Tell students that there are job cards at each computer to help them accomplish their task. Then say, "Please distribute these among your team members. You may make suggestions to help the reference person and the recorder do their jobs. All of you are to use the social skill of asking for a reason and listening to the response."
   6. Explain that every group that catches a thief will be permitted to put a marble in the jar on the teacher's desk and that the class will have a party when the jar is filled. Explain that, in the meantime, every group that puts a marble in the jar will have a day when they will be first in the lunch line.
D. Guided Practice
   1. Students work in their teams to catch a thief.
   2. The teacher observes and records instances of team members' asking others for the reason behind their ideas. The teacher also records instances of students listening for the responses of others.
E. Closure
   1. Each individual fills out an evaluation form.
   2. With the total class together, the teacher calls on students to give comments on work in their group. Afterwards, the teacher gives comments with examples of what asking for a reason sounded like and what the behavior of listening to a response looked like.
F. Independent Practice
   1. Teams work on additional cases in succeeding days, adding marbles to the class jar as they are solved.
   2. Teams can gather their members together to work on cases before or after school or during unscheduled times.

Notetaking Guide for "Where in the World is Carmen Sandiego?"

Country	Capital	Population	Geography	Flag	Money	Products

FIGURE 13.2

(continued)

Scenario 2

A group around the computer is using problem-solving simulation software. Each group member is performing a task role (e.g., ecologist) and a group maintenance role (e.g., recorder). The students work together talking over the information on the computer screen and the options available to solve the problem. When the problem is finally solved, they share their success. For the next session, they change group maintenance and task roles so that everyone has a chance to master a variety of content and social skill roles. At the end of the lesson, they discuss successful strategies with the class and reflect on how the group process worked in their team.

Scenario 3

Students read different reference books, each focusing on one aspect of the topic being studied. Then they gather at the computer to use a database. Together they have the information to complete each of the fields for the database entries. Later they may merge this information with the information the rest of the class has collected and analyze all of the information.

A list of software that is appropriate for these scenarios is included in Table 13.3. Research has documented the effectiveness of classroom activities such as those described in the scenarios. In one study (Mevarech, Stern, & Levita, 1987), students were given an achievement test and then assigned at random to an individualistic setting or a paired learning setting, with each pair being approximately equivalent in scores on the achievement test. After 2 months, the students were asked

TABLE 13.3
Social Development Software and Publishers

Software	Publisher
Yukon Trail	MECC
Oregon Trail	MECC
Maya Quest	Sunburst
Pilgrim Quest	Sunburst
Africa Trail	Sunburst
Colony Quest	Sunburst
Decisions, Decisions	Tom Snyder
Rainforest Researchers	Tom Snyder
The Great Solar System Rescue	Tom Snyder
Nigel's World	Lawrence Productions
Where in the . . . series	Broderbund
SimCity	Maxis
Dig It: Egyptians	Terrapin
Microsoft Works	Microsoft

to complete questionnaires on their attitudes toward their classmates, computer learning, and cooperative learning. The results showed that students became more altruistic toward their partners in the cooperative setting and preferred cooperative to individualistic learning. The achievement of students in the cooperative learning groups was also slightly higher than that of the students in the individualistic setting, although the differences were not statistically significant. Additional studies e.g. (Bruder, 1992; Mevarech & Light, 1992) have confirmed the beneficial effects of combining cooperative learning with computers.

Summary

In this chapter, I discussed the synergy of cooperative learning and computer activities. The computer can be a powerful catalyst for communication and social skill development with appropriate software and carefully structured lessons. Several sample lesson plan ideas and suggestions for software were presented for exploration. Now you're ready to get started on your own! Here are some steps to begin:

1. Select a "foolproof" lesson—one that has worked well in almost every situation that you've tried.
2. Select software that enhances or expands students' ability to complete the lesson (word processing? drawing? simulation?).
3. Structure the lesson so that students work in pairs or triads at the computer.
4. Follow the essential elements of cooperative learning, including positive interdependence, individual accountability, social skills instruction, and processing.
5. Monitor the groups after you have introduced the lesson. Evaluate for fine-tuning next time!

References

Anderson, M. (1989). *Partnerships: Teambuilding at the computer.* Arlington, VA: Ma-jo Press.

Anderson, M. (1995). *Using HyperStudio in a resource room.* Presentation given at San José State University, May.

Broad, C. (1991). *The writing team with the writing machine.* Santa Cruz, CA: Educational Apple-cations.

Bruder, I. (1992). Can technology help? *Electronic Learning,* 12(3), 18–19.

Center for Special Education Technology. (1991). *Computers and cooperative learning.* Reston, VA: Council for Exceptional Children.

Dishon, D., & O'Leary, P. W. (1984). *A guidebook for cooperative learning.* Holmes Beach, FL: Learning Publications.

Hooper, S. (1992). Cooperative learning and computer-based instruction. *Educational Technology, Research and Development, 40*(3), 21–38.

Johnson, D. & Johnson, R. (1994). *Learning together and alone.* Englewood Cliffs, NJ: Prentice-Hall.

Johnson, D., Johnson, R., and Holubec, E. (1993). *Circles of learning.* Edina, MN: Interaction Book Company.

Johnson, D., Johnson, R., Holubec, E. & Roy, P. (1984). *Circles of learning.* Alexandria, VA: Association for Supervision and Curriculum Development.

Johnson, R., Johnson, D., & Stanne, M. (1986a). Computer-assisted instruction: A comparison of cooperative, competitive, and individualistic goal structures. *American Educational Research Journal, 23,* 382–391.

Johnson, R., Johnson, D., & Stanne, M. (1986b). The effects of cooperative, competitive, and individualistic goal structures on computer-assisted instruction. *Journal of Educational Psychology, 77*(6), 668–677.

Kagan, S. (1997). *Cooperative learning resources for teachers.* San Juan Capistrano, CA: Kagan Cooperative Learning.

Male, M., Johnson, D., Johnson, R., & Anderson, M. (1986). *Cooperative learning and computers: An activity guide for teachers.* Santa Cruz, CA: Educational Apple-cations.

Mevarech, Z., & Light, P. (Eds. 1992). Cooperative learning with computers. *Learning and Instruction, 2*(3), 155-285.

Mevarech, Z., Stern, D., & Levita, I. (1987). To cooperate or not to cooperate in CAI: That is the question. *Journal of Educational Research, 60*(2), 68–72.

Parr, D. (1995). *Increasing social awareness and geographical skills of fourth grade students with technology, on-line communications, and cooperative activities.* Unpublished manuscript, Nova Southeastern University (ERIC Document Reproduction Service No. ED 389 270), Tallahasse, FL.

Polin, L. (1992). Collegial learning: Life with the boyz. *The Writing Notebook, 9*(4), 28–32.

Signer, B. (1992). A model of cooperative learning with intergroup competition and findings when applied to an interactive video reading program. *Journal of Research on Computing in Education, 25*(2), 141–158.

Creating Opportunities for Success by Teaching Study Skill Strategies

14

Mary M. Gleason and Anita L. Archer

Increasingly, students with learning disabilities remain in general education classrooms all day. They potentially profit from this practice by having more access to the content-rich knowledge of science, social studies, art, music, and other disciplines, thus building background knowledge for comprehension. Not all aspects of this practice are positive, however. Students with learning disabilities struggle with task demands in general education classrooms. Many of the activities draw upon organizational, cognitive, and social skills with which students with learning disabilities have been notoriously weak. General education and special education teachers alike wonder how to meet the needs of students with learning disabilities within the general education classroom.

Additionally, the general education curriculum has tended to move progressively from didactic instruction to project-based instruction. This progression has not necessarily made it easier for students with learning disabilities. Whether general education task demands are embedded in teacher-directed or student-directed instruction, students with learning disabilities are still being asked to use multiple skills to gain, record, organize, and use information.

One response to the challenges faced by students with learning disabilities has been to place them in cooperative groups, such as those formed for project-based learning (Ellis's and Male's chapters in this book) and those formed for reciprocal teaching and completion of science booklets (Campione, Rutherford, Gordon, Walker, & Brown, 1994). Although these projects have shown many benefits for students with learning disabilities, group work does not guarantee achievement for these students. O'Connor and Jenkins (1986) observed students with learning disabilities making few contributions to cooperative learning groups. The students with learning disabilities usually contribute to cooperative groups according to their strengths and potentially avoid working on their areas of weakness. For example, while students with reading and writing skills dominate the literacy aspects of these projects by taking notes and writing the reports, students with fewer reading and writing skills contribute the illustrations and participate in discussions. Having students with learning disabilities participate with their peers, make friends, learn content information, and contribute to class discussions is laudable. However, that these same students fail to develop and use other academic skills is undesirable. It is important to ensure that students with learning disabilities develop and use all of the various skills required by project-based learning. If students with learning disabilities are to participate in the general education curriculum successfully, they must be taught ways of participating in content-rich and cognitively challenging activities without waiting until they have achieved grade level skills in reading, writing, and math. Therefore, they must be taught the learning strategies, study skills, and organizational skills that assist in successful and active participation in these group experiences.

Students with learning disabilities can acquire the necessary skills if they are directly taught the skills and then given the type and amount of practice needed for the transfer of the skills across all subjects and all settings. Developing independence with these skills is as important to participating in everyday classroom activities as having basic skills in reading, writing, and math. Consequently, general and special educators must plan and implement study skills instruction (learning strategies and organization skills), particularly for students with learning challenges. In this chapter, we present strategies to use with elementary and middle school students, along with the necessary teaching and maintenance procedures for use by teachers.

Selection of Study Skill Strategies for Instruction

When selecting study skill strategies for instruction, the teacher should follow several curriculum guidelines. First, the study skill should be *useful* to the students. For example, it would be useful to teach middle school students to take notes. They could use notetaking strategies when reading expository textbooks, collecting information for writing a report, or researching a topic for a verbal presentation. Notetaking skills would also be useful when recording information from a lecture, a video, or from the Internet. Of course, the determination of usefulness is dependent upon the age of the students and the tasks they are commonly requested to complete.

Second, the strategies selected should *generalize* to other settings and across time. A notetaking strategy for a science textbook should also work for a social studies textbook, a health article, or a math teacher's demonstration. The strategies taught in elementary school should continue to be empowering in middle school and high school. Strategies taught in middle school should still be of assistance when students enter high school, college, or vocational training. Because many students attach a study skill to a specific subject or time, teachers must show students how the strategy can also be used in other settings and in other subjects.

Third, the strategies that are taught should actually *work*. While this criterion seems obvious, a number of study strategies do not actually empower students. For example, you may have learned formal outlining as a notetaking strategy in high school. You learned to show the subordination of ideas using Roman numerals, capital and lowercase letters, and numbers. In the process of developing notetaking strategies for *Skills for School Success* (Archer & Gleason, 1994a, 1994b), we introduced this strategy to fifth- and sixth-grade students for taking notes on expository material. The students were so concerned with the appropriate use of numbers and letters that their attention was actually taken away from the content. We then taught the students an alternative strategy that involved showing the subordination of ideas through simple indention. We taught the students to record the topic of the paragraph, then indent and record brief notes about important details. We found that this strategy was not only easier for students to learn, but it also increased their attention on the content of the chapter. To ensure you are using strategies that work, be sure that it has been field-tested with students or test the strategy yourself with a small number of students.

All of the strategies described in the following sections meet these criteria: They are useful, will generalize to other settings and time, and have proven effectiveness. We have divided these study skill strategies into two groups: learning strategies and organization skills.

Teaching Learning Strategies

Learning strategies refer to systematic procedures for responding to common, consistent school tasks such as reading textbooks, studying for tests, and proofreading papers. Learning strategies generally involve a few steps designed to actively involve students in task completion and increase cognitive processing while studying. Even though a wealth of research-based learning strategies exist, we focus here on learning strategies for reading and writing expository material, reading and writing narrative selections, learning from lectures and other verbal presentations, and studying material for increased retention. Many of the strategies described are drawn from the study skills curricula entitled *Skills for School Success* (Archer & Gleason, 1991a, 1991b, 1994a, 1994b) and *Advanced Skills for School Success* (Archer & Gleason, 1992, 1993a, 1993b, 1994c, 2000).

Expository Reading Strategies

DECODING UNKNOWN WORDS

One of the challenges of reading expository materials for students with learning disabilities is difficulty in decoding unknown, multisyllabic words. As a teacher, you can follow either of two approaches to offer assistance. First, you can directly assist students in decoding the words. Second, you can teach students an independent strategy for reading longer words.

For the first strategy, directly assisting students with decoding, you would use the following procedures: Preread the material. Write difficult-to-read words on the chalkboard and indicate the word parts by drawing lines under the word parts as shown here.

electromagnet   electric   magnetize

When presenting a word, you would loop your finger from part to part, asking students to read each part and then asking them to read the entire word. If a word was not in their oral language, you would probably have to model the word's pronunciation. This teaching procedure (loop, loop, loop) models for students a strategy for decoding words independently by breaking the word into manageable parts.

The second approach, teaching students an independent strategy for reading longer words (Archer, Gleason, & Vachon, 2000), works like this: Students would first locate any common word parts at the beginning or end of the word (prefixes and suffixes). Next, students would locate vowel graphemes in the remainder of the word. Each vowel grapheme would also indicate a word part. Finally, the students would move their finger under and say each word part, say the word quickly, and correct the pronunciation to match their aural/oral language. This strategy requires that students have systematic preskill instruction on the pronunciation of common prefixes and suffixes and the identification and pronunciation of vowel graphemes.

DETERMINING THE MEANING OF UNKNOWN WORDS

Students have difficulty not only in decoding multisyllabic words found in expository materials but also in inferring the meanings of unfamiliar words. While the teacher may elect to preteach the meanings of words, students should also be taught strategies for independently determining the meaning of new words. For example, the following strategy can be taught:

1. Use context clues, the glossary, or a dictionary to determine meaning.
2. Restate the definition in a brief form.
3. Substitute your meaning in the context and ask yourself, "Does it make sense?"

Another approach is one that teaches students to use context clues within the unknown word (Pressley & Associates, 1990). For example, when elementary students read "dissimilar," they can be taught to realize that "dis" means "not" and "similar" means "the same." Putting this information together, the students can infer that the meaning of the unknown word is "not similar." In the same manner, middle school students may be unfamiliar with the meaning of "biosphere." Using known words, students can infer the meaning. First, the students would divide the word into meaningful parts, "bio" and "sphere." The students would then think: "*In the word biology, bio means living things, and in the word hemisphere, sphere means part of the earth. Thus, biosphere may refer to the living part of the earth.*" This hypothesis could be validated by substituting the meaning in a sentence and asking: "Does it make sense?"

UNDERSTANDING AND CREATING GRAPHICS

In addition to strategies needed for decoding and vocabulary, students must be taught to gain information from pictures, maps, and other graphics that accompany the text and, ultimately, to create their own graphics to display information gained from various sources. Frequently, graphics that accompany text contain valuable information that is not repeated in the text itself, yet students neglect the information found in graphics because they are unsure how to access and interpret the information. While field-testing *Skills for School Success,* we found that students benefited the most when we directly taught interpretation of information in pictographs, pie graphs, tables, bar graphs, and line graphs. Most students were able to answer questions at a 90% level or above after 2 or 3 days of brief instruction on each type (Archer & Gleason, 1991a, 1991b, 1994a, 1994b).

Before students read a new section of expository material, the teacher should examine the material and note the graphics that are included. If students are not familiar with a particular type of graphic, the teacher should preteach that type. The teacher would provide samples of the relevant graphic and show students a number of steps for interpreting it. First, the teacher would explain what the particular type of graphic is used for. Then, the teacher and students would determine the kinds of information gained from that type of graphic by interpreting the title, caption, and/or legend accompanying the graphic. If necessary, the teacher would explain how to apply a specific legend, especially if it involved using other skills. For example, in looking at the legend for the pictograph in Figure 14.1, the teacher would make sure that the students knew to multiply the number of farm pictures by the number 10,000 and knew how to determine and add the number for a half picture (5,000). Next, the teacher and students would determine the organization of the graphic by examining the numbers and words across the bottom or top and up and down the left side or around the circle, if the graphic was a pie graph. The teacher would then show the students how to answer literal questions about the information contained in the graphic. In addition to asking about numerical information, the teacher would ask questions that require students to compare nonnumerical information in the graph (e.g., lengths of rows in the pictographs, the relative sizes of pie pieces). Finally, the students should be taught how to respond to questions that require mathematical computation, such as adding or subtracting, and questions that require making inferences based on the information (see questions in Figure 14.1).

It is also helpful to teach students how to compare information gained from two or more graphs. For example, students might be shown two related pie graphs, one

A. Pictograph

Approximate Number of Farms per State

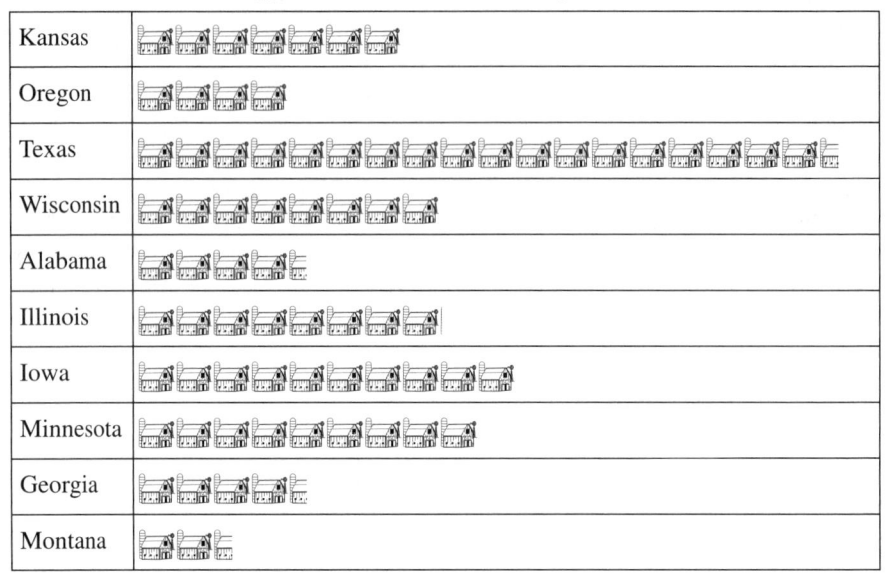

Kansas	🏠🏠🏠🏠🏠🏠🏠
Oregon	🏠🏠🏠🏠
Texas	🏠🏠🏠🏠🏠🏠🏠🏠🏠🏠🏠🏠🏠🏠🏠
Wisconsin	🏠🏠🏠🏠🏠🏠🏠🏠
Alabama	🏠🏠🏠🏠🏠
Illinois	🏠🏠🏠🏠🏠🏠🏠🏠
Iowa	🏠🏠🏠🏠🏠🏠🏠🏠🏠
Minnesota	🏠🏠🏠🏠🏠🏠🏠🏠
Georgia	🏠🏠🏠🏠🏠
Montana	🏠🏠🏠

🏠 = 10,000 farms

B. Use the pictograph to answer these questions.

1. Approximately how many farms are there in Minnesota? _____

2. Circle the state that has the most farms.

    Kansas   Texas   Iowa

3. Which state has approximately 25,000 farms? _____

4. Circle the state that has the fewest farms.

    Wisconsin   Oregon   Kansas

5. Which state has more than 90,000 farms but fewer than 150,000? _____

6. What is the combined number of farms in Alabama, Illinois, and Georgia? _____

7. Approximately how many more farms are there in Texas than in Minnesota? _____

8. Approximately how many fewer farms are there in Kansas than in Texas? _____

Source: From *Skills for School Success: Student Workbook, Book 5* by A. Archer and M. Gleason (North Billerica, MA: Curriculum Associates, 1994), 83. Used with permission of Curriculum Associates.

FIGURE 14.1

Learning to Interpret Pictographs

illustrating income sources of the federal budget and the other illustrating expense outlays of the budget. Because students would have already learned to interpret a single pie graph, the teacher would not need to demonstrate how a pie graph works. The instructional focus would, instead, be on how to use information across two graphs at once. The teacher would provide a series of structured questions, such as: Where does the federal government get money? What is the biggest item the money is spent on? Do excise taxes provide enough income to pay for national defense?

After students have learned to interpret graphics, they must also be taught to access graphics while they are reading expository material. Occasionally, the text refers the reader directly to the accompanying graphic; usually, the reference to the graphic is implied by a general discussion of related information. Students should be taught to peruse graphics and captions before reading the text and then to refer to the graphics again when the related discussion occurs. Teachers must remind students not to ignore the wealth of information provided in content area textbooks via graphics, including graphs, illustrations, sidebars, diagrams, maps, and timelines.

Once students have learned to interpret and use graphics effectively, they can use graphics for displaying information they've gathered from print or electronic resources, project-based learning, science experiments, or other data-gathering activities. Teachers must guide students in determining the best graphic for displaying information. Students can then design titles, captions, and legends, lay out an organizational scheme, and, finally, display the data so the information can be communicated to others.

STRATEGIES TO BE USED BEFORE READING EXPOSITORY MATERIAL

In addition to preteaching difficult words, meanings, and types of graphics before students read expository material, it is useful to activate students' prior knowledge about a topic and to activate cognition or thinking. A variety of strategies can assist in this process, but the following two can be used in many situations.

KWL. Among others, Ogle (1986) found that using a KWL chart prior to reading assisted students in comprehending expository text. The chart is usually presented as three columns, with headings at the top of each column that ask: What do we already KNOW (**K**) about this topic? What do we WANT (**W**) to learn? What did we LEARN (**L**)? Prior to having the students read the text, the teacher leads the students in brainstorming what they already know about the topic and writes what they say in the first column of the chart. To facilitate brainstorming, the teacher can use the cooperative learning strategy called Think-Pair-Share. First, the teacher asks the students *Think* about and record what they already know about the topic. Next, the teacher has them *Pair* up and tell a partner what they already know. As the students complete the Think and Pair steps of the strategy, the teacher moves from desk to desk and writes down what the students already know about the topic on an overhead transparency. Then, he or she *shares* the list on the transparency with the entire class while also collecting additional suggestions from class members. This brainstorming strategy can be repeated to generate what the students want to learn. The final step, generating what was learned, is completed after the students read the material. For this step, too, the Think-Pair-Share strategy can be used for summarizing.

Preview Strategies. Another way for students to prepare for reading is to preview the chapter to infer what the chapter is about and the chapter's organization. One of the earliest learning strategies developed, SQ3R (**S**urvey, **Q**uestion, **R**ead, **R**ecite, **R**eview), began with a survey of the chapter (Robinson, 1946). Subsequently, a number of preview strategies have been developed. Each of these strategies has students examine, prior to reading, chapter parts that are particularly salient in revealing the content of the chapter and its organization. When using the Warm-Up strategy (Archer & Gleason, 1991b, 1993b, 1994a, 1994b), for example, students first read the title and introduction of the chapter, asking themselves what the chapter is about. The students then examine the headings and subheadings throughout the chapter, thinking about the overall organization of the chapter and the content included in each section. Finally, the students examine the end of the chapter, reading the chapter summary and questions, thus expanding their understanding of the chapter content before reading it.

STRATEGIES TO BE USED WHILE READING EXPOSITORY MATERIAL

Students can be taught a variety of strategies for increasing their comprehension of expository materials. Most expository reading strategies are based on exposing the pattern of the underlying text structure. Consistently, factual material is divided into sections that are delineated by headings and subheadings. In addition, each paragraph also has a pattern. First, the paragraph has a topic, which is what the whole paragraph is about. Next, it has a number of important details that expand on the topic. As a result, all expository strategies direct students' attention to the text structure: the headings and subheadings and the topic and details for each paragraph.

Verbal Rehearsal Strategies. One set of strategies directs the students to read a paragraph, the natural unit of thought in most expository materials, reflect on the topic and the important details found in the paragraph, and then recite the information. For example, in the Paraphrasing strategy (Schumaker, Denton, & Deshler, 1984), also referred to as the RAP strategy, students use these steps to read factual material: 1. **R**ead a paragraph. 2. **A**sk yourself, "What were the main idea and details in this paragraph?" 3. **P**ut the main idea and details into your own words. The Active Reading strategy (Archer & Gleason, 1991b, 1993b, 1994a, 1994b), which is built on the Read, Cover, Recite, Check (RCRC) strategy (Archer & Gleason, 1991a, 1991b, 1993a, 1994a, 1994b), also has students use verbal rehearsal to increase the retention of content. When using Active Reading, students *read* a single paragraph and think about the topic (a word or phrase that tells what the whole paragraph is about) and important details. Next, students *cover* the paragraph and *recite* the topic and important details. Finally, they lift their hands and *check* the paragraph, repeating the process if they missed critical information. This strategy has also been adapted to a cooperative learning structure. When used with a partner, one student *reads* a paragraph, then both students silently reread the paragraph and think about the topic and important details. Next, the second partner *covers* the paragraph and *recites* the content, gaining input from the first partner, if needed. Finally, both partners *check* the paragraph to ensure that all important information was included in the recitation.

Verbal rehearsal strategies are appropriate when the content to be read is not difficult or students are young enough to be encountering their first expository selections. However, when students mature in their reading strategies and the difficulty of the material increases, the need for retention also increases. At that point, notetaking strategies should be introduced.

Notetaking Strategies. In both the RAP and Active Reading strategies, students read a paragraph and determine the topic and important details. These same skills can be translated into formal notetaking. With one such strategy, Indentation Notes (Archer & Gleason, 1993b, 1994a, 1994b, 1994c), the students copy the heading or subheading into their notes and then carefully read the first paragraph. After reading the paragraph, the students write down the topic of the paragraph, and then indent under the topic and record the important details. Students continue the same steps for each paragraph (see examples in Figure 14.2).

When teaching students to take notes, it is important to teach guidelines that make notetaking more efficient and avoid plagiarism. First, to enhance the depth of processing, students should avoid copying; instead, they should translate ideas into their own words. Second, students should record only words and phrases rather than sentences. Using abbreviations and symbols is also helpful for increasing the brevity of the notes. Finally, students must be sure that they understand their own notes. To test their personal understanding, they may retell their notes to themselves or to a partner. This rehearsal will not only increase the depth of their cognitive processing (Spires & Stone, 1989) but will also give them feedback on the quality of their notes.

An alternative to Indentation Notes that appeals to many students with learning disabilities is referred to as mapping, webbing, or clustering. When mapping, students create a visual array that graphically shows relationships between ideas. The students first draw a preliminary map on their paper for one section of the chapter. This preliminary map includes large ovals in which heading and subheadings are written. The students then proceed by reading the paragraphs under a particular subheading and thinking about topics and important details. Next, the students draw more ovals and record the topics of the paragraphs inside the ovals. Under each topic, important details are recorded (see Figure 14.3). Mapping is a particularly powerful tool when reading information in expository texts from which conceptual relationships can be drawn or inferred (DiCecco & Gleason, 2000).

Indentation Notes and mapping strategies can be enacted within the context of cooperative learning. Working with a partner, students would read a paragraph silently or orally. Next, they would determine and record the topic of the paragraph. Finally, they would add important details to their notes.

ANSWERING QUESTIONS ON EXPOSITORY MATERIAL

A common classroom activity is writing answers to questions. Having students answer questions about content they've read is beneficial for two reasons. First, if

246   New Ways of Looking at Learning Disabilities: Connections to Classroom Practice

```
                    heading or
                    subheading        Internal Structure of Earth (p.35)
                                                          topic of the
    How many layers    Model of earth                    first paragraph
    does the earth have?   -developed by scientists from bits of info.
                              -3 layers      topic of the
    What is the              Crust          next paragraph        important
    crust like?                                                   details
                              -thin layer of solid rock
                              -covered w/rock, soil, sand,
                                oceans, seas           topic of the
    How does the           Thickness of crust         next paragraph   important
    thickness of the         -different thicknesses                    details
    crust vary?              -thinner under oceans and seas
```

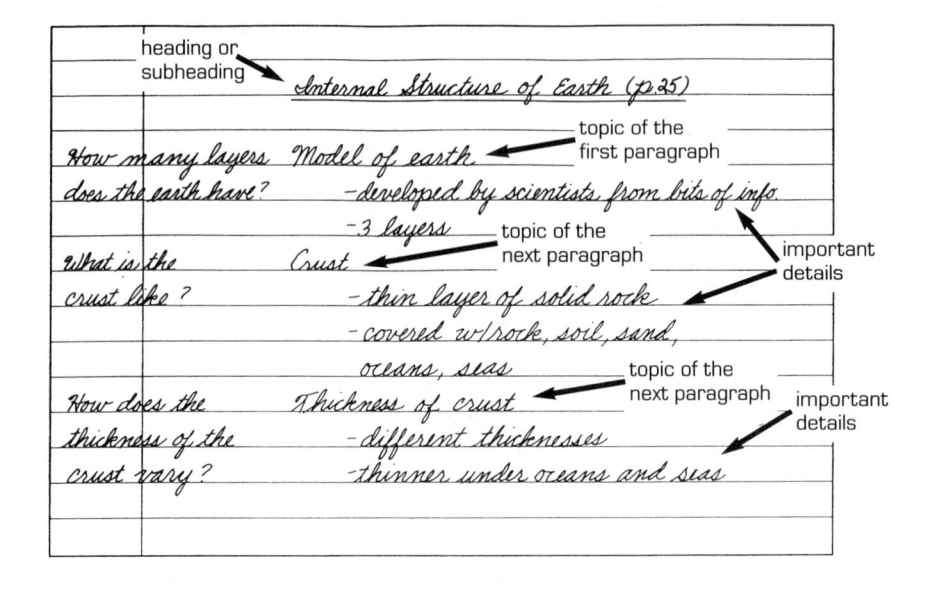

Hints for Taking Good Notes

1. Write your notes in your own words.
2. Make your notes brief.
3. Use abbreviations and symbols.
4. Be sure you understand your notes.

Source: From *Advanced Skills for School Success: Teacher Guide, Module 3* by A. Archer and M. Gleason (North Billerica, MA: Curriculum Associates, 1993), 83. Used with permission of Curriculum Associates.

FIGURE 14.2

Sample of Indentation Notes

---

the questions are well written, they will assist students in attending to the most important information and give students an opportunity to process and summarize that information. Second, the answers form a study guide that students can use in preparing for tests, discussions, and verbal presentations.

Unfortunately, the quality of many students' answers don't support these goals. For example, students often write a word or phrase rather than a complete sentence as their answer. In some cases, students don't carefully read the questions, and thus

Successful Participation **247**

1. Draw circles for the heading and subheadings.
2. Take notes on each paragraph.
   a. Write the topic in the circle.
   b. Write an important detail on each line.

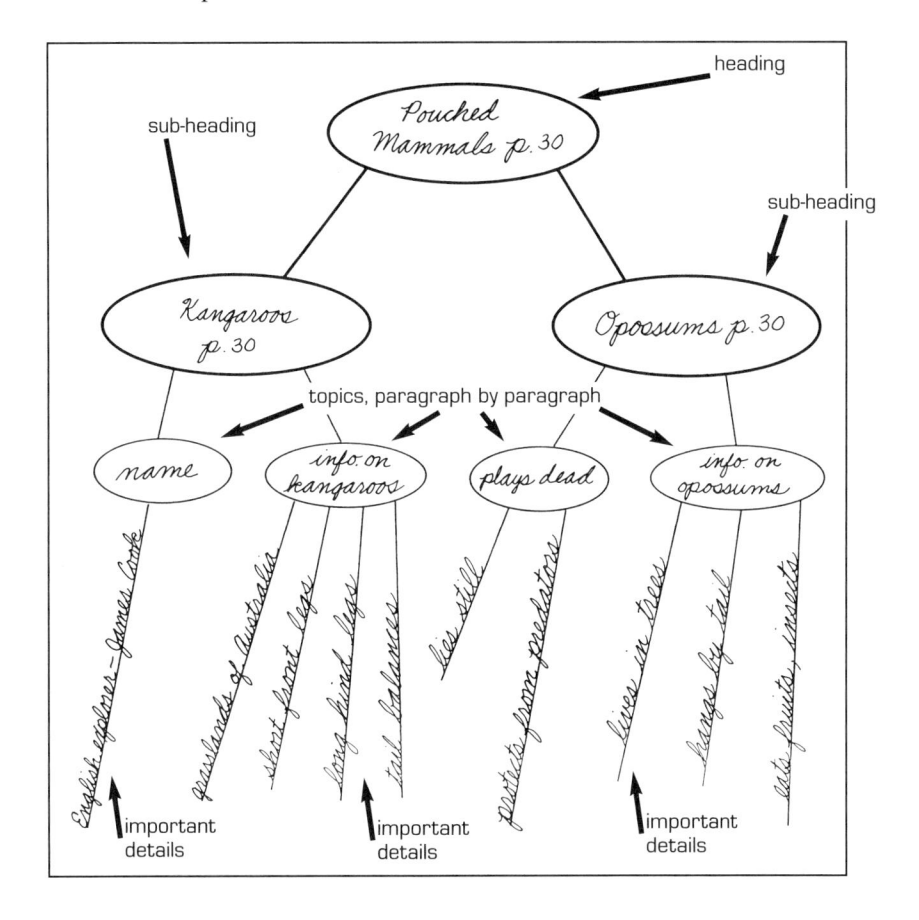

Source: From *Advanced Skills for School Success: Teacher Guide, Module 3* by A. Archer and M. Gleason (North Billerica, MA: Curriculum Associates, 1993), 84. Used with permission of Curriculum Associates.

FIGURE 14.3

Sample of Mapping

their answers don't correlate with the questions. Finally, many of their answers are in a truncated form (e.g., "There are three."), which does not allow for careful subsequent study if the students no longer have access to the questions. For all of these reasons, students need to be taught a strategy for answering chapter questions that will increase the accuracy and quality of their answers. In *Skills for School Success* (Archer & Gleason, 1991a, 1991b, 1994a, 1994b), we have students read a question, change the question into part of the answer, and write it down. For example, if the question was, "What are the three branches of the federal government?" students would write the partial answer, "The three branches of the federal government are . . ." Next, students would use headings and subheadings of the material they read to locate the desired topic. When they locate the section, students would reread it and complete their answers.

In a related strategy, Garner, McCready, and Wagoner (1984) taught students to use lookbacks. They taught students with comprehension challenges to look back at the text when they could not answer postreading questions. Students were taught why you should look back (you cannot remember everything you read), when to look back (the question asks about what the author said, not what you think), and where they should look (skim the article and find the part that might have the answer). Students trained to use lookbacks were more apt than control subjects to use lookbacks when they could not answer a question and were thus more likely to answer the question correctly.

WRITING SUMMARIES

Although summary writing is a difficult skill to teach (e.g., Brown & Day, 1983; Hare & Borchardt, 1984), it is an important skill for students. Writing summaries of what has been read has been shown to assist in comprehension and long-term retention (Murrell & Surber, 1987; Rinehart, Stahl, & Erickson, 1986). In addition, summary writing helps students learn to paraphrase others' ideas and write in a way that is useful for writing longer reports and research papers. The keys to successful summary writing are the abilities to sort important information from less important details and to restate the information in a condensed, concise form.

In *Advanced Skills for School Success,* we applied what Stevens and Fear (1987) called POWER steps to summary writing (Archer & Gleason, 1993b). Stevens and Fear utilized the acronym POWER to refer to **P**lan, **O**rganize, **W**rite, **E**dit, **R**evise. However, we modified the POWER strategy to include the following steps: **P**repare, **O**rganize, **W**rite, **E**dit, and **R**ewrite (Archer & Gleason, 2000). With this strategy, students *prepare* for writing a summary by taking brief notes on what they read using words and phrases and then checking the most important information in their notes. Then, the students *organize* the information by taking the most important information, mapping it around topics and subtopics, using brackets to overtly connect the ideas that could be combined into one sentence, and numbering the ideas in the order they should appear in the summary. During the connecting and numbering process, students can also cross out any ideas or details they've decided not to use. Next, students *write* a first draft by translating the organized information into full sentences and making sure to state the topic first and then tell important information about the topic. Students then *edit* the draft by rereading it to see that it explicitly states the topic, tells the most important information about the topic, and seems easy for a reader to understand. Finally, students proofread their summary for mechanical conventions and *rewrite* their draft to become the final summary.

Expository Writing Strategies

The strategies that have been developed for assisting students in writing have been universally based on the natural steps of the writing process. Early models included three steps: prewriting, writing, and rewriting. More recently, Hayes and Flower (1980) presented a more sophisticated model. They utilized the steps of planning (generating, organizing, and goal setting), translating (transforming ideas using a plan into meaningful sentences), and reviewing (reading and editing). Similarly, Graham and Harris (1989) taught four steps for planning and writing: Think, Plan, Write, and Say More. The following sections describe a strategy we developed (Archer & Gleason, 2000) that applies the modified POWER steps to the teaching of report writing. Each step is explained in relationship to writing a short, factual report. The strategy illustrates the type of systematic strategies that are needed to support the writing of many students, but particularly those with learning disabilities.

PREPARE

When *preparing* to write a factual report, the student must do several things. First, the student must select a report subject within the parameters of the teacher's assignment. For example, when Jessica's sixth-grade class was completing a unit on oceans, the teacher told the students to select a report subject related to oceans. Jessica listed possible topics that interested her (whales, seashells, ocean currents, coral reefs) and finally selected one for her report (seashells).

The next step in preparing to write a factual report is to determine topics that will be covered in the report. In *Advanced Skills for School Success* (Archer & Gleason, 2000), students are taught to generate questions they would like to answer in their report and then turn those questions into topics. These are some of the questions and topics that Jessica generated:

Question	Topic
What are the characteristics of seashells?	Characteristics
How are seashells formed?	Formation
What are the different types of seashells?	Types

Jessica would not need to limit her report to these topics, but her list would assist her in accessing appropriate reference materials. Reference materials can include trade books on the subject, encyclopedias, magazines, and electronic reference materials. The number of reference materials should not be fewer than three, though the actual number of materials used depends on the length of the proposed report, its desired depth, and the extensiveness of the report subject.

As a final step in preparing to write a factual report, the student would take notes from appropriate reference materials on information related to the designated topics. Two effective notetaking strategies are Indentation Notes and mapping, which were described earlier for recording information from lectures and textbooks.

ORGANIZE

When students have completed their research, they are ready to *organize* their notes for writing. We recommend that students write their topics at the top of separate pieces of paper and put the pages in the order they wish the topics to appear in the body of their report. The students then use the following steps to organize their information for writing: list, cross out, connect, and number. First, the students *list* details on the topic pages by rewriting the details from their notes or by cutting and pasting their notes onto these pages. Second, the students review their listed details and *cross out* any details that they have decided not to include within their report. Third, the students physically *connect* ideas that can go into one sentence. (During the field-testing of this strategy, we found that many students wrote one sentence per detail. The connecting step resulted in a greater variety of sentence types, including compound and complex sentences.) Finally, the students *number* the listed ideas in the order they will appear in the paragraph.

WRITE

After carefully organizing topics and details, students proceed in *writing* the body of their paper. Our field-testing showed that student products were improved when students first wrote the body of the report and then generated the introduction and conclusion. Whether the draft is handwritten or word processed, the draft should be double-spaced to allow subsequent editing.

EDIT

Editing any written product should proceed through a number of levels, leading from the general to the specific. First, the writer should read and revise the product to ensure clarity of communication. Second, the product should be examined to see if it reflects the structure of the genre. For example, at this stage, Jessica read her report, evaluated it against the rubric for a factual report that is shown in Figure 14.4, and revised the content.

The third level of editing involves proofreading for mechanics. A number of strategies may be shared with students to facilitate proofreading. In the Error Monitoring strategy that is a part of the Learning Strategies Curriculum (Schumaker, Nolan, & Deshler, 1985), students are taught to monitor written work for **C**apitalization, **O**verall appearance, **P**unctuation, and **S**pelling (COPS). Similarly, the proofreading strategy that we developed (Archer & Gleason, 1991a, 1991b, 1994a, 1994b) directs students to proofread for sense, capitalization, punctuation, and spelling.

Name: _____ Date: _____

No				Yes
0	1	2	3	4
Not Evident				Very Evident

INTRODUCTION

0 1 2 3 4   1. Does the introduction tell you what the report is about?

0 1 2 3 4   2. Does the introduction capture the interest of the reader?

BODY

0 1 2 3 4   3. Does the body tell important information about the report topic? Does each paragraph in the body:

0 1 2 3 4   4. Focus on one subtopic?

0 1 2 3 4   5. Present important details about the subtopic?

0 1 2 3 4   6. Use linking words to connect sentences when appropriate?

0 1 2 3 4   7. Are the paragraphs in the body easy to understand?

CONCLUSION

0 1 2 3 4   8. Does the conclusion retell the most important information about the report topic?

0 1 2 3 4   9. Does the report have a definite end?

FIGURE 14.4

Rubric for Evaluating a Factual Report

REWRITE

Because the report is a form of public communication, after all revisions have been made, students must *rewrite* the draft to produce a clean copy and add, if relevant, a cover page, illustrations, and bibliography.

Narrative Reading Strategies

Narrative stories have a text structure pattern that includes setting (the time and place of the story), a main character, a problem or conflict generally experienced by the main character, attempts to resolve the problem, a resolution of the problem, the emotional responses of the main characters to the resolution, and an ending. Because of this consistent text pattern, narrative reading strategies attempt to draw students' attention to these story grammar elements.

STRATEGIES FOR RECOGNIZING STORY GRAMMAR ELEMENTS

While training students to recognize story grammar elements always focuses on recognizing the general pattern of the story, the strategies have differed across researchers. Short and Ryan (1984) taught fourth-grade students who were reading below grade level to ask the themselves the following questions as they read a story: (a) Who is the main character? (b) Where and when did the story take place? (c) What did the main character do? (d) How did the story end? and (e) How did the main character feel? After training with this strategy, students remembered the story better than did students who hadn't received the training.

In other studies investigating the effects of story grammar training, students were taught to construct story maps during reading (e.g., Idol, 1987; Idol & Croll, 1987). In the studies by Idol and colleagues, students recorded information about the story grammar elements on a worksheet that had spaces that were labeled for each element. The reading comprehension of 9- to 12-year-old poor readers was enhanced by this intervention.

STRATEGIES FOR ANSWERING QUESTIONS

Upon completion of a narrative selection, students are often asked to answer written questions. Raphael and colleagues (e.g., Raphael & McKinney, 1983) developed a strategy for teaching students to answer such questions. This strategy shows students the relationship between the questions and answers to assist them in locating answers. Students are taught to analyze questions to see if they can be answered by information in the selection ("right there" questions), by information they can infer by combining pieces of information in the selection ("think and search" questions), or by information in the reader's prior knowledge ("on your own" questions). If a question was in the "right there" category (e.g., "Where did the story take place?"), students would examine the story to locate the literal answer. If a question fell into the "think and search" category (e.g., "What were three of Matthew's favorite activities?"), the students would locate segments of the answer throughout the story and put them together to formulate an answer. Finally, "on your own" questions required no story information though they could be tangentially related to the story theme (e.g., "What qualities are most important to you when selecting a friend?"). With this type of question, the student must rely entirely on his or her prior knowledge and ideas. When these relationships between questions and answers were taught and practiced, an increase in correct responding occurred.

Narrative Writing Strategies

The strategies for writing stories, like the strategies for reading stories, focus on the consistent story grammar elements. For example, in a study by Graham, Harris, and Sawyer (1987), fifth- and sixth-grade students with learning disabilities were taught a story grammar strategy for developing and writing narrative stories that included the following steps:

1. Look at the picture (stimulus item).
2. Let your mind be free.
3. Write down the story part reminder "W-W-W; What = 2; How =2." (This is explained in the next paragraph.)
4. Write down story ideas for each part.
5. Write your story—use good parts and make sense.

Before being introduced to the entire strategy, students received training on the mnemonic device in Step 3. The students were presented with a chart containing the mnemonic and were taught to generate the following story grammar questions: **Who** is the main character? **Who** else is in the story? **When** does the story take place? **Where** does the story take place? **What** does the main character do? **What** happens when he/she tries to do it? **How** does the story end? **How** does the main character feel? Students used the content generated from answering these questions as a blueprint for their stories. As a result of this strategy training, students wrote stories containing more of the story grammar elements.

An alternative to teaching students a self-questioning strategy is to provide them with a think sheet for planning stories (Englert & Mariage, 1991). Think sheets can be developed to support the organizational phase of writing for many different genres. Figure 14.5 presents a think sheet for a short story that one of us (Anita) developed. The numbers indicate the order the student would proceed in planning his or her story. In thinking about the story, the student would first select a main character and a problem or conflict. Next, the student would determine a setting for the story and outline the events in the story leading to the resolution or end of the story. Finally, the student would devise a title for the story that summarized what the story was about, or its theme. When the student moved to the writing phase of the writing process, he or she would write the story in the order it appeared on the think sheet: first recording the title, then writing a paragraph to introduce the setting, and next writing a paragraph introducing the main character. Using his or her plot outline, the student would then elaborate on the story events in which the problem or conflict would emerge and would continue until a resolution was reached. An organizational think sheet is a type of scaffold or procedural facilitation (Bereiter & Scardamalia, 1982) for planning stories that benefits many students with learning disabilities.

Strategies for Learning From Lectures and Other Verbal Presentations

Earlier we introduced a flexible style of notetaking referred to as Indentation Notes (Archer & Gleason, 1993b, 1994a, 1994b, 1994c) for recording information when reading a textbook or collecting information for a written or verbal report. It is an equally useful strategy for taking notes on verbal material (Archer & Gleason, 1994c). Students often learn from lectures or other auditory presentations (films,

| (6) | Title |

| (3) | Setting |

| (1) | Main Character(s) |

| (2) | Problem |

| (4) | Events |

| (5) | End |

FIGURE 14.5

Short Story Think Sheet

videos). Recording notes and later studying the notes assist in comprehension and recall. The notes are also useful for preparing for tests, discussions, and verbal presentations. Huffman and Spires (1994) found that instruction in notetaking improved sixth-graders' comprehension of lecture material. Not surprising, this recall was strengthened if students reviewed and studied their notes (Laidlaw, Skok, & McLaughlin, 1993). In addition, as described by Seitz (1997), becoming proficient in notetaking and recall may motivate students to become interested in other tasks. Seitz described how at-risk middle school students who became proficient with notetaking and summarization skills using daily newscasts ultimately became engaged in current events, news analysis, and the analysis of commercials.

In addition to learning that they need to record a lecture's title, topics, and important details, students need assistance in learning how to determine what points are important (Archer & Gleason, 1994c). For example, a point in a lecture is often important if the teacher emphasizes the point with his or her voice or hands, repeats the point, writes information on the chalkboard or a transparency, or pauses to allow students time to write. Unfortunately, even with good strategy training, the quality of student's notes is still dependent on the clarity and organization of the lectures or other verbal presentations.

Strategies for Studying Material

VERBAL REHEARSAL STRATEGIES

Often, students attempt to learn material simply by reading the material again and again. However, some students read the material "mindlessly" and retain little information. One strategy to activate cognition during studying is Read, Cover, Recite, Check (RCRC). Using this strategy for studying, students read a small amount of the material to be studied, cover up the material, recite the important information, and, finally, lift their hands and check. This simple strategy shows one of the important benefits of teaching learning strategies: It empowers students with a strategy that generalizes across curricular areas and settings. Students could use RCRC to study social studies notes, a science study guide, steps in a math algorithm, lines for a play, content for a speech, math facts, a driver's manual, or spelling words. Third graders, high school juniors, and college seniors could all employ this strategy when study or memorization is necessary.

QUESTIONING STRATEGIES

Another way to study material is to generate self-study questions. For example, after taking notes on a content area chapter, students could write self-study questions in the margin. This practice not only would lead to deeper processing of the information but would also create a self- or cooperative study tool. Individually, students could use RCRC to study the material. The students would *read* the question they wrote and the related material, *cover* up the material, *recite* the answer to the question, and lift his or her hands and *check*. When studying with a peer partner, students could alternately ask their partner one of the questions and check responses with their notes. While student-generated questions certainly enhance notes, teachers could also add such questions to study guides and handouts. Good study questions are also often included in chapter summaries.

MNEMONIC STRATEGIES

Occasionally, students need to learn a list of elements. Such a requirement is not uncommon in science, social studies, and health material. Students may also need to recall a list of steps in a math algorithm, a list of music elements, or a list of artists in a certain period. Such recall is often enhanced by creating a mnemonic device to facilitate memory (e.g., Mastropieri, Scruggs, & Levin, 1985). A mnemonic device is formed from the first letters of the list items. The student recalls the letters or creates a sentence comprising words corresponding to the items in the list. Some examples follow:

Topic: Why people eat?
  List: Hunger, Energy, Habit, Emotion
  Mnemonic device: Letters—H E H E

Topic: Great Lakes
  List: Huron, Ontario, Michigan, Erie, Superior
  Mnemonic device: A word—HOMES

Topic: Nutrients
  List: Protein, Carbohydrates, Fats, Vitamins, Minerals
  Mnemonic device: Sentence—Pretty Carol Felt Very Merry.

Teaching Organization Skills

Organization of Materials

Many students struggle to achieve success in school because they lack systems for storing, organizing, and retrieving written materials, pens and pencils, blank notebook paper, textbooks, and other materials necessary for participating in individual and group activities. For students in third grade and above, one of the most important and effective mechanisms for establishing such a system is an organized notebook. The notebook should assist students in being prepared for class, transporting materials between home and school, and storing materials that need to be used later.

To get students started, teachers should make sure each student has a three-ring notebook with dividers for each subject area or school activity. One section should be labeled "Blank Paper" and another labeled "Take Home." The notebook should also contain a pen and pencil pouch and a monthly calendar at the front. If the students have desks, they should put a pen and pencil box or other container that will help keep supplies in place inside their desks as well.

Several practices will help students and teachers use notebooks to their full advantage. As a first step, teachers should use their own notebooks to show students what an organized notebook looks like. Next, teachers should guide students in putting their notebooks together and labeling the dividers. Then, they should simulate the use of the notebook by asking students to pretend, for example, that a math assignment was being handed back and asking them to show where they would put it in their notebook. Teachers should refer to the notebooks frequently as well as provide daily opportunities for students to practice putting completed written products into and retrieving them from the respective sections. To help students maintain organization, teachers should give them frequent feedback. A checklist can also be used that allows students to give themselves daily feedback regarding notebook and desk organization. Similarly, a list of suggestions can be sent home prompting parents to regularly assist in placing homework in appropriate sections, complimenting their child on good organization, and reminding their child to take the notebook back to school on a daily basis.

Periodically, the teacher can conduct a goal-setting session with students in which the students examine their self-monitoring checklists, determine their strengths and weaknesses in organization skills, and set goals for improvement during the subsequent time period. Certificates of accomplishment, access to special events, or other positive consequences can be rewarded in recognition of individual efforts at working on organization.

Organization of Time

Just as many students lack a system for the organization of materials, many also lack a system for time management. They forget when assignments are due, leave homework assignments undone until it's nearly too late to complete them, or neglect to plan what tasks need be completed on a daily basis. Third graders and above can begin to build time-management habits that will help them be successful in school in the present as well as in the future and in employment situations. A time-management system will help students track class assignments and important events, plan for class and homework activities, and complete long-term assignments in a timely fashion. The monthly calendar seems to be the most effective, as well as generalizable, tool for reaching these goals.

Teaching students to use a monthly calendar requires teaching them a number of component skills first. They need to learn the meaning of "due date" and to learn to locate due dates on the calendar in relation to common phrases teachers use to indicate when assignments must be completed (e.g., day after tomorrow, in 2 weeks, a week from Tuesday). In addition, students must learn to write abbreviations that will assist them in writing notes to themselves in small calendar spaces. For example, students might learn to write abbreviations for various subject areas and for words such as *chapter, page,* and *exercise.* Finally, students should be given practice in recording assignments on the calendar in a number of simulated exercises.

Once students learn to record entries on the calendar, they can begin to plan for nightly activities. Each day for several weeks and then periodically, the teacher should have students look at their calendars to see what is due the next day, so that students remember to bring materials home and to complete their short homework assignments.

For assignments that are due further ahead, older students must learn to look ahead, break a larger task into smaller tasks, and plan for completion across time, rather than leave a large assignment for the night before it is due. Teachers might show students how to create a task list by breaking the larger assignment into smaller parts, create a timeline, and then write the smaller parts onto their assignment calendars. For example, if students are to read a novel and write a description and analysis of one of the main characters, they might indicate these smaller parts: select a book, read enough of the book to decide on the focus character, read and take notes on each chapter, organize the notes regarding the description of the character, organize the notes for analysis of the character, write a first draft, rewrite and prepare the final report. For a novel containing 10 chapters, these smaller parts might be indicated on 15 different days. During completion of this large task, it would be particularly important for the teacher to set aside time each day to have students consult their calendars and plan how much of the task should be completed that evening and to assist students on following through. Daily positive feedback and consequences would encourage students to persist in completing their long-term assignments.

Organization of Written Products

The appearance and organization of written products is equally important to the organization of materials and time. Many students must be taught how to create a neater, more organized appearance for their papers. One set of standards, introduced in a strategy called HOW (Archer & Gleason, 1991a, 1991b, 1993a, 1994a, 1994b), is presented in Figure 14.6. These standards include the use of a **h**eading, an **o**rganized appearance, and a neatly **w**ritten appearance. Using the checklist in Figure 14.6, students would circle yes or no for each standard, then trade papers. Peers would use the last column to do the same. Using a self-monitoring checklist has been shown to be an effective procedure for promoting the transfer of neatness skills to other settings (Anderson-Inman, Paine, & Deutchman, 1984).

Prior to having students use such a checklist, however, the teacher would first have to show students an assignment that demonstrated each desired attribute. Then, the teacher would present examples of unacceptable assignments and show how they did not meet the standard. Finally, students would be asked to evaluate a mix of examples to see if they could tell which would be acceptable and which would be unacceptable. Once they successfully discriminated the two, students would be asked to evaluate their own written work.

As with the organizational strategies for notebooks, desks, and assignment calendars, once skills for organizing written products are taught, the teacher's primary challenge is in getting students to consistently use the skills for the entire school year. The teacher might post a large sample of an acceptable paper and remind students on a frequent basis to use HOW when they complete written products. To encourage attention to the standards, teachers might ask students to redo unacceptable papers. Neat, organized papers can be displayed in the classroom or in public hallways. Teachers can provide checklists to assist students in monitoring their own and their peers' work.

Name _____

Teacher _____ Date _____

HOW Should Your Papers Look?

H = Heading

1. First and last name	1.	yes	no	yes	no
2. Date	2.	yes	no	yes	no
3. Subject	3.	yes	no	yes	no
4. Page number if needed	4.	yes	no	yes	no

O = Organized

1. On the front side of the paper	1.	yes	no	yes	no
2. Left margin	2.	yes	no	yes	no
3. Right margin	3.	yes	no	yes	no
4. At least one blank line at the top	4.	yes	no	yes	no
5. At least one blank line at the bottom	5.	yes	no	yes	no
6. Good spacing	6.	yes	no	yes	no

W = Written neatly

1. Words and numbers on the lines	1.	yes	no	yes	no
2. Words and numbers written neatly	2.	yes	no	yes	no
3. Neat erasing or crossing out	3.	yes	no	yes	no

Comments: _____

_____

_____

_____

_____

_____

_____

_____

Source: From *Advanced Skills for School Success: Teacher Guide, Module 3* by A. Archer and M. Gleason (North Billerica, MA: Curriculum Associates, 1993), 168. Used with permission of Curriculum Associates.

FIGURE 14.6

How; Standards for the Appearance and Organization of Written Products

Teaching Study Skills

If students are to apply study skill strategies to daily task completion, the strategies must be carefully taught. There are many effective models for teaching learning strategies and organization skills (e.g., Deshler, Schumaker, & Lenz, 1984; Deshler, Schumaker, Lenz, & Ellis, 1984; Graham, Harris, & Sawyer, 1987; Paris, Cross, & Lipson, 1984). The model presented here employs the same instructional steps that are used for teaching reading, mathematics, and language arts: modeling the strategy, guiding students in applying the strategy, and, when proficiency is evidenced, checking the students' understanding.

1. Model the strategy. When teaching any strategy for which performance is the desired outcome, the teacher should model or demonstrate the strategy rather than just talk about how it should be performed. Thus, when teaching learning strategies and organization skills, the teacher should provide a dynamic demonstration of each strategy. First, the teacher should clearly demonstrate each step in the strategy, exaggerating the critical attributes of the steps to enhance student attention. Second, while modeling each of the steps, the teacher should describe exactly what he or she is doing, using clear, easy-to-understand language. The teacher should also engage in thinking aloud, telling students not only what he or she is doing but also what he or she is thinking while modeling the strategy. For example, when teaching Indentation Notes (Archer & Gleason, 1993b, 1994a, 1994b, 1994c), the teacher would read a paragraph out loud and tell students a possible topic and the thinking that led him or her to select that topic, before recording it in the notes. Finally, the teacher must actively involve students in the demonstration. This can be done by asking students to repeat critical information or answer questions concerning the strategy steps (e.g., "The first step in the strategy is READ. What is the first step in the strategy?" *Read.* "Yes, first we read a small bit of information. If we were studying words and definitions, would you read one definition or many definitions?" *One definition.*)

2. Prompt students in use of the strategy. As soon as a strategy has been modeled, students should be given immediate practice that involves guidance or prompting by the teacher. Teachers can prompt students in their application of the strategy with such instructional procedures as (a) telling students a strategy step or asking them to say or read the step, (b) having students perform the step while monitoring their performance, and (c) giving students feedback on their performance. Prompting in this manner should proceed through the entire strategy and should be repeated until students demonstrate proficiency on the strategy.

3. Check students on their application of the strategy. When students have demonstrated proficiency in use of the strategy steps when prompted, they should practice the strategy without any assistance. While the students are practicing the strategy, the teacher should carefully monitor their performance, acknowledging correct use of the strategy and correcting any errors that are observed.

While the instructional steps of model, prompt, and check can be used for teaching any academic strategy or social skill, a few modifications might be made when teaching learning strategies. First, to enhance student understanding, the teacher may wish to describe the strategy steps and the rationale for each step *before* beginning to model the steps. Second, the teacher may wish to have the students verbally rehearse the strategy steps after the model or to prompt steps of instruction (Deshler, Alley, Warner, & Schumaker, 1981). If the wording of the steps is simple and generalization would be facilitated by being able to state the strategy steps, verbal rehearsal should be included. For example, students should be able to state the steps in the writing strategy POWER: Prepare, Organize, Write, Edit, Rewrite.

Maintenance of Study Skill Strategies

When effective instructional procedures are used to introduce study strategies, students generally do not have difficulty learning the strategy steps or applying them. However, getting students to *use* the strategies consistently and independently is a challenge. If the teacher never tells the students to use the strategy, never provides opportunities for strategy use, or doesn't provide feedback on strategy application, strategy use will disappear. It is vital that teachers place as much emphasis on the maintenance of study skill strategies as on their initial instruction. The following guidelines can be used to increase the use of all of the strategies presented in this chapter.

1. Tell students that you expect them to use the skill or strategy. Clearly stating expectations is a simple procedure that will increase the probability that students will employ the skill. An example of a clearly stated expectation is: *"When I give an assignment, I expect you to record it on your calendar."* If expectations are not explicit, generalization and maintenance of the strategy are likely to be minimal (Ellis, Lenz, & Sabornie, 1987).

2. Remind students to use the skill or strategy. Students can be reminded verbally to use a specific strategy before they begin a specific task in class (e.g., *"As you read Chapter 4, map the content"* or *"Now, proofread your paragraph. Check each sentence for sense, capitals, punctuation, and spelling"*). Visual prompts can also be used to encourage strategy use. For example, students can be given reference copies of the strategies to retain in their notebooks. In addition, posters with strategy steps can be displayed in classrooms to remind teachers and students about the strategy.

As students become more proficient in strategy use, the teacher should engage students in determining the appropriate strategy to apply to a task. For example, the teacher might say, *"We just previewed Chapter 5 using Warm-up. Now, you are going to read Chapter 5. Turn to the strategy in your notebook that you will use as you read the chapter. Be ready to tell me the strategy you will be using and why you have selected it."* This type of discussion will be immensely helpful in meeting the main goal of study skills instruction, which is independent application of the strategies.

3. Review the strategy periodically. As with academic strategies, study skills should be reviewed periodically within the context of well-organized lessons. During these lessons, the steps in the strategy can be reviewed, the steps can be verbally rehearsed, the importance of the steps and the strategy can be reemphasized, and the strategy can be practiced. Such "booster sessions" are often necessary for long-term maintenance of a strategy (Harris & Graham, 1985).

4. Discuss why, when, and where the strategy could be applied and the environmental cues that tell the student when to use the strategy. Students' knowledge and beliefs about when and where a study skill might be used are important if students are to take control of their cognitive processing (Pressley, Snyder, & Cariglia-Bull, 1987; Swanson, 1989). Thus, when reminding students to use a strategy or when reviewing a strategy, it is important to discuss why, when, and where the study skill might be appropriately utilized. For example, when reviewing the proofreading strategy, the teacher should discuss the types of written products that could be proofread (e.g., written reports, notes, essay tests) and the environments in which the strategy could be used. The teacher should also have students suggest their own examples of where the proofreading strategy could be employed. Further, it is useful to discuss the characteristics of tasks that would cue strategy use (Deshler & Schumaker, 1986; Gelzheiser, Shepherd, & Wozniak, 1986). For example, cues for taking specific notes include a teacher repeating a point, emphasizing a point with gestures, writing important information on the board, or telling students that information is important.

5. Provide opportunities to use and practice the skill or strategy. As with all learning, if students do not have opportunities to use the skills taught, the skills will not be maintained. Students must be given opportunities to utilize the strategies that they have been taught. For example, if they have learned how to take notes on textbook readings, the teacher must require that they take notes on factual selections. A strategy without the opportunity for application is useless.

6. Provide feedback on performance and use of the strategy. While students are using study skill strategies, the teacher should provide feedback that stresses the relationship between the students' performance and their use of the strategy to promote future generalization. For example, if a student correctly uses a strategy for answering written questions, the teacher should give feedback that stresses the student's successful use of the strategy (e.g., *"You used all the strategy steps when you answered the chapter questions. As a result, your answers are correct and written in complete sentences."*). In addition, students can be encouraged to analyze their performance in relation to their use of the strategy (e.g., *"You got seven of eight questions correct. Why do you think you did so well?"*). Reid and Borkowski (1985) showed that encouraging students with learning disabilities to attribute performance improvements to strategy use caused students to continue using the strategy after the initial instruction ended.

7. Engage students in self-monitoring and self-evaluation activities. Independent initiation of any study skill or strategy will be highly related to the students' beliefs about why, when, and where the strategy should be applied and the students' ability to self-monitor their performance (Gelzheiser et al., 1986). When teaching a skill or strategy, it is important to also teach self-management skills, such as self-questioning, self-monitoring, and self-evaluation (Gelzheiser et al., 1986; Wong & Jones, 1982), or self-recording procedures such as graphing daily progress (Harris & Graham, 1985). For example, after students have learned the strategy for creating neat, well-organized papers, they could be given a checklist to evaluate their application of each of the attributes (see Figure 14.6). In addition, on an informal level, teachers can have students verbally report on their successful and less successful applications of skills or strategies.

Summary

Jason enters his sixth-grade classroom. It is social studies period, and the students are studying the countries of South America. Jason picks up his notebook and joins three team members. After the group examines their task list and calendar entries, they decide to do some research and take notes on their country. Jason will work with Matthew while Peter will work with Rose.

Jason and Matthew set off to learn more about the products, landforms, waterways, and natural resources of Peru. After locating encyclopedia entries and a book on South America, the boys settle into their task. They read a paragraph together, decide if it relates to one of the designated topics, discuss the topic of the paragraph, and record the topic and related details using an Indentation Notes strategy. At the end of the work session, they have completed their notes for two of the topics and have set a task for the next day.

The power of learning strategies and organization skills is clearly evident in this scenario. Jason, a student with learning disabilities, could not have participated in this cooperative group or gained access to the general education curriculum without the power of learning strategies and organization skills. Equally noteworthy is the importance of the same strategies to Matthew, a normally progressing sixth-grade student. Just a few visits to a classroom reminds us that these strategies must be carefully selected, systematically taught, and maintained so that all students can experience the joy of success.

References

Anderson-Inman, L., Paine, S. C., & Deutchman, L. (1984). Neatness counts: Effects of direct instruction and self-monitoring on the transfer of neat-paper skills to nontraining setting. *Analysis and Intervention in Developmental Disabilities, 4,* 137–155.

Archer, A., & Gleason, M. (1991a). *Skills for school success, Book 3.* North Billerica, MA: Curriculum Associates.

Archer, A., & Gleason, M. (1991b). *Skills for school success, Book 4.* North Billerica, MA: Curriculum Associates.

Archer, A., & Gleason, M. (1992). *Advanced skills for school success: Module 1. School behaviors and organization skills.* North Billerica, MA: Curriculum Associates.

Archer, A., & Gleason, M. (1993a). *Advanced skills for school success: Module 2. Completing daily assignments.* North Billerica, MA: Curriculum Associates.

Archer, A., & Gleason, M. (1993b). *Advanced skills for school success: Module 3. Effective reading of textbooks.* North Billerica, MA: Curriculum Associates.

Archer, A., & Gleason, M. (1994a). *Skills for school success, Book 5.* North Billerica, MA: Curriculum Associates.

Archer, A., & Gleason, M. (1994b). *Skills for school success, Book 6.* North Billerica, MA: Curriculum Associates.

Archer, A., & Gleason, M. (1994c). *Advanced skills for school success: Module 4. Learning from verbal presentations and participating in discussions.* North Billerica, MA: Curriculum Associates.

Archer, A., & Gleason, M. (2000). *Advanced skills for school success: Module 5. Report writing.* Manuscript submitted for publication.

Archer, A., Gleason, M., & Vachon, V. (2000). *Effects of teaching multisyllabic word reading to skill-deficient fourth and fifth graders.* Unpublished manuscript.

Bereiter, C., & Scardamalia, M. (1982). From conversation to composition: The role of instruction in a developmental process. In R. Glaser (Ed.), *Advances in instructional psychology* (Vol. 2, pp. 1–64). Hillsdale, NJ: Erlbaum.

Brown, A. L., & Day, J. D. (1983). Macro-rules for summarizing texts: The development of expertise. *Journal of Verbal Learning and Verbal Behavior, 22,* 1–14.

Campione, J. C., Rutherford, M., Gordon, A., Walker, J., & Brown, A. L. (1994). "Now I'm a real boy": Zones of proximal development for those at risk. In N. C. Jordan & J. Goldsmith-Phillips (Eds.), *Learning disabilities: New directions for assessment and intervention* (pp. 245–274). Boston: Allyn & Bacon.

Deshler, D. D., Alley, G. R., Warner, M. M., & Schumaker, J. B. (1981). Instructional practices for promoting skill acquisition and generalization in severely learning disabled adolescents. *Learning Disability Quarterly, 4,* 415–421.

Deshler, D. D., & Schumaker, J. B. (1986). Learning strategies: An instructional alternative for low-achieving adolescents. *Exceptional Children, 52,* 583–590.

Deshler, D. D., Schumaker, J. B., & Lenz, B. K. (1984). Academic and cognitive interventions for LD adolescents: Part I. *Journal of Learning Disabilities, 17,* 108–117.

Deshler, D. D., Schumaker, J. B., Lenz, B. K., & Ellis, E. (1984). Academic and cognitive interventions for LD adolescents: Part II. *Journal of Learning Disabilities, 17,* 170–179.

DiCecco, Y. M., & Gleason, M. M. (2000). *Graphic organizers as an aid in fostering comprehension of expository text.* Manuscript submitted for publication.

Ellis, E. S., Lenz, B. K., & Sabornie, E. J. (1987). Generalization and adaptation of learning strategies to natural environments: Part 2. Research into practice. *Remedial and Special Education, 8*(2), 6–23.

Englert, C. S., & Mariage, T. V. (1991). Shared understandings: Structuring the writing experience through dialogue. *Journal of Learning Disabilities, 24,* 330–342.

Garner, R., McCready, G. B., & Wagoner, S. (1984). Readers' acquisition of the components of the text lookback strategy. *Journal of Educational Psychology, 76,* 300–309.

Gelzheiser, L. M., Shepherd, M. J., & Wozniak, R. H. (1986). The development of instruction to induce skill transfer. *Exceptional Children, 53,* 125–129.

Graham, S., & Harris, K. R. (1989). Improving learning disabled students' skills at composing essays: Self-instructional strategy training. *Exceptional Children, 56,* 201–214.

Graham, S., Harris, K. R., & Sawyer, R. (1987). Composition instruction with learning disabled students: Self-instructional strategy training. *Focus on Exceptional Children, 20*(4), 1–11.

Hare, V. C., & Borchardt, K. M. (1984). Direct instruction of summarization skills. *Reading Research Quarterly, 21,* 62–78.

Harris, K. R., & Graham, S. (1985). Improving learning disabled students' composition skills: Self-control strategy training. *Learning Disability Quarterly, 8,* 27–36.

Hayes, J. R., & Flower, L. S. (1980). Identifying the organization of writing processes. In L. W. Gregg & E. R. Steinberg (Eds.), *Cognitive processes in writing* (pp. 3–30). Hillsdale, NJ: Erlbaum.

Huffman, L. E., & Spires, H. A. (1994). Effects of explicit instruction in notetaking on sixth graders' lecture comprehension and attitudes toward notetaking. *Reading Improvement, 31,* 72–76.

Idol, L. (1987). Group story mapping: A comprehension strategy for both skilled and unskilled readers. *Journal of Learning Disabilities, 20,* 196–205.

Idol, L., & Croll, V. J. (1987). Story-mapping training as a means of improving reading comprehension. *Learning Disability Quarterly, 10,* 214–229.

Laidlaw, E. N., Skok, R. L., & McLaughlin, T. F. (1993). The effects of notetaking and self-questioning on quiz performance. *Science Education, 77,* 75–82.

Mastropieri, M. A., Scruggs, T. E., & Levin, J. R. (1985). Mnemonic strategy instruction with learning disabled adolescents. *Journal of Learning Disabilities, 18,* 94–100.

Murrell, P. C., Jr., & Surber, J. R. (1987, April). *The effect of generative summarization on the comprehension of main ideas from lengthy expository text.* Paper presented at the annual meeting of the American Educational Research Association, Washington, DC.

O'Connor, R., & Jenkins, J. (1986). Cooperative learning as an inclusion strategy: A closer look. *Exceptionality, 6*(1), 29–52.

Ogle, D. M. (1986). K-W-L: A teaching model that develops active reading of expository text. *The Reading Teacher, 39,* 564–570.

Paris, S. G., Cross, D. R., & Lipson, M. Y. (1984). Informed strategies for learning: A program to improve children's reading awareness and comprehension. *Journal of Educational Psychology, 76,* 1239–1252.

Pressley, M., & Associates. (1990). *Cognitive strategy instruction that really improves children's academic performance.* Cambridge, MA: Brookline Books.

Pressley, M., Snyder, B. L., & Cariglia-Bull, T. (1987). How can good strategy use be taught to children? Evaluation of six alternative approaches. In S. M. Cormier & J. D. Hagman (Eds.), *Transfer of learning: Contemporary research and applications* (pp. 81–120). Orlando, FL: Academic Press.

Raphael, T. E., & McKinney, J. (1983). An examination of fifth- and eighth-grade children's question-answering behavior: An instructional study in metacognition. *Journal of Reading Behavior, 15,* 67–86.

Reid, M. K., & Borkowski, J. G. (1985, April). *The influence of attribution training on strategic behaviors, self-management, and beliefs about control in hyperactive children.* Paper presented at the annual meeting of the Society for Research in Child Development, Toronto, Canada.

Rinehart, S. D., Stahl, S. A., & Erickson, L. G. (1986). Some effects of summarization training on reading and studying. *Reading Research Quarterly, 21,* 422–438.

Robinson, F. P. (1946). *Effective study.* New York: Harper & Brothers.

Schumaker, J. B., Denton, P. H., & Deshler, D. (1984). *Learning strategies curriculum: The paraphrasing strategy.* Lawrence: University of Kansas.

Schumaker, J. B., Nolan, S. M., & Deshler, D. D. (1985). *Learning strategies curriculum: The error monitoring strategy.* Lawrence: University of Kansas.

Seitz, E. R., Jr., (1997). Using media presentations to teach notetaking, main idea, and summarization skills. *Journal of Adolescent and Adult Literacy, 40,* 562–563.

Short, E. J., & Ryan, E. B. (1984). Metacognitive differences between skilled and less skilled readers: Remediating deficits through story grammar and attribution training. *Journal of Educational Psychology, 76,* 225–235.

Spires, H. A., & Stone, P. D. (1989). The directed notetaking activity: A self-questioning approach. *Journal of Reading, 33,* pp. 36–39.

Stevens, P., & Fear, K. L. (1987). *Metacognitive knowledge about writing informational text: Effects of cognitive strategy instruction.* Paper presented at the National Reading Conference, St. Petersburg, FL.

Swanson, H. L. (1989). Strategy instruction: Overview of principles and procedures for effective use. *Learning Disability Quarterly, 12,* 3–14.

Wong, B. Y. L., & Jones, W. (1982). Increasing metacomprehension in learning disabled and normally achieving students through self-questioning training. *Learning Disability Quarterly, 5,* 228–240.

15

High-Access Instruction: Practical Strategies to Increase Active Learning in Diverse Classrooms

Kevin Feldman and Lou Denti

Determining how to enhance teaching and motivate students to learn continues to present a challenge for educators. The challenge today is, perhaps, greater than ever, as more diverse students with complex academic and emotional needs look to teachers for social support and academic assistance. Adding to the problem is the fact that creating opportunities for students with learning challenges to access the district's or school's core curriculum of study requires a significant shift in teaching attitude and focus. Research-validated instructional methods have made a substantial difference for students with diverse learning needs, but all too often, creating the time for teachers to learn these methods is not of high priority for the district or school. Further, the organization of schools is sometimes structured in a way that prevents powerful teaching, innovative organizational arrangements, and new curricular approaches. As Peter Senge, organizational expert, stated, "Schools may fail to incorporate research-validated practices for students with learning disabilities because schools themselves suffer from learning disabilities" (cited in Knight, 1998, p. 1). To truly meet the academic and social needs of a diverse population of students, organizations will need to re-create themselves to meet this diversity head-on, or they will be left sideswiped by an anachronistic system geared for a student who no longer exists (Katz & Denti, 1996).

The ensuing discourse challenges schools to redesign themselves based on the given that every classroom contains a diverse group of students with large variances in prior knowledge, skills, motivation, and ability in English. More specifically, it responds to the demands of classroom diversity by providing empirically valid and practical learning strategies that teachers can implement without extensive training. Further, it suggests that traditional approaches (e.g., undifferentiated curriculum, "sage on the stage" teaching, removing children who do not fit) only serve to widen the gaps between successful and struggling students. Challenging the notion that schools are for those students who "do school well," the chapter offers teachers a view of powerful instruction that empowers all students. The focus of the chapter is the following question: *How can teachers more effectively respond to classroom diversity and help all students improve or "get smarter"?*

Why Change the Way We Teach?

The data over the past 25 years suggest that lower level classes and special classes for students with learning difficulties often produce an opposite effect from the original intent, which was to provide intensive individualized instruction to improve or ameliorate the identified problem (Ensminger, 1991; Stainback & Stainback, 1984; Steinberg, 1991; Wang, Reynolds, & Walberg, 1986). By their very nature, these classes dilute or supplant the core curriculum, often rescuing or enabling students via a tutorial or remedial approach (Deshler & Schumaker, 1986). The result has been a less capable learner unequipped to deal with the exigencies of the general education classroom or the real world (Zigmond & Thorton, 1985). Just as distressing, many students with learning problems give up, give in, act out, become indifferent, or drop out—an indictment, so to speak, of a system unable to adapt to meet students' needs.

To offset the negative aspects of separate schooling for students with learning disabilities, educators in the past decade have touted inclusion as educationally sound and "right." Though inclusionary efforts have been meritorious, they have not garnered the necessary support and resources to gain unilateral acceptance at most schools. Further, teachers lack the training and time to develop an appropriate opportunity structure for students with learning disabilities in general education classrooms (Denti, 1994). Whether a school is using pullout programs or inclusive programs, the need to provide more intensive focused instruction to students labeled learning disabled and other low-achieving students is critical.

On that note, we now turn to what we have called high-access instruction (HAI). High-access instruction is a method of teaching that uses instructional strategies designed to ensure that all teachers and students are actively engaged in the learning process. The remainder of this chapter defines HAI, contrasts high- and low-access strategies, and describes how high-access instruction can be implemented by classroom teachers.

The Challenge of Incorporating High-Access Instruction in School Classrooms

As a society, we can legislate and mandate opportunity—think, for example, of desegregation and inclusion—but legislation does not ensure access. That is, we can place students with learning disabilities in general education classrooms and tell ourselves that they have expanded opportunities, but the actual research data (Vaughn & Schumm, 1995; Vaughn, Schumm, Jallad, Slusher, & Saumell, 1996; Zigmond & Baker, 1995) document that students with learning disabilities do not have the same access to classroom activities as their peers.

According to a growing body of research (McIntosh, Vaughn, Schumm, Haager, & Lee, 1993; Schumm, Vaughn, Gordon, & Rothlein, 1994), general education teachers have provided opportunities for students with learning disabilities to participate in the same activities as nonlabeled peers, but few adaptations or enhancements have been made. Differentiation of the curriculum to support students with learning challenges has rarely been observed. Moreover, Vaughn and Schumm (1995) found that students with learning disabilities participated minimally in general education classes. For these students, they observed low levels of participating in class, asking for help, answering and asking questions, engaging with peers, participating in teacher-directed activities, and following through with homework. Further, they found that general education classroom teachers expected less of students with learning disabilities. The teachers asked the students with learning disabilities fewer questions, interacted with them less in discussion, provided them with less feedback, and monitored their group work less. These findings occurred across grade levels and were exaggerated at middle and high school levels. The authors concluded that there appeared to be a tacit assumption between general education teachers and students with learning disabilities that went something like this: "You don't bother me, and I won't bother you!"

Any rethinking of the learning disabilities paradigm must go beyond concepts of inclusion and mainstreaming to address learning activities in the classroom that empower and engage all learners. Significant changes are required on the part of general and specialist teachers to ensure that high-access instruction becomes the norm in schools serving diverse learners.

What we propose fundamentally challenges the very nature of instruction in classrooms. High-access instruction sees all students as potential assets rather than problems. It also asks teachers to analyze their teaching and look for areas where instruction may be "breaking down," rather than blaming their students for not understanding the content. By shifting the paradigm of instruction to variables the teacher controls, high-access instruction lays the groundwork for more interaction between teachers, students, ancillary staff, and parent volunteers.

High-Access Instruction: What is it?

High-access instruction is a way of teaching that uses empirically sound and valid learning strategies to (a) actively engage all learners in a classroom, (b) maximize student participation, and (c) ensure that diverse learners focus their attention on critical concepts and big ideas (Kameenui & Carnine, 1998). High-access instruction combines many strategies that have their roots in cooperative learning, direct instruction, and critical thinking. These approaches have a sound research base and can be effectively implemented in almost any type of classroom at any grade level.

High-access instruction frames teaching from the perspective of "everyone does everything" in the classroom. The teacher's role shifts from disseminator of information to choreographer of learning. The lesson/unit design incorporates dynamic interaction with students. The teacher's job is to get all students actively engaged and participating. Simply put, HAI encourages students to think, speak, write, touch, build, listen, practice—to actively learn. It frames the issue of student diversity in terms of variables that teachers can powerfully respond to, rather than in terms of problems to be eliminated via administrative fiat. As Keogh (1990) indicated nearly a decade ago, major changes are needed in the delivery of services to problem learners, and these services need to be the responsibility of general and special educators. She further pointed out that teachers are the central players in bringing about change in practice and that our most pressing challenge is to determine how to improve the quality of instruction at the classroom level.

High-access instruction is an answer to Keogh's cry for change at the classroom level. It provides teachers with a means for employing concrete learning strategies at every stage of a lesson or unit, from brainstorming and predicting before new content is taught to structured review after a lesson. Many examples of high-access learning strategies are provided in this chapter to help teachers gain an understanding of how to employ these powerful teaching methods in their classrooms. In addition, the chapter points out the limited viability of low-access instruction.

What Does Not Work: A Brief Look at Common Low-Access Teaching Practices

Before we examine the details of high-access instructional strategies, we present a brief look at some common low-access teaching practices to provide a point of comparison. The majority of these low-access teaching routines are not harmful or "bad" in and of themselves; however, they are likely to be ineffective in today's diverse classrooms because they assume homogeneity among very diverse students. Low-access practices tend to treat all students as if they have the same skill levels, motivation, fluency in English, and prior knowledge about various content area subjects. As such, they limit the ability of many students to interact with the teacher, think critically, or construct new meaning.

A significant first step to crafting schools and classrooms that truly work for all kinds of learners is to ensure that teachers' instructional "tool kits" are well stocked with validated strategies that engage every student in the learning process so that teachers may better resist using low-access strategies.

Hand Raising

The most powerful thing a teacher can do to ensure real access to powerful learning experiences may be deceptively simple: Stop the age-old practice of hand raising as the primary way to structure discussion and other forms of discourse in the classroom. It has been repeatedly documented (e.g., Cohen, 1994; Goodlad, 1984) that dramatic inequity exists in classroom verbal interactions as early as kindergarten and that these troubling social structures persist through graduate school. Some students can't get enough of the teacher's attention, continually having their hands in the air, responding to every question, blurting out answers, and so forth, while others sit quietly, either bored or daydreaming, fearful of looking inept, or otherwise disengaged from the instructional conversation. It comes as no surprise that the correlation between classroom interaction and student achievement is significant and that the "dye gets cast" at an early age. All teachers know it is not the low-achieving student, the second language learner, the student with disabilities, or the less confident student who raises his or her hand to contribute. Thus, a logical first step for a teacher desiring to change this inequitable classroom sociology is to stop engaging in the practice of asking questions and waiting for students to raise their hands with a response.

Allowing Students to Blurt Out Answers

Blurting out answers as soon as the teacher poses a question is the primary-grade "cousin" to hand raising. Eager students often want to show their enthusiasm and intelligence by shouting out the answer before much of the class has even figured out the question! While teachers may admonish students who blurt out answers, subtle cues often communicate that this behavior is acceptable and indicative of a quick mind. However, the student who shouts out answers is unwittingly depriving his or her classmates of the valuable thinking time that they need to cognitively process the question and construct a viable response.

Round-Robin Reading

One of the most common forms of passage reading in schools is known as round-robin reading, where students take turns reading aloud while the rest of the class or group follow along. Though this is practice fraught with difficulties, just one of which being that only one student is actively engaged in the reading activity, it persists as a salient teaching method in most classrooms. Teachers who dismiss this method have reported that many students are so busy counting the lines until their turn to read that they pay little attention to the student who is reading aloud. In addition, less able students are often anxiety ridden awaiting their turn and then humiliated by demonstrating to the whole class their lack of skill in oral reading.

Unstructured Group Work

"Get into groups and discuss the meaning of the homework," exhorts a well-intended middle school teacher. The problem with this type of instruction is that, lacking a clear objective, the groups will simply replicate the inequities of the larger classroom. One student will likely dominate and take over the conversation while others, will be uninvolved or off task. Group work can be a powerful alternative to whole class instruction or independent seat work (Slavin, 1984), but only if the groups are carefully structured to ensure positive interdependence and individual accountability for learning the information.

Undifferentiated Curriculum—"One Size Fits All"

Assigning everyone the same homework assignment, the same stories for individual reading, the same format for projects, and so on, ensures frustration for students who do not have the required prior knowledge and skills to derive benefit from the activity. Yet teachers often find themselves confronting the reality of using an elementary reading anthology ordered by their district's central office for use with all students at their grade, regardless of the fact that one half or more of their students cannot independently read the books. Vygotsky (1978) and others have documented that instruction must be provided at a student's instructional level, or zone of proximal development. This cannot be done with a "straitjacket" curriculum that assumes homogeneity in heterogeneous classrooms.

Undifferentiated Teaching—"Sage on the Stage"

The corollary to undifferentiated curriculum is undifferentiated instruction. The teacher who views teaching as essentially communicating information via oral recitation to a group of students limits opportunities for learning. Goodlad's (1984) groundbreaking study documented that "sage on the stage" teaching was the most established and universal form of classroom instruction and was especially commonplace at the secondary level. Very little has changed since that study. Yet oral recitation ignores the fact that classrooms with many diverse learners require teachers to do more than simply cover the material. They need to *scaffold* new information via the effective use of various instructional strategies designed to teach students how to learn (Simmons & Kameenui, 1996).

In sum, many of the most common general instructional practices are not effective because they assume homogeneity among students. It is not enough, however, to simply stop engaging in nonproductive instructional routines such as hand raising: Teachers need clear alternatives that increase *access* to critical skills and information for the wide variety of students in today's classrooms. Classroom teachers of the 21st century need to be equipped with a "tool kit" of instructional tactics and strategies that have been documented to work with diverse learners, including students labeled learning disabled. High-access instructional strategies are one set of tools that research suggests can significantly assist teachers in meeting the challenge of creating classrooms that truly work for all students.

High-Access Instructional Strategies

The goal of high-access instructional strategies is to ensure that all students have meaningful access to the content of lessons through active-engagement learning activities. The instructional tactics assume that diverse students will have varying amounts of prior knowledge about any given topic as well as varying proficiency in English and a wide range of basic skills in reading, writing, and mathematics. Additionally, high-access instructional strategies strive to provide a safe, nonthreatening environment within which students can practice developing skills and explore new information. The following sections briefly describe the high-access strategies and provide examples that demonstrate how teachers can incorporate the strategies into their lessons to effectively accommodate the needs of diverse learners.

Choral, or Group, Responding

1. Ask a question and tell students, "Think—don't blurt out."
2. Provide thinking time.
3. Provide a simple oral or visual cue that will signal all students to respond together.

Choral or group, responding is an age-old strategy that works very well when the answers are *short* and the *same* (Archer, Gleason, & Issacson, 1995; Carnine, Silbert, & Kameenui, 1997). It provides a safe environment for practicing new skills while keeping engagement and attention focused for all students. The teacher teaches the students how to think first and then, upon a signal such as lowering both hands, to respond as a group.

Consider, for example, a first-grade teacher reviewing the sight word "was." He or she could use choral responding to ensure that all students look at the word, think about how to say it, and then say it together. The teacher would point at the word on the overhead projector and ask everyone to look at it and think about what it says. After a minute or two, the teacher would give a signal for the class to respond as a group. Individual mistakes in the group responses would cue the teacher to review the sight word in more detail before going on with the lesson.

Thumbs Up When You Know

1. Ask a question and tell students, "Think—don't blurt out, and put your thumb up when you know."
2. Provide thinking time.
3. Check to see that most students have their thumbs up.
4. Either call on students randomly or cue students to respond chorally as a group (if the answer is short and the same).

Thumbs Up allows students to demonstrate that they know an answer without blurting it out, which, as noted earlier, deprives other students of the critical time they may need to cognitively process the question and form an answer. Secondary teachers often use a modification of the Thumbs Up approach by asking students to make eye contact with them when they are ready to answer. Both approaches provide all students with valuable thinking time, prevent the blurting out of answers, and give the teacher a quick and immediate assessment of student knowledge and ability to respond successfully. In addition, they avoid the pitfalls of calling on students who are not prepared or do not feel comfortable responding.

A fifth-grade teacher might, for example, ask students to reflect on the critical attributes of cold-blooded animals just reviewed in a video on the subject and to put their thumbs up when they can identify at least one. The teacher would then randomly call on individual students or ask the students to whisper the answer to their partners. Thus, all students would be actively engaged in reflecting on key aspects of the video and would have a nonthreatening opportunity to participate in the class dialogue.

Classroom Whip Around

1. Pose an open-ended question. Answers must be a word or a phrase, 10-word limit.
2. Provide thinking time, and model a response if needed (partner responses can be used instead to better ensure that all students have something to contribute).
3. Start anywhere in the class and "whip around the room" having students quickly share their answers. Allow no discussion or comments.
4. Students have the right to pass.

The Classroom Whip Around is a fun, engaging strategy that provides students with the opportunity to practice summarization and oral recitation in a safe classroom environment. The whip is particularly useful for encouraging students to identify key big ideas, themes, and summative information at the end of a lesson or activity. Teachers can modify the whip by having students write their answer on a sheet of paper and simply stand to show the class their written response as the "wave" circulates around the classroom.

The following scenarios illustrates the classroom Whip Around strategy. At the end of an eighth-grade geography lesson, students are asked to reflect on one important attribute of the region they have been studying. The teacher provides thinking time, inviting the students to put their thumbs up or make eye contact when they are ready to respond. Then he or she "whips around" the classroom giving each student a brief chance to share one attribute. Further discussion took place after all students had the chance to respond.

Partner Strategies

Perhaps the most flexible set of HAI strategies involve various forms of structured partner responding. In all of these partner strategies, the teacher matches each student to an appropriate partner (i.e., high-performing students with middle-performing, middle-performing with lower-performing students) and provides the partners with specific roles for the activity. Partner responding works well across the educational spectrum, from kindergarten through graduate school classrooms.

THINK-(WRITE)-PAIR-SHARE

1. Pose an open-ended question (no single answer).
2. Provide time for students to think of answers (useful to have older students write responses in a notebook/double-entry journal).
3. Have students form pairs. Designate students in each pair as a "one" or a "two." Direct "ones" to share answers for a minute or two, then reverse the process.
4. Randomly call on individuals to share with the class.

Think-Pair-Share (Kagan, 1992) is a versatile high-access strategy. It is particularly useful for open-ended questions that have many possible answers, such as used in brainstorming. Success with this and other partner strategies revolves around carefully structuring each detail involved in the activity. Care should be taken, for example, to structure the time frame (start short, 1–2 minutes), topic, role, and social expectations.

This example illustrates the Think-(Write)-Pair-Share strategy. A high school English teacher asks students to reflect on a character in a novel they are reading and then to individually write a list of as many attributes as they can that are distinctive about the character. After a few minutes, the teacher directs the students to work in pairs. The teacher instructs the "ones" to share what they have written about the character while the "twos" practice good listening skills. At the end of 2 minutes, he instructs the "twos" to share what they found distinctive about the character. He encourages the students to add useful items learned from their partner to their own master list. The teacher carefully monitors student responses by listening to selected pairs as they converse. This provides him with an opportunity to informally assess how well students understand the information and if more examples or practice would be helpful. After Think-(Write)-Pair-Share, the teacher asks the students to compose, as a homework assignment, a brief essay comparing and contrasting the key attributes of this character with the protagonist of the novel they have read earlier in the semester.

TELL-HELP-CHECK

1. Assign partners. Designate students in each pair as a "one" or a "two."
2. Pose a closed-ended question (one right answer).
3. Give thinking time.
4. Have one partner in each pair *tell* the other all he or she can recall about the topic/subject/question (encourage students to make educated guesses—tell them to "give it a go").
5. Explain that the other partner *helps* by adding anything the "teller" left out, by correcting, by elaborating, and so on.
6. Explain that both partners will then *check* in the book, notes, overhead, etc., and validate, correct, or elaborate on their answers.

Research (Rosenshine, 1987) and common sense suggest that review of critical information is vital for all students, especially those most at risk for school failure. Evidence also suggests that teachers and higher achieving students actually do most of the reviewing that takes place in the typical classroom (Schumm & Vaughn, 1995; Thomas & Rohwer, 1987). In fact, the students who most need to generate a response or practice their emerging English are the very students least likely to be actively engaged in classroom review activities. Tell-Help-Check (Archer, 1999) offers teachers a robust strategy for ensuring that all students are actively involved in systematic review of critical information, regardless of their prior knowledge or proficiency in English. This strategy works well when reviewing factual information that has discrete right and wrong answers.

As an example, a high school science teacher could ask her students to describe the key phases of the convection cycle they have been studying. Ones would *tell* "twos" all they could, "twos" would *help* by adding, correcting, or elaborating on "ones'" responses. Finally, the partners together would *check* the response by reviewing a graphic in their text that summarizes the information. Whole class discussion could then be conducted to provide additional information or examples the teacher felt were necessary. Tell-Help-Check is a textbook example of a high-access instructional strategy that dramatically increases the active participation of all learners, thus ensuring that the students, not the teacher, are actually doing the cognitive work of reviewing.

DO-CHECK-TEACH

1. Assign students to partners with adjacent achievement levels. Have them number off as "ones" and "twos."[1]
2. Pass out the problems/worksheet and the answer key.
3. Instruct partners to individually (independently) answer the first question without looking at the answer key.
4. Have partners compare answers and compare their answers to the answer key.
5. If either partner missed the question, the other student should teach him or her how to work it out correctly.
6. If both partners missed the problem, they should ask another pair or you for assistance.

Do-Check-Teach is a simple partner strategy that is ideal for enhancing independent seat work in math. Similar in nature to Kagan's (1992) Pairs Check, Do-Check-Teach helps students focus on the purpose of practice by providing them with the answers for checking their work. Students are reminded that the reason for doing the worksheet is to become fluent with the process or strategy recently covered in class, not simply to arrive at the right answers. If both partners struggle, they can ask

---

[1] A quick format for determining adjacent levels in reading is to rank order your classroom and then place the top student with the middle student and so forth. For example, in a class of 30, Student 1 would partner with Student 16, Student 2 with Student 17, and so on.

a nearby pair for assistance or summon the teacher. Use of Do-Check-Teach also gives teachers time to circulate and provide individual pairs with additional instruction, modeling, and other personalized assistance.

A first-grade teacher might use Do-Check-Teach with her students to practice recently taught math skills. By having the time to circulate, the teacher would be able to differentiate her teaching and provide individual pairs with the exact practice they need, thereby avoiding a"one-size-fits-all" approach. Topics could range from single column addition to addition with regrouping to subtraction with borrowing. The students would also benefit from the immediate feedback by their assigned peers.

CLASSWIDE PEER TUTORING/PEER-ASSISTED LEARNING

1. Partner students via adjacent achievement levels.
2. Structure partner activity (e.g. for reading fluency, "ones" could read for 5 minutes followed by "twos" rereading the same passage for 5 minutes; continue for 20 minutes).
3. Partners earn points for on-task behavior.
4. Tutors provide partners with error correction as needed.
5. Team points are totaled weekly.

Classwide Peer Tutoring (CWPT) offers a wide range of effective high-access instructional opportunities. An extensive research base documents its effectiveness in heterogeneous elementary and secondary classrooms for developing basic skills in reading, math, and spelling (Greenwood & Delquadri, 1995). Peer-Assisted Learning Strategies (PALS), elaborations of CWPT (Fuchs, Fuchs, Mathes, & Simmons, 1997), are particularly helpful for teachers in Grades 2–8 facing the challenge of diverse reading levels among their students. To implement PALS Reading, for example, the teacher structures partner reading wherein students take turns engaging in the following sequence of activities to promote reading fluency and comprehension:

Peer-Assisted Learning Strategies Reading

1. Partner 1 predicts what will happen next in a reading passage at the partners' instructional level.
2. Partner 1 then reads the section of text orally and monitors his or her prediction.
3. Partner 1 summarizes the text and says who/what the section was about—that is, the topic.
4. Partner 1 tells the most important thing about the topic, adding pertinent details.
5. Partner 1 paraphrases in 10 words or fewer the "gist" of the section.
6. Partner 2 makes a new prediction about the same section and repeats the sequence.
7. With PALS Reading, the partners take turns reading and asking each other the comprehension questions while the teacher monitors individual pairs.

Like CWPT, Peer-Assisted Learning Strategies allow teachers to differentiate instruction by having students read in texts at their instructional level while the whole class is practicing the same reading strategy (e.g., prediction, summarization). Mathes, Howard, Allen, and Fuchs (1998) recently demonstrated that a modification of PALS is equally effective for assisting first-grade readers in the acquisition of beginning reading skills.

The following example shows how PALS can be used: A fourth-grade teacher might set up PALS reading practice for 40 minutes a day. He would partner students with adjacent reading levels and find appropriate texts to match their average instructional level, ranging from second- to seventh-grade texts. The partners would take turns reading and practicing comprehension strategies using the PALS guidelines. The teacher would circulate to listen to students as they read orally and practiced their comprehension strategies.

Cloze Reading With Choral Responding

1. Read material from the text aloud to the class.
2. Have students follow along in their books.
3. Leave out selected words every sentence or so.
4. Have students read the left out words chorally.

A powerful alternative to round-robin reading is cloze reading with choral responding. This strategy gives all students access to the information in the text, focuses their attention, and allows for diverse reading levels among students. The teacher reads aloud while the students follow along in their books (primary students can use their fingers as well). The teacher leaves out selected words that most students will be able to read, and the whole class reads those words together chorally. Care should be taken to keep the pace lively to encourage all students to read the words that are left out.

Consider this scenario: A seventh-grade history teacher realizes that one half of her class cannot independently read the text. Moreover, when she reads aloud, many students are inattentive. By leaving out a word every sentence or two and prompting students to respond as a group, attentiveness increases. She makes sure that the majority of the words she leaves out are words that most of the students can read independently. With this strategy, less confident readers as well as English language learners have a safe environment in which to practice their emerging language skills without holding the class back from exploring content area concepts.

Random Questioning With 3 × 5 Name Cards

1. Write all the students' names on 3 × 5 cards.
2. Pose a question and give thinking time.
3. Use Thumbs Up or partners to ensure that all students are prepared to respond productively.
4. Randomly select a student to give the answer by picking the next card in the pile of 3 × 5 cards.

Students often enjoy game-like formats, which enliven class discussion. The use of 3 × 5 cards adds an enjoyable element to the discussion process while making students accountable for their learning. Step 3 is the key to success when using this strategy. It ensures that all students have access to the information prior to the teacher having a student answer the question.

A middle school teacher might conduct the review of study questions at the end of a history chapter by combining Think-Pair-Share and 3 × 5 cards to create a lively discussion. If extra pizzazz is desired, the teacher could place half of the class on one team and half on another and keep a running score of correct responses for each team.

Give one–Get One

1. Pose a question that requires a list of answers. Have students brainstorm the answers individually and write them down in a list.
2. Have students draw a line after the final idea they noted.
3. At your signal, invite students to move around the classroom to *get* at least one additional idea to add to their list and to *give* at least one idea from their list to a classmate.
4. Have students return to their seats, review their new lists, and discuss the items with a partner or the whole class.

Brainstorming is an important classroom activity with endless permutations. Give One–Get One provides an interesting brainstorming variation by giving students a chance to get up and move around the classroom in a structured manner while at the same time holding them accountable for a productive outcome.

For example, a sixth grade teacher could ask students to list all of the possible reasons people immigrated to the United States in the 1840s. Then, using Give One–Get One, she could give students 4 minutes to add reasons to their lists ("below the line" on their papers) as they circulate around the classroom. After 4 minutes, the teacher would give a "wrap it up" signal, and the students would return to their seats to review their new lists. Using Think-Pair-Share, the teacher might then direct the students to select the three most compelling reasons from their newly expanded lists and discuss with a partner why they chose them. Whole class discussion using 3 × 5 cards could follow with the teacher helping students to grapple with the key ideas behind immigration to the United States in the mid-19th century.

Heads Together

1. Place students in heterogeneous teams of three or four (combine two pairs if using partners regularly).
2. Have students number off (e.g., 1, 2, 3, 4).
3. Explain that you will pose a question and set a time limit for the groups to discuss the answer.
4. Inform the teams that you will randomly select one number and the person in each team with that number will be accountable for sharing the group's answer.

5. Pose a question that requires conversation and elaboration. Set a time limit.
6. Have the students put their heads together to find the answer.
7. Randomly select one number. Have the "lucky" students share answers with the class.

Classroom discussions are notorious for lack of equitable student participation. At a recent conference session on curricular adaptations for secondary students, one teacher quipped, "The same kids participate in high school who did in third grade!" Unfortunately, the research data support this observation. Heads Together offers teachers a simple, yet elegant alternative to traditional classroom discussions driven by hand raising. It provides all students with access to critical information while making each student responsible for responding to the question at hand. Heads Together increases performance in content area discussions and content tests for all levels of students in diverse classroom settings (Maheady, Mallette, Harper, & Sacca, 1988). Our observations suggest that teachers may want to assign additional roles of "checker" and "discussion facilitator" to provide even more structure for the discussion. The checker simply checks to make sure that all group members can answer appropriately if called upon; the discussion facilitator's job is to ensure that all group members participate and share information.

Here's an example of classroom use of the Heads Together strategy. A third-grade teacher places students into heterogeneous teams of four and asks them to think about and discuss four questions they would like to ask the author of the novel they have just finished. After 7 minutes of intense dialogue, the teacher brings the class back together, using the predetermined signal of turning the lights off and on once to get student attention. After the signal, the students stop talking and watch intently as the teacher spins a spinner on his desk to see who the "lucky winners" will be. The spinner lands on 4. All "fours" stand up, and the teacher randomly calls on each to share one idea. The whole class claps for each student as he or she shares an idea. After each student shares, he or she takes a seat. At the conclusion of the sharing, the teacher adds additional comments to tie the ideas together. For homework, each individual student composes a letter to the author using one or two of the questions generated in their Heads Together team.

Ambassadors

1. Follow the same procedures as for Heads Together.
2. After choosing the lucky number, have each of the selected students go to the group closest, clockwise, to him or her. Explain that each group is a foreign country and that each selected student is an "ambassador."
3. Have the ambassadors share their groups' answers with the "foreign country" and ask for one different answer that they can take back "home" to share.
4. Have the ambassadors return home to share what they have learned with their team members.

Ambassadors can be a particularly effective strategy for increasing access to learning in diverse classrooms. It allows students to practice oral recitation in the relatively nonthreatening context of a small group, instead of before the entire class. Like Heads Together, Ambassadors allows students with less prior knowledge to benefit from the team's combined knowledge, while at the same time holds individuals accountable for learning, because no one knows who will be selected until the number is chosen. If the topic is particularly open ended and complex, teachers may want to have the ambassadors make rotations to two or more different groups. Doing so not only expands the knowledge base of each group but provides each individual ambassador with repeated practice presenting his or her information. This type of authentic practice is exactly what English language learners, low achievers, and other diverse learners need to master critical information in a safe learning community.

The following scenario shows a classroom situation that is ideal for Ambassadors. A ninth-grade social studies teacher is working with her students to understand why Sumaria was an important civilization in the ancient world. She assigns each team of four the task of determining the four major reasons for why Sumaria was an important civilization. At the end of a Heads Together type discussion, she randomly selects "threes" to be the appointed ambassadors. All "threes" stand and "fly" to the country to their right with a "visa" that expires in 5 minutes. They must share their group's four reasons and rationales and then must come back "home" with at least one new reason learned from the "foreign country." At the end of 5 minutes the teacher gives the signal for the ambassadors to return "home" and share what they learned. A classwide discussion follows bringing to light interesting answers from all countries. For homework, each student writes a short paper describing why ancient Sumaria was an important civilization.

Reciprocal Teaching

1. Demonstrate and model the four strategies of reciprocal teaching: predictions (cover what are they, why use them, and what makes a good one); questions (cover how to phrase them and why they are so helpful in reading); clarifications (cover what are they, how to phrase them, and why they are useful); and summaries (cover what are they, examples of paraphrasing, and how summaries help text understanding).
2. Read aloud, or have students silently read (if students have the decoding skills), a section of text (a paragraph or page).
3. Then lead students through a dialogue using the relevant reciprocal teaching strategies, taking care to model the thinking that would be used when applying each strategy.
4. Provide on going practice by shifting control for leading discussion to the students as longer passages of text are being read.

Palinscar and Brown (1984) documented the effectiveness of reciprocal teaching for developing reading comprehension with diverse students. The demonstrations and modeling show students exactly how to perform a task so that they can better comprehend narrative and factual text. The key to success with reciprocal teaching, as well as other reading comprehension strategies, is to overtly model the thinking one might use when applying the strategy (Pressley, El-Dinary, et al., 1992).

For example, a sixth-grade teacher modeling prediction when prereading a science textbook might say, "Let's see. We know these plants capture insects to eat, but the author hasn't told us anything about how the plants actually attract and seize them. I predict in the next section the author will tell us . . ." As the class continued to read the selection, the teacher would stop to model each of the four reciprocal teaching strategies and would prompt the students to practice using the strategies with their partners. Over the next 4–6 weeks, the students would take more and more control of the modeling and of directing the reciprocal teaching process in content area texts.

Low- and High-Access Instruction Contrasted

The purpose of HAI extends beyond incorporating a few calculated instructional tricks into classroom instruction. The challenge rests in the responsibility of the teacher to create a classroom that honors active thinking and discussion while at the same time advocates for and promotes student construction of meaning either individually or as a group. In high-access classrooms, teachers are accountable for ensuring that all students are active participants in each instructional activity. These teachers understand that "learning is not a spectator sport" (Archer, 1999). The differences between high-access and low-access instruction are summarized in Table 15.1.

Summary

Low-access classroom activities go on in almost every classroom in America that unintentionally exclude many diverse students from having meaningful access to learning. This typical, or generic, instruction is a product of years of creating schools as assembly lines, with the underlying assumption that diversity was a problem to either ignore or eliminate. Yet, American schools are continuing to become more diverse in terms of achievement level, educational background, home language, and ethnicity. Traditional "teach to the middle" approaches to instruction and unintentional tracking into high, middle, and low groups simply do not work. Mounting research (Pressley, Harris, & Marks, 1992; Pressley, Hogan, Whareon-McDonald, & Mistretta, 1996) suggests that when teachers systematically apply high-access strategies across the curriculum, learning gains accrue for all levels of students. In essence, high-access instruction offers educators an opportunity to capitalize on the diversity in their classrooms without compromising the integrity of classroom expectations and while meeting state and district standards.

We believe that teachers need specific research-validated instructional tools, such as those described in this chapter, that will empower them to effectively

TABLE 15.1
Contrast Between Low- and High-Access Strategies

Low-Access Strategies	High-Access Strategies
Engage students one at a time	Engage all students simultaneously
Little or no thinking time	Prioritize thinking time for all
Assume adequate prior knowledge and skills	Assume diverse prior knowledge and skills
Focus on coverage of content and skills	Focus on learning of skills and content
High levels of threat/discomfort for diverse learners	Low levels of threat; diverse learners are "set up for success"
No differentiation for skill levels ("one size fits all")	Differentiates instruction to different skill levels and learning needs
Little or no structuring of student interaction ("sage on the stage")	Careful structuring of student interaction (teacher acts as "learning choreographer")

respond to the challenges posed by increased academic diversity, including serving students identified as learning disabled. Teachers and other professionals are encouraged to use these and other high-access practices, to dialogue with others who are attempting to implement them, and to work together to transform the learning landscape from providing generic opportunity to truly providing meaningful access for all.

References

Archer, A. (1999). *Skills for school success.* Workshop presentation. San Jose State University Summer Educators Workshop (June), San Jose, CA.

Archer, A., Gleason, M., & Issacson, S. (1995). Effective instructional delivery. In P. T. Celgelka & W. H. Berdine (Eds.), *Effective instruction for students with learning difficulties* (pp. 161–194). Boston: Allyn & Bacon.

Carnine, D. W., Silbert, J., & Kameenui, E. J. (1997). *Direct instruction reading.* Englewood Cliffs, NJ: Prentice-Hall.

Cohen, E. (1994). *Designing group work: Strategies for the heterogeneous classroom.* New York: Teachers College Press.

Denti, L. (1994). Walling students with disabilities out of the mainstream: Revealing the illusions of inclusion. *International Journal of Group Tensions, 24*(1), 69–78.

Deshler, D. D., & Schumacker, J. B. (1986). Learning strategies: An instructional alternative for low-achieving adolescents. *Exceptional Children, 52,* 583–589.

Ensminger, G. (1991). Defragmenting fragmented learners. *Hands On: A Journal for Teachers, 39,* 44–48.

Fuchs, D., Fuchs, L., Mathes, P., & Simmons, D. C. (1997). Peer assisted learning strategies: Making classrooms more responsive to diversity. *American Educational Research Journal, 34*(1), 174–206.

Goodlad, J. I. (1984). *A place called school: Prospects for the future.* New York: McGraw-Hill.

Greenwood, C. R., & Delquadri, J. (1995). Classwide peer tutoring and the prevention of school failure. *Preventing School Failure, 39*(4), 21–25.

Kagan, S. (1992). *Cooperative learning resources for teachers.* San Juan Capistrano, CA: Kagan Cooperative Learning.

Kameenui, E. J., & Carnine, D. W. (Eds.). (1998). *Effective teaching strategies that accommodate diverse learners.* Columbus, OH: Merrill.

Katz, M., & Denti, L. (1996). The road to nowhere begins with where we are: Rethinking the future of American education. *Interchange, 27*(3–4), 261–277.

Keogh, B. K. (1990). Narrowing the gap between policy and practice. *Exceptional Children, 57,* 186–190.

Knight, J. (1998). Do schools have learning disabilities? *Focus on Exceptional Children, 30*(9), 1–14.

Maheady, L., Mallette, B., Harper, G., & Sacca, M. K. (1988). Heads together: A peer mediated option for improving the academic achievement of heterogeneous learning groups. *Remedial and Special Education, 12*(2), 25–33.

Mathes, P. G., Howard, J. K., Allen, S. H., & Fuchs, D. (1998). Peer assisted learning strategies for first grade readers: Responding to the needs of diverse learners. *Reading Research Quarterly, 33,* 62–93.

McIntosh, R., Vaughn, S., Schumm, J. S., Haager, D., & Lee, O. (1993). Observations of students with learning disabilities in general education classrooms. *Exceptional Children, 60,* 249–261.

Palincsar, A. S., & Brown, A. L. (1984). Reciprocal teaching of comprehension fostering and comprehension monitoring activities. *Cognition and Instruction, 1*(2), 117–175.

Palincsar, A., & Klenk, L. (1992). Fostering literacy learning in supportive contexts. *Journal of Learning Disabilities, 25*(4), 211–215, 229.

Pressley, M., El-Dinary, P. B., Gaskins, I., Schudder, T., Bergman, J. L., & Brown, R. (1992). Beyond direct explanation: Transactional instruction of reading comprehension strategies. *Elementary School Journal, 92,* 511–554.

Pressley, M., Harris, K. R., & Marks, M. B. (1992). But good strategy instructors are constructivists!! *Educational Psychology Review, 4,* 1–32.

Pressley, M., Hogan, K., Wharton-McDonald, R., & Mistretta, J. (1996). The challenges of instructional scaffolding: The challenges of instruction that supports student thinking. *LD Research and Practice, 11*(3), 138–146.

Rosenshine, B. (1987). Explicit teaching. In D. Berliner & B. Rosenshine (Eds.), *Talks to teachers* (pp. 75–92). New York: Random House.

Schumm, J. S., & Vaughn, S. (1995). Getting ready for inclusion: Is the stage set? *LD Research and Practice, 10*(3), 169–179.

Schumm, J. S., Vaughn, S., Gordon, J., & Rothlein, L. (1994). General education teachers' beliefs, skills, and practices in planning for mainstreamed students with learning disabilities. *Teacher Education and Special Education, 17*(1), 22–37.

Simmons, D. C., & Kameenui, E. J. (1996). A focus on curriculum design: When children fail. *Focus on Exceptional Children, 28*(7), 1–16.

Slavin, R. E. (1984). Team assisted individualization: Cooperative learning and individualized instruction in the mainstreamed classroom. *Remedial and Special Education, 5*(6), 33–42.

Stainback, W., & Stainback, S. (1984). A rationale for the merger of regular and special education. *Exceptional Children, 51*(2), 102–111.
Steinberg, Z. (1991). Pandora's children. *Beyond Behavior, 2*(3), 5–14.
Thomas, J. W., & Rohwer, W. D., Jr. (1987). Grade-level and course-specific differences in academic studying: Summary. *Contemporary Educational Psychology, 12,* 381–385.
Vaughn, S., Schumm, J. S., Jallad, B., Slusher, J., & Saumell, L. (1996). Teachers' views of inclusion. *LD Research and Practice, 11*(2), 96–106.
Vaughn, S., & Schumm, J. S. (1995). Responsible inclusion for students with learning disabilities. *Journal of Learning Disabilities, 28,* 264–270.
Wang, M. C., Reynolds, M. C., & Walberg, H. J. (1986). Rethinking special education. *Educational Leadership, 44,* 26–31.
Zigmond, N., & Baker, J. M. (1995). Concluding comments: Current and future practices in inclusive schooling. *Journal of Special Education, 29,* 245–250.
Zigmond, N., & Thorton, H. (1985). Follow-up of postsecondary-age learning disabled graduates and drop-outs. *Learning Disabilities Research* (1), 50–55.
Vygotsky, L. S. (1978). *Mind and society.* Cambridge, MA: Harvard University Press.

16

Using Student Investigation to Water Up Content-Area Instruction for Adolescents With Learning Disabilities

Edwin S. Ellis, Carol Schlichter, and Charlotte A. Sonnier-York

*T*he four-year project started when one student brought in a box of rocks that her father had collected on a trip to Antarctica. That same day, Schafer [the teacher] read a story in the local newspaper about living brachiopods discovered off the coast of New Zealand. As they talked about the rock samples and the newspaper article, the students wondered if the prime minister of New Zealand would send them samples of the brachiopods. "So we wrote to him, and about two weeks later, a beautifully wrapped box came in the mail," Schafer says. The box contained two dozen brachiopods, pictures of the ship that collected them, and information about them.

Schafer's students were off and running. That year, they wrote to other heads of state and received samples and support materials, along with lots of encouraging and enthusiastic letters. The next year's class wrote to governors and mayors, and the third year's students contacted rock and mineral clubs.

The best result came during the project's fourth year, though, when the students wrote to business

CEOs. "There seemed to be no limit to what businesses would do and what they would send," Schafer says. For example, when students wrote to a coal company, they received a 50-pound box, sent air express, containing a coal ball. The students looked at thin slices of the ball through the microscope to see the imprints of vegetation that lived 300 million years ago.

Besides becoming good letter writers and skilled scientists, the kids learned a few other lessons. For example, when one governor's office replied to their request with a nasty letter, Schafer took the opportunity to teach the kids to write back and redefine their purpose and needs. The students received an apologetic letter from the governor's assistant—along with the samples requested." (Adapted from Shafer, 1996, pp. 43–44, with permission of the author).

What Is Project-Based Learning?

Schooling in our nation has been dominated by traditional methods of instruction that tend to limit inquiry and flexibility within the classroom. These traditional methods of schooling are typically conducted in a manner that promotes information accumulation; that is, school success is measured by the degree to which students accumulate information that is provided by the teacher (Rallis, 1995).

To accommodate this model, instruction and curriculum are often watered down for adolescents with learning disabilities. However, the following problems have been associated with watering down the curriculum (Ellis, 1997, 1998):

A watered-down curriculum often emphasizes memorization of loosely related facts.

- ▶ Watering down the curriculum reduces opportunities to learn content.
- ▶ Watering down the curriculum reduces opportunities to develop thinking skills.
- ▶ Watering down the curriculum can inhibit the "learnability" of subject matter.
- ▶ Watering down the curriculum may reduce investment in learning.

Over the years, the mind-sets of many educators have evolved from such traditional methods to constructivistic methods that are more student centered (Thornton & McEntee, 1995). As an alternative to traditional instruction, constructivistic approaches to learning are used to help students build their own knowledge in the classroom. In short, the goal is to water up the curriculum by placing greater emphasis on the authentic use of the thinking and problem-solving skills that are necessary for functioning in today's world.

How Projects Address Goals of a Watered-Up Classroom

Abundant evidence exists that students display their intelligence in different ways (Rallis, 1995). Some students perform well with traditional instruction and lesson learning, whereas others may not be skilled at academic achievement which focuses on retention of predetermined information but *can* become more successful at expressing their intelligence through creating new ideas, making judgments, planning projects, predicting causes and effects of events and circumstances, and communicating verbally and nonverbally (Schlichter, 1993). Rallis (1995) noted that the implementation of a project-based, learner-centered environment is an affirmation that all students learn differently and that each has a different approach and brings something different to the learning process. With project-based instruction, all students contribute to their learning experience without the reduction or watering down of the curriculum. The approach thus creates an experience that is authentic and enriching.

There are a number of compelling reasons why emphasis should be placed on project-based instruction that *waters up* the curriculum. In a manner similar to the practice of gifted education teachers who "water up" the curriculum through enrichment, project-based instruction provides students with learning experiences that require them to grapple with core ideas of the content and develop sophisticated relational understanding of these ideas. Furthermore, the students engage in a variety of analytical, critical, creative, and productive thinking and problem-solving activities, which helps develop their cognitive skills. In addition, students receive a curriculum where instruction in effective and efficient learning strategies is integrated into the ongoing interest-based content instruction (Ellis, 1997a, 1997b).

Among the problems associated with *watering down* the curriculum are that the practice tends to concomitantly water down the expectations of students with mild cognitive disabilities. Furthermore, although there are effective techniques for promoting self-reliance and independence among these students, such as teaching learning strategies, many of the actual practices in special education for adolescents do not emphasize these procedures (Ellis, 1997a). In addition, practices, especially in inclusive settings, tend to be oriented toward accommodation, especially in inclusive settings.

The goals of a watered-up curriculum for adolescents with learning disabilities (Ellis, 1997a), as summarized in the following paragraph, sharply contrast with this picture:

1. *More emphasis on students constructing knowledge.* Traditional approaches to teaching content subjects take into account little of what is understood about the construction of knowledge, the learning process, and critical cognitive actions that must take place for meaningful learning to occur (Jones, Palincsar, Ogle, & Carr, 1987). To construct knowledge (as opposed to memorizing someone else's understanding of it), learners must understand the information in relation to what they already know from their own repertoire of experiences (for a review, see Reid, Kurkjian, & Carruthers, 1994). With the exception of specific facts, knowledge of information is relative and never static. One's understanding is constantly changed as one views information from different contexts and in relation to other background knowledge or new information. Knowledge of facts may be right or wrong, recalled or forgotten. Similarly, the understanding of facts is continuously changing. Thus, it is also relative and never static (Wansart, 1995).

2. *More depth, less superficial coverage.* Teachers who strive to provide a watered-up curriculum are concerned with facilitating in-depth understanding and developing deep knowledge structures of essential concepts rather than emphasizing content coverage. The watered-up curriculum focuses on the students' understanding of core ideas of the curriculum, how they interrelate, and how these core ideas can help the students understand the current world and solve real-world problems (Cushman, 1994; Newman & Wehlage, 1993).

3. *More emphasis on the redundancy of archetype concepts and patterns.* An archetype concept is an idea that is universal and is manifested across genre, settings, and contexts. An example of an archetype concept is that *all living beings have a need for self-preservation and procreation, and much of their behavior is centered around these two goals.* An archetype pattern is a predictable sequence of events that also is manifested across situations and settings. An example of a simple archetype pattern is that *for every action, there is a reaction.*

In watered-up classrooms, emphasis is placed on facilitating the discovery and identification of archetype concepts, patterns, and strategies, and how they are manifested across genre, settings, and contexts. The more students understand the archetype concept and are able to recognize its manifestations and patterns in content subjects, the more likely they will readily understand material being taught in classrooms.

4. *More emphasis on developing relational understanding and knowledge connections to real-world contexts.* The watered-up classroom is designed to facilitate the connection of new knowledge to background experience and knowledge (Wansart, 1995). The intent is for students to develop metaphoric connections as a result of exploration of the core content ideas. These connections occur when students recognize how the central idea or its critical features relate to other ideas in a different genre. Metaphoric connections may be the strongest contributor to the students' learning, as the students relate new ideas to something from their real-world or actual experience. It is important to expand students' learning beyond the school context and into the real world.

5. *More student elaboration.* The human brain is like a "language toolbox" that contains a variety of tools for learning. One of the most powerful tools in that box is elaboration. Furthermore, just as there are many different sizes and types of pliers, there are many forms of elaboration. Elaboration strategies include paraphrasing or summarizing ideas or otherwise using one's own words to discuss a concept, generate questions about the materials, form predictions or hypotheses regarding what the material is really about, and creating mental images about how something looks, tastes, sounds, or feels. These cognitive strategies require the learner to interact with the information, relate it to background knowledge in some way, and convert it in some manner while retaining its essential meaning.

6. *More emphasis on developing effective habits of the mind, higher order thinking and information-processing skills, and learning strategies.* One distinguishing characteristic of a watered-up curriculum is the commitment of teachers to merge the development of cognitive skills with the acquisition of conceptual knowledge.

Higher order thinking requires students to be active participants in problem solving rather than passive receivers of information. Furthermore, students receiving watered-up curriculum learn how to "be smart" as they learn the content subjects. Thinking skills are an integral part of the curriculum; they are of equal importance to the content being taught (Marzano,1988; Schlichter & Brown, 1985).

7. *More student reflection, risk taking, and active participation.* Traditional methods of learning require students to memorize the teacher's words from a set of notes, definitions of terms, or details from a text chapter, requiring little reflection or risk on the student's part in relation to developing an understanding of a concept. Such methods can result in students channeling their energy into learning information that will not be included in the assessment. More powerful learning occurs when students stretch their understanding and generate their own connections between ideas, form relationships, and develop an awareness of many applications or extensions of the ideas. The intent of "stretching" is to require the student to take risks; unfortunately, a history of academic failure makes many adolescents with learning disabilities unwilling to take risks because they do not feel safe in doing so. (Helping students to feel safe taking risks is another goal of watered-up instruction.)

8. *More emphasis on developing social responsibility and collaboration skills among students.* Meaningful learning is more likely to take place in environments where students feel safe and free to take risks with their understanding and do not feel inhibited or punished for doing so. In classrooms where collaborative learning is employed effectively, students with learning disabilities usually engage in these activities with enthusiasm and risk taking (Schrag, 1993). They seem to wrestle openly with ideas and are less concerned with generating the right answer. Furthermore, they engage in the give-and-take exchange of ideas with other students, challenging ideas that others put forth and accepting others' challenges of their own ideas.

9. *More emphasis on fostering a sense of personal potency and enhancement of academic and social self-esteem.* Students' success in school and in life will be influenced by the sense of personal potency students have about themselves. Personal potency means that students have a sense that they are in control of their destinies and are positively influencing others and contributing to their world. It means that they feel valued and possess a sense of belonging (Glenn & Nelson, 1987). There are a number of elements that make the development of personal potency particularly challenging for many adolescents with learning disabilities, including low academic concept, heterogeneous classroom environments with large enrollments, delayed development of internal locus of control, uninteresting curriculum that is watered down, sheltering of students from the nature of their problem, and provision of services that are primarily reactive, such as tutoring (Ellis, 1997a).

Teachers who create a watered-up curriculum strive to foster and develop a sense of personal potency in each student in a variety of ways. For example, in watered-up classrooms, students frequently make decisions or choices, and student-teacher dialogue frequently addresses the meaning of specific choices that students make. The teacher works hard to ensure that all students, regardless of their ability, feel they belong and are contributing, valuable members of the class. Creating such an environment requires that teachers be flexible with regard to tasks and assignments while still providing challenging instruction. Furthermore, the teacher must identify the unique abilities that each student possesses so that they can be recognized and can contribute to the learning for all students.

10. *More social support for student achievement.* Social support for student achievement means not only that achievement is valued but also that the environment reflects this value and is conducive to emphasizing and reinforcing achievement. Watered-up classrooms are success oriented in relation to achievement and include several elements that make them so: challenging tasks, high expectations for all students, success-oriented instruction, a learning environment permeated with goal setting, frequent evaluation of and meaningful feedback on performance, celebration of achievement, achievable goals for all students, and a learning environment conducive to mutual respect for achievement among all students.

11. *More intensive and extensive instruction.* A significant body of research collectively shows that the quality of interactions between teachers and students, regardless of their respective labels, is the most predictive variable in successful classroom learning (Kauffman, 1993). Quality instruction is considerably more important to educational success than is the label a child or teacher is given or the setting in which instruction is provided. The following are some specific techniques positively associated with improving the quality of interactions between teachers and students: mediated elaboration, interactive modeling and coaching, meaningful and frequent feedback, sufficient opportunities to learn, and interesting and meaningful experiences.

To summarize, the goal of a watered-up curriculum is to enhance opportunities to learn for all students by creating highly robust learning environments. In contrast, the watered-down curriculum which tends to be accommodation oriented, as indicated by the common practices of reducing academic content and lowering the student's academic expectations for students with learning disabilities.

Project-Based Instruction

One method being used by educators to assist students in constructing their knowledge is project-based instruction. The project-based classroom is an instructional concept that promotes flexibility, and individuality and explores the reality that there is no single right way of doing things (Thornton & McEntee, 1995). Teachers who promote project-based learning recognize students as the center of the learning experience. Thus, they create an environment that acknowledges that children construct their own meanings for the events, objects, and people with whom they interact. Furthermore, students make discoveries instead of following teacher directions or memorizing facts (Rallis, 1995). There is considerable evidence that students representing a wide range of intellectual abilities have potential for creative and critical thinking and that training enhances the development of that potential (Schlichter

& Palmer, 1993). Thornton and McEntee (1995) noted that a project-based environment requires students to mindfully attend to information as they make discoveries.

In project-based instruction, students are in charge of their own learning. The teacher's role goes beyond one of traditional instruction. In contrast to traditional learning, the teacher allows the students to be the center of instruction. The teacher of project-based instruction is able to create conditions that enable children to interpret and understand learning for themselves (Haynes, 1996; Rallis, 1995).

How the Characteristics of Adolescents With Learning Disabilities Compel the Need for Project-Based Instruction

Adolescence is a time period marked by conflicting feelings about security and independence, rapid physical changes, and peer pressure. These factors can greatly affect the learning process, especially for students with learning disabilities (Hammachek, 1990; Kerr, Nelson, & Lambert, 1987). Project-based learning is one way that educators can water up the meaningfulness of content-area instruction for adolescents with learning disabilities. Furthermore, project-based instruction can address academic skills that are authentic for students and provide learning environments where all students participate.

Adolescents with learning disabilities commonly have difficulty in school and social life not only because of their learning disability but also because they must cope with the normal challenges and adjustments that all adolescents face (Ellis & Friend, 1991; Schumaker, Deshler, & Ellis, 1986; Zigmond, 1990). These adolescents experience a variety of cognitive difficulties that may inhibit meaningful learning. More specifically, adolescents with learning disabilities often have difficulty with cognitive functioning and with developing academic skills, social skills, and motivation for learning. Challenges that adolescents with learning disabilities may experience in school and ways project-based learning can address these difficulties are described in the following sections.

COGNITIVE CHARACTERISTICS

Some adolescents with learning disabilities have poor impulse control and, as a result, experience difficulty taking notes from lectures or focusing on a timed writing assignment (Levine, 1988; Sileo, 1989). When assigned projects, students with learning disabilities often rush to begin without reflecting about the parameters of the task or the best approach for attacking the task. Secondary education environments commonly require long periods of concentration, making it hard for students with hyperactivity or attention deficit disorder to attend. Considering the long periods of concentration needed for studying and listening in class, these deficits can seriously hinder a student's progress in school (Levine, 1988).

Project-based instruction can be beneficial to students with poor impulse control because it promotes proactive thinking and requires students to anticipate or forecast an outcome. Rather than trying to take notes on a teacher's lecture for an extended period of time, the students acquire information on their own by engaging in a meaningful project. Because the learners are actively engaged in a project, they are mindfully attending to their construction of the project. Taking notes or listening to a lecture does not provide the students with the same meaningful learning (Thornton & McEntee, 1995).

Although the difficulty adolescents with learning disabilities experience accessing background knowledge is typically attributed to their cognitive deficits, this problem could also be due to educators failing to provide these students with authentic learning experiences that require them to become actively involved in the learning process in a manner that facilitates *relational* understandings. For example, it is common for educators to provide accommodations for these students by watering down the curriculum with less intellectually demanding and less interesting activities. When educators reduce the content, the result may be a disjointed curriculum that is composed largely of insignificant concepts and facts to be memorized (Ellis, 1997a). As a repercussion, students may have a limited knowledge base and limited skills for using information-processing strategies. It is commonly assumed that since students with learning disabilities appear to lack sophisticated cognitive skills, they are unable to develop them. This belief, unfortunately, may result in educators providing students with few opportunities to engage in creative, analytical, or productive thinking activities. Although special education practices often allow little time or encouragement for this type of instruction, adolescents with learning disabilities could benefit from it greatly (Schlichter & Brown, 1985). Because project-based instruction requires students to construct their own knowledge, they develop a foundation to which they can refer when trying to access background knowledge (Rallis, 1995). Furthermore, as skills become increasingly difficult, the students' repertoire of knowledge and ability to recall this knowledge become more sophisticated.

Adolescents with learning disabilities also face the challenges of limited language skills; they may have difficulty processing or expressing oral or written language. Learning at the secondary level often calls for identifying main ideas and pertinent details, using verbal and written elaboration, problem solving, and identifying cause-and-effect relationships. Adolescents with language disabilities may struggle with some of these skills, especially if they are called on to elaborate about ideas for which they have little background knowledge. For this reason, it is important that language be considered an integrated, whole system rather than a collection of isolated skills (Mann, 1991; Sawyer & Butler, 1991). Students' ability to elaborate using their own words requires them to interact with the information and relate it to background knowledge in some way (Pressley, Johnson, & Symons, 1987). Through project-based instruction, students may develop an understanding of the relationship between oral language, reading, and writing. As students gain competence and intimacy with learning language in one form, they will build knowledge and experience with learning language in another form (Mann, 1991; Sawyer & Butler, 1991).

By the time adolescents with learning disabilities reach the secondary level, they may have experienced many failures in school. As a consequence, many have begun to doubt their intellectual abilities and give up quickly when something appears to be difficult. In turn, they resist taking risks or engaging in learning situations that may reinforce past failure. Thus, educators find it difficult to motivate them. The decisions educators make about what and how to teach will be successful only if students are motivated to learn and can attribute success to their own efforts (Zigmond, 1990; Zigmond & Thornton, 1988).

Because adolescents with learning disabilities are poor risk takers, it is important to establish environments and learning experiences that are risk-friendly. Teachers who implement project-based instruction encourage, nurture, and legitimize nontraditional methods of retaining knowledge, thereby accommodating different types and styles of learners. Furthermore, they consider all learners as participants in the learning environment (Thornton & McEntee, 1995). Rallis (1995) noted that the project-based classroom offers each student many opportunities to learn. Rather than expecting all students to conform to a norm, the teacher broadens expectations to encompass the diversity within the classroom. Furthermore, the teacher acknowledges the difficulties, talents, and life experiences that each student brings to the classroom. If a student does not meet "criteria," then the teacher examines what can be done to enable this student to learn and experience school success (Rallis, 1995).

ACADEMIC CHARACTERISTICS

It is common for adolescents with learning disabilities to have limited reading comprehension skills as well as limited oral and written expression skills. Approximately 80% of students with learning disabilities have difficulty in reading (Kirk & Elkins, 1975; Lyon, 1985). Because reading is such an important part of the integrated language system, these students also may have difficulty in oral and written expression (Stanovich, 1986; Wiig & Semmel, 1984; Vogel, 1974). For this reason, adolescents with learning disabilities need to be provided with active and meaningful experiences in writing and using oral language that will eventually improve their integrated language skills.

SOCIAL CHARACTERISTICS

Another trait common to adolescents with learning disabilities is inadequate social skills. Many doubt their success in many aspects of their own life. Their fear of failure often leads to avoidance of new challenges and experiences. Furthermore, they may be tempted to engage in maladaptive behavior rather than to risk failure. Thus, alternatives to traditional methods of instruction that are more student centered can provide a means for teaching students sophisticated social skills in "real-life" situations. (Sileo, 1989).

Adolescents with learning disabilities commonly have difficulty making friends and collaborating with their peers (Vaughn, McIntosh, & Spencer-Rowe, 1991). As a result, they often are not accepted by their classmates, and they are often viewed negatively by their teachers. When adolescents with learning disabilities do attempt to interact socially, they are often given negative reinforcement from other students and their teachers (Bryan, 1991; Pearl, Donahue, & Bryan, 1986). For these reasons, adolescents with learning disabilities need learning experiences that teach them how to interact with others efficiently and effectively.

It is important to provide adolescents with social support as they engage in learning experiences. Because project-based learning is success oriented, this instructional method naturally provides students with social support for their achievement. Social support for student achievement, as noted earlier, means that achievement is valued by the student and that the environment reflects this value and is conducive to emphasizing and reinforcing achievement (Ellis, 1997a).

MOTIVATIONAL CHARACTERISTICS

Because many adolescents with learning disabilities have low academic self-concepts due to prolonged failure experiences, they often do not attribute the success they may experience to their own efforts. Thus, even experiencing success is not enough to raise their confidence. It can be especially challenging for a teacher to motivate such students (Licht & Kistner, 1986; Zigmond, 1990; Zigmond & Thornton, 1988).

When the curriculum is watered down, students' investment in learning may be further reduced. The uninteresting instruction associated with a watered-down curriculum may result in the students viewing the secondary school experience as less than meaningful. In traditional classrooms, teachers generally do not help the situation by resorting to extrinsic reward systems such as behavior modification to entice students to engage in academic tasks. In such cases, the emphasis of the classroom often becomes focused on ensuring that students comply with the norms of schooling, and students' grades are often based on how well they comply with others' norms rather than how well they actually understand the content being taught (Ellis, 1997b).

Glenn and Nelson (1987) noted that one of the primary goals in an adolescent's life is to have a sense of being in control of one's own destiny and a feeling of personal potency. The enrichment students receive from project-based instruction can be motivating to them as they embark on their learning adventures. Further, because students are directing their own construction of knowledge, they have the opportunity to take ownership of the experience and thus have control over it (Ellis, 1997a).

Impact of Projects on Heterogeneous Research Teams: Benefits to Students With High, Average, and Low Learning Abilities

Education for adolescents with learning disabilities tends to focus on the development of academic and social skills through traditional methods of instruction. However, the environments provided for students may have a greater impact on subsequent success than the academic skills they master. Educators face the challenge of teaching academic content and skills while ensuring that students substantively and positively develop in the affective dimension (Ellis, 1996). The learning environment created by the teacher should be one that cultivates participation and questioning and allows trial by error (Gabella, 1995).

The project-based classroom is heterogeneous and flexible in that it uses developmentally appropriate practices, integrated/thematic curriculum, and hands-on activities while giving special attention to the cognitive, physical, aesthetic, social, and emotional development of each child (Haynes, 1996). Educators who promote the learner-centered, project-based classroom recognize the importance of choosing learning activities that make it possible for all children to participate (i.e., activities that do not limit students with special needs or for whom English is not the primary language). In addition, students' learning is not limited by existing expectations for what the students can learn (Rallis, 1995).

Because project-based learning requires children to use information, think critically and creatively, and communicate their constructs, there are no ceilings placed on their learning. Teachers question and probe to help the students make meaning of their own learning rather than directing the students' learning (Rallis, 1995). Furthermore, as students encounter new experiences, they are prompted by new meaning that is related to something that they already know (i.e., students are learning through their own construction of meaning). In such situations, the teacher's responsibility is to provide opportunities for active learning where the students build, discuss, compare, collaborate, and experiment. Rather than delivering information, the teacher is the provider of opportunities for students to gather their own information (Anderson & Barrera, 1995).

Capitalizing on Multiple Talents

The notion that students should be active thinkers rather than passive memorizers and that teachers should be talent developers rather than disseminators of knowledge is not a new idea. Calvin W. Taylor proposed multiple talent theory in 1967 as a system for helping teachers identify and nurture students' multiple thinking talents, and it was subsequently translated into classroom practice through Talents Unlimited, a national staff development model for creative and critical thinking skills instruction (Schlichter, 1981). Schlichter and Palmer (1993) noted that multiple talent development emphasizes the important role of *academic* talent in helping students acquire basic knowledge and skills. However, five other talents in the Talents Unlimited model (see Table 16.1) help students learn to process and use their knowledge base to think creatively and critically about concepts and issues in curricular areas and to solve problems that require the application of basic knowledge and skills in new contexts. Recent reports on the declining success of elementary and secondary school programs in nurturing students' ability to think creatively and critically about ideas and issues have led to a renewal of interest in research on thinking skill instruction and the development of programs to enhance higher order thinking of all students (Schlichter, 1993). If the multiple talent approach is used in the classroom, the band of talents would be deliberately widened as a by-product, and the scope and type of knowledge acquired by the students would be widened as well. When teachers cultivate components of curiosity and creativity, the students are required to expand their experience by working at and beyond the fringe of knowledge. For

TABLE 16.1
The Talents Unlimited Model

Talent Area	Definition	Sample Activity
Productive Thinking	To generate many varied and unusual ideas or solutions and to add detail to the ideas to improve them or make them more interesting.	In a composition class, students generate a variety of clever ways the element of surprise could be used to create interest in a given story situation.
Decision Making	To outline, weigh, make final judgments about, and defend a decision on the many alternatives to a problem.	On the basis of research on various American presidents, students present cases for "the ideal president" using such criteria as education, experience, magnitude of events during presidency, impact of media, handling of crises, etc.
Planning	To design a means for implementing an idea by describing what is to be done, identifying the resources needed, outlining a sequence of steps to take, pinpointing possible problems and making improvements in the plan.	Students who are studying the unusual characteristics of slime mold are asked to design experiments to answer questions they have generated about the behavior of the mold.
Forecasting	To make a variety of predictions about the possible causes and/or effects of various phenomena.	Students in a business math class are asked to predict the possible consequences if a company does not prepare departmental margin statements.
Communication	To use and interpret both verbal and nonverbal forms of communication to express ideas, feelings, and needs to others.	Students in a biology lab are given practice in writing research reports by completing an activity in which they express in varied and interesting ways all the statements that could be made on the traits observed for sets of cell specimens based on a completed chart of data.
Academic	To develop a base of knowledge and/or skill about a topic or an issue through the acquisition of information and concepts.	Students read from a variety of resources to gain information about the Impressionist period and then share the information in a discussion of a painting by Monet.

teachers to accomplish this particular expansion of knowledge and of talents, they must break away from solely nurturing academic talents and begin helping students to apply creative talents as well (Taylor, 1993).

Project-Based Strategies

Project-based strategies generally require three basic phases for carrying out projects in the classroom (see Figure 16.1). The first phase involves identifying the parameters of the project and planning its implementation. Critical for adolescents with learning disabilities, this phase requires students not only to think proactively by forecasting and anticipating the outcome of the project but also to identify potential resources that could contribute information to the project. During this phase, students begin to visualize and sketch out plans for completing the project.

The second phase is investigative in nature and requires students to determine and find a variety of resources needed to complete a quality project. Because students with learning disabilities are typically given few opportunities to engage in productive thinking activities, tasks such as brainstorming, predicting, and anticipating can be difficult for them (Schlichter & Brown, 1985). However, providing students with a systematic means of investigating and prioritizing sources can help these students to accept such a task as less difficult and intimidating. As students enter this phase of the project, they investigate the resources that were identified during the first phase. As a rule, students should be encouraged to perform multisource investigations.

The third phase involves an organized presentation of the project, using multiple communication formats and a little imagination. (Because adolescents with learning disabilities typically lack some of the necessary language and communication skills to launch such a presentation, many of these students will need to be taught how to develop these skills [Ellis, 1997a]). This phase involves systematic steps that assist students in planning a presentation. During this phase, students are encouraged to develop visually appealing and imaginative presentations that require them to stretch beyond the simple methods of communication with which they may be most familiar.

The planning, investigating, and presenting phases can be addressed with strategies that serve as organizers for completing the tasks in an effective and efficient manner. The following sections present effective strategies for addressing each of these three phases.

PROJECT: A Project Planning Strategy

The PROJECT strategy provides students with a procedure for planning a project (see Figure 16.2). The first step of this strategy involves *previewing the task*. Often, students plunge into a project without giving thought to the way it should be approached or how it could be organized into sequential steps that could lead to the completion of a project. This step requires students to visualize what they have to do

STUDENT VARIABLES That Water Up the Quality of Projects

	Collaborative Processes	Commitment to Quality	Task-Specific Variables
PLANNING	▲ Use of brainstorming. ▲ Total team involvement while identifying ideas, making decisions. ▲ Consensus-based decision making.	▲ Utilizes goal setting/making commitments. ▲ Investigations planned that extend beyond the textbook. ▲ Potential "to-be-answered" questions identified. ▲ Potential resources identified.	*Metacognition/organization* ▲ Project parameters identified and explored (intended audience, due date, specific expectations of evaluators, rubrics, etc.). ▲ Within-team assets/talents/resources identified. ▲ Research strategy developed or adopted by team, clear plan established. ▲ Tasks identified, assignments made, due dates established. ▲ Timelines utilized. ▲ Team reflects on and self-evaluates their use of effective planning processes.
INVESTIGATING	▲ Each team member has significant role in investigation process. ▲ Each team member has a significant role in the "making sense" process (constructing and organizing information, comparing/contrasting, prioritizing, justifying, identifying cause/effect relationships, etc.). ▲ Investigations utilize individual talents of team members.	▲ Members adhere to timelines. ▲ Members utilize self- and team evaluations regarding: – effectiveness of collaboration – effectiveness of investigation process – quality of information gathered – quality of the organization of information.	*Multisource investigations* ▲ Variety of print sources (not just text). ▲ Variety of nonprint sources (interviews, videos, museums, observations, etc.). ▲ Use of technological sources (CD ROM, Net, Worldwide Web, etc.). *Recursive flexible alignment processes* ▲ Investigate/revisit original questions/align/investigate/revisit . . .

(continued)

FIGURE 16.1

Three Basic Phases of Projects

	Collaborative Processes	Commitment to Quality	Task-Specific Variables
PRESENTING	▲ Presentation provides opportunities for students with multiple intellectual abilities to show competence. ▲ Presentation substantively includes *all* team members in the communication of important ideas (does not just have the most verbally skilled team member make the entire presentation).	▲ Members adhere to timelines. ▲ Members utilize self- and team evaluations regarding effectiveness of collaboration and quality of presentation.	*Content of presentation* ▲ Overall content has a clear focus: ideas/concepts are tied together via a theme. ▲ Ideas are important, accurate, clear, meaningfully organized and synthesized. ▲ Presentation extends, elaborates and connects ideas/concepts to student interests/relevant "real-life" issues, or problems to be solved/personal themes, etc. ▲ Presentation reflects many and varied ways of viewing an idea. *Presentation performance* ▲ Presentation is appropriate for a specific audience (classmates, parents, community, staff, etc.). ▲ Content of presentation is linked to *audience* background knowledge, concerns, etc.; engages audience. ▲ Multiple communication formats are used. Beyond the simple "report," includes many and varied ways of presenting an idea (i.e., performance, products, multimedia, manipulatives, and/or activities; novelty and creativity). ▲ Presentation is visually appealing and imaginative. ▲ Effective communication process tools are used (e.g., advance organizer, opening, body, closing); ideas are presented in a logical manner.

Source: From *Designing Quality Projects for Group Investigation* by E. S. Ellis (Lawrence, KS: Edge Enterprises, in preparation).

FIGURE 16.1

(continued)

Preview the task
- ▶ nature of project
- ▶ audience
- ▶ expectations
  - what will be evaluated? how? rubric?
  - due date?
  - presentation expectations (format? length? graphics? etc.)
  - content expectations (theme? how detailed? topics to include?)
  - collaboration/individual accountability expectations?

Rough out a plan
- ▶ topic and subtopics
- ▶ research plan
- ▶ presentation plan

Organize tasks and resources
- ▶ brainstorm to identify specific tasks
- ▶ determine priority and order for tasks that need to be completed
- ▶ brainstorm to identify potential resources for each task

Job assignments
- ▶ dissect each task and identify specific jobs
- ▶ match jobs with unique talents and abilities

Expected obstacles identified
- ▶ brainstorm to identify potential obstacles that might be encountered for each task
- ▶ brainstorm to identify potential solutions to each obstacle

Commitments
- ▶ make commitments with regard to quality of project and presentation
- ▶ make commitments regarding use of collaboration skills
- ▶ make commitments regarding use of mind habits

Timeline
- ▶ note due date for finished project
- ▶ determine order of tasks and indicate due dates for each
- ▶ identify team-meeting dates and record
- ▶ make a copy of the timeline for each member of team

Source: From *Designing Quality Projects for Group Investigation* by E. S. Ellis, (Lawrence, KS: Edge Enterprises, in preparation).

FIGURE 16.2

PROJECT: A Project Planning Strategy

in order to finish the project. It also requires them to establish the general nature of the project and to consider who their audience may be. The characteristics of the audience will often determine the direction a project should take. Finally, this step requires students to determine expectations for the completed project, including due dates, what will be evaluated, presentation expectations, content expectations, and collaborative and/or individual accountability expectations.

The second step in this strategy is for students to *rough out a plan* for the project. This step requires students to determine *how* the project will be completed. Sketching out the plan helps students visualize what they need to do sequentially in order to complete the project. During this step, students engage in brainstorming activities that assist them in visualizing an outline or sketch of the key topics to be addressed, the way in which information will be attained, and the way in which it might be communicated. Students first brainstorm about topics and subtopics that are related to the main idea. They can use question starters (who, what, why, when, where, and how) to start their thinking as they generate potential topics and subtopics. After establishing a variety of topics, the students develop a draft of an initial research plan that contains each component necessary for completion of the project. Finally, the students outline a tentative plan for presenting the completed project. Figure 16.3 illustrates a computed graphic organizer that students developed

---

Overview of Basic Topics and Subtopics (tentative)

The French and Indian War

Why	*What*	*Who*	*How*
Why did problems arise in the Ohio Valley?	What were some of the reasons for going to war?	Who was fighting in the French and Indian War?	How was the problem resolved?

Basic Plan for Investigating, Experimenting, and/or Inventing

- Grolier's CD Encyclopedia
- Text
- Internet
- World Book Encyclopedia
- National Geographic
- Published books from the library
- Library films and videos
- Interviews with history teachers

Tentative Plan for Presenting

- Design and display map that shows territories owned by Great Britain and France.
- Develop and display timeline of events that led to the French and Indian War.
- Develop handouts for presentation: presentation outline, list of natural resources, and a summary of the French and Indian War.
- Information that was obtained through the interviews.

Source: From *Designing Quality Projects for Group Investigation* by E. S. Ellis, (Lawrence, KS: Edge Enterprises, in preparation).

FIGURE 16.3

Roughing Out a Plan

as they were "roughing out a plan" about a project concerning the French and Indian War.

After the students have developed a clear plan for completing and presenting the project, they begin the next step, *organizing tasks and resources.* This step requires students to organize the various tasks involved in completing the project and brainstorm about various resources that they can use. Once the specific tasks have been identified, the students determine priority and order for each task. Finally, the students identify potential resources that may be useful in completing each task. The first two columns in Figure 16.4 illustrate how students used a graphic organizer to complete this step as they planned their project about the French and Indian War.

After organizing tasks and resources, the students consider *job assignments* for individuals within the collaborative group. This step requires the students to give thought to the individual strengths of the group and, based on this observation, to assign well-balanced tasks to each team member. To accomplish this, the students must dissect each task into specific jobs that can be designated to each team member. Then, they attempt to match jobs with each team member's unique talents and abilities (see Column 3 in Figure 16.4).

During the next step, the students delineate *expected obstacles.* This step requires the students to brainstorm about potential obstacles that may be encountered for each task and to identify possible solutions for the obstacles. Although the students may, in actuality, encounter few or no obstacles, this step requires them to forecast potential problems and methods for solving problems if and when they emerge (see last column in Figure 16.4).

After delineating obstacles, the team members make a number of *commitments* to the project. Each team member is required to commit, foremost, to the quality of the project and the presentation. To do so, he or she must also commit to the collaboration process. This requires each student to strengthen the collaboration skills that he or she already possesses. By committing to this, students establish the will to work together and to do well as a group (Kagan, 1992). Finally, the students must commit to using effective habits of the mind (Marzano, 1988). Therefore, as they engage in the project, the students must think about how they learn best and their most efficient methods for creating a quality project. Then, they must take responsibility for their strengths and contribute these strengths to the project whenever possible. Figure 16.5 illustrates a form of contract students can use to indicate their commitments to quality. On the top portion of the form, students sign their names indicating their commitment to quality performance in overall areas. In the second section, the students indicate three collaboration skills they agree to practice as they work on the project. The teacher can use the contract as a rubric when evaluating how well each team used the specific collaboration skills that it targeted as goals. The contract can also be used by team members as they provide peer feedback and as a means for facilitating self-evaluation. Similar processes can be applied to the bottom section of the form to set goals and evaluate the use of various mind habits.

The final step of this strategy addresses *timelines* that the students should consider. This step is especially important for adolescents with learning disabilities, as

Water Up Content-Area 305

Organizing Tasks and Resources		Job Assignments	Expected Obstacles
Task Develop questions for interviews. ▲ conducting ▲ tape-recording ▲ summarizing information	**Potential Resources** ▲ text ▲ World Book Encyclopedia ▲ Internet ▲ tape recorder	**Who... Does What?... By When?** ▲ Mary, Matthew, & Rick—develop questions (4/12) ▲ Mary & Rick—conduct interviews (4/15) ▲ Matthew—tape-record (4/15) ▲ Mary, Matthew, Rick & Sharon—summarize information (4/16)	**Potential Obstacles/Ways to Overcome** Teachers may not be willing to be interviewed. → Provide incentive for participating in the interview.
Task Design maps of the New World territories.	**Potential Resources** ▲ text ▲ World Book Encyclopedia ▲ Grolier's CD Encyclopedia	**Who... Does What?... By When?** ▲ Sharon, William, David, & Joan—search for different maps (4/12) ▲ William & Joan—draw map on poster board (4/14) ▲ Sharon, William, David & Joan—color and label map (4/17)	**Potential Obstacles/Ways to Overcome** There may be geographical differences in some of the maps that are located. → Turn into class brainstorming activity.
Task Develop timeline of events that led to the French and Indian War.	**Potential Resources** ▲ text ▲ information from interviews ▲ World Book Encyclopedia ▲ Grolier's CD Encyclopedia ▲ published books ▲ library videos and films	**Who... Does What?... By When?** ▲ Mary, William & Suzi—develop a rough draft of events (4/12) ▲ Mary, William, Suzi, Rick & Kim—design the final timeline (4/17)	**Potential Obstacles/Ways to Overcome** Cannot find enough information. → Call or write to history professors at nearest college.
Task Develop handouts for presentation. ▲ outline ▲ natural resources ▲ summary	**Potential Resources** ▲ text ▲ information from interviews ▲ Grolier's CD Encyclopedia ▲ World Book Encyclopedia	**Who... Does What?... By When?** ▲ John, Kim, & Suzi—search for handout information (4/12) ▲ Kim & Suzi—design rough draft of each handout (4/14) ▲ John—type handouts on computer (4/17)	**Potential Obstacles/Ways to Overcome** John may have difficulty developing handout on his computer at home. → David will help John complete the handouts.

Source: From *Designing Quality Projects for Group Investigation* by E. S. Ellis (Lawrence, KS: Edge Enterprises, in preparation).

FIGURE 16.4

Organizing Tasks and Resources, Job Assignments, and Expected Obstacles

Commitments to quality of project and presentation

By signing my name below, I am making a commitment to:
1. Developing a high-quality product that I will be proud of.
2. Creating a product that will make sense and will be interesting and informative to my audience.
3. Being neat and careful.
4. Doing my share on time.
5. Doing my best.

Signatures of team members

Commitments to collaborating effectively
(Check 3 that will be <u>primary</u> goals.)

___ Listening without interrupting	___ Respecting different opinions, skills, and abilities	___ Recognizing unique talents of others
___ Taking turns and involving everyone	___ Encouraging and complimenting others	___ Giving "I" messages
___ Offering assistance	___ Recognizing and celebrating others' successes	___ Consensus building
___ Communicating about difficulties		___ Giving negative feedback
		___ Peacefully resolving conflicts

Other_____

Commitments to using effective habits of the mind
(Check 3 that will be <u>primary</u> goals.)

___ Using and keeping timelines	___ Organizing ideas and being clear	___ Being open minded
___ Resisting impulsiveness	___ Being accurate	___ Being creative
___ Engaging in challenging tasks	___ Noticing how you and others think	___ Viewing an idea in unusual ways
___ Persisting during tough times	___ Using information resources	___ Presenting an idea in unusual ways

Source: From *Designing Quality Projects for Group Investigation* by E. S. Ellis, (Lawrence, KS: Edge Enterprises, in preparation).

FIGURE 16.5

Commitments to Quality of Project and Presentation

they typically have limited planning experience and skills (Schlichter & Brown, 1985). Thus, these students may engage in a project without anticipating the amount of time each task may take. As a result, they may spend too much time on some tasks and too little time on others, producing a project that is lacking in some critical components. The timelines step of the strategy requires students to note the due date for the completed project, to determine the order of each task and assign a due date for each, and to identify on the timeline all team-meeting dates. When the timeline is completed, copies are made and distributed to each team member.

FIND: An Information Gathering Strategy

The FIND strategy helps students to organize their research of a topic (see Figure 16.6). During the use of this strategy, teachers should place emphasis on multisource

---

Filter the database
- ▶ Determine available data sources.
  - electronic (Internet, CD ROM, library)
  - written and/or electronic abstracts
  - persons to interview or survey
  - places to visit or things to experience (museums, displays, tours, etc.)
- ▶ Brainstorm keywords that directly relate to the topic.
- ▶ Explore the information within the database.
- ▶ Create a list of primary sources.

Investigate source material
- ▶ Determine priority (which primary sources to access first).
- ▶ Determine location of primary sources, library call numbers, Internet addresses, etc.).
- ▶ Find and evaluate source material.

Note ideas
- ▶ Code important ideas and key phrases from source material that you might want to use.
  *Copy key ideas onto sticky tags, cards, or computer file.

Determine organization
- ▶ Decide which information to use.
- ▶ Decide what additional information is needed (FIND IT).
- ▶ Graphically organize into main ideas and supporting details.
  - hierarchic   - compare/contrast
  - cause/effect   - sequence

Source: From *Designing Quality Projects for Group Investigation* by E. S. Ellis, (Lawrence, KS: Edge Enterprises, in preparation).

FIGURE 16.6

FIND: An Information Gathering Strategy

investigations. Students should be encouraged to identify people who could be interviewed, videos, museums, observations, and texts. During the first step of this strategy, the students *filter the database*. This step requires students to locate a variety of resources. Initially, students determine which data sources or resources are available (e.g., Internet, CD ROM, library, persons to interview, surveys that might be conducted, written and electronic abstracts, data yields, and experiments). Once students have outlined their database of available resources, they brainstorm about keywords that directly relate to the topic. Using the keywords, they then explore what information is available about the topics within the database. Finally, students create a list of primary resources.

Next, the students *investigate* the resources that they located in the previous step. This step requires the students to determine if the selected resources will be useful. To begin, the students prioritize the primary resources that they chose by determining which sources to access first. After the primary resources have been prioritized, the students determine the location of the primary resources (library call numbers, Internet addresses, etc.). Finally, the students find and evaluate the resource material. If students are conducting experiments or surveys, they need to design and implement them during this step.

As the students investigate the available resources, they should begin the next step of the strategy, *noting ideas*. This step requires the students to dissect each resource for important information that can contribute to the project. The students first code important ideas and key phrases from the resource material that they may want to use. As the students note key ideas, they should report them on sticky tags, cards, or computer files. If experiments or surveys are being conducted, the students should note what they learned or obtained from them.

During the final step, students *determine the organization* for the source material that they have noted. This step requires students to think about how the information can be combined and organized. Initially, the students decide which of the information is useful. Then, they determine what additional information is needed and locate it. Finally, they graphically organize the information into main ideas and supporting details (hierarchic, cause/effect, compare/contrast, sequence).

CLEAR: A Communicating Ideas Strategy

The CLEAR communication strategy provides students with a systematic plan of attack for communicating ideas in a presentation or written report (see Figure 16.7). To begin this strategy, the students *clarify goals, expectations, and audience needs*. This step requires students not only to determine goals of the presentation or report but also to reflect about the messages they want to portray to their audience. Initially, the students identify their *own* goals for the presentation or report and consider what *they* want to happen as a result of giving it. Next, the students identify the expectations of those who will receive the presentation or report. What do they want to happen as a result of the presentation or report? How brief or extensive do they want the presentation or report to be? What do they expect to learn from it? What format/style

Clarify goals, expectations, and audience needs
- Identify what your own goals are for the report, and what you want to happen as a result of giving the report.
- Identify the expectations of those who will receive the report.
  - What do they want to happen as a result of the report?
  - How brief or extensive do they want the report to be?
  - What do they expect to learn from the report?
  - What format/style do they expect?
- Identify audience needs.
  - How familiar will the audience be with the topic? (novice? expert?)
  - Will the audience need handouts?

List questions and organize responses
- List specific questions your report is designed to answer.
- Order the questions in a manner that makes the most sense.
- Organize responses to each question by outlining and creating a graphic.

Elaborate answers
- Introduce the big ideas, the problems, or the questions your report is designed to address.
- List questions as headings.
- Using your organizers, answer each of the questions.
- If appropriate, convert questions to heading titles.

Anchor key ideas with graphics or pictures
- Decide which key ideas should be enhanced with a graphic or picture.
- Decide if any of your organizers could be included as graphics and refine as needed.
- Refer to and explain the graphics in the report.

Review key ideas
- Provide closure to the report by summarizing key ideas and reviewing your position.

Source: From *Designing Quality Projects for Group Investigation* by E. S. Ellis, (Lawrence, KS: Edge Enterprises, in preparation).

FIGURE 16.7

CLEAR: A Communicating Strategy

do they expect? Once students have addressed these questions, they then identify the needs of the audience. The students consider how familiar the audience is with the topic (novice or expert) and if the audience will need handouts.

During the next step of the strategy, *list questions and organize responses,* the students sequentially organize the information that they want to portray to the audience. During this step, the students first list specific questions that their presentation or report is designed to answer. Then, they order the questions in a sequential manner that makes sense. Once they have done so, they organize responses for each question sequentially and outline the responses using a graphic organizer.

After the students have organized responses to the questions that their presentation or report will address, they *elaborate answers*. This step requires students to determine the key ideas that will be addressed in the presentation or report and refine those ideas. To begin this step, the students note the big ideas, the problems, or the questions that their presentation or report is designed to address. Then, they list each question as a heading and use the responses outlined on their graphic organizer to answer each of the questions. If it is appropriate, the students can convert the questions into heading titles.

During the next step, the students *anchor key ideas with graphics or pictures*. This step is important because it requires students to locate pictures and other visuals that can be used to enhance their presentation or report. The students first decide which key ideas should be enhanced with a graphic or picture. Then, they decide if any graphic organizers could be included as visuals. Finally, they refer to and explain the graphics.

The last stage of the strategy involves *reviewing key ideas* of the presentation or report. This step requires the students to determine and summarize the key ideas. Before giving the presentation or report, students should rehearse and review their position and provide closure to the report or presentation by summarizing the key ideas.

Facilitating the Use of Project Strategies

The teacher who plans to implement project-based instruction should also plan for time to teach the students how to use project strategies efficiently. Generally speaking, instruction in the use of the three project strategies should be scaffolded so that just enough assistance is provided by the teacher to ensure successful performance. The first time the strategies are introduced, use of a classwide project is recommended. Later, once students have become familiar with the strategies, other instructional arrangements can be used. For example, groups can use the strategies collaboratively as they undertake team projects or group investigations. Eventually, individual students can use the strategies independently.

To implement a classwide project, the teacher can have the whole class select a specific topic and use the three strategies to explore it. The teacher would have multiple roles. One of these roles requires the teacher to provide direct explanation of the strategies, modeling, and coaching in the strategy applications. Another role is that of co-planner, co-researcher, and co-presenter. Here, the teacher becomes one of the learners and engages in the strategic activities side-by-side with students.

After the class has completed at least one classwide project, the nature of instruction in the use of the strategies shifts, so that more responsibility is given to individual groups of students. Instead of the entire class working together to use the three strategies to plan, research, and present about a specific topic, each group selects its own topic and uses the strategies collaboratively within their group. The role of the teacher is much more as a guide or "resource on the side" than as a mediator of the strategies themselves.

Eventually, students learn to use the three project strategies individually without assistance from the teacher or peers. Here, each student targets a specific topic and then independently plans, researches, and presents.

Specific suggestions for facilitating performance in each of the strategies within the context of a classwide project and group investigations are presented in the following sections.

Facilitating the Use of PROJECT: The Project Planning Strategy

One way to develop students' knowledge of the strategies is to begin project-based instruction using PROJECT as a class activity. Because students may spend a week or more to complete each step of the PROJECT strategy, the teacher would have ample time to coach the students through each step.

The teacher's responsibility in this situation is that of an "executive." As the classroom executive, the teacher's role is to establish the parameters, or basic requirements, of the task. The challenge is to design the task in a manner that maximizes the attainment of effective and productive outcomes. As the executive, the teacher must consider several components for the project. First, the project should provide students with opportunities to develop higher order thinking skills and problem-solving strategies in uncertain, open-ended situations. Second, because the development of students' multiple perspectives will be facilitated by establishing parameters that allow for *controlled ambiguity,* the teacher should establish learning parameters that require students to stretch their problem-solving and thinking skills. For example, through questioning, the teacher can guide students in the correct direction without giving the students correct answers or solutions. This "direction" establishes parameters, but students are still left with the understanding that there is no single solution or correct way to approach the problem. Third, the project should require students to "stretch," so that scaffolded assistance is needed. Students should not be expected to complete the project without a *little* help from the teacher. However, the teacher should avoid helping the students when help is not needed. Fourth, the teacher should develop a central theme for the project or across all projects. Thematic units promote conceptual redundancy or an overarching conceptual framework that integrates ideas and activities and allows for students at different cognitive levels to struggle with the same ideas.

Facilitating the Use of FIND: The Information Gatherings Strategy

Once the students have completed the PROJECT strategy successfully, they are ready to engage in the FIND strategy. At this point, the teacher may choose to divide the students into small teams. As the students begin using the FIND strategy within their teams, the teacher plays the role of a facilitator. That is, he or she is responsible for creating an environment that is conducive to effective project development and for facilitating all of the teams' successes for all of the outcome areas. However, the teacher must remember that doing something for the team that they can do on their own is not facilitating success. In assisting the teams, the teacher should make ample use of "Wh" questions, which often serve as the best verbal facilitators. Sample "Wh" questions include the following:

"What would happen if . . . ?"
"What would be a different way to do that?"
"What are some other ways to view this problem?"
"Who would be the best person to do that?"
"Who might be a good resource?"
"When would be the best time?"
"When should you seek help, and when should you keep trying without help?"
"Where would be another place to find information?"

The teacher must also facilitate team-building activities, helping the students to learn and develop collaborative skills and team rapport, which strengthen the collaborative process. Further, the teacher should facilitate or promote discussion about controversial issues that incorporate different perspectives. Finally, the teacher facilitates by arranging for peer-evaluation throughout the collaborative process. Each student should understand that he or she is being held accountable for participating in the collaborative process and the completion of the project. Each student's self-evaluation and peer-evaluations should reflect his or her contribution to the team project.

Facilitating CLEAR: A Communicating Ideas Strategy

As the students conclude the FIND strategy, the teacher should begin preparing for the final strategy. As the students begin applying each step of CLEAR, the teacher should continue to be the executive facilitator but should also begin to play the role of executive *evaluator*. As the executive evaluator, the teacher is responsible for the ultimate evaluation of both the students' products and the processes the students used to create and present the project. Furthermore, the teacher is responsible for facilitating student reflection and self-evaluation throughout the process. Each team should have specific responsibilities for evaluating the quality of their work process and product.

As the evaluator of the project, the teacher has four roles. First, the teacher determines which dimensions of the completed project and the presentation will be evaluated. In doing so, the teacher should keep each student's individual abilities in mind. Second, the teacher establishes the criteria for evaluating each dimension. The teacher could use rubrics to establish the standards and measures of success for *each* outcome. When appropriate, the teacher could allow the students to develop the rubrics. Students should have a good understanding of the standards and expectations for evaluation in advance. The student's knowledge of the evaluation standards will guide the student's work plus define the "quality" project. Third, the teacher periodically facilitates team and individual self-evaluations. As mentioned previously, these evaluations should indicate each student's contribution to the completed product. Fourth, the teacher provides a formal evaluation and feedback of the team's product and process. The teacher should avoid placing too much emphasis on grades. Instead, the teacher should place emphasis on the quality of the project.

References

Anderson, G., & Barrera, I. (1995). Critical constructivist research and special education. *Remedial and Special Education, 16*(3), 142–149.

Bryan, T. (1991). Social problems and learning disabilities. In B. Wong (Ed.), *Learning about learning disabilities* (pp. 195–231). San Diego, CA: Academic Press.

Cushman, K. (1994). Less is more: The secret of being essential. *Horace, 11*(2), 1–12.

Ellis, E., & Friend, P. (1991). Adolescents with learning disabilities. In B. Wong (Ed.), *Learning about learning disabilities* (pp. 506–563). San Diego, CA: Academic Press.

Ellis, E. S. (1996). *Watering-up the curriculum using graphic organizers.* Lawrence, KS: Edge Enterprises.

Ellis, E. S. (1997). Watering up the curriculum for adolescents with learning disabilities: Part 1. Goals of the knowledge dimension. *Remedial and Special Education 18,* 326–347.

Gabella, M. S. (1995). Unlearning certainty: Toward a culture of student inquiry. *Theory Into Practice, 34,* 236–242.

Glenn, H. S., & Nelson, J. (1987). *Raising children for success: Blueprints and building blocks for developing capable people.* Fair Oaks, CA: Sunrise Press.

Hammachek, D. (1990). *Psychology in teaching, learning, and growth.* Boston: Allyn & Bacon.

Haynes, H. L. (1996). Observations for the panicked: How to implement a multi-age classroom. *Rural Educator, 17,* 41–44.

Jones, B. F., Palincsar, A. S., Ogle, D. S., & Carr, E. G. (1987). *Strategic teaching and learning: Cognitive instruction in the content areas.* Alexandria, VA: ASCD.

Kagan, S. (1992). *Cooperative learning.* San Juan Capistrano, CA: Kagan Cooperative Learning.

Kerr, M., Nelson, C., & Lambert, D. (1987). *Helping adolescents with learning and behavior problems.* Columbus, OH: Merrill.

Kirk, S. A., & Elkins, J. (1975). Characteristics of children enrolled in Child Service Demonstration Centers. *Journal of Learning Disabilities, 8,* 630–637.

Levine, M. (1988). Learning disability: What is it? *ACLD Newsbriefs, 173,* 1–2.

Licht, B., & Kistner, J. (1986). Motivational problems of learning-disabled children: Individual differences and their implications for treatment. In J. Torgesen & B. Wong (Eds.), *Psychological and education perspectives on learning disabilities* (pp. 225–255). New York: Academic Press.

Lyon, R. (1985). Educational validation studies of learning disability subtypes. In B. Rourke (Ed.), *Learning disabilities in children: Advances in subtype analysis.* New York: Guilford.

Mann, V. (1991). Language problems: A key to early reading problems. In B. Wong (Ed.), *Learning about learning disabilities* (pp. 130–163). San Diego, CA: Academic Press.

Marzano, R. (1988). *Dimensions of thinking: A framework for curriculum and instruction.* Alexandria, VA: ASCD.

Newman, F. M., & Wehlage, G. G. (1993). Five standards of authentic instruction. *Educational Leadership, 50*(7), 8–12.

Pearl, R., Donahue, M., & Bryan, T. (1986). Social relationships of learning disabled children. In J. Torgesen & B. Wong (Eds.), *Psychological and educational perspectives on learning disabilities* (pp. 193–225). New York: Academic Press.

Pressley, M., Johnson, C. J., & Symons, S. (1987). Elaborating to learn and learning to elaborate. *Journal of Learning Disabilities, 20,* 76–91.

Rallis, S. F. (1995). Creating learner centered schools: Dreams and practices. *Theory Into Practice, 34,* 224–229.

Reid, D. K., Kurkjian, C., & Carruthers, S. S. (1994). Special education teachers interpret constructivist teaching. *Remedial and Special Education, 15*(5), 267–280.

Sawyer, D., & Butler, K. (1991). Early language intervention: A deterrent to reading disability. *Annals of Dyslexia, 41,* 55–79.

Schlichter, C. L. (1981). The multiple talent approach in mainstream and gifted programs. *Exceptional Children, 48,* 144–150.

Schlichter, C. L. (1993). Talents Unlimited: Implementing the multiple talent approach in mainstream and gifted programs. In C. L. Schlichter & W. R. Palmer (Eds.), *Thinking smart: A primer of the Talents Unlimited model* (pp. 21–44). Mansfield Center, CT: Creative Learning Press.

Schlichter, C. L., & Brown, V. (1985). Application of the Renzulli Model for the education of the gifted and talented to other areas of special education. *Remedial and Special Education, 6*(5), 49–55.

Schlichter, C. L., & Palmer, W. R. (Eds.). (1993). If you're thinking smart, read this first. *Thinking smart: A primer of the Talents Unlimited model.* Mansfield Center, CT: Creative Learning Press.

Schumaker, J., Deshler, D., & Ellis, E. (1986). Intervention issues related to the education of LD adolescents. In J. Torgesen & B. Wong (Eds.), *Psychological and educational perspectives on learning disabilities* (pp. 329–366). New York: Academic Press.

Sileo, T. W. (1989). Programs for adolescents and adults. In B. R. Gearheart & C. J. Gearheart (Eds.), *Learning disabilities: Educational strategies* (pp. 227–256). Columbus, OH: Merrill.

Stanovich, K. E. (1986). Cognitive processes and the reading problems of learning-disabled children: Evaluating the assumption of specificity. In J. Torgesen & B. Wong (Eds.), *Psychological and educational perspectives on learning disabilities* (pp. 87–132). New York: Academic Press.

Taylor, C. W. (1993). Cultivating new talents: A way to reach the educationally deprived. In C. L. Schlichter & W. R. Palmer (Eds.), *Thinking smart: A primer of the Talents Unlimited model* (pp. 21–44). Mansfield Center, CT: Creative Learning Press.

Thornton, L. J., & McEntee, M. E. (1995). Learner centered schools as a mindset, and the connection with mindfulness and multiculturalism. *Theory Into Practice, 34,* 250–257.

Vaughn, S., McIntosh, R., & Spencer-Rowe, J. (1991). Peer rejection is a stubborn thing: Increasing peer acceptance of rejected students with learning disabilities. *LD Research and Practice, 6,* 83–88.

Vogel, S. (1974). Syntactic abilities in normal and dyslexic children. *Journal of Learning Disabilities, 7,* 103–109.

Wansart, W. L. (1995). Teaching as a way of knowing: Observing and responding to students' abilities. *Remedial and Special Education, 16*(3), 166–177.

Wiig, E., & Semmel, E. M. (1984). *Language assessment and intervention for the learning disabled.* Columbus, OH: Merrill.

Zigmond, N. (1990). Rethinking secondary school programs for students with learning disabilities. *Focus on Exceptional Children, 23,* 1–22.

Zigmond, N., & Thornton, H. (1988). Learning disabilities in adolescents and adults. In K. Kavale (Ed.), *Learning disabilities: State of the art and practice.* San Diego, CA: College Hill Press.

17

Sociocultural Scaffolding as a Means Toward Academic Self-Regulation: Paraeducators as Cultural Brokers

Robert Rueda and Michael Genzuk

One of the major developments in both general and special education has been the "cognitive revolution" and its impact on instructional practice. While perceptual-motor training and related "ability training" models predominated in earlier special education interventions (Meyers & Hammill, 1990), research failed to substantiate their impact on academic achievement (Arter & Jenkins, 1979; Kavale & Forness, 1985). Subsequently, this "ability training" perspective has been replaced by a cognitive orientation to learning that is now increasingly dominant in both general and special education. The reason for the increased influence of the cognitive model in special education practice is the realization that many of the learning problems that characterize students with mild learning disabilities are due to problems in the use of learning strategies and self-regulation (Brown, 1978; Brown, Armbruster, & Baker, 1986; Brown & Campione, 1986).

Contemporary cognitive psychology focuses on the cognitive processes that learners use to actively make sense of incoming information. More specifically, this perspective focuses on an individual learner's use of strategies for problem solving, his or her metacognitive awareness about when, where, and why to use specific strategies, strategies for self-monitoring, how the individual stores and uses background knowledge, and motivational factors (especially beliefs) that impact learning (Gagné, Yekovich, & Yekovich, 1993; Pressley & McCormick, 1995). The impact of this perspective on the education of students with mild learning disabilities has been substantial (Graham & Harris, 1993; Reid, Hresko, & Swanson, 1996). Students with mild learning problems have been shown to be passive, nonstrategic learners with poor self-monitoring and an often inadequate store of background knowledge. As a result, various interventions have been developed that focus on one or more of these specific aspects. These powerful interventions emphasize the active construction of knowledge and meaning, with a goal of self-regulation, to address poor academic achievement.

An example of a successful intervention from this orientation is the reciprocal teaching method for reading comprehension instruction described by Palincsar and Brown (1986). Using explanations and modeling, four strategic activities were taught to groups of at-risk students to increase reading comprehension: self-questioning about the main idea, summarizing, predicting, and clarifying difficult sections of the text. These strategic activities then became a script to guide discussions about the text, where students took turns playing teacher. Discussions centered on the effectiveness of the text summary, the clues used to make predictions, students' differing interpretations of the text, and differing use of strategies. Variations of this procedure have been successful with a wide variety of students with learning disabilities. A review of other successful applications of the cognitive orientation in reading, writing, and other areas can be found in Reid and Kuykendall (1996).

Cognition and Learning: Sociocultural Considerations

As powerful as the cognitive psychology framework has been in reformulating thinking about the nature of learning problems and promoting active instruction, the cognitive model has some shortcomings. For example, one characteristic of the cognitive orientation has been the search for universals in human cognition and learning (Strauss, 1996). One of the consequences of this goal has been a de-emphasis on context and on sociocultural factors in learning and development. Recently, researchers and theorists have begun to acknowledge the limitations that this narrow focus has imposed on research and the development of relevant interventions (Greeno, 1998; Rogoff & Chavajay, 1995) and have pointed to sociocultural theory as a useful expansion of the learning research (Keogh, Gallimore, & Weisner, 1997).

An especially relevant addition to sociocultural theory is found in work by Rogoff and colleagues. Sociocultural theory in general, and the work by Rogoff and colleagues (Rogoff, 1994, 1995; Rogoff, Baker-Sennett, La Casa, & Goldsmith, 1995) in particular, focus on the social, cultural, and interactional aspects of learning, cognition, and development. Briefly, Rogoff proposed a view of learning and development as a dynamic process of *transformation of participation* in a given community of learners. Rogoff's framework orients the researcher to answer such questions as, What are the activities in which people participate? Why and with whom and with what do they participate? How do the activity, its purpose, and peoples' roles in it transform? How do different activities relate to one another currently, historically, and prospectively?

Participation in any sociocultural activity occurs on many planes or levels of interaction. Rogoff (1995) suggested that a complete account of learning and development must take into account a minimum of three levels or planes of development: the *personal plane,* involving individual cognition, emotion, behavior, values, and beliefs; the *interpersonal or social plane,* including communication, role performances, dialogue, cooperation, conflict, assistance, and assessment; and the *community or institutional plane,* involving shared history, languages, rules, values, beliefs, and identities. Sociocultural theory in general emphasizes that these three planes are inseparable. Moreover, language is the primary force that defines and connects these planes. While one plane might be "foregrounded" for a particular study or analysis and the other planes "backgrounded," a complete account of learning and development needs to consider all three simultaneously.

In practice, the smallest unit of analysis that contains all three planes is the *activity setting,* or the "who, what, when, where, why, and how" of the routines that constitute everyday life. Although perhaps confusing at first, an activity setting can simply be seen as a more concrete way of talking about what is often called "context." What is often harder to understand, however, is that adopting the activity setting as one's unit of analysis means that the individual is no longer the exclusive focus. The target for study or intervention is rather the individual in interaction with others in a specific activity setting. This unit of analysis, along with the practice of "foregrounding" and "backgrounding" various planes of development for different purposes, offers a useful way of talking about the social and cultural features of learning.

One of the important implications of this view of learning and cognition as consisting of interacting planes of development is that all of the planes must be taken into account when building and implementing a comprehensive instructional program. Most public discussions about improving school performance and academic achievement fail to consider this interaction. Moreover, as powerful as existing cognitive theory and interventions are, one shortcoming is that they focus almost exclusively on the individual (Greeno, 1998). This relatively narrow focus has been especially prominent in special education, where the focus on individual deficits is deeply embedded in tradition, law, and practice (Trent, Artiles, & Englert, 1998).

From Theory to Practice: A Focus on Diverse Learners

As schools have become increasingly diverse, they have been forced to deal with cultural and linguistic factors in learning, often in the absence of well-developed theoretical frameworks for guiding practice. Research has substantiated the important role that sociocultural factors play in academic success for diverse learners and how neglect of these factors can be detrimental to childrens' school careers (Au & Kawakami, 1994).

Crago, Eriks-Brophy, Pesco, and McAlpine (1997), as well as others, have described how sociocultural factors can impede learning when they are ignored. Their work suggests that the discourse and interaction that take place in the classroom are the foundation for learning and that the social events in which these factors are embedded and through which meaning is co-constructed by participants are key factors in successful academic achievement. Thus, instances of miscommunication may originate and manifest themselves in cultural differences regarding language use, participation, and interaction structures in the classroom as well as differences in the nature and use of narrative forms and other aspects of literacy. As the authors pointed out, these factors are often mediated by the imbalance in power relationships based on culture, race, and socioeconomic status. In short, learning takes place in the context of social relationships in the classroom, and both success and failure can be considered socially organized activities.

For learners from diverse sociocultural and linguistic backgrounds, these factors are especially critical. A classic example of how these considerations can make a difference in educational success is found in the KEEP reading program implemented in Hawaii, which was designed to make reading instruction culturally compatible with the backgrounds of native Hawaiian children (Au, 1997; Au et al., 1986; Tharp & Gallimore, 1988). In addition to changing the focus of instruction from low level to more challenging content (word identification vs. comprehension), specific sociocultural features of students' everyday lives were incorporated into the instructional program. Specific elements addressed included opportunities to use out-of-school discourse forms such as cooperative production of responses by two or more children ("talk story"), modifications in the exercise of authority, attention to fair allocation of students' speaking time, and other features. Dramatic gains in students' achievement resulted from the use of these classroom features.

There are many other examples that also substantiate the importance of sociocultural factors in learning in both special education and general education settings. In theoretical terms, the issue of cultural congruence in instruction (Au & Kawakami, 1994) belies the importance of the planes of development that extend beyond the individual. For English learners and other diverse learners, the interpersonal and community planes of development take on increased importance. The argument being made here is that while students with learning problems benefit from cognitively based self-regulatory strategies, *of equal importance are consideration of students' existing sociocultural knowledge and the role of linkages and connections to out-of-school community-related factors*. In short, contextualized instruction is good instruction. Although many teachers are equipped to provide cognitive scaffolding to assist their students to increase their self-regulatory repertoires, relatively few are equipped to provide the "sociocultural scaffolding" that is so critical for many students.

Conceptualizing Everyday Knowledge

One useful way of thinking about children's backgrounds and home environments as resources and not as deficits is found in the work on funds of knowledge (Moll &

Greenberg, 1990). This body of research studies households' social and community histories and attempts to derive instructional innovations and insights from such analysis. The basic concept is that every household is an educational setting in which the major function is to transmit knowledge that enhances the survival of its dependents. One way to look at "funds of knowledge" is as a guidebook of sorts of the essential information and strategies that families and communities need to maintain their well-being and continued survival. In other words, funds of knowledge are wide ranging and abundant. They are central to the family and to the relationship of the family to others in the community. They have been referred to as the nuts and bolts for survival (Moll & Greenberg, 1990).

Given what is known about the contextualized nature of teaching and learning, these social relationships provide a motive and a context for applying and for acquiring knowledge. The key point is that funds of knowledge are constructed through daily events or activities. That is, funds of knowledge are not possessions or idiosyncrasies of people in the family but are characteristics of people in an activity (Moll & Greenberg, 1990). Knowledge is therefore obtained and constructed by the children, not imposed by the adults. This kind of knowledge is most often content or knowledge based and is rarely insignificant. Funds of knowledge usually matter; that is, they are authentic. For it is only when the content of an interaction is significant or necessary that people are motivated to establish the social contexts for the transfer or the use of knowledge and other resources. It is these social relationships that are so intriguing and carry with them the potential to form the foundation for academic learning. Without specific, deliberate attention to these social relationships and persons in activities, it is very easy for educators to underestimate the abundance of funds of knowledge available in ethnic or working-class environments. It is this third plane of development, in Rogoff's terms, that is so often neglected in curriculum and instructional practice.

Many educators and researchers continue to undervalue the background knowledge of nonmainstream children. For many at-risk children, especially those in special education, background knowledge and experience are often viewed as information from which the student must be rescued rather than as reserve of knowledge that can foster the child's cognitive growth (Gonzalez et al., 1993). Funds of knowledge are available in all households and communities regardless of families' years of formal schooling or the prominence that families assign to school-based literacy. Yet this type knowledge and the forms of transmission families use for sharing it rarely make their way into classrooms in any substantive way (Moll & Greenberg, 1990). Funds of knowledge represent a major, undeveloped resource for academic instruction that many schools have not learned to tap.

Lending support to this contention, researchers have noted an increase in motivation and engagement in schools where students, especially those labeled at risk, are able to develop personal bonds with adults (Foster, 1994; McLaughlin & Talbert, 1990; Wigfield, Eccles, & Rodriguez, 1998). For example, a personalized style and an intimate and nurturing relationship between Latino teachers and pupils, characterized as *cariño* (affectionate kindness), has been identified as one of several influential elements in classrooms that exhibit high degrees of co-membership and success (Cazden, 1988).

The Role of Paraeducators in Effective Instructional Programs

In seeking ways to address this issue in diverse classrooms, we have focused our recent work on paraeducators. The nation's nearly 500,000 paraeducators working in K–12 classrooms embody a promising source of prospective instructors for the nation's diverse student population in both special and general education. Paraeducators are school employees whose responsibilities are instructional in nature or who deliver other services to students. They work under the supervision of teachers or other professional personnel who have the ultimate responsibility for educational programs (Pickett, 1994). Often they live in the community in which the school is located and are familiar with students' home language and discourse forms, whereas teachers often reside elsewhere and may not speak the language. Paraeducators can therefore potentially bring a wealth of community and relevant background knowledge to their practice, attributes that are greatly needed in today's diverse classrooms (Haselkorn & Fideler, 1996).

As suggested earlier, students may have fewer opportunities to learn when school lessons and other activities are conducted, or socially organized, in a manner that is inconsistent with the values and norms of their home culture. A related hypothesis is that students of diverse backgrounds will have better learning opportunities if classroom instruction is conducted in a manner that is congruent with the culture of the home. This type of instruction has been labeled culturally compatible instruction (Jordan, 1985) and culturally responsive instruction (Erickson, 1984).

Zapata (1988), discussing shared identity in teaching and learning, argued that instructors more often predicate their instructional choices on their own ways of learning than base them on how their students learn. He argued that instructors generally pattern their teaching based upon the methods of learning that were successful for them.

In the majority of cases, especially those where the teachers and their students are from different sociocultural backgrounds, shared identity of teachers and students is rare. However, if learning is influenced by one's sociocultural environment, then teachers and students from similar backgrounds have a greater likelihood of having shared understandings and similar background knowledge. Accordingly, teachers with these shared understandings may be better prepared than teachers from other backgrounds to meet the learning needs of an ever growing proportion of the school population (Zapata, 1988).

Paraeducators as Teachers: Some Classroom Examples

We are currently engaged in research examining the instructional activities of Latino paraeducators in classrooms with English language learners. Because of the trend toward reducing special education placements, most of these classrooms, which are not special education placements, include students who have been diagnosed as having learning disabilities. We are particularly focused on how the funds of knowledge that these paraeducators bring to the classroom impact their teaching behaviors. Although we are collecting a variety of measures, we are relying primarily on field notes of classroom observers visiting classrooms on numerous occasions over an extended period of time to capture ongoing instructional events.

Although this work is at an early stage, we have begun to identify various ways that the paraeducators' funds of knowledge enter into their teaching. Some of our observers (graduate students who are often of the same ethnic and language background as the children and paraeducators), for example, have noted the almost "grandmotherly" quality that some of the paraeducators evoke and its effect on children's engagement. The following excerpt from a first-grade Spanish language arts class illustrates this point (observer's comments in italics):

> When children gave the correct response, the paraeducator would say "muy bien" [very good] or "excelente" [excellent] with a very enthusiastic and encouraging facial expression and voice. (*This behavior seemed to increase childrens' attention and interest.*) During this exercise, one young boy was biting his fingernails to which the paraeducator said as she took his hand away from his mouth, "No te comas el dedo" [Don't eat your finger]. (*She did this in an authoritative, motherly fashion, in a way that reminded me of the way teachers interact with children in my hometown in Mexico, and it seemed that the children perceived the paraeducator with high respect and appreciation.*)

Other data from our research also illustrate the simple but effective way that discourse forms can accomplish this effect. For example, we have found that it is common for paraeducators to use terms of endearment, such as "mi amor" (literally, my love), which are common, affectionate forms of address normally used by parents and grandparents. It may be that in the efforts to professionalize teaching, an emphasis on maintaining professional distance has become a value that discourages this type of interaction with students. The following excerpt from our field notes from this same first-grade Spanish language arts class illustrate other ways that these special forms of knowledge come into play:

> The final exercise was in a dictation of words. The paraeducator would pronounce a word and the children were to write the words down on a sheet of paper. In one occasion a boy was missing a letter, so the paraeducator got near the boy's ear and pronounced the dictated word "sorpresa" [surprise] with an emphasis on the letter he was missing, which was the second "r" in the word. After two more pronunciations of the word by the teacher and a bit of thinking on the child's part, he included the missing letter. Both the child and the paraeducator had a smile. To another boy who spelled the word "encontrar" [to find] wrong, the paraeducator repeated the word out loud. The boy paused to think, and the paraeducator encouraged him by saying "Tu lo puedes hacer" [You can do it]. The boy attempted to correct the word but is wrong again. The paraeducator says "come on Raul," encouraging the boy, and pronounces the word one more time. The boy writes it correctly this time, to

which the paraeducator enthusiastically responds "muy bien" [very good], and the boy smiles. Another boy had a problem writing the word "ustedes" (you—plural). He had written the letter "a" instead of the second letter "e" in the word, but after a short pause to reason, the boy was successful. To this the paraeducator knocked on the boy's head and said "knock, knock". The paraeducator said "Excelente, si usa la cabeza, muy bien" [Excellent, if you use your head that is very good]. *(All this was done in a very positive/comic voice to which the young boy and his classmates expressed themselves with a big smile.)*

This excerpt illustrates several interesting features of the way that this paraeducator manages instructional activities. For example, it is important to notice how errors were handled. At the beginning of the excerpt, where a student was missing a letter in his response, the paraeducator chose not to publicly correct the student. Rather, she physically approached the child and pronounced the complete word emphasizing the missing letter, and he was able to produce the correct answer. This approach is a significant change from the question-answer-evaluate sequence seen in so many classrooms.

With a second student, she used a different strategy, providing simple encouragement and confidence in the child's ability to produce the correct answer. Rather than producing the answer herself, or calling on another student, or rebuking the child for not knowing the answer, she chose to provide encouragement and confidence in the child's abilities, and he was able to succeed.

Finally, at the end of the excerpt, the paraeducator affectionately knocked on a child's head in a comedic fashion after the child made an error. Although the students were amused, the paraeducator managed to communicate that the boy needed to think harder, but she did so in a way that did not humiliate the student or penalize his error.

For this paraeducator, the social relationships she maintains with the students are of great importance. She uses a variety of strategies to engage her students, many of which are rooted in the cultural and linguistic shared knowledge that she has with these students. This type of cultural and linguistic scaffolding that we have repeatedly noted in our observations appears to be a key aspect of maintaining engagement for these students, who for a variety of reasons are at risk for low academic achievement.

It is likely that other aspects of classroom instruction and interaction are also influenced by the backgrounds of the paraeducators we are studying. For example, many researchers have begun to study teachers' belief systems as important mediators of their classroom teaching practices. We have found intriguing examples of how the belief systems of paraeducators and teachers differ. In describing the nature of learning problems exhibited by their students with learning disabilities, teachers in our study have tended to refer to factors such as "visual-motor processing" and other related constructs that are focused on presumed within-child deficits. Paraeducators, conversely, have tended to focus more on specific knowledge of the family related to such factors as unemployment, economic problems, the influence of older siblings, and the presence of gangs in the neighborhood.

We have only begun to categorize and catalog the ways that the paraeducators in our study are able to utilize their background knowledge and experiences in their teaching. Even at this early stage, however, it is clear that the cultural and language-based scaffolding on which they draw are important resources that can help provide a bridge to those students who need it. While cognitive interventions are clearly important in promoting academic success, our research has supported the contention that there is a social side to learning that must be addressed as well. It is important to note that we are not arguing that one must be of the same ethnic or racial group to be a successful teacher of diverse students. However, we are arguing that special attention needs to be paid to recognizing and validating the unique backgrounds that many students bring to school and that would otherwise be seen as deficits and impediments to learning. Unfortunately, the type of teaching knowledge that we have been documenting is rarely recognized or promoted in teacher training programs.

While many teachers do not share the backgrounds of their students, they should be able to learn about the communities in which they work. A useful resource that they can use for instructing students in diverse classrooms is the pool of paraeducators who can help bridge the academic content of the school with the social and discourse knowledge of students from diverse backgrounds. In short, paraeducators have enormous potential to bridge the three planes of development referred to earlier.

A Note on Collaborative Practice

It is paradoxical that at the same time that paraeducators represent an important addition to the classroom, they are often undervalued by the teachers and schools in which they work. Although still in its very early stages, our study suggests that many paraeducators are assigned low-level activities and are given little freedom in terms of instructional activities. It is rare to find a truly collaborative relationship where the paraeducator and teacher discuss and plan instruction, each contributing his or her own expertise. Many paraeducators report a wide gap in terms of status, which is made concrete in a variety of ways. Although there are notable exceptions, we have found that many teachers do not take full advantage of the special skills and expertise that paraeducators might contribute. While paraeducators do not have the formal training and credentials that teachers do, they do have a great deal to contribute especially in diverse classrooms. It would be wise for teachers to consider carefully the role of paraeducators in their classrooms and to evaluate whether there are better ways to incorporate and build on this resource.

Summary

As the literature has clearly documented, diverse students who are in special education or who perform poorly in school most often are not self-regulated, strategic learners. However, there is another factor that appears to greatly contribute to their difficulties. In almost all cases, the background knowledge and experiences that these students bring to school are not valued or are not visible in their classroom activities and materials. While cognitive interventions may be useful to these students, many need additional scaffolding to help them build upon their background knowledge and experiences and connect them to the academic content of the classroom.

We believe that a valuable and underappreciated resource to help address this need is found in the numbers of paraeducators who work in a variety of classroom settings. Given the numbers of students whose native language is not English in American public schools and the numbers of teachers who are monolingual, paraeducators represent an important educational tool. For language minority students, paraeducators who speak the students' first language can deliver subject matter instruction and provide literacy development in that language as one part of a larger instructional program.

These arguments should not be seen as in any way diminishing the role of the teacher in the classroom. There is no substitute for the research-based academic knowledge and instructional strategies that teachers bring to the classroom. However, as noted earlier, the social aspects of learning are important factors, especially for students from diverse backgrounds. Teacher/paraeducator pairing is one useful way to promote classroom environments that are conducive to learning. While the teacher may provide formal schooling and powerful academic interventions such as cognitive strategy training, the paraeducator may possess the everyday, non-school-based knowledge that provides cultural and linguistic scaffolds when and where they are needed. Respecting the special competence that each brings to the classroom, together the teacher and paraeducator can provide an effective approach for English learners and other students of diverse backgrounds in general and for children with learning problems in particular.

References

Arter, J. A., & Jenkins, J. R. (1979). Differential diagnostic prescriptive teaching: A critical appraisal. *Review of Educational Research, 49,* 517–555.

Au, K. H. (1997). Ownership, literacy achievement, and students of diverse cultural backgrounds. In J. T. Guthrie & A. Wigfield (Eds.), *Reading engagement: Motivating readers through integrated instruction* (pp. 168–182). Newark, DE: International Reading Association.

Au, K. H., Crowell, D. C., Jordan, C., Sloat, O. C. M., Speidel, G. E., Klein, T. W., & Tharp, R. G. (1986). Development and implementation of the KEEP reading program. In J. Orasanu (Ed.), *Reading comprehension: From research to practice* (pp. 235–252). Hillsdale, NJ: Erlbaum.

Au, K. H., & Kawakami, A. J. (1994). Cultural congruence in instruction. In E. R. Hollins, J. E. King, & W. C. Hayman (Eds.), *Teaching diverse populations: Formulating a knowledge base.* (pp. 5–24). Albany, NY: State University of New York Press.

Brown, A. L. (1978). Knowing when, where, and how to remember: A problem of metacognition. In R. Glaser (Ed.), *Advances in instructional psychology* (Vol. 1, pp. 77–165). Hillsdale, NJ: Erlbaum.

Brown, A. L., Armbruster, B. B., & Baker, L. (1986). The role of metacognition in reading and studying. In J. Orasanu (Ed.), *A decade of reading research: Implications for practice* (pp. 49–75). Hillsdale, NJ: Erlbaum.

Brown, A. L., & Campione, J. C. (1986). Psychological theory and the study of learning disabilities. *American Psychologist, 14,* 1059–1068.

Cazden, C. B. (1988). *Classroom discourse: The language of teaching and learning.* Portsmouth, NH: Heinemann.

Crago, M. B., Eriks-Brophy, A., Pesco, D., & McAlpine, L. (1997). Culturally-based miscommunication in classroom interaction. *Language, Speech, and Hearing Services in Schools, 28,* 245–254.

Erickson, F. (1984). School literacy, reasoning, and civility: An anthropologist's perspective. *Review of Educational Research, 54,* 525–546.

Foster, M. (1994). Effective black teachers: A literature review. In E. R. Hollins, J. E. King, & W. C.Hayman (Eds.), *Teaching diverse populations* (pp. 225–241). Albany, NY: State University of New York Press.

Gagné, E. D., Yekovich, C. W., & Yekovich, F. R. (1993). *The cognitive psychology of school learning.* New York: HarperCollins College Publishers.

Gonzalez, N., Moll, L. C., Floyd-Tenery, M., Rivera, A., Rendon, P., Gonzales, R., & Amanti, C. (1993). *Teacher research on funds of knowledge: Learning from households* (Educational Practice Reports 6). Santa Cruz, CA: University of California, National Center for Research on Cultural Diversity and Second Language Learning.

Graham, S. & Harris, K. R. (1993). Self-regulated strategy development: Helping students with learning problems develop as writers, Special Issue: Strategies Instruction. *Elementary School Journal, 94,* 169–181.

Greeno, J. G., and the Middle School Mathematics Through Applications Project Group. (1998). The situativity of knowing, learning, and research. *American Psychologist, 53,* 5–26.

Haselkorn, D., & Fideler, E. (1996). *Breaking the class ceiling: Paraeducator pathways to teaching.* Belmont, MA: Recruiting New Teachers.

Jordan, C. (1985). Translating culture: From ethnographic information to educational program. *Anthropology and Education Quarterly, 16,* 105–123.

Kavale, K. A., & Forness, S. R. (1985). *The science of learning disabilities.* San Diego, CA: College Hill Press.

Keogh, B. K., Gallimore, R., & Weisner, T. (1997). A sociocultural perspective on learning and learning disabilities. *LD Research and Practice, 12,* 107–113.

McLaughlin, M., & Talbert, J. (1990). Constructing a personalized school environment. *Phi Delta Kappan, 72,* 230–235.

Meyers, P. L., & Hammill, D. D. (1990). *Learning disabilities: Basic concepts, assessment practices, and instructional strategies.* Austin, TX: PRO-ED.

Moll, L. C., & Greenberg, J. B. (1990). Creating zones of possibilities: Combining social contexts for instruction. In L.C. Moll (Ed.), *Vygotsky and education: Instructional implications and applications of sociohistorical psychology* (pp. 319–348). New York: Cambridge University Press.

Palincsar, A. S., & Brown, A. L. (1986). Interactive teaching to promote independent learning from text. *The Reading Teacher, 39,* 771–777.

Pickett, A. L. (1994). *Paraprofessionals in the education workforce.* Washington, DC: National Education Association.

Pressley, M., & McCormick, C. B. (1995). *Cognition, teaching, and assessment.* New York: HarperCollins College Publishers.

Reid, D. K., Hresko, W. P., & Swanson, H. L. (Eds.) (1996). *Cognitive approaches to learning disabilities.* Austin, TX: PRO-ED.

Reid, D. K., & Kuykendall, M. (1996). Literacy: A tale of different belief systems. In D. K. Reid, W. P. Hresko, & H. L. Swanson (Eds.), *Cognitive approaches to learning disabilities* (pp. 497–544). Austin, TX: PRO-ED.

Rogoff, B. (1994). Developing understanding of the idea of communities of learners. *Mind, Culture, and Activity, 1,* 209–229.

Rogoff, B. (1995). Observing sociocultural activity on three planes: Participatory appropriation, guided participation, and apprenticeship. In J. V. Wertsch, P. Del Rio, and A. Alvarez (Eds.), *Sociocultural studies of mind* (pp. 139–164). Cambridge, UK: Cambridge University Press.

Rogoff, B., Baker-Sennett, J., Lacasa, P., & Goldsmith, D. (1995). Development through participation in sociocultural activity. In J. Goodnow, P. Miller, & F. Kessel (Eds.), *Cultural practices as contexts for development.* (Pp. 45–65). San Francisco: Jossey-Bass.

Rogoff, B., & Chavajay, P. (1995). What's become of research on the cultural basis of cognitive development? *American Psychologist, 50,* 859–877.

Strauss, S. (1996). Confessions of a born-again constructivist. *Educational Psychologist, 31,* 15–21.

Tharp, R., & Gallimore, R. (1988). *Rousing minds to life: Teaching, learning, and schooling in social contexts.* Cambridge: Cambridge University Press.

Trent, S. C., Artiles, A. J., & Englert, C. S. (1998). From deficit thinking to social constructivism: A review of theory, research, and practice in special education. In P. D. Pearson & A. Iran-Nejad (Eds.), *Review of research in education* (Vol. 23, pp. 277–307). Washington, DC: American Educational Research Association.

Wigfield, A., Eccles, J.S., & Rodriguez, D. (1998). The development of children's motivation in school contexts. In P. D. Pearson & A. Iran-Nejad (Eds.), *Review of research in education* (Vol. 23, pp. 73–118). Washington, DC: American Educational Research Association.

Zapata, J. T. (1988). Early identification and recruitment of Hispanic teacher candidates. *Journal of Teacher Education,* Vol. 2, 19–23.

The work described herein was supported under the Education Research and Development Program, PR/Award No. R306A60001, the Center for Research on Education, Diversity & Excellence, as administered by the Office of Educational Research and Improvement (OERI), National Institute on the Education of At-Risk Students (NIEARS), U.S. Department of Education (USDE). The contents, findings, and opinions expressed in this chapter are those of the authors and do not necessarily represent the positions or policies of OERI, NIEARS, or the USDOE.

Index

A

Academic achievement
  concept of normality and, 12–13
  curriculum-based measurement and, 94, 96–97
  discrepancy between potential and, 22–23
  factors related to, 7–9, 23
  normal distribution and, 12–13
  social support for, 292, 296
  teacher expectations and, 177, 179
Accountability, 228
Active Reading strategy, 244–245
Adapted instruction, 118–119
Administrators
  critical cultural mirroring and culturally focused dialogue and, 55–56
  curriculum development and, 56–58
  disembedding cultural bias and, 54–55
  need for culturally responsive, 51–53
  parent involvement and, 58–62
Adolescents with learning disabilities. *See also* Project-based instruction; Students with learning disabilities
  academic characteristics of, 295
  cognitive characteristics of, 293–295
  impact of projects on, 296–297
  motivational characteristics of, 296
  overview of, 293
  social characteristics of, 295–296
  watered-down curriculum for, 288
  watered-up curriculum for, 289–292
African American Vernacular English (Ebonics), 10, 13

African Americans. *See also* Ethnic minorities
  Black Church and, 177, 184–186
  deficits perspective and, 20
  mental retardation classification and, 23
  narrative text and, 182–183
  power of the word and, 177
  in special education programs, 28, 53
Allington, R. L., 5–6
Ambassadors strategy, 280–281
American Indians, 28. *See also* Ethnic minorities
Anderson, Walter, 73, 74
Angelo, Maya, 207
Answers, blurting out, 271
Archetype concepts, 290
Archetype patterns, 290
Asian Americans, 28. *See also* Ethnic minorities
Assessment. *See also* Curriculum-based measurement (CBM)
  cheaper and faster, 92–93
  curriculum-based measurement *vs.* medical, 91–92
  explanation of, 86
  focus of, 86–88
  frequency of, 88–89
  function of, 153
  intensity of, 90–91
  new views about, 151–152
  Peter's Story and, 151–152, 159–171
  of students with learning disabilities in general education programs, 197
  use of curriculum-based measurement for, 93–107

327

B

The Bell Curve (Herrnstein & Murray), 12
Bias. *See* Cultural bias
Bilingual students, 53
Black Church
    discourse techniques in, 185–186
    power of the word and, 177
    seating procedures in, 184–185
Black English, 10, 13
Blurting out answers, 271
Brotherton, S., 73
Brown v. Board of Education, 26, 32
Bullivant, B., 52
Burke, C., 154–155
Byrd, H. B., 29–31

C

Calendar use, 257
Canada, 7
Carr, Linda, 216
Center for Special Education Technology, 230
Choral responding, 273
Church-based discipline, 184–186
Circle Time Read Aloud, 208–209
Cities in Schools project, 32
Classroom seating procedures, 184–185
Classroom Whip Around, 274
Classwide Peer Tutoring (CWPT), 277, 278
CLEAR communication strategy, 308–310, 312–313
Cloze reading with choral responding, 278
Clustering, 245
Cognitive processes
    of adolescents with learning disabilities, 293–295
    multicultural multicognitive model and, 29–31
    students with mild learning disabilities and, 315–316
Cognitive psychology, 315
Coles, Gerald, 46
Collaborative teaching
    in general education environments, 194–198
    with paraeducators, 323
Committee of Fifteen, 154
Communities in Schools project, 32
Community resources
    collaboration between schools and, 31–32
    development of parent empowerment skills by, 33
    three-phase preservice/inservice model for promoting networks using, 33–34

Computer lab, 230
Computers
    in cooperative learning situations, 225–228
    Learning Together strategy using, 229–233
    overview of, 223–224
    social development scenarios using, 230, 234
    social development software for, 234
Conferences, with minority parents, 59–62
Cooperative learning
    in computer labs, 230
    computer use for, 225–228, 234–235
    cultivation of, 14
    explanation of, 224
    expository reading strategies for, 245
    individual accountability and, 228
    Learning Together strategy for, 229–233
    positive interdependence during, 227–228
    social and academic development during, 228–230, 234–235, 291
    student processing of outcomes and, 228
    student with learning disabilities and, 237–238
    team assignment and team preparation for, 226–227
    traditional *vs.,* 224–225
Counseling, 72–75
Crichlow, W., 7
Cultural bias, 54–55
Cultural context, 29–31
Cultural diversity. *See* Multicultural issues
Cultural mirroring
    administrators and, 55–56
    curriculum dialogues and, 57
Culturally and linguistically diverse students. *See also* Shared Reading for Older Emergent Readers
    learning environment for, 200
    literacy instruction in special education classes for, 200–203
    test results for, 199
Culturally focused dialogue
    about curriculum, 56–58
    need for, 55–56
Culture, 52
Curriculum
    assumptions for building, 152
    culturally focused dialogue about, 56–58
    in multicultural language arts classroom, 180–181
    multicultural multicognitive model and, 31
    undifferentiated, 272
    watered-down, 288

watered-up, 288–292
Curriculum-based measurement (CBM)
  broader focus and continuous database and, 93–94
  case studies using, 97–107
  cheaper and faster testing and, 93
  IDEA assessment language and, 94–96
  improved student achievement outcomes and, 94, 96–97
  medical assessment and, 91
  problem certification and, 100–102
  problem identification and, 97–100
  problem solution and, 105–107
  solution evaluation and, 104–105
  solution exploration and, 102–103
  testing strategies used in, 91–92

D

DEAR Time, 211, 219
Decontextualized phonics, 202
Deficits perspective
  African Americans and, 20
  problems with, 47–48
  in special education, 317
Democracy, 14
Diagnostic and Statistical Manual of Mental Disorders (DSM-IV), 71–72
Discipline
  church-based, 184–186
  in collaborative classrooms, 197–198
Discrepancy clause, 22–23
Discrimination, 7–8
DISTAR program, 45
Do-Check-Teach, 276–277
Doherty, William, 73
Drabble, Margaret, 154

E

Ebonics, 10, 13
Editing strategies, 250, 251
Education
  assumptions implicit in traditional, 7–13
  ideological perspective and, 9–11
  as key to success, 7–9
  meaning of learning disability and meaning of, 13–14
  performance distributions and, 12–13
  reconceptualizing, 13–14
Education of All Handicapped Childrens Act of 1975, 94
Elaboration strategies, 290
Emotional disabilities, 28
English proficiency limitations, 53

Epston, David, 75
Error Monitoring strategy, 250
Escalante, Jaime, 186
Ethnic minorities. *See also specific minority groups*
  demographic change and, 25–26
  discrepancy clause and, 22–23
  in learning disabilities programs, 24, 27–29, 34
  multicultural multicognitive model for, 29–31
  parental involvement and, 31–34
  reconceptualization of learning disabilities and, 20
Exclusionary clause, 23–24
Expository reading strategies
  answering questions and, 245–246, 248
  decoding unknown words and, 240
  determining meaning of unknown words and, 240–241
  prereading, 243–244
  during reading, 244–247
  understanding and creating graphics and, 241–243
  writing summaries and, 248–249
Expository writing strategies, 249–251

F

FIND strategy, 307–308, 311–312
First Steps (Heinemann), 47
Fisher, Ronald, 12
Foorman study, 202
Ford, B. A., 33
Foundations of Literacy (Holdaway), 44

G

Gallery Walk, 211–212
Gee, James, 11
Geertz, C., 52
Gender, 28
General education classrooms
  adapted instruction in, 118
  inclusion and, 193–198
  meeting needs of students with learning disabilities in, 237–238, 268, 269
  teacher training for, 268
Give One - Get One, 279
Goodlad, J. I., 272
Grading
  example of, 123–125
  function of, 113
  of students with learning disabilities, 111–112

Grading adaptations
    curricular adaptations and, 118–119
    district policies regarding, 114
    future transitions to school and work and, 114, 118
    options for, 113–117, 126
    proposed process for implementing, 121–123
    teachers' and students' perceptions of, 119–120, 126
Graff, H. J., 7
Graphics, 241–243
Graves, Donald, 43
Group responding, 273
Group work, 271–272. *See also* Cooperative learning

H

Hamilton, Susan, 152, 153
Hand raising, 271
Harste, J., 154–155
Heads Together, 279–280
Heard, Georgia, 219
Heath, S. B., 182–183
Herrnstein, R. J., 12
High-access instruction (HAI)
    benefits of, 282–283
    explanation of, 268–270
    incorporation of, 269
    low-access *vs.*, 282, 283
High-access instructional strategies
    ambassadors, 280–281
    choral, or group, responding, 273
    classroom whip around, 274
    cloze reading with choral responding, 278
    give one-get one, 279
    goals of, 273
    heads together, 279–280
    partner, 274–277
    peer-assisted learning, 277–278
    random questioning with 3 x 5 cards, 278–279
    reciprocal teaching, 281–282
    thumbs up when you know, 273–274
Higher-order thinking, 290–291
Hispanic Americans, 28, 53, 319–320. *See also* Ethnic minorities
    as paraeducators, 320–322
    relationship between teachers and students and, 319–320
    in special education programs, 28, 53
Holdaway, Don, 203, 205
HOW strategy, 258, 259

Hubbard, R., 155
HyperStudio Vacation Lesson Plan, 231

I

In-service teacher training, 29–30
Inclusion
    co-teaching issues and, 196–198
    drawbacks of, 268
    explanation of, 194–195
    strategies for dealing with, 195–196
Indentation Notes
    for verbal information, 253, 255
    for written material, 245, 246
Individualized educational program (IEP)
    curriculum-based measurement and, 94, 103
    grading adaptations and, 114, 120, 122
    parental participation in development of, 32, 59
    students with learning disabilities in general education programs and, 195, 197
Individuals With Disabilities Education Act (IDEA)
    curriculum-based measurement and, 94–96, 103
    learning disabilities definition in, 21
    parental participation requirements of, 32, 59, 60
    provisions of, 196
    structures for labeling and, 71–72
Inquiry, 156–157
Insult to Intelligence (Smith), 44
Intelligence tests, 22–23
Interview model (White & Epston), 75

J

John-Steiner, V., 154

K

Kingsolver, Barbara, 8
Knowledge
    conceptualizing everyday, 318–320
    connected to background experience, 290, 318–320, 323–324
    emphasis on constructing, 289
    as objective and ideologically neutral, 9–11
Kress, G., 166
KWL, 243–244

L

Labeling
    cultural differences and, 53–54
    problems related to, 69–71
    taxonomic structures for, 71–72

Langer, J., 158
Language arts classroom study
  background of, 173–174
  church-based discipline in, 184–186
  curriculum choices in, 180–181
  innovative instructional techniques in, 179–184
  multicultural classroom design strategies in, 175–176
  narrative comprehension questioning techniques in, 182–184
  strategies for teaching writing in, 184
  strategies to inspire and challenge students in, 177–179
  student profile in, 174–175
Language assessment, 53
Language use
  of dominant groups, 10–11
  to inspire and challenge students, 177–179
Latinos. *See* Hispanic Americans
Lax, W. D., 74
Leading and Managing for Performance (NASDSE), 89
Learning. *See also* Cooperative learning
  cognition and, 315–317
  cultural and linguistic factors in, 317–318
Learning disabilities
  meaning of school and meaning of, 13–14
  problems with definition of, 22–24
Learning disabilities construct
  background of, 21
  multicultural perspective for, 25–34
  reconceptualization of, 5, 19–21, 47
  reformation of, 34–35, 316
Learning disabilities programs
  effectiveness of, 5–6
  ethnic minorities in, 24, 27–29, 34
  outcome of lower-level and special, 268
Learning groups, 224–225
Learning strategies
  emphasis on development of, 290–291
  explanation of, 239
  for expository reading, 240–249
  for expository writing, 249–252
  for narrative reading, 251–252
  for narrative writing, 252–253
  for studying, 255–256
  for verbal presentations, 253, 255
Learning Strategies Curriculum, 250
Learning Together strategy
  elements of, 229–230
  lesson plans for, 231–233
The Learning Mystique: A Critical Look at "Learning Disabilities (Coles), 46

Lectures, 253, 255
Linguistically diverse students. *See* Bilingual students; Culturally and linguistically diverse students
Literacy
  assumptions regarding, 152, 153
  learner's theories and, 157–159
  multiple sign systems and, 154–156
  Peter's Story and, 151–152, 159–171
  process of inquiry and, 156–157
Literature, multicultural, 180, 181
Low-access teaching
  explanation of, 270
  high-access *vs.*, 282, 283
  practices of, 271–272

M

Males, 53
Mapping, 245, 247
Maze, 91
McCarthy, C., 7
McGill-Franzen, A., 5–6
Medical assessment
  curriculum-based measurement and, 91–92
  explanation of, 86
  focus of, 86–88
  frequency of, 88–89
  intensity of, 90–91
Medical model
  disability identification and, 60, 71–72
  emphasis on, 85
Mental retardation, 23, 53
Metacognitive awareness, 146
Miscue analysis
  application of, 134–138
  explanation of, 132
  markings for, 133, 134, 149, 150
Mnemonic strategies, 256
Modernism, 72–73
Multicultural classrooms. *See also* Language arts classroom study
  literature for, 180, 181
  strategies for design of, 175–176
Multicultural issues
  curriculum development and, 56–58
  critical cultural mirroring and, 52, 55–56
  cultural differences and labeling and, 53–54
  ethnic minority representation in learning disabilities programs and, 24, 27–29, 34
  function of education and, 53
  leadership through disembedding cultural biases and, 54–55

overview of, 51–53
parental involvement and, 31–34, 58–62
personnel preparation deficits and, 28–31
student demographic changes and, 25–26
teaching staff inadequacies and, 26–27
Multicultural multicognitive model (Byrd), 29–31
Multiple intelligences model (Gardner), 29
Multiple sign systems
　case study on use of, 159–171
　explanation of, 154
　literacy development and, 154–158
Multiple talent theory, 297
Murray, C. A., 12

N

Narrative strategies
　for reading, 251–252
　for writing, 252–253
Narrative therapy
　case example of, 75–79
　classroom use of, 79–81
　explanation of, 74
　postmodern approach of, 74–75
Narrative thinking, 80
National Advisory Committee on Handicapped Children, 21
National Agenda for Achieving Better Results for Children and Youth With Disabilities (Department of Education), 89
National Association of State Directors of Special Education (NASSDE), 89
National Longitudinal Transition Study of Education Students (NLTS), 28–29
Newkirk, T., 155
Notebooks, 256–257
Notetaking strategies
　outlining and, 239
　types of, 245
　for verbal presentations, 253, 255

O

Office of Civil Rights (OCR), 28, 53
O'Hara, Maureen, 73, 74
Oládélé, Folásadé, 177, 188
OLE Curriculum Guide (Ruiz, Garcia, & Figueroa), 206
OLE Project (Optimal Learning Environment Project). *See also* Shared Reading for Older Emergent Readers
　explanation of, 203
　function of, 200

shared reading as part of, 204–205, 207
O'Leary, Lauren, 213
Oliver, Mary, 219
Organization skills
　for organizing materials, 256–257
　for time management, 257–258
　for written products, 258–259
Outlining strategies, 239

P

Pairs Check, 276
Paraeducators
　collaboration with, 323
　role of, 320
　as teachers, 320–323
Paraphrasing strategy, 244, 245, 290
Parental involvement
　administrators and, 58–62
　ethnic minority, 31–34
　positive effects of, 31–34
Parents
　conferences with minority, 59–62
　school favoring middle- and upper-middle-class, 8
Partner strategies, 274–277
Pathology
　explanation of, 71
　medical model of, 60, 71–72, 82, 83, 85
Paz, Octavio, 207–208
Pedagogical strategies, 31
Peer-Assisted Learning Strategies (PALS), 277–278
Personal potency, 291
Peter's Story, 151–152, 159–171
Pictographs, 241, 242
Poetry, 206–219. *See also* Shared Reading for Older Emergent Readers
　eliciting personal reactions from, 212–215
　games with, 215–218
　getting started writing, 218–219
　performances using, 218
　Shared Reading with, 206–212
Pollock, Margie, 219
Postmodernism
　counseling approaches to, 73–74
　narrative therapy and, 74–75
Poverty
　education and, 7–8
　gap between wealth and, 12
POWER steps
　to report writing, 249–251
　to summary writing, 248–249
Preservice trainees, 33

Preview strategies, 244
Principals. *See* Administrators
Problem-solving model
    curriculum-based measurement in, 94, 97–107
    problem certification in, 100–102
    problem identification in, 97–100
    problem solution in, 105–107
    solution evaluation in, 104–105
    solution exploration in, 102–103
Project-based instruction
    for adolescents, 293–296
    benefits of, 288–292
    to develop multiple talents, 297–299
    explanation of, 288, 292–293
    for heterogeneous research teams, 296–297
Project-based strategies
    CLEAR communication strategy step in, 308–310, 312–313
    facilitating use of, 310–313
    FIND strategy step in, 307–308, 311–312
    phases of, 299–301
    PROJECT strategy step in, 299, 302–307, 311
Project Zero (Harvard), 154
Proofreading, 250
Purcell-Gates, V., 158

Q

Questions
    following expository reading, 245–246, 248
    following expository writing, 252
    following narrative reading, 182–184, 252
    following narrative writing, 253
    self-study, 255–256

R

Random questioning with 3 x 5 cards, 278–279
RAP strategy, 244, 245
RCRC strategy, 244, 255
Readers and Writers With a Difference (Rhodes & Dudley-Marling), 44
Reading
    efferent, 153
    round-robin, 271
Reading case study
    background information and, 129–131
    metacognitive awareness and, 146–147
    miscue analysis and, 132–138
    reader confidence and, 147
    reading words and, 131–132
    retrospective miscue analysis and, 140–142
    revaluing process and, 138–140
    strategy use and, 142–145
Reading strategies
    cloze with choral response, 278
    expository, 240–249
    narrative, 251–252
    peer-assisted, 277–278
    writing skills and, 43–46
Reciprocal teaching, 281–282, 316
Reflection, 291
Retrospective miscue analysis (RMA)
    application of, 140–145
    explanation of, 140
    metacognitive awareness and, 146
Revaluing
    explanation of, 138
    focus of, 138–140
    reader confidence and, 147, 148
    retrospective miscue analysis for, 140
Rewriting, 251
Risk taking, 291, 295
Rogoff, B., 316, 317, 319
Romo, Dana, 219
Rosenblatt, Louise, 153, 158
Round-Robin Read, 209–210
Round-robin reading, 271
Rural areas, 28–29

S

"Sage on the stage" teaching, 272
School drop-out rate, 28–29
Schools
    collaborative relationships between parents and, 32–33
    expectations for, 14
    types of specialists in, 70–72
Seating arrangements, 175–176
Second language acquisition (SLA), 201
Self-esteem, 291
Self-evaluation activities, 262–263
Self-monitoring activities, 262–263
Self-questioning strategy, 253
Self-study questions, 255–256
Semiotics, 154
Senge, Peter, 267
Shapiro, J. P., 28
Shared Reading for Older Emergent Readers
    constructing meaning in, 213–215
    explanation of, 200
    implementation of, 206–212
    as link between classroom research and practice, 203–206
    performance and extension and, 218
    poetry and, 218–219

skill work in, 215–218
Short story think sheets, 253, 254
Sign systems
　application of, 154–155
　explanation of, 154
　use of multiple, 154–158
Sing Along, 210–211
Skrtic, Tom, 6
Sleeter, Christine, 6
Social contact theory, 58–59
Social development
　in adolescents with learning disabilities, 295–296
　cooperative computer use and, 230, 234–235
　cooperative learning situations and, 228
　skills for various grade levels, 229
　software for, 234
Sociocultural factors
　background knowledge and experience and, 318–320, 323–324
　diverse learners and, 317–318
　learning and, 316–318
　paraeducators and, 320–323
Socioeconomic status
　academic variance and, 23
　schools and, 7–8, 11
　special education referrals and, 54
Special education programs. *See also* Learning disabilities programs
　deficits focus of, 317
　ethnic minorities in, 28, 53–54
　males in, 53
　writing strategies for, 42–46
Special education teachers. *See also* Teachers
　function of, 47
　personal account of, 41–49
　recruitment of ethnic minority, 35
SQ3R, 244
Story grammar elements, 252–253
Students with learning disabilities. *See also* Adolescents with learning disabilities
　cognitive processes and, 315–316
　effectiveness of programs for, 5–6
　in general education environments, 194–198
　goals for, 196
　identification of, 34–35, 46–48
　outcome for urban, 28–29
　perceptions of grading adaptations by, 119–120
　watered-down curriculum for, 288
　watered-up curriculum for, 288–292
Study-skill strategies
　guidelines for increasing use of, 261–263
　guidelines for teaching, 260–261
　importance of teaching, 238
　learning strategies and, 238–259 (*See also* Learning strategies)
　organization skills and, 256–259
　selection of, 238–239
　types of, 255–256
Suburban areas, 28–29
Summary writing, 248–249
Survey-level assessment (SLA), 100–103
Symbol weaving, 155

T

Talents Unlimited model, 297, 298
Tan, Amy, 181
Taylor, Calvin W., 297
Teacher education/training
　in collaborative teaching, 195
　In-service, 29–30
　multicultural perspectives and, 29–30
　for students with learning disabilities on general education classrooms, 268
Teachers. *See also* Special education teachers
　decline in number of male, 27
　interaction between students and, 292, 319–320
　with learning disabilities, 194
　paraeducators as, 320–323
　perceptions of grading adaptations by, 119–120
　recruitment of ethnic minority, 35
　shortage of ethnic minority, 26–27, 32
Teaching. *See also* High-access instruction (HAI)
　low-assess, 270–272, 282
　reciprocal, 281–282, 316
　undifferentiated, 272
Tell-Help-Check, 275–276
Think-Pair-Share, 275, 279
Think sheets, 253, 254
Three-phase preservice/inservice model for promoting school-community collaborative networks, 33–34
Thumbs Up, 273–274
Time-management strategies, 257–258
Tong, Rosina, 219
Traditional learning groups, 224–225
Transitions (Routman), 44

U

Urban areas, 28
U.S. Office of Special Education Research Strategic Targets, 89

V

Verbal presentations, 253, 255
Verbal rehearsal strategies, 244–245, 255

W

Warm-Up Strategy, 244
Watered-down curriculum, 288
Watered-up curriculum, 288–292
Watson, Dorothy, 43
Webbing, 245
Where in the World Is Carmen Sandiego Lesson Plan, 232–233
White, Michael, 75
Whole language movement, 156
The Whole Story (Cambourne), 44
Witty, E. P., 26
Women, 27
Woodward, V., 154–155
Words
   decoding, 240
   determining meaning of, 240–241
   power of, 177
Writing strategies
   for appearance and organization, 258, 259
   for at-risk students, 184
   expository, 249–251
   narrative, 252–253
   for special education classes, 42–46

Z

Zapata, J. T., 320